W Juliet™

Volume 12

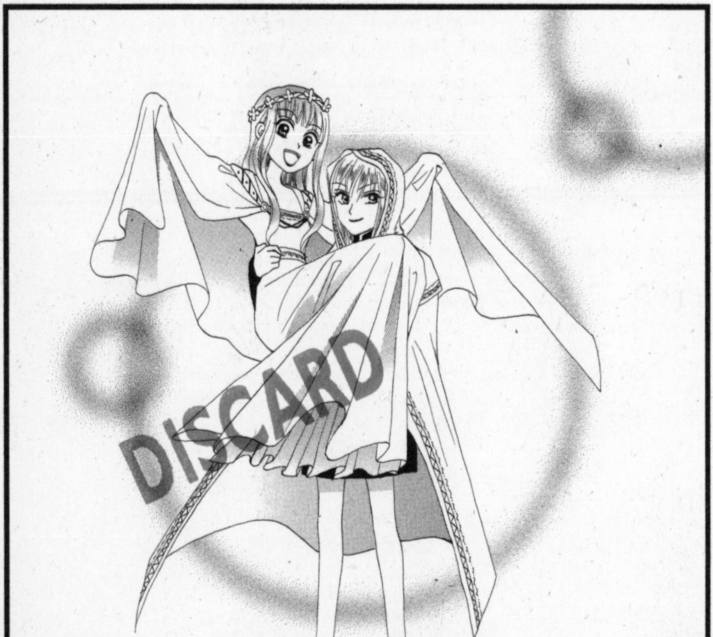
DISCARD

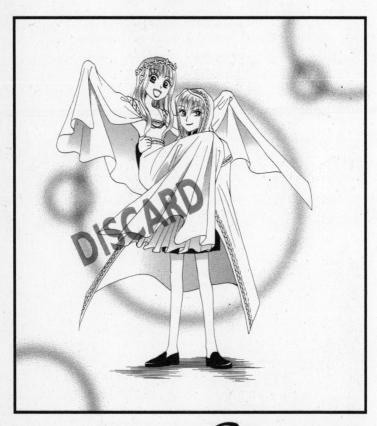

Story & Art by Emura

W Juliet
Volume 12

Story and Art by Emura

Translation & English Adaptation/Naomi Kokubo & Jeff Carlson
Touch-up Art & Lettering/Krysta Lau, Imaginary Friends Studios
Graphic Design/Hidemi Sahara
Editor/Carrie Shepherd

Editor in Chief, Books/Alvin Lu
Editor in Chief, Magazines/Marc Weidenbaum
VP of Publishing Licensing/Rika Inouye
VP of Sales/Gonzalo Ferreyra
Sr. VP of Marketing/Liza Coppola
Publisher/Hyoe Narita

Printed in the U.S.A.

Published by VIZ Media, LLC
P.O. Box 77010
San Francisco, CA 94107

10 9 8 7 6 5 4 3 2
First printing, September 2006
Second printing, March 2007

www.viz.com
store.viz.com

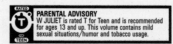

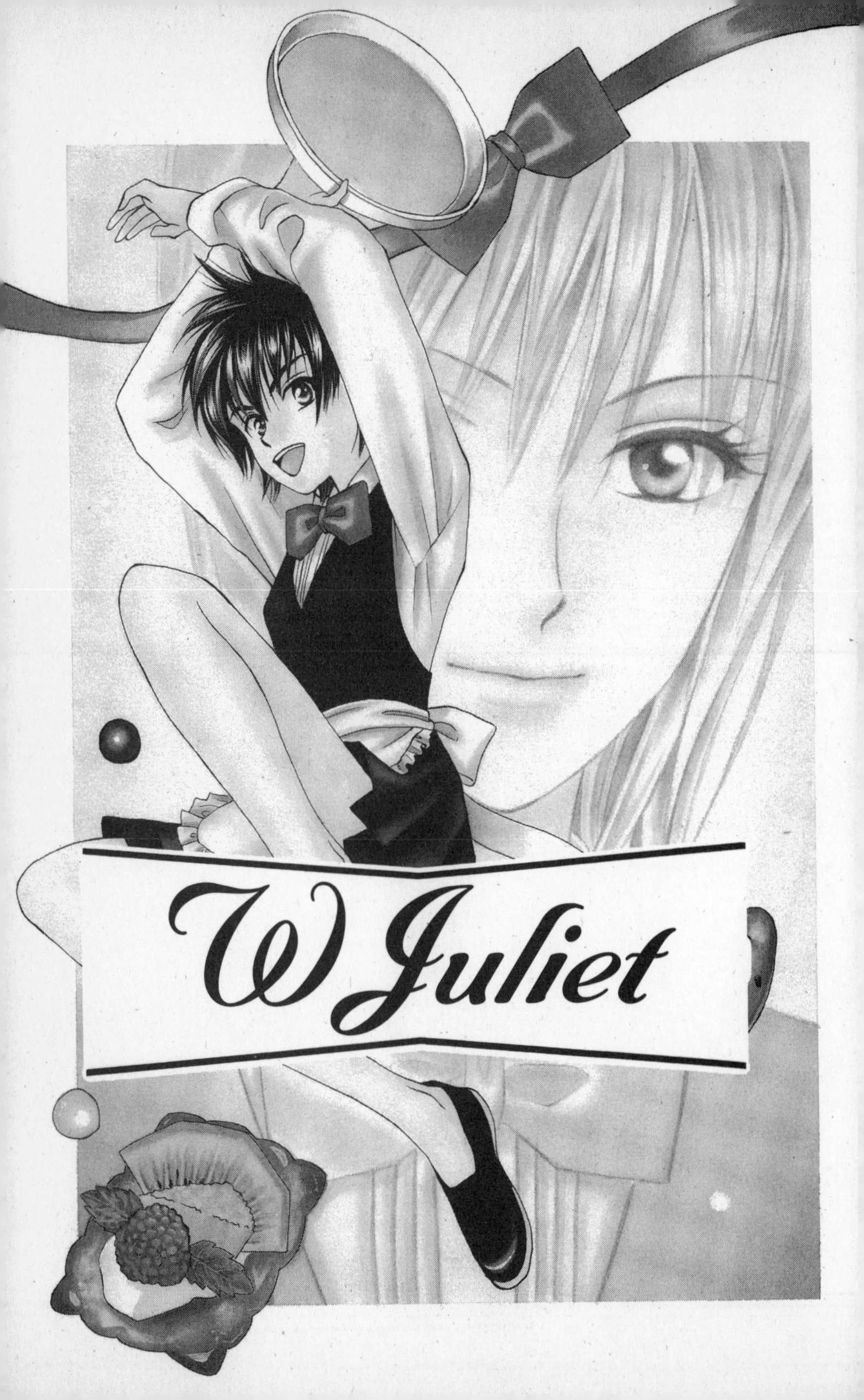
W Juliet

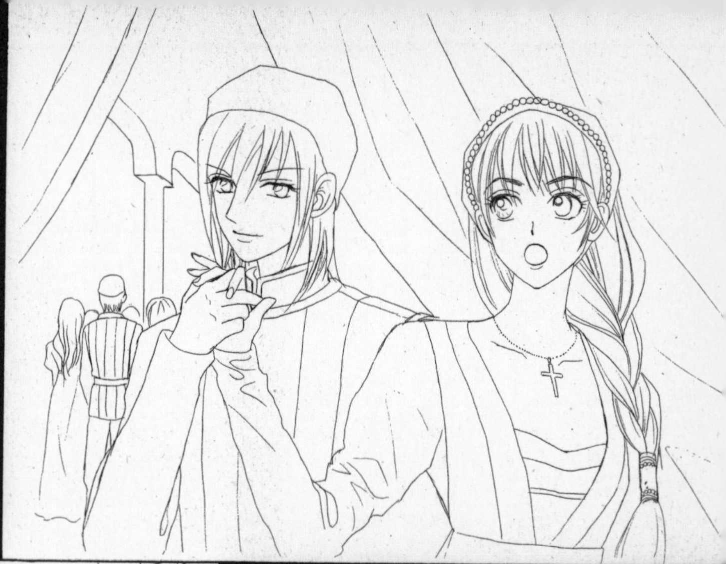

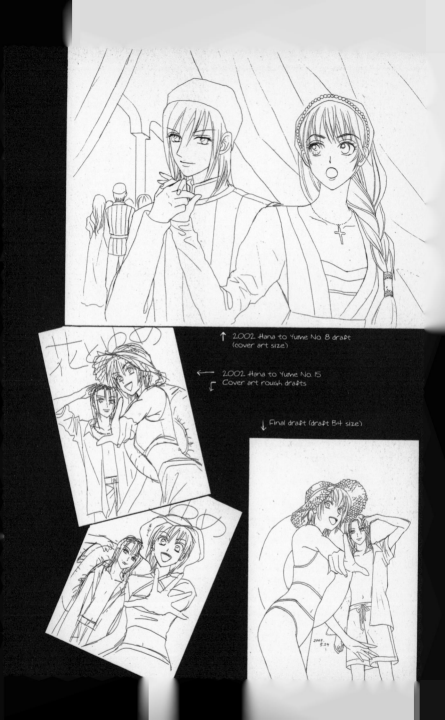

↑ 2002 Hana to Yume No. 8 draft
(cover art size)

← 2002 Hana to Yume No. 15
Cover art rough drafts

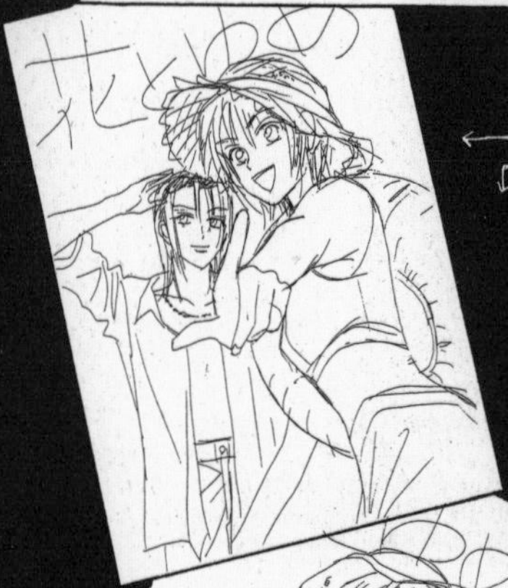

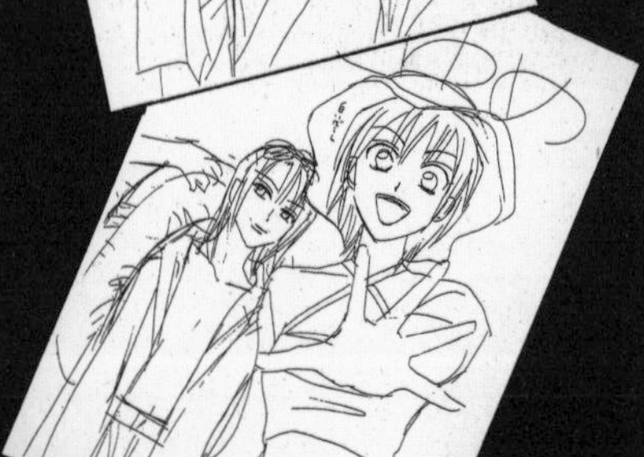

↓ Final draft (draft B4 size)

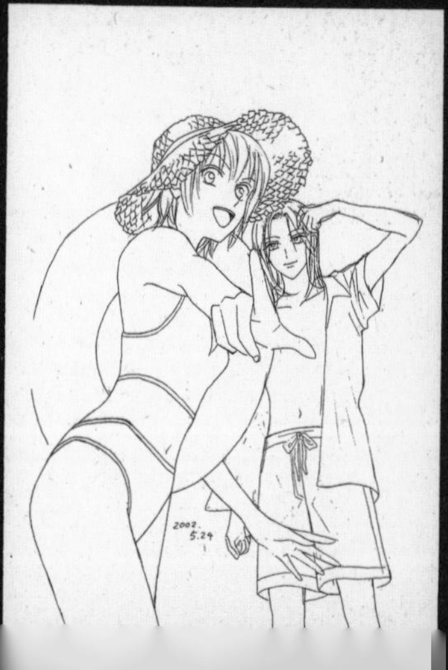
2002.
5.24

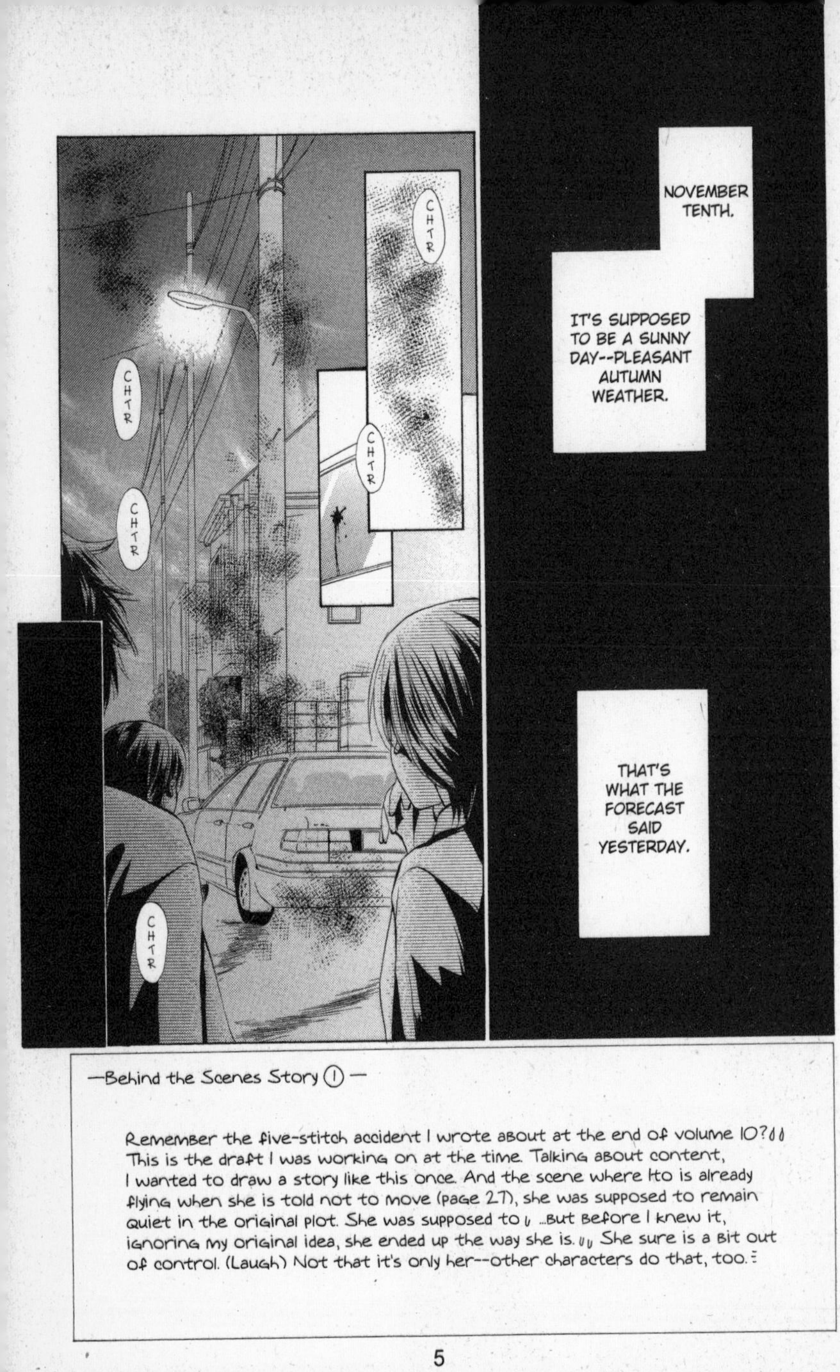
NOVEMBER TENTH.
IT'S SUPPOSED TO BE A SUNNY DAY--PLEASANT AUTUMN WEATHER.
THAT'S WHAT THE FORECAST SAID YESTERDAY.
CHTR
CHTR
CHTR
CHTR
CHTR

—Behind the Scenes Story ① —

Remember the five-stitch accident I wrote about at the end of volume 10? This is the draft I was working on at the time. Talking about content, I wanted to draw a story like this once. And the scene where Ito is already flying when she is told not to move (page 27), she was supposed to remain quiet in the original plot. She was supposed to ...But before I knew it, ignoring my original idea, she ended up the way she is. She sure is a bit out of control. (Laugh) Not that it's only her--other characters do that, too.

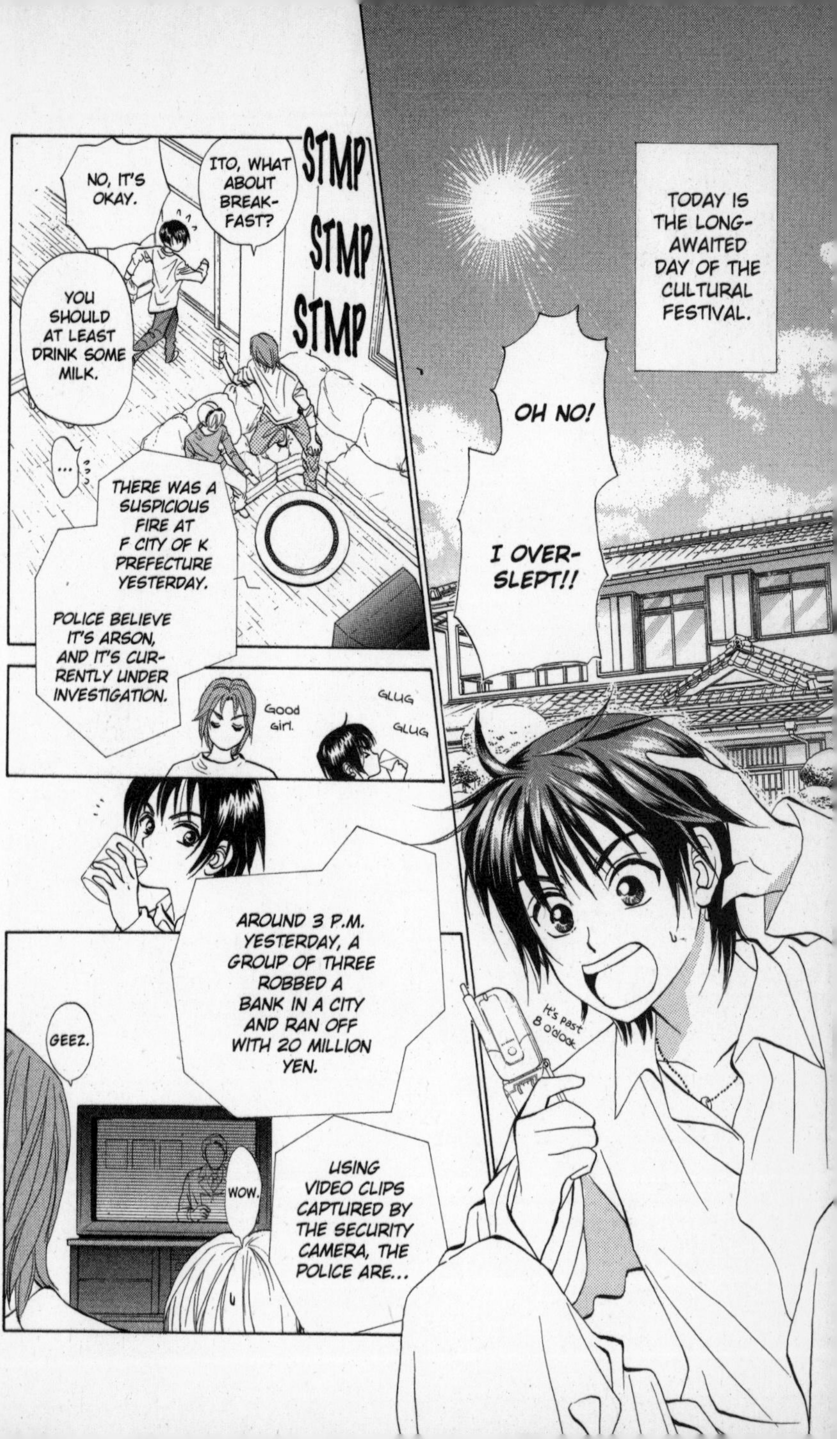
TODAY IS THE LONG-AWAITED DAY OF THE CULTURAL FESTIVAL.
OH NO!
I OVER-SLEPT!!
It's past 8 o'clock
STMP
STMP
STMP
ITO, WHAT ABOUT BREAK-FAST?
NO, IT'S OKAY.
YOU SHOULD AT LEAST DRINK SOME MILK.
...
THERE WAS A SUSPICIOUS FIRE AT F CITY OF K PREFECTURE YESTERDAY.
POLICE BELIEVE IT'S ARSON, AND IT'S CUR-RENTLY UNDER INVESTIGATION.
GLUG
GLUG
Good girl.
AROUND 3 P.M. YESTERDAY, A GROUP OF THREE ROBBED A BANK IN A CITY AND RAN OFF WITH 20 MILLION YEN.
GEEZ.
USING VIDEO CLIPS CAPTURED BY THE SECURITY CAMERA, THE POLICE ARE...
WOW.

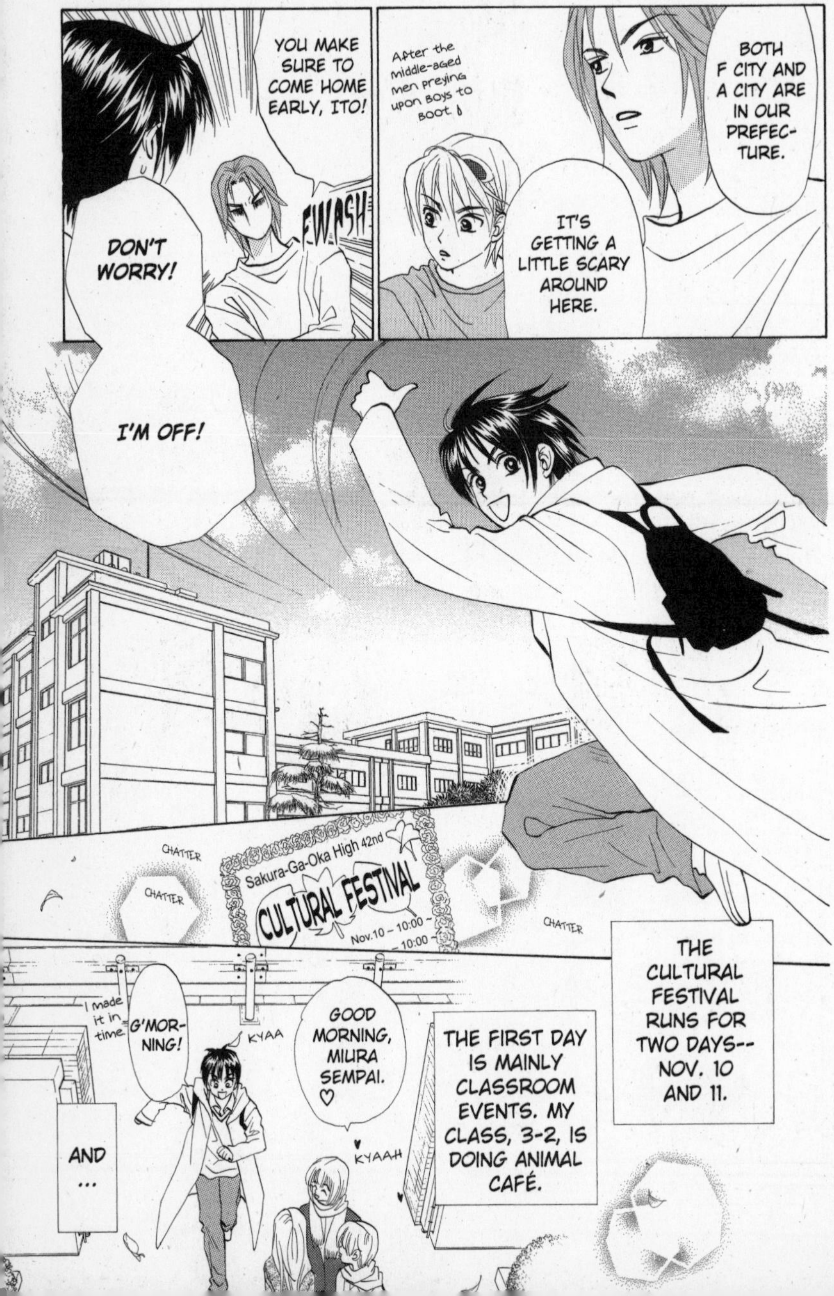

BOTH F CITY AND A CITY ARE IN OUR PREFECTURE.
IT'S GETTING A LITTLE SCARY AROUND HERE.
After the middle-aged men preying upon Boys to Boot.
YOU MAKE SURE TO COME HOME EARLY, ITO!
FWASH
DON'T WORRY!
I'M OFF!
THE CULTURAL FESTIVAL RUNS FOR TWO DAYS-- NOV. 10 AND 11.
CHATTER
Sakura-Ga-Oka High 42nd
CULTURAL FESTIVAL
Nov.10 – 10:00 ~
– 10:00 ~
CHATTER
CHATTER
THE FIRST DAY IS MAINLY CLASSROOM EVENTS. MY CLASS, 3-2, IS DOING ANIMAL CAFÉ.
GOOD MORNING, MIURA SEMPAI. ♡
KYAAH
KYAA
G'MOR-NING!
I made it in time.
AND ...

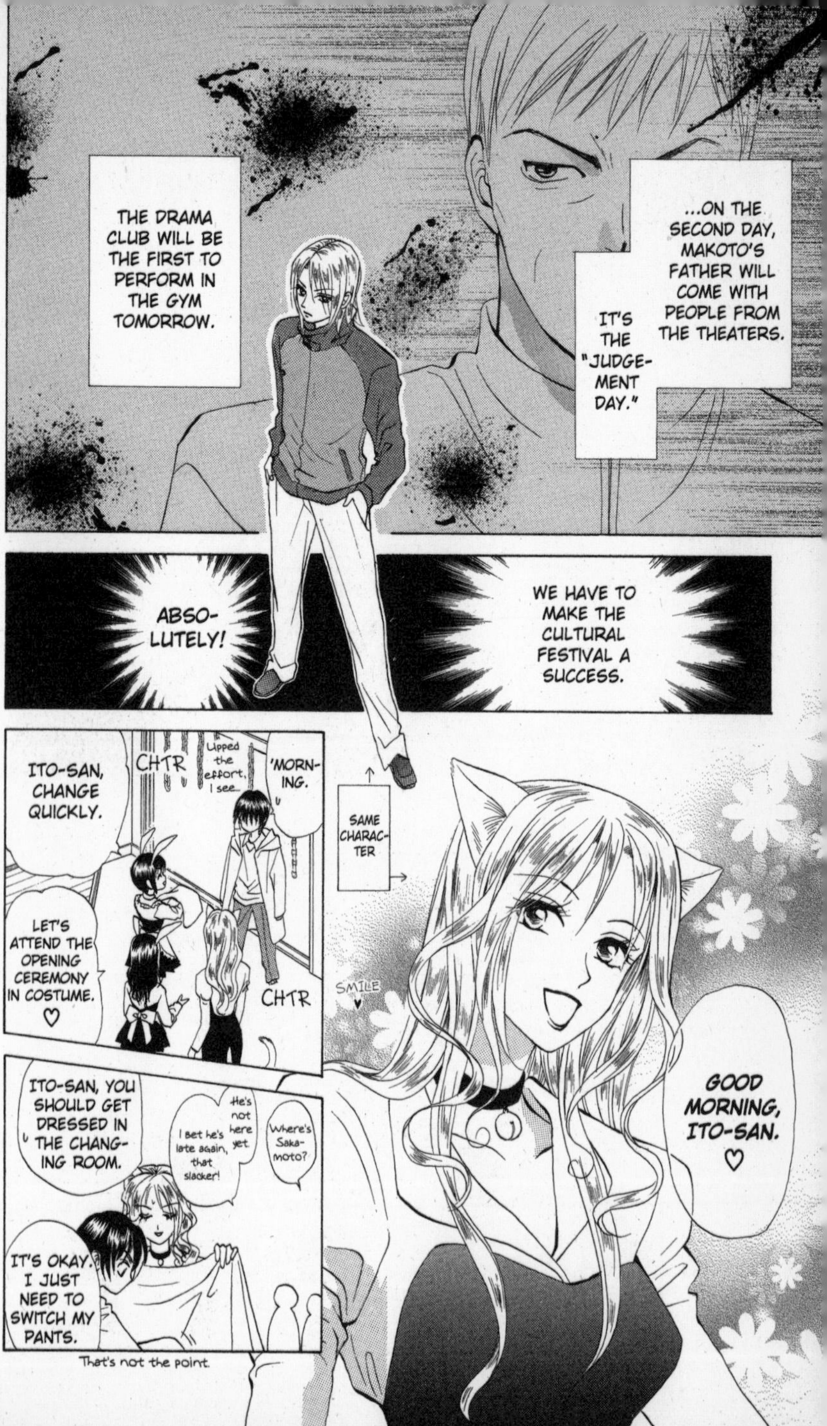
...ON THE SECOND DAY, MAKOTO'S FATHER WILL COME WITH PEOPLE FROM THE THEATERS.
IT'S THE "JUDGEMENT DAY."
THE DRAMA CLUB WILL BE THE FIRST TO PERFORM IN THE GYM TOMORROW.
WE HAVE TO MAKE THE CULTURAL FESTIVAL A SUCCESS.
ABSOLUTELY!
GOOD MORNING, ITO-SAN. ♡
SMILE
SAME CHARACTER
'MORNING.
Upped the effort, I see...
CHTR
ITO-SAN, CHANGE QUICKLY.
LET'S ATTEND THE OPENING CEREMONY IN COSTUME. ♡
CHTR
Where's Sakamoto?
He's not here yet.
I bet he's late again, that slacker!
ITO-SAN, YOU SHOULD GET DRESSED IN THE CHANGING ROOM.
IT'S OKAY. I JUST NEED TO SWITCH MY PANTS.
That's not the point.

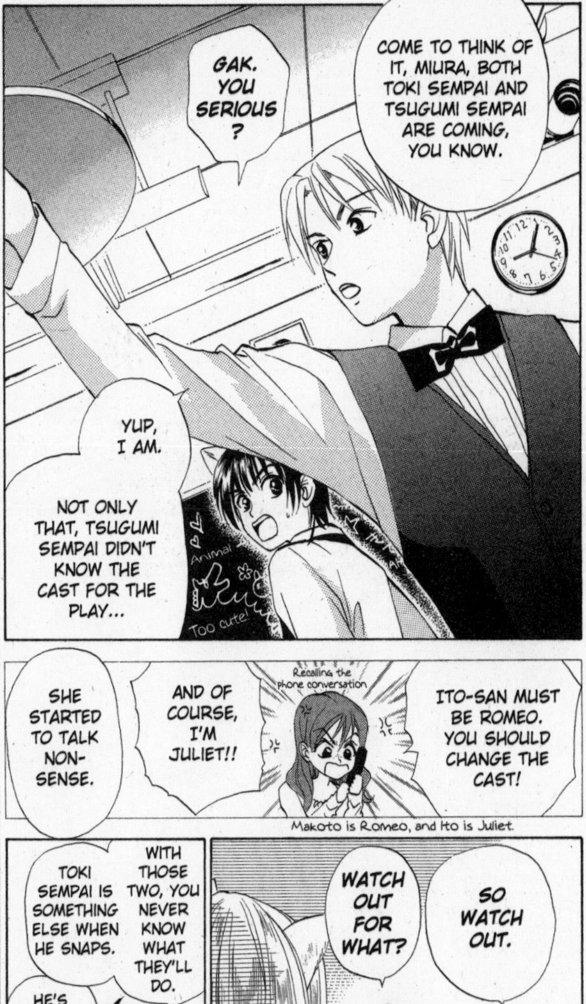
COME TO THINK OF IT, MIURA, BOTH TOKI SEMPAI AND TSUGUMI SEMPAI ARE COMING, YOU KNOW.
GAK. YOU SERIOUS?
YUP, I AM.
NOT ONLY THAT, TSUGUMI SEMPAI DIDN'T KNOW THE CAST FOR THE PLAY...
Animal
Too cute!
ITO-SAN MUST BE ROMEO. YOU SHOULD CHANGE THE CAST!
Recalling the phone conversation
AND OF COURSE, I'M JULIET!!
SHE STARTED TO TALK NON-SENSE.
Makoto is Romeo, and Ito is Juliet.
SO WATCH OUT.
WATCH OUT FOR WHAT?
JUST DON'T GET KIDNAPPED.
WITH THOSE TWO, YOU NEVER KNOW WHAT THEY'LL DO.
TOKI SEMPAI IS SOMETHING ELSE WHEN HE SNAPS.
HE'S SCARY EVEN WHEN HE'S CALM.
WHAT? YOU THINK SO?

GREETINGS.

Hello, this is Emura. Since volume 12 is being released two months sooner than usual, I'm dizzy drafting the story.

As a matter of fact, in the magazine, the story is in the cool final stage, and we know which volume will be the last. I won't announce it here, but I'm sure you'll quickly figure that out. That's why this one is released early...

For the cover art, the Romeo-Juliet motif is used to match the content, but their costumes are quite out of control. (Laugh). I say there's an original touch to it.

I play with each volume, but this time, it's unusual that the Cultural Festival alone covered six installments. Please enjoy. ♪

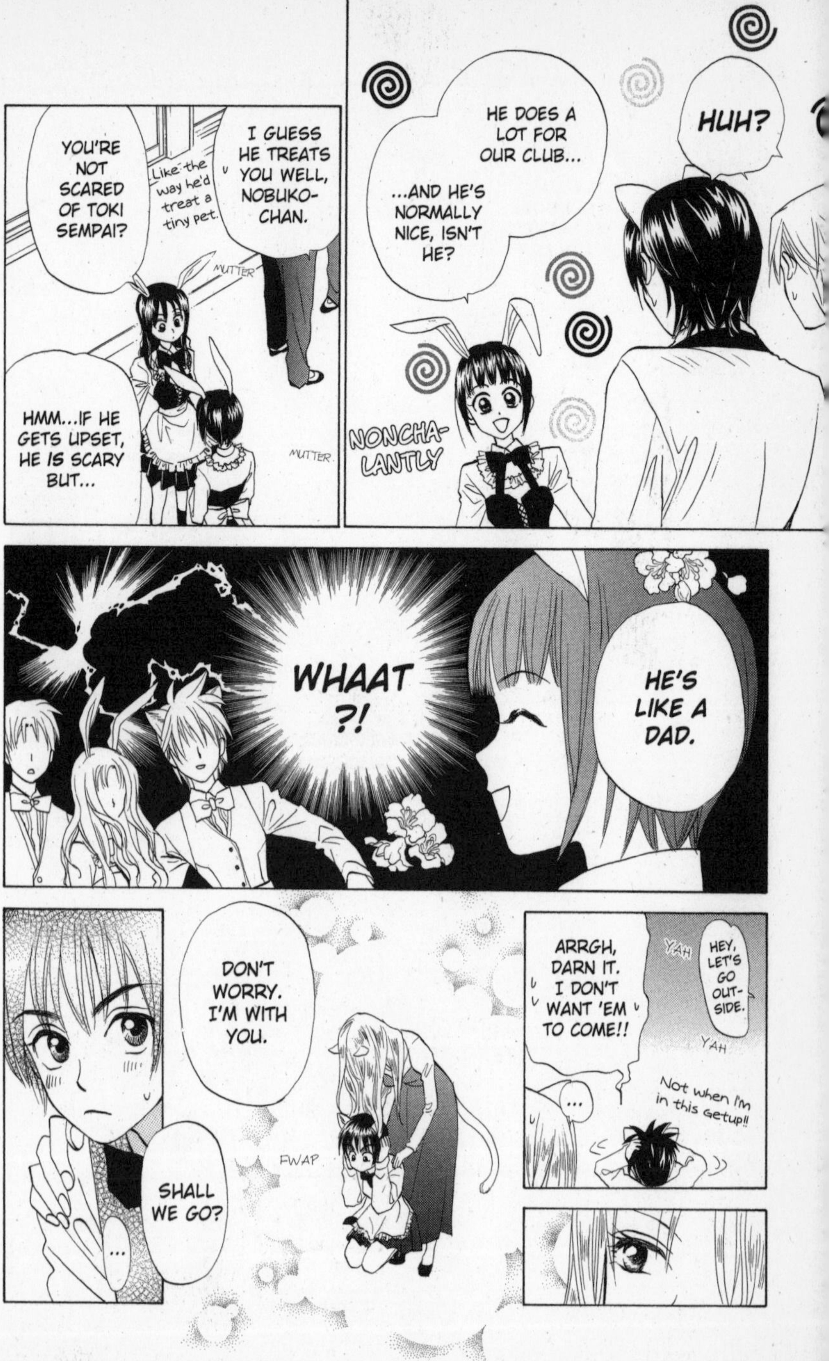
HUH?
HE DOES A LOT FOR OUR CLUB...
...AND HE'S NORMALLY NICE, ISN'T HE?
NONCHALANTLY
I GUESS HE TREATS YOU WELL, NOBUKO-CHAN.
Like the way he'd treat a tiny pet.
YOU'RE NOT SCARED OF TOKI SEMPAI?
MUTTER
HMM...IF HE GETS UPSET, HE IS SCARY BUT...
MUTTER
HE'S LIKE A DAD.
WHAAT ?!
HEY, LET'S GO OUTSIDE.
YAH
YAH
ARRGH, DARN IT. I DON'T WANT 'EM TO COME!!
Not when I'm in this Getup!!
...
DON'T WORRY. I'M WITH YOU.
FWAP
SHALL WE GO?
...

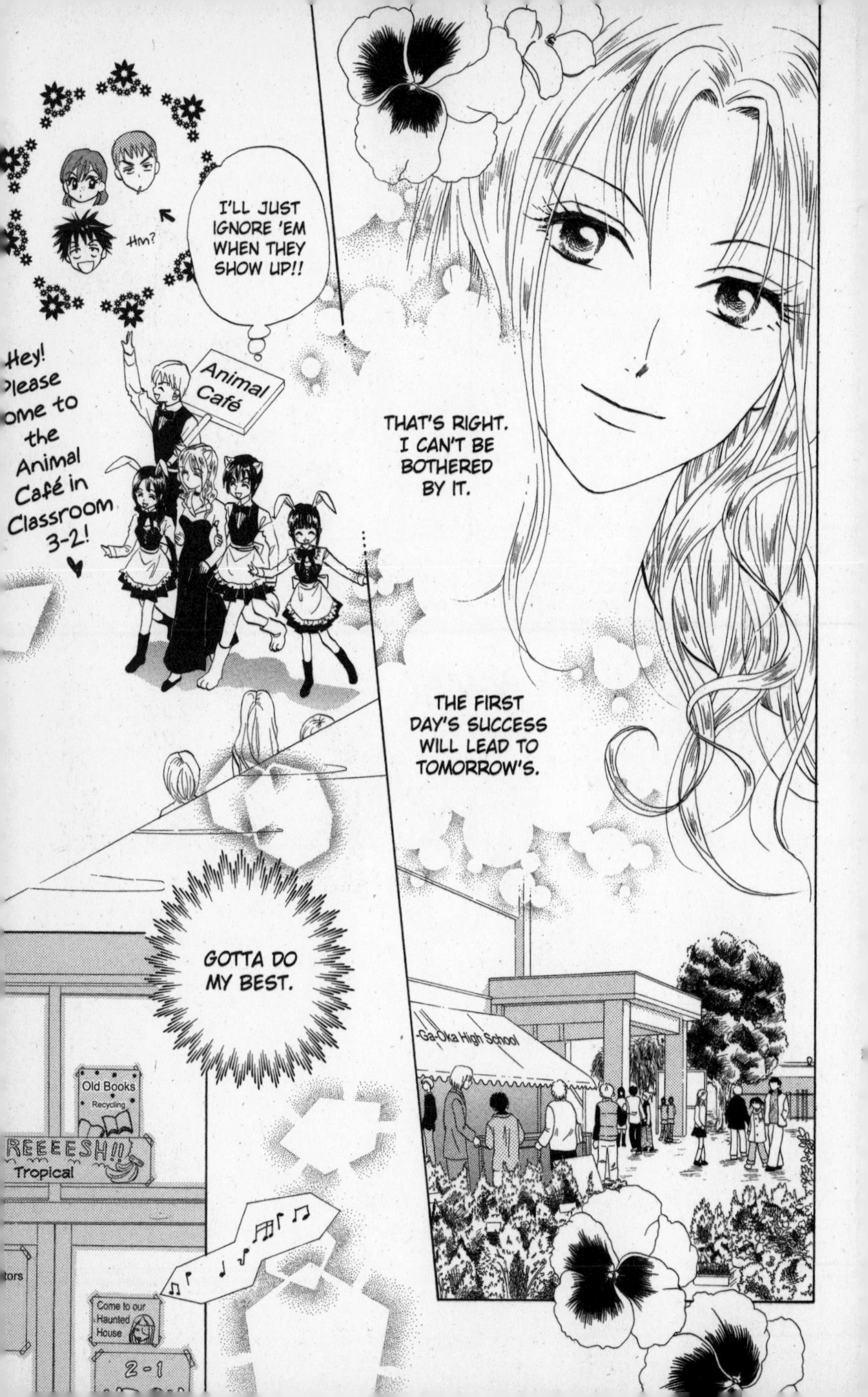
THAT'S RIGHT. I CAN'T BE BOTHERED BY IT.
THE FIRST DAY'S SUCCESS WILL LEAD TO TOMORROW'S.
-Ga-Oka High School
I'LL JUST IGNORE 'EM WHEN THEY SHOW UP!!
Hm?
Hey! Please ome to the Animal Café in Classroom 3-2!
Animal Café
GOTTA DO MY BEST.
Old Books Recycling
REEEESH!! Tropical
tors
Come to our Haunted House
2-1

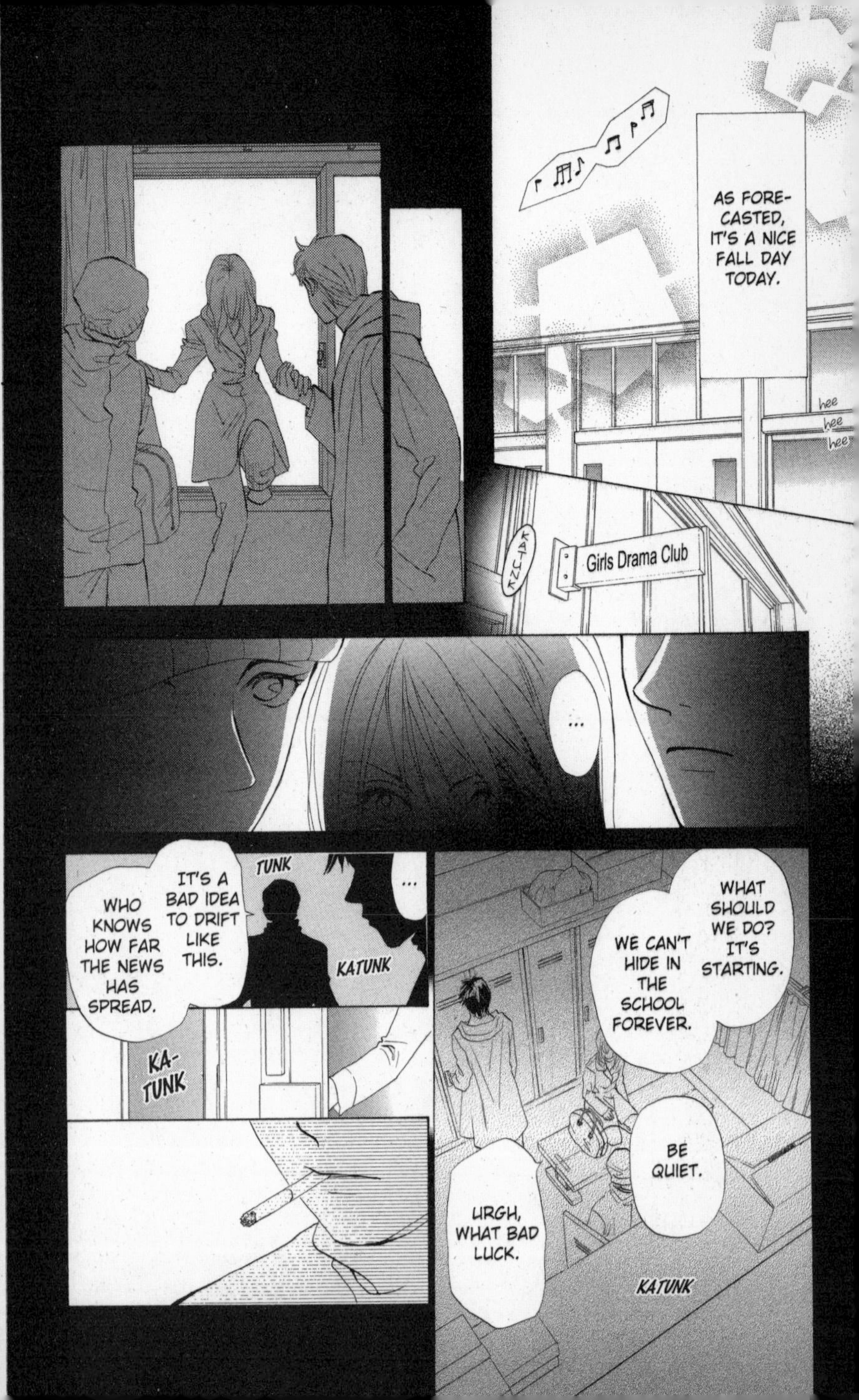

AS FORE-CASTED, IT'S A NICE FALL DAY TODAY.
hee hee hee
KATUNK
Girls Drama Club
...
WHAT SHOULD WE DO? IT'S STARTING.
WE CAN'T HIDE IN THE SCHOOL FOREVER.
BE QUIET.
URGH, WHAT BAD LUCK.
KATUNK
...
TUNK
KATUNK
IT'S A BAD IDEA TO DRIFT LIKE THIS.
WHO KNOWS HOW FAR THE NEWS HAS SPREAD.
KA-TUNK

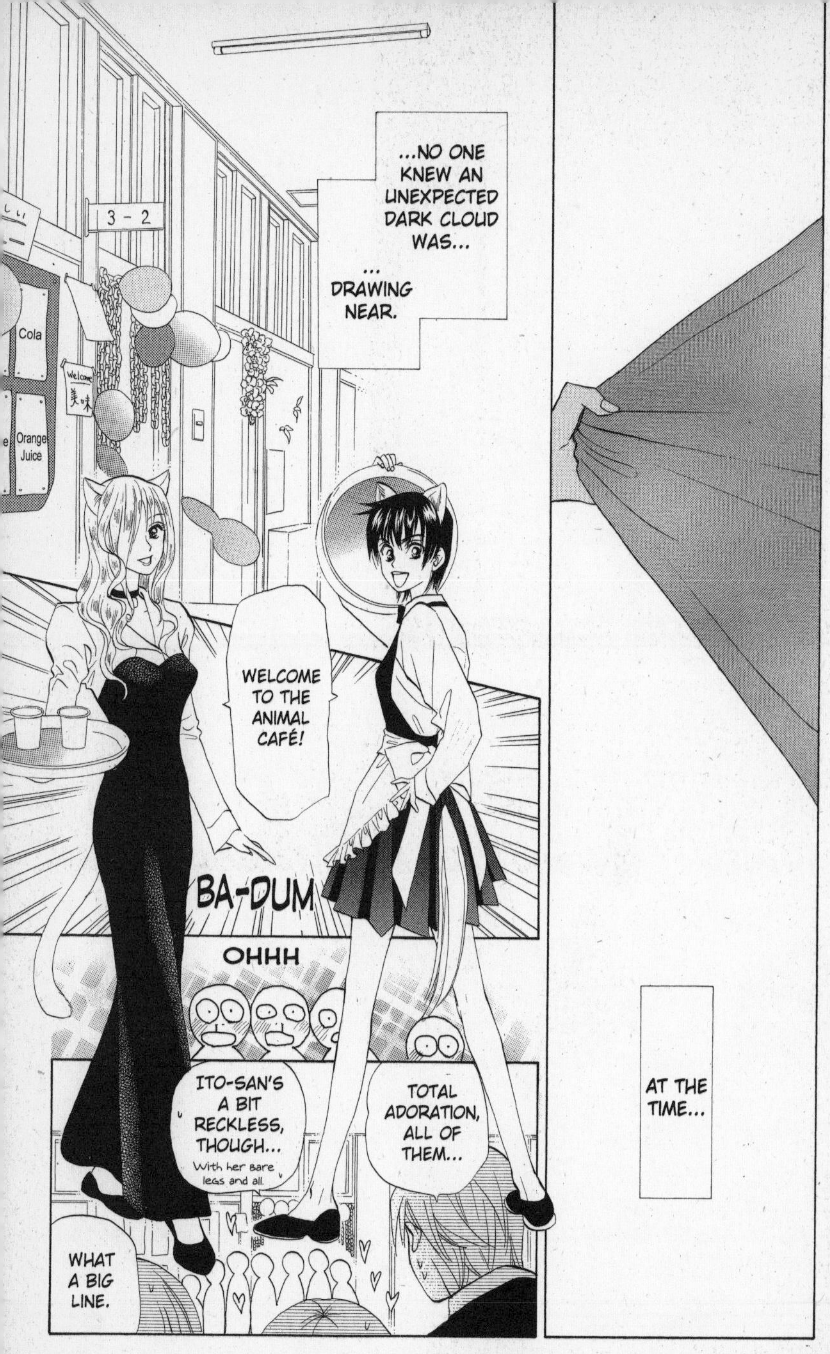
AT THE TIME...
...NO ONE KNEW AN UNEXPECTED DARK CLOUD WAS...
... DRAWING NEAR.
3 - 2
Cola
Orange Juice
WELCOME TO THE ANIMAL CAFÉ!
BA-DUM
OHHH
TOTAL ADORATION, ALL OF THEM...
ITO-SAN'S A BIT RECKLESS, THOUGH...
With her bare legs and all.
WHAT A BIG LINE.

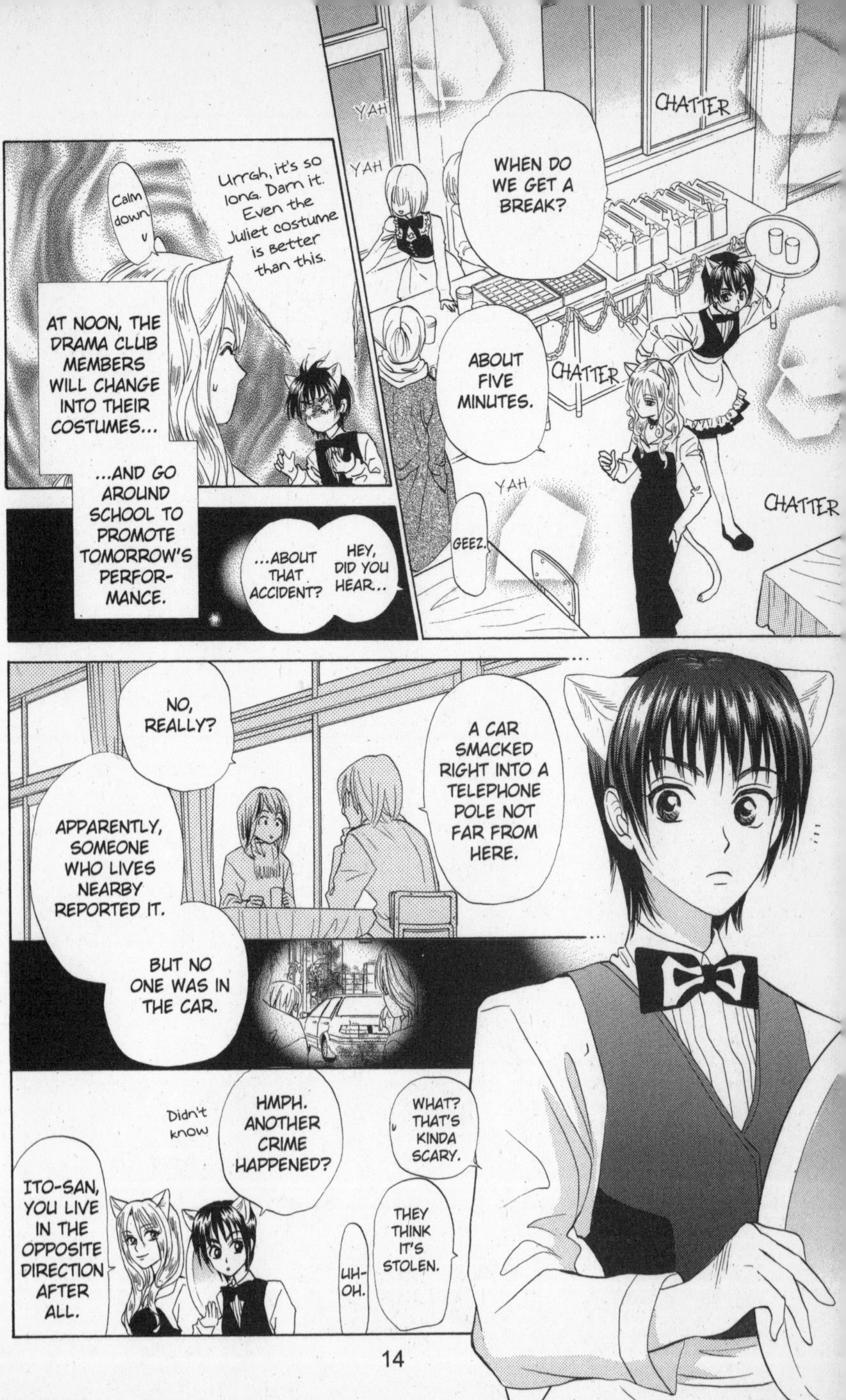
CHATTER
YAH
YAH
WHEN DO WE GET A BREAK?
ABOUT FIVE MINUTES.
CHATTER
CHATTER
YAH
GEEZ.
Urrgh, it's so long. Darn it. Even the Juliet costume is better than this.
Calm down
AT NOON, THE DRAMA CLUB MEMBERS WILL CHANGE INTO THEIR COSTUMES...
...AND GO AROUND SCHOOL TO PROMOTE TOMORROW'S PERFORMANCE.
HEY, DID YOU HEAR...
...ABOUT THAT ACCIDENT?
A CAR SMACKED RIGHT INTO A TELEPHONE POLE NOT FAR FROM HERE.
NO, REALLY?
APPARENTLY, SOMEONE WHO LIVES NEARBY REPORTED IT.
BUT NO ONE WAS IN THE CAR.
WHAT? THAT'S KINDA SCARY.
THEY THINK IT'S STOLEN.
UH-OH.
HMPH. ANOTHER CRIME HAPPENED?
Didn't know
ITO-SAN, YOU LIVE IN THE OPPOSITE DIRECTION AFTER ALL.

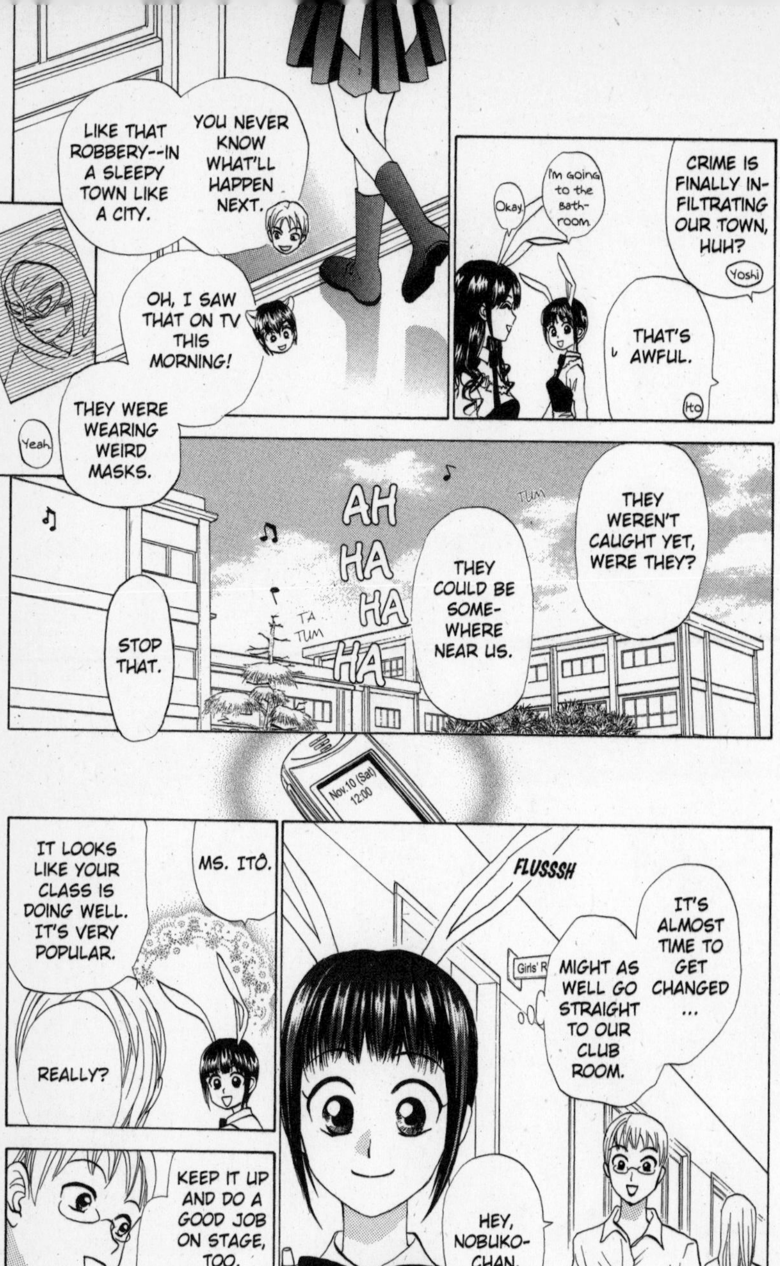
CRIME IS FINALLY IN-FILTRATING OUR TOWN, HUH?
Yoshi
I'm going to the bath-room.
Okay.
THAT'S AWFUL.
Ito
YOU NEVER KNOW WHAT'LL HAPPEN NEXT.
LIKE THAT ROBBERY--IN A SLEEPY TOWN LIKE A CITY.
OH, I SAW THAT ON TV THIS MORNING!
THEY WERE WEARING WEIRD MASKS.
Yeah.
THEY WEREN'T CAUGHT YET, WERE THEY?
TUM
THEY COULD BE SOME-WHERE NEAR US.
AH HA HA HA
TA TUM
STOP THAT.
Nov.10 (Sat) 12:00
FLUSSSH
IT'S ALMOST TIME TO GET CHANGED ...
MIGHT AS WELL GO STRAIGHT TO OUR CLUB ROOM.
Girls' R
HEY, NOBUKO-CHAN.
MS. ITÔ.
IT LOOKS LIKE YOUR CLASS IS DOING WELL. IT'S VERY POPULAR.
REALLY?
KEEP IT UP AND DO A GOOD JOB ON STAGE, TOO.
HUH?

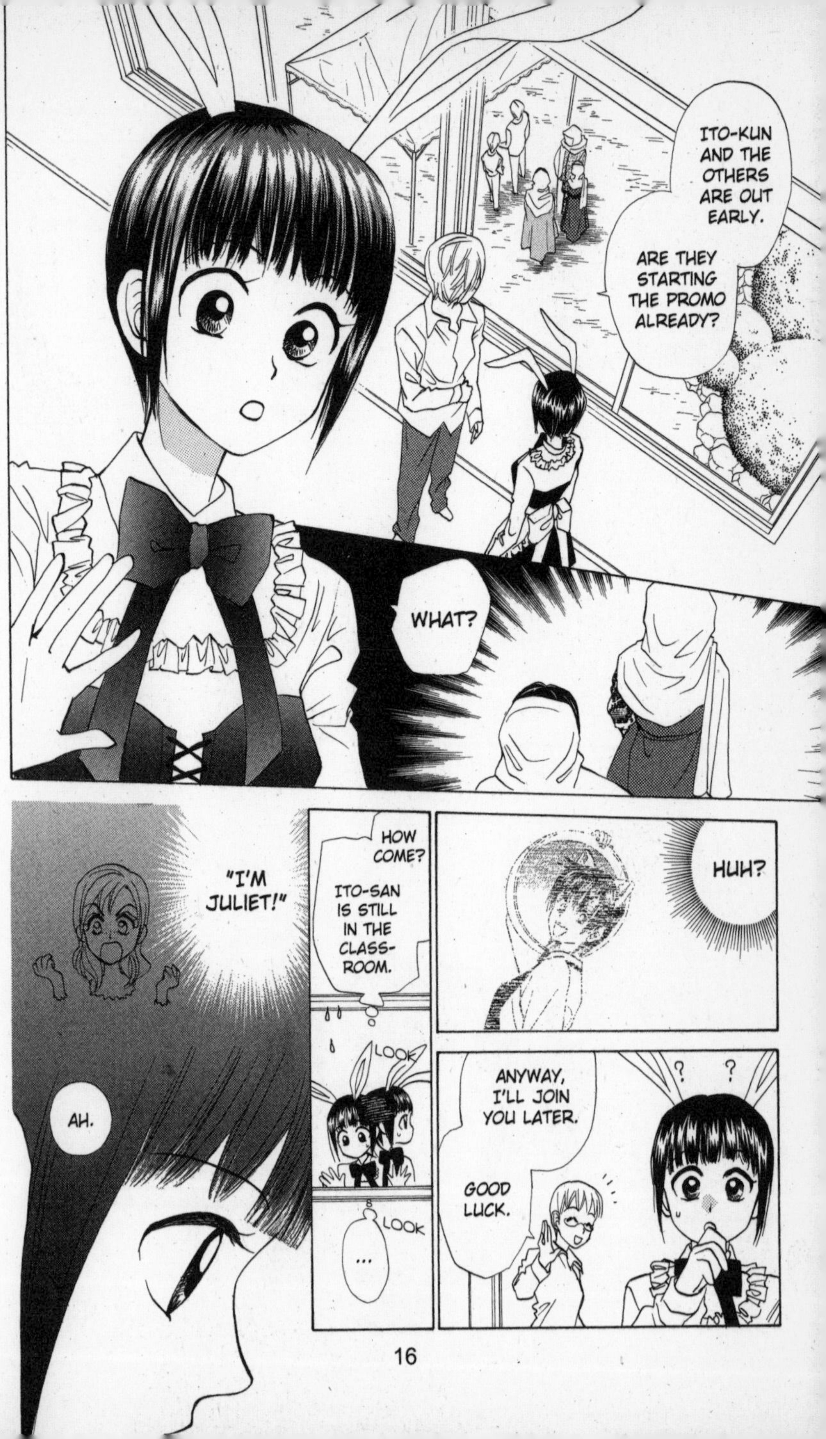
ITO-KUN AND THE OTHERS ARE OUT EARLY.
ARE THEY STARTING THE PROMO ALREADY?
WHAT?
HUH?
ANYWAY, I'LL JOIN YOU LATER.
GOOD LUCK.
HOW COME?
ITO-SAN IS STILL IN THE CLASS-ROOM.
LOOK
LOOK
...
"I'M JULIET!"
AH.

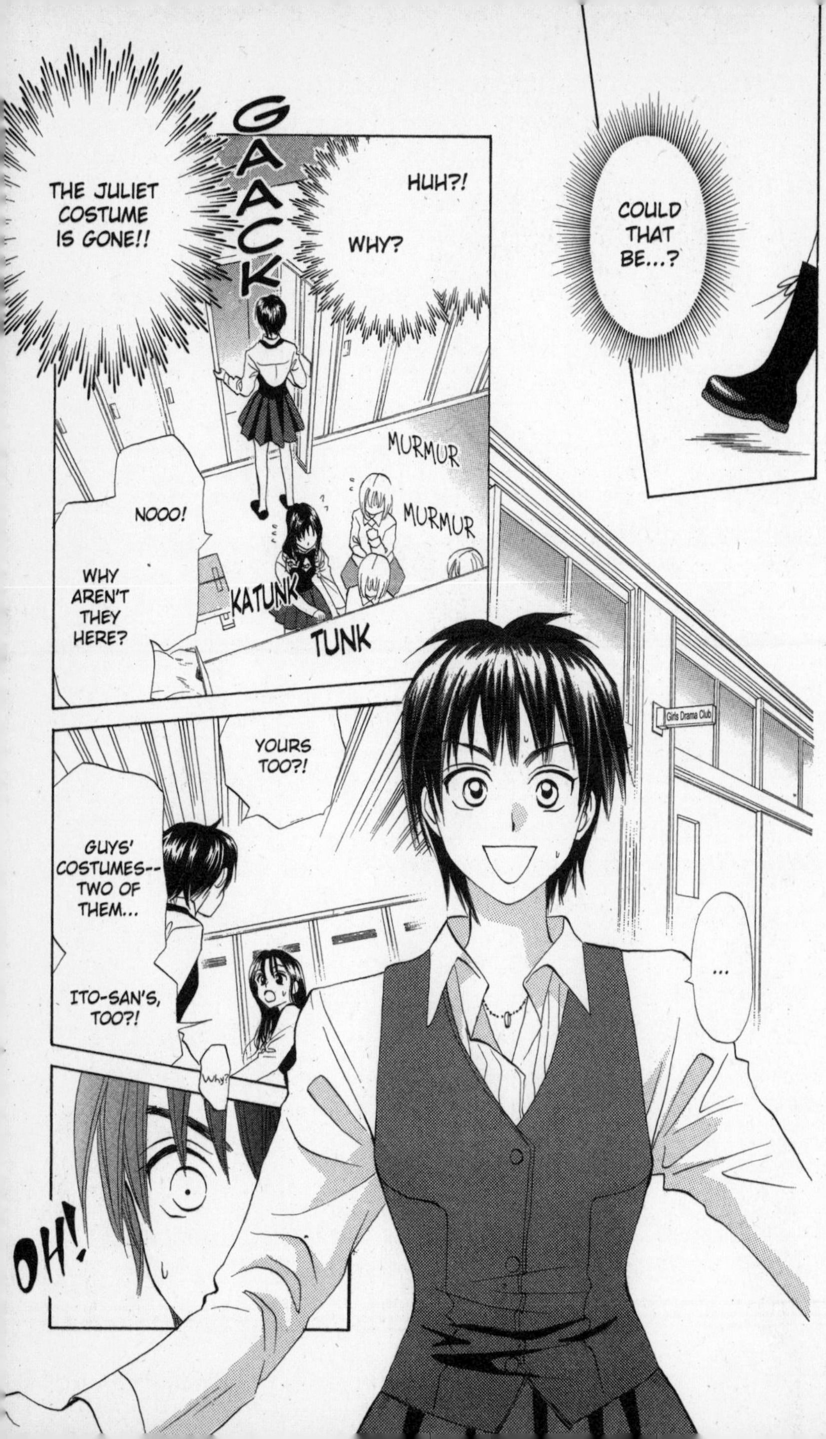
COULD THAT BE...?
GAACK
HUH?!
WHY?
THE JULIET COSTUME IS GONE!!
MURMUR
MURMUR
NOOO!
WHY AREN'T THEY HERE?
KATUNK
TUNK
...
Girls Drama Club
YOURS TOO?!
GUYS' COSTUMES--TWO OF THEM...
ITO-SAN'S, TOO?!
Why?
OH!

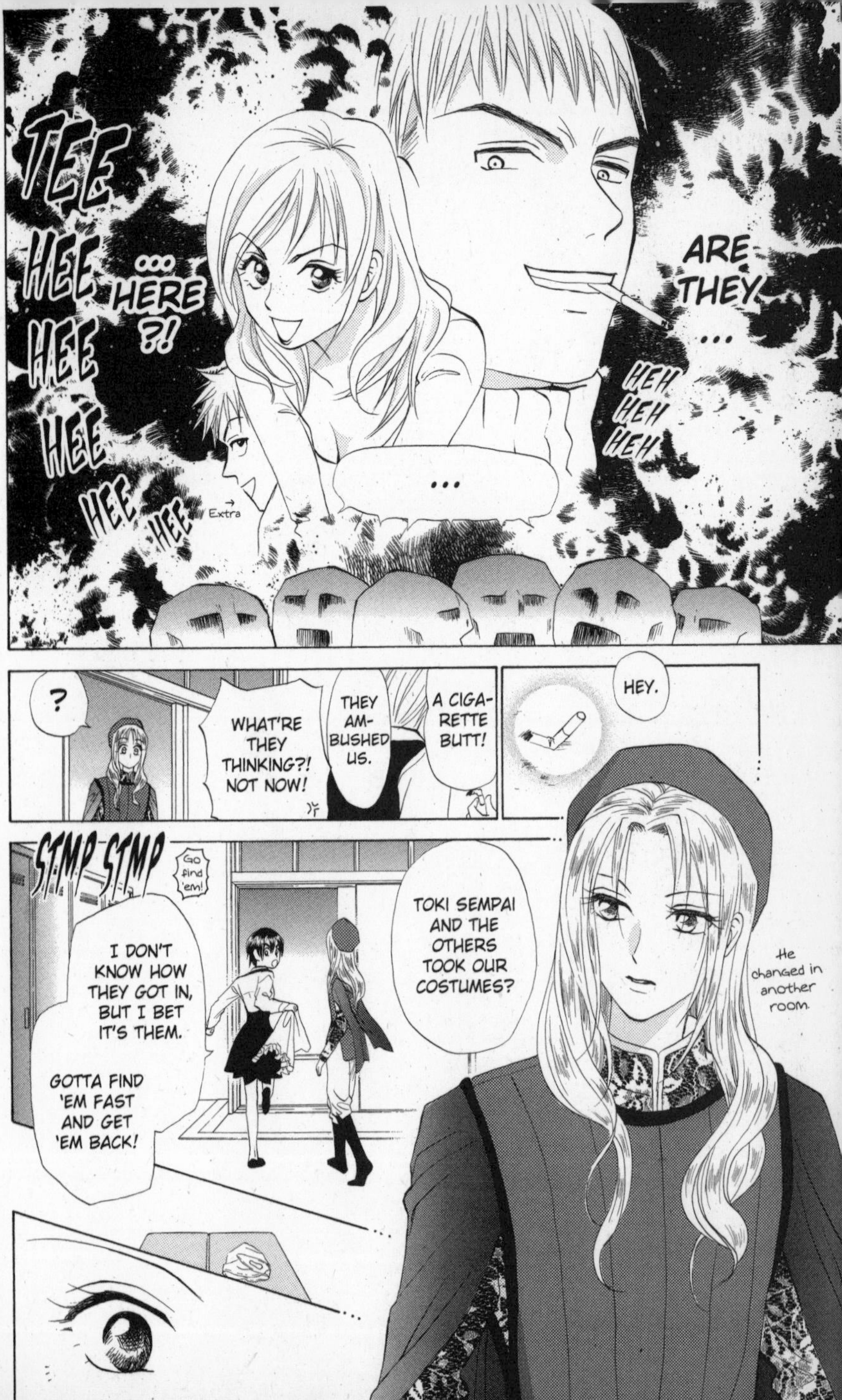
ARE THEY...
HEH HEH HEH
...HERE?!
TEE HEE HEE HEE HEE HEE
...
Extra
HEY.
A CIGARETTE BUTT!
THEY AMBUSHED US.
WHAT'RE THEY THINKING?! NOT NOW!
?
TOKI SEMPAI AND THE OTHERS TOOK OUR COSTUMES?
He changed in another room.
STMP STMP
Go find 'em!
I DON'T KNOW HOW THEY GOT IN, BUT I BET IT'S THEM.
GOTTA FIND 'EM FAST AND GET 'EM BACK!

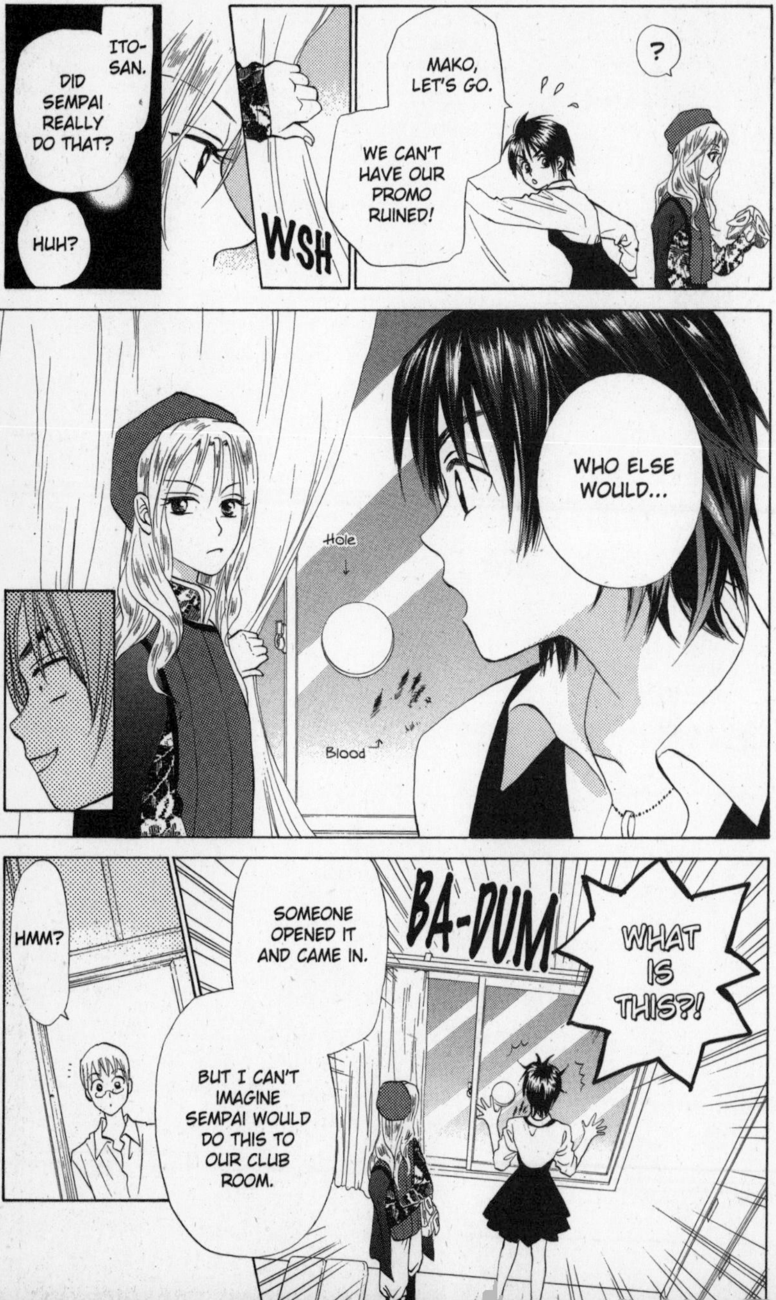
?
MAKO, LET'S GO.
WE CAN'T HAVE OUR PROMO RUINED!
WSH
ITO-SAN.
DID SEMPAI REALLY DO THAT?
HUH?
WHO ELSE WOULD...
Hole
Blood
WHAT IS THIS?!
BA-DUM
SOMEONE OPENED IT AND CAME IN.
BUT I CAN'T IMAGINE SEMPAI WOULD DO THIS TO OUR CLUB ROOM.
HMM?

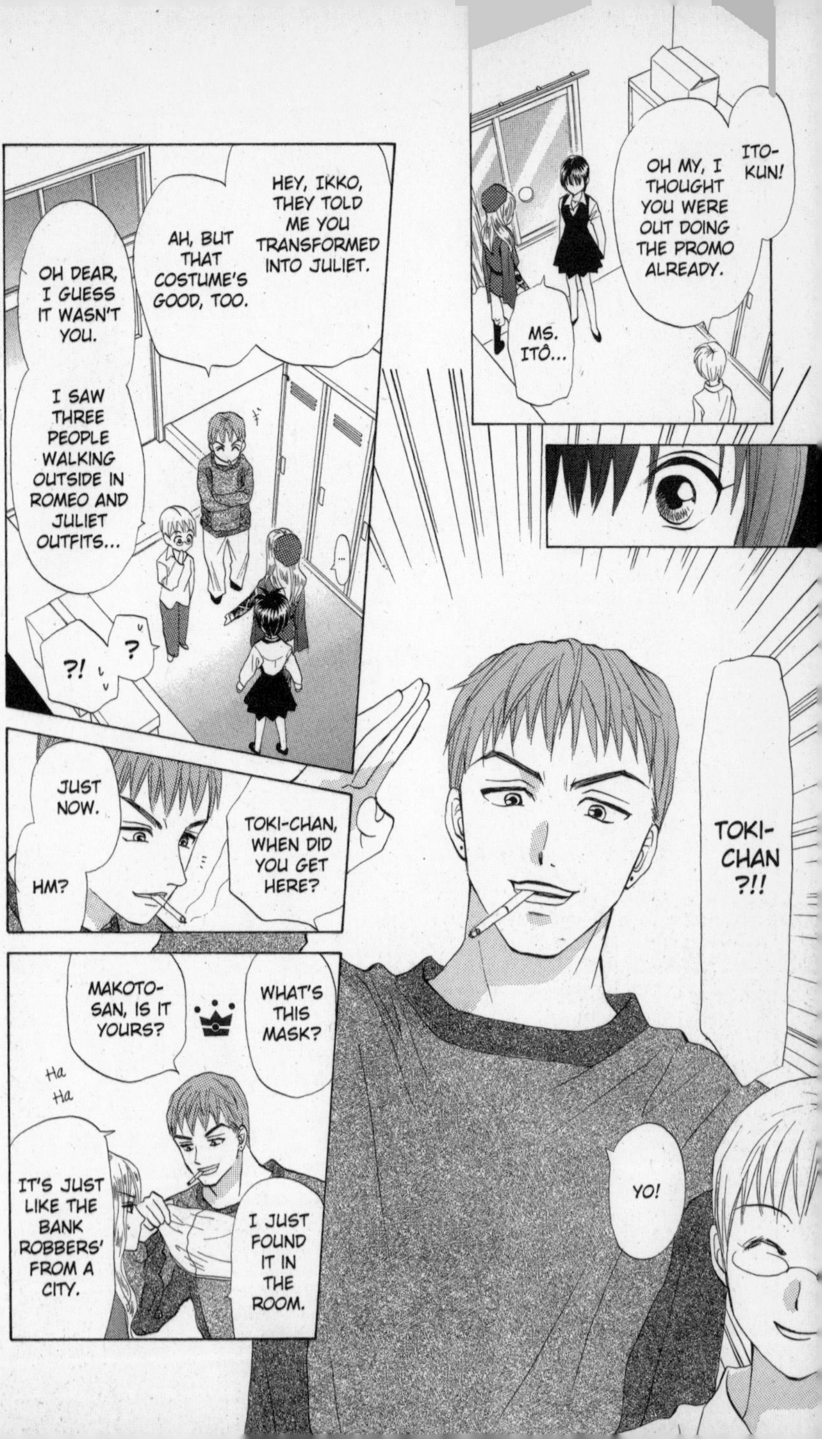
ITO-KUN!
OH MY, I THOUGHT YOU WERE OUT DOING THE PROMO ALREADY.
MS. ITÔ...
HEY, IKKO, THEY TOLD ME YOU TRANSFORMED INTO JULIET.
AH, BUT THAT COSTUME'S GOOD, TOO.
OH DEAR, I GUESS IT WASN'T YOU.
I SAW THREE PEOPLE WALKING OUTSIDE IN ROMEO AND JULIET OUTFITS...
...
?
?!
TOKI-CHAN?!!
YO!
TOKI-CHAN, WHEN DID YOU GET HERE?
HM?
JUST NOW.
WHAT'S THIS MASK?
MAKOTO-SAN, IS IT YOURS?
I JUST FOUND IT IN THE ROOM.
IT'S JUST LIKE THE BANK ROBBERS' FROM A CITY.
Ha Ha

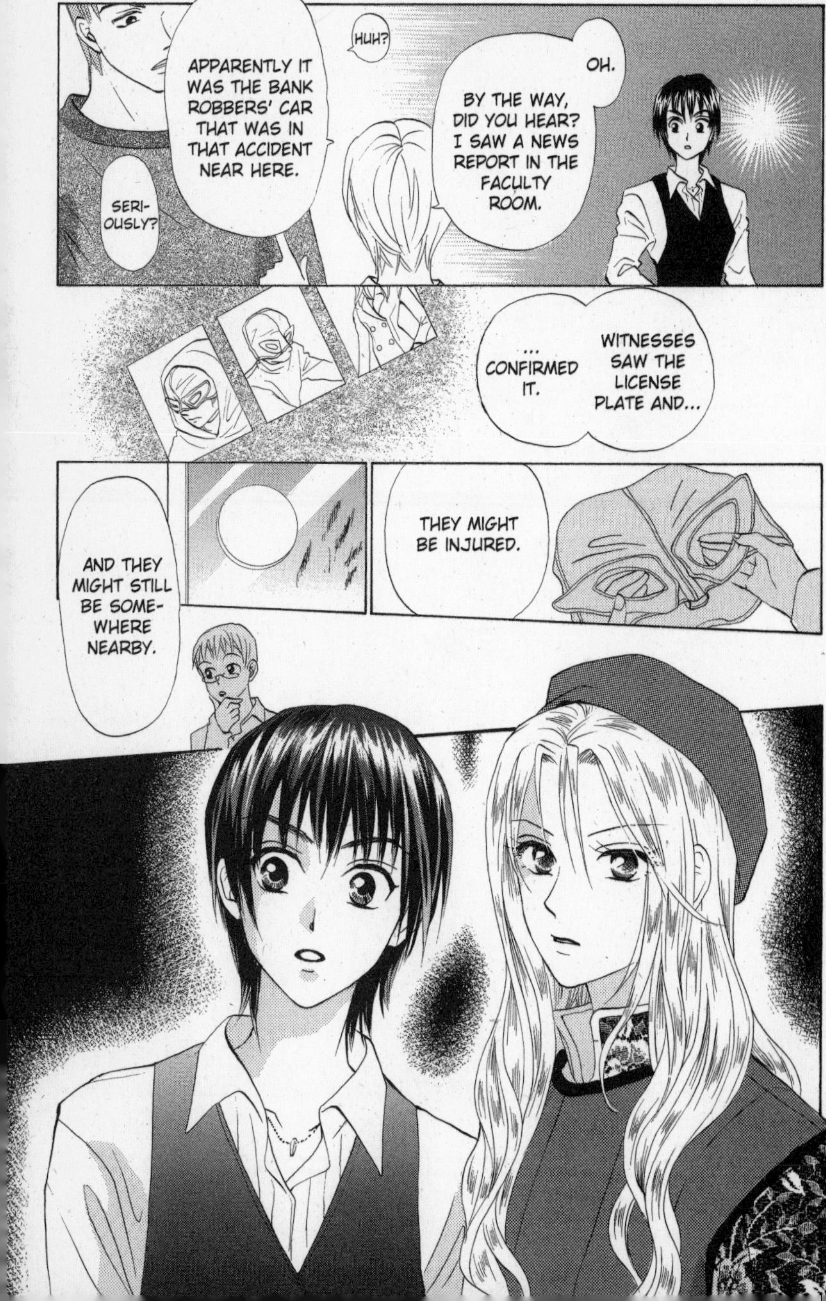
OH.
BY THE WAY, DID YOU HEAR? I SAW A NEWS REPORT IN THE FACULTY ROOM.
HUH?
APPARENTLY IT WAS THE BANK ROBBERS' CAR THAT WAS IN THAT ACCIDENT NEAR HERE.
SERI-OUSLY?
WITNESSES SAW THE LICENSE PLATE AND...
...CONFIRMED IT.
THEY MIGHT BE INJURED.
AND THEY MIGHT STILL BE SOME-WHERE NEARBY.

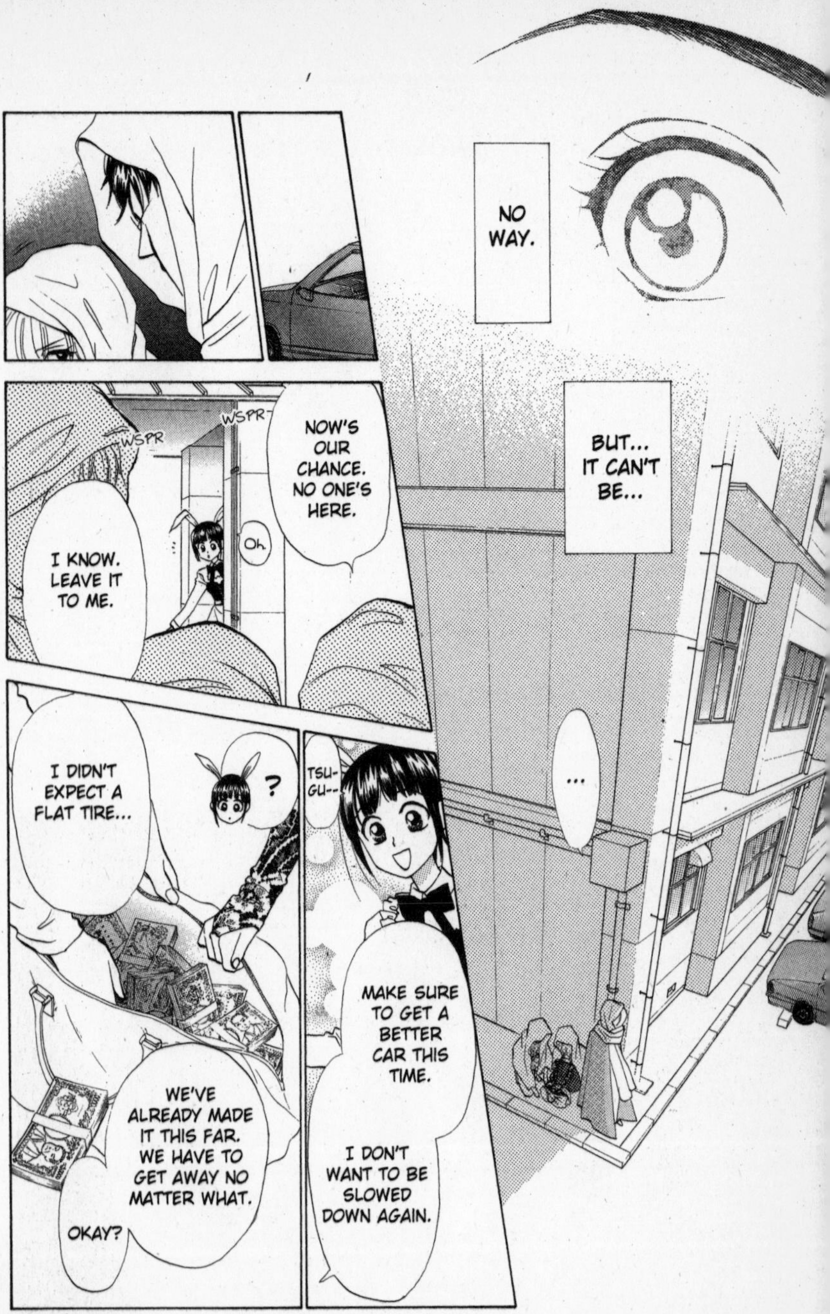
NO WAY.
BUT... IT CAN'T BE...
...
WSPR
WSPR
NOW'S OUR CHANCE. NO ONE'S HERE.
Oh.
I KNOW. LEAVE IT TO ME.
TSU-GU--
MAKE SURE TO GET A BETTER CAR THIS TIME.
I DON'T WANT TO BE SLOWED DOWN AGAIN.
?
I DIDN'T EXPECT A FLAT TIRE...
WE'VE ALREADY MADE IT THIS FAR. WE HAVE TO GET AWAY NO MATTER WHAT.
OKAY?

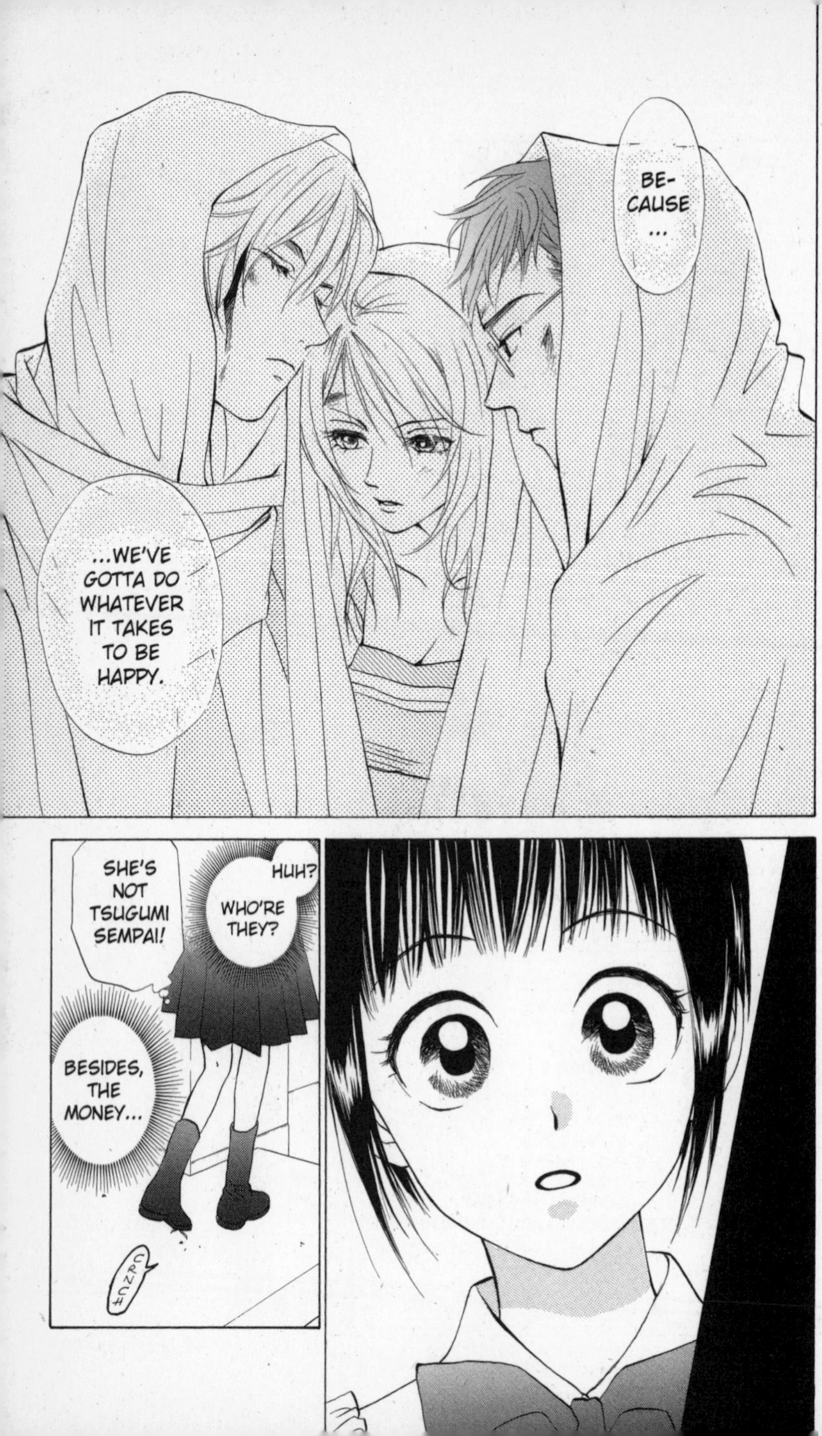
BE-CAUSE ...
...WE'VE GOTTA DO WHATEVER IT TAKES TO BE HAPPY.
HUH?
WHO'RE THEY?
SHE'S NOT TSUGUMI SEMPAI!
BESIDES, THE MONEY...
CRNCH

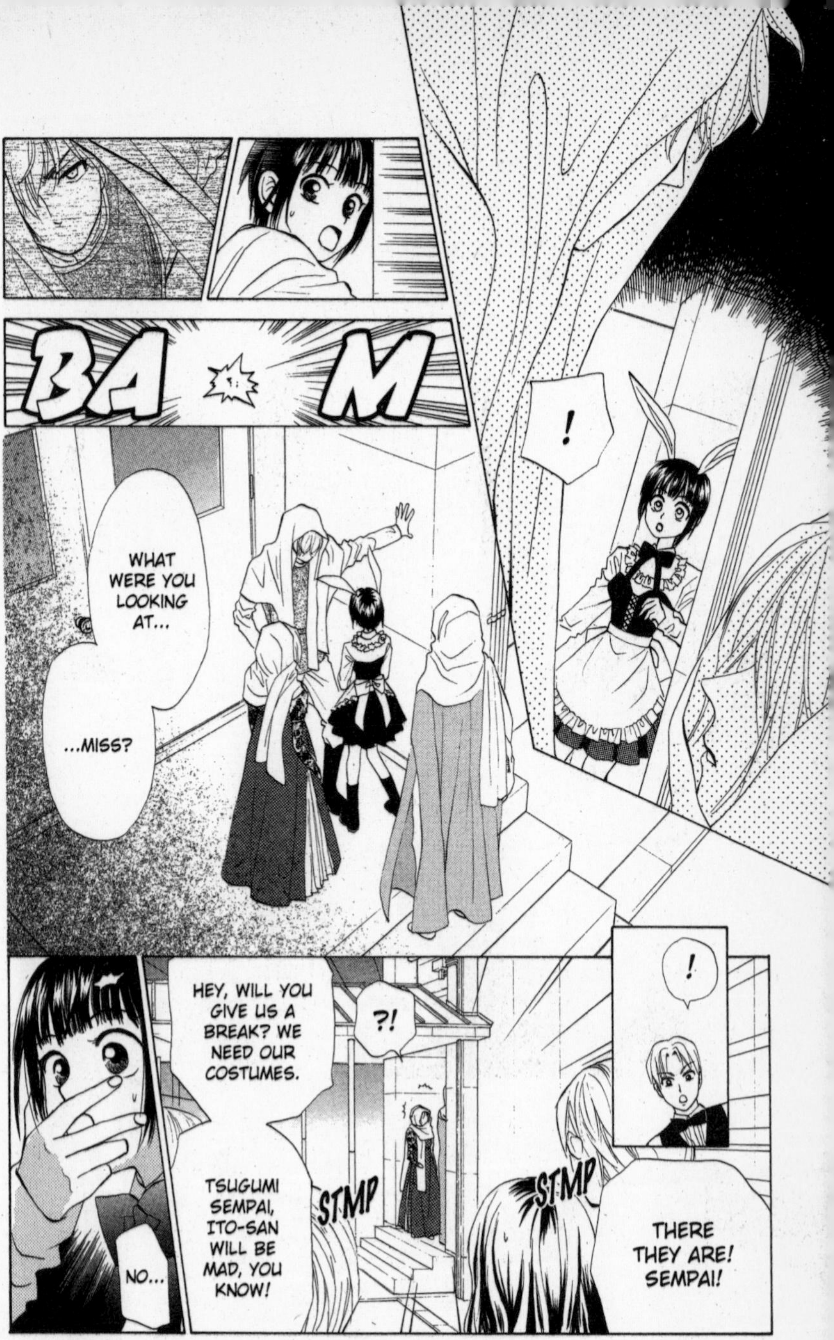
!
BA M
WHAT WERE YOU LOOKING AT...
...MISS?
!
THERE THEY ARE! SEMPAI!
STMP
?!
HEY, WILL YOU GIVE US A BREAK? WE NEED OUR COSTUMES.
STMP
TSUGUMI SEMPAI, ITO-SAN WILL BE MAD, YOU KNOW!
NO...

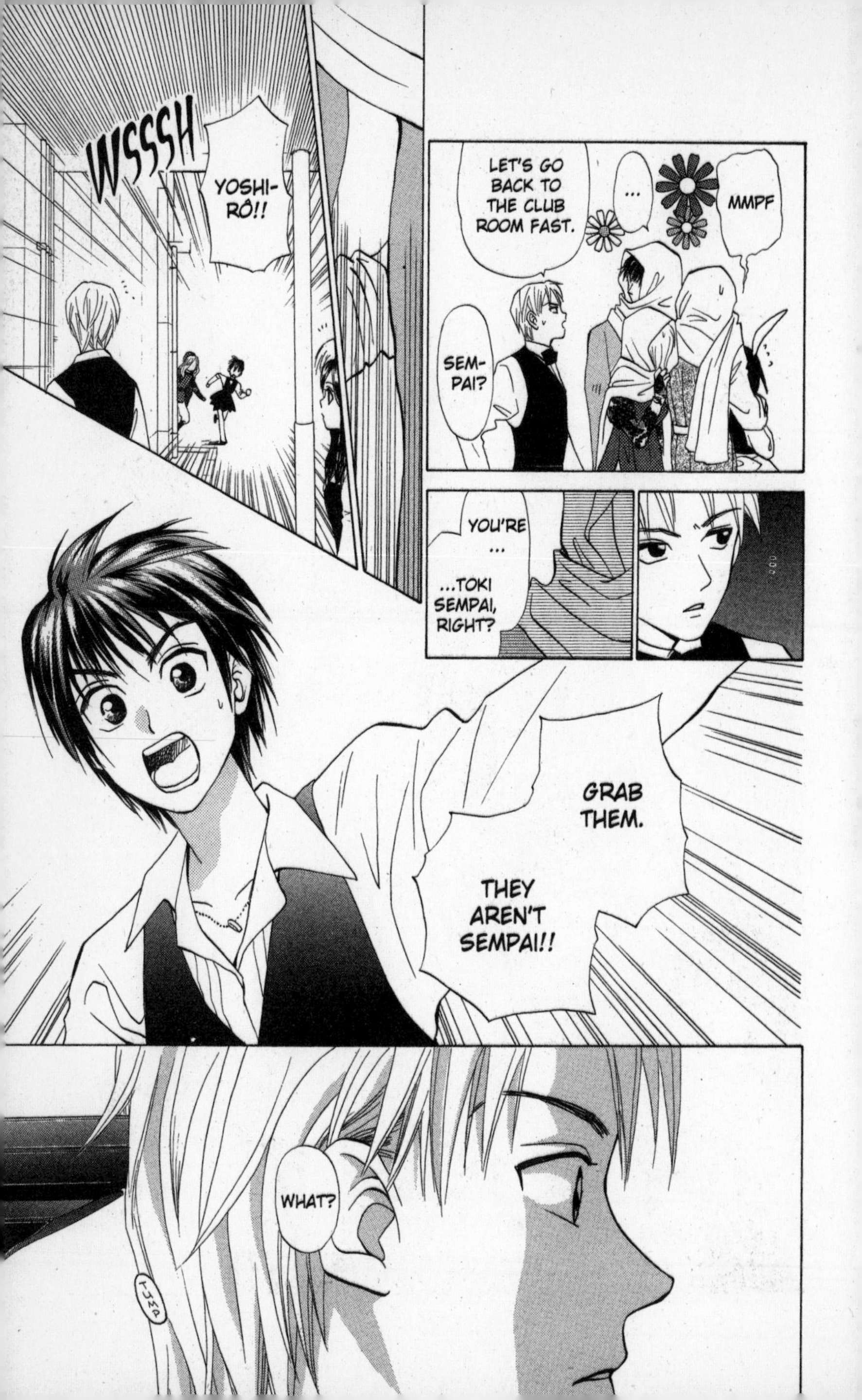
MMPF
...
LET'S GO BACK TO THE CLUB ROOM FAST.
SEMPAI?
YOU'RE ...
...TOKI SEMPAI, RIGHT?
WSSSH
YOSHI-RÔ!!
GRAB THEM.
THEY AREN'T SEMPAI!!
WHAT?
TUMP

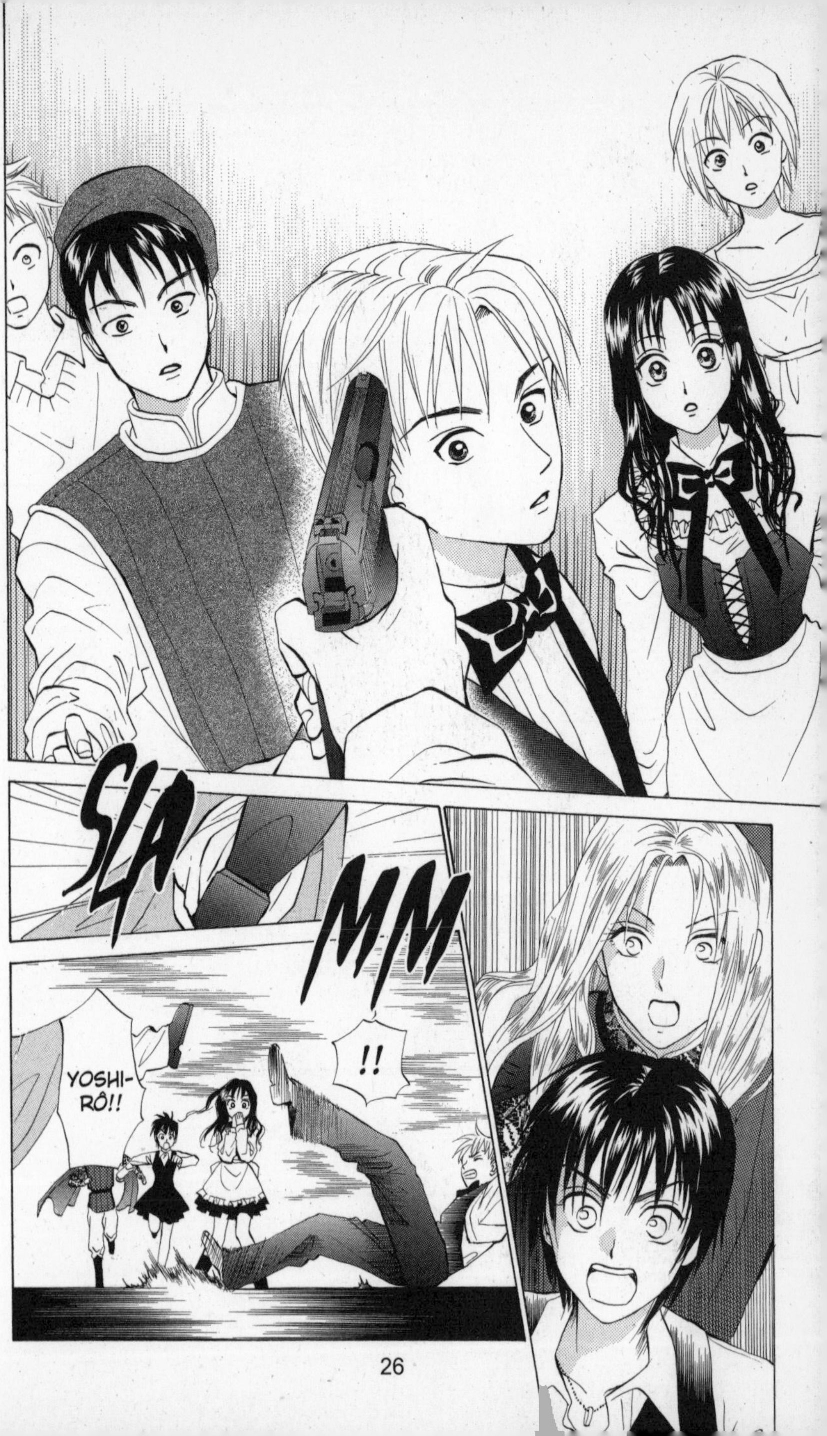
SLAMM
!!
YOSHI-RÔ!!

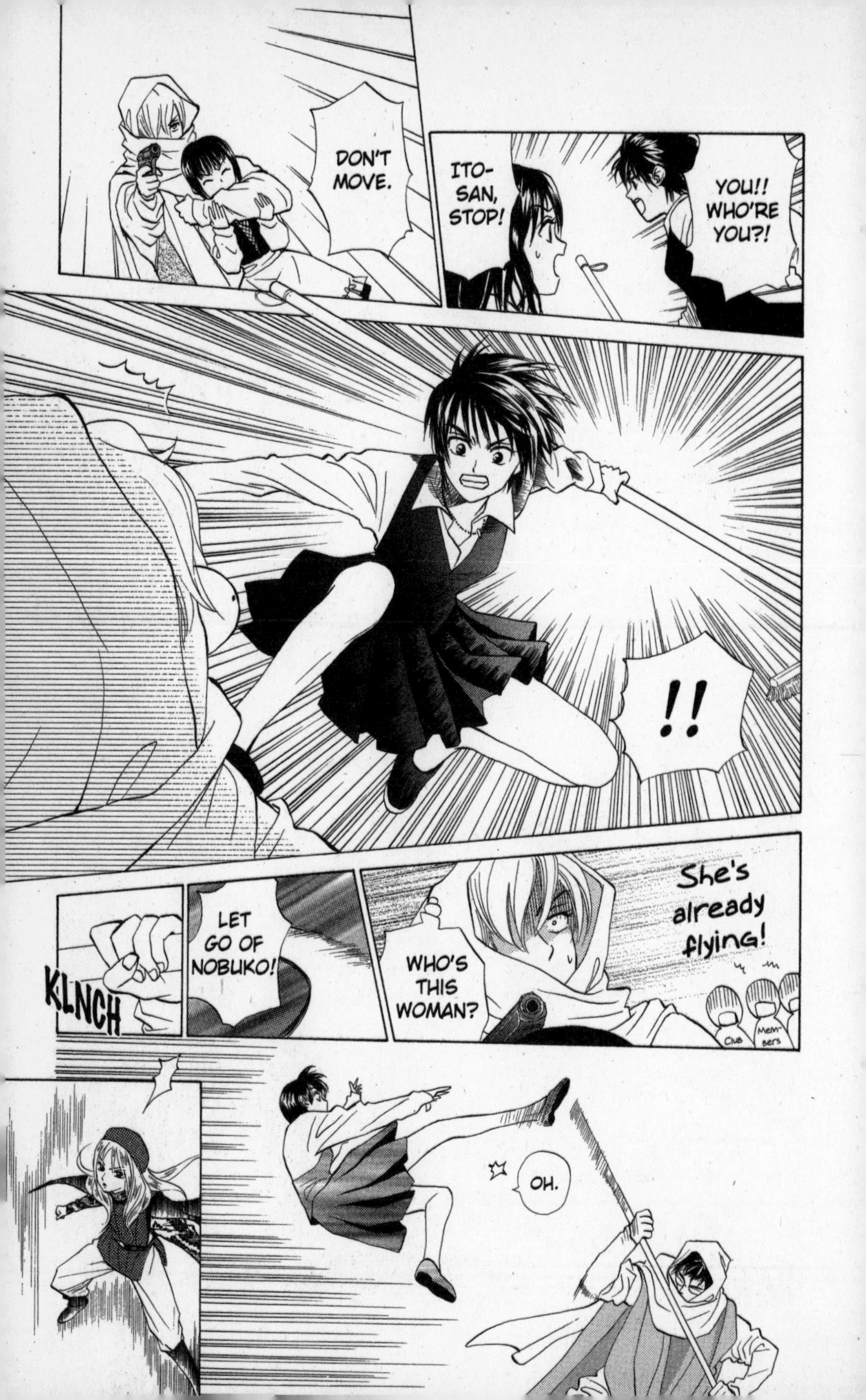
YOU!! WHO'RE YOU?!
ITO-SAN, STOP!
DON'T MOVE.
!!
She's already flying!
Club Members
WHO'S THIS WOMAN?
LET GO OF NOBUKO!
KLNCH
OH.

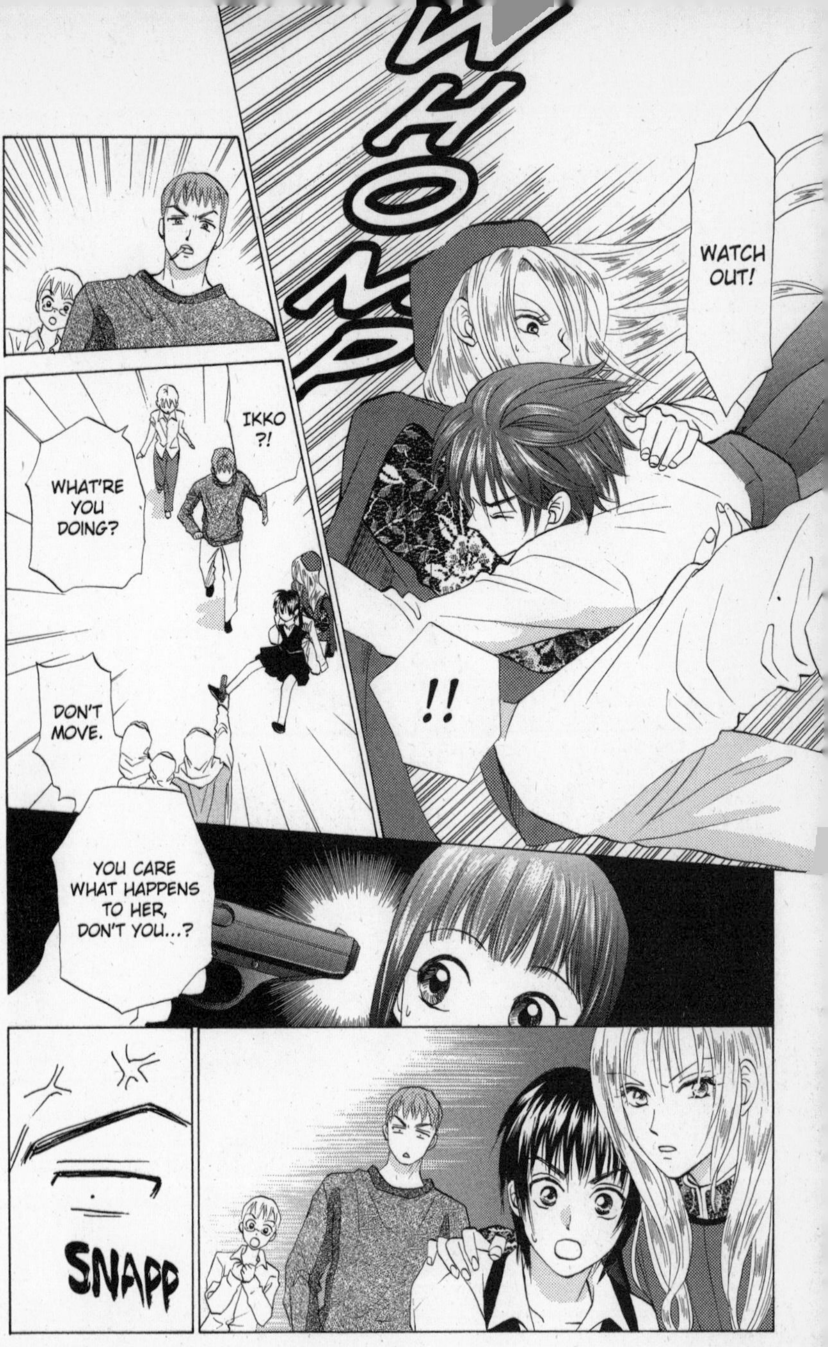
WHOMP
WATCH OUT!
!!
IKKO ?!
WHAT'RE YOU DOING?
DON'T MOVE.
YOU CARE WHAT HAPPENS TO HER, DON'T YOU...?
SNAPP

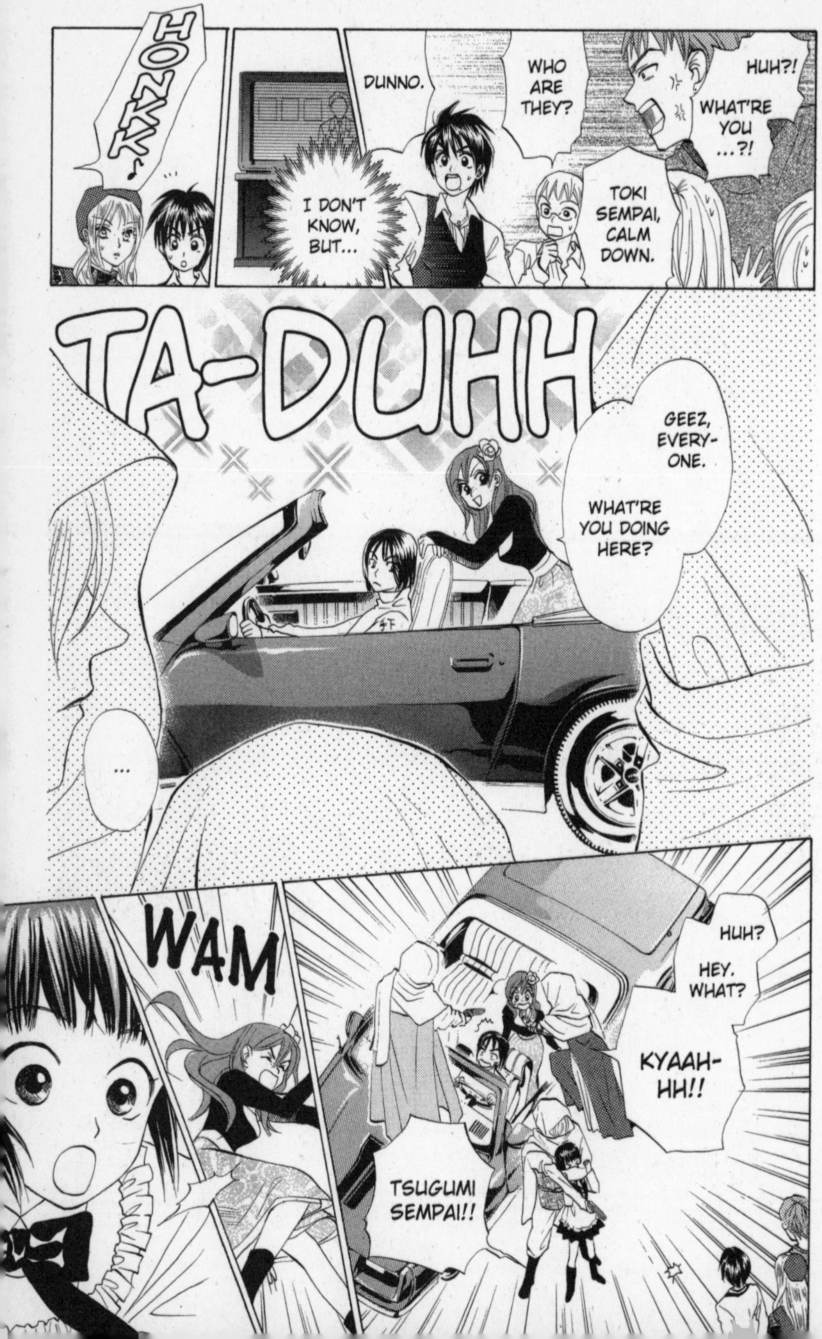
HUH?!
WHAT'RE YOU ...?!
WHO ARE THEY?
TOKI SEMPAI, CALM DOWN.
DUNNO.
I DON'T KNOW, BUT...
...
HONKK♪
TA-DUHH
GEEZ, EVERY-ONE.
WHAT'RE YOU DOING HERE?
...
HUH?
HEY. WHAT?
KYAAH-HH!!
TSUGUMI SEMPAI!!
WAM

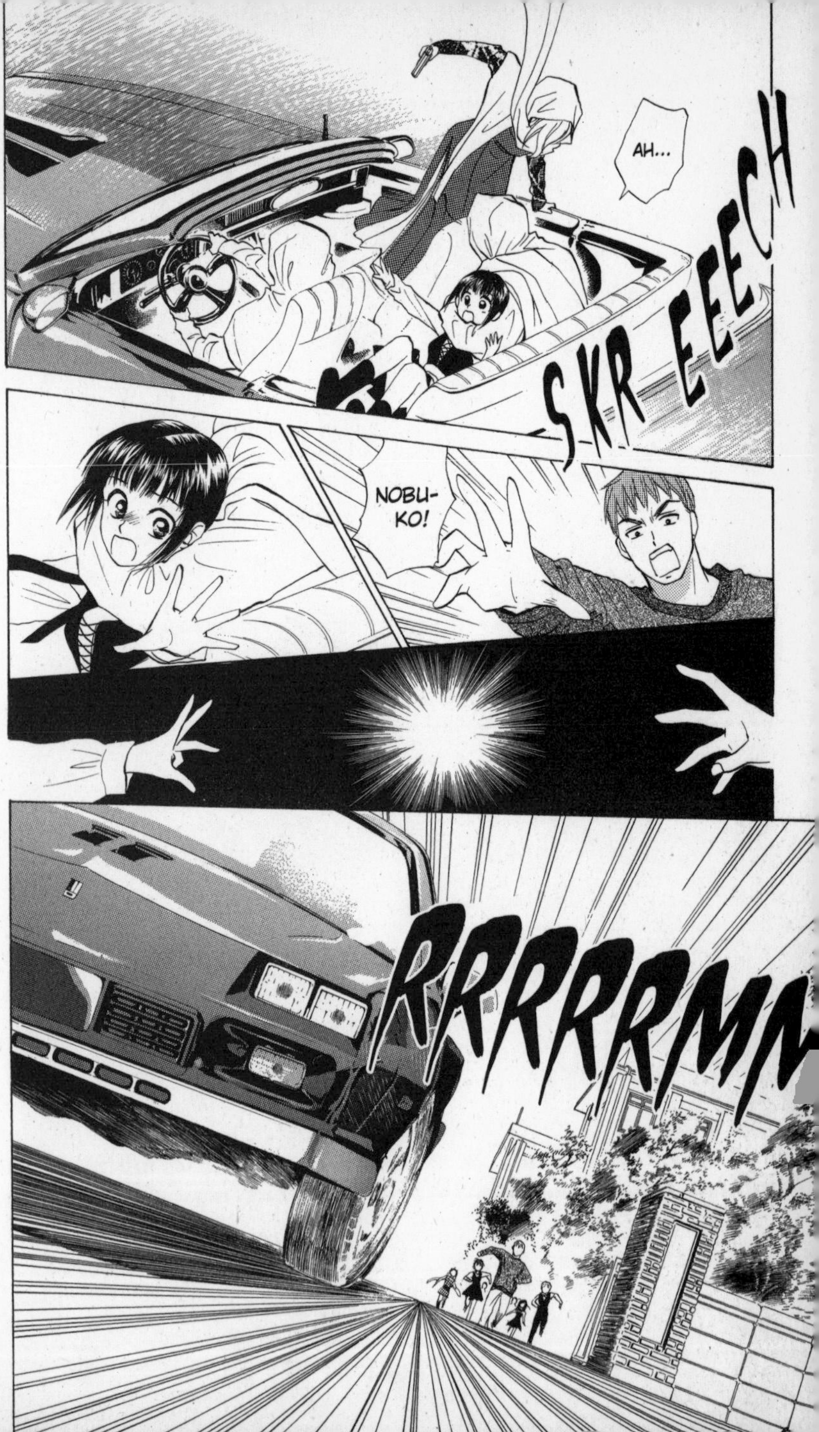
AH...
SKREEECH
NOBUKO!
RRRRRRMMM

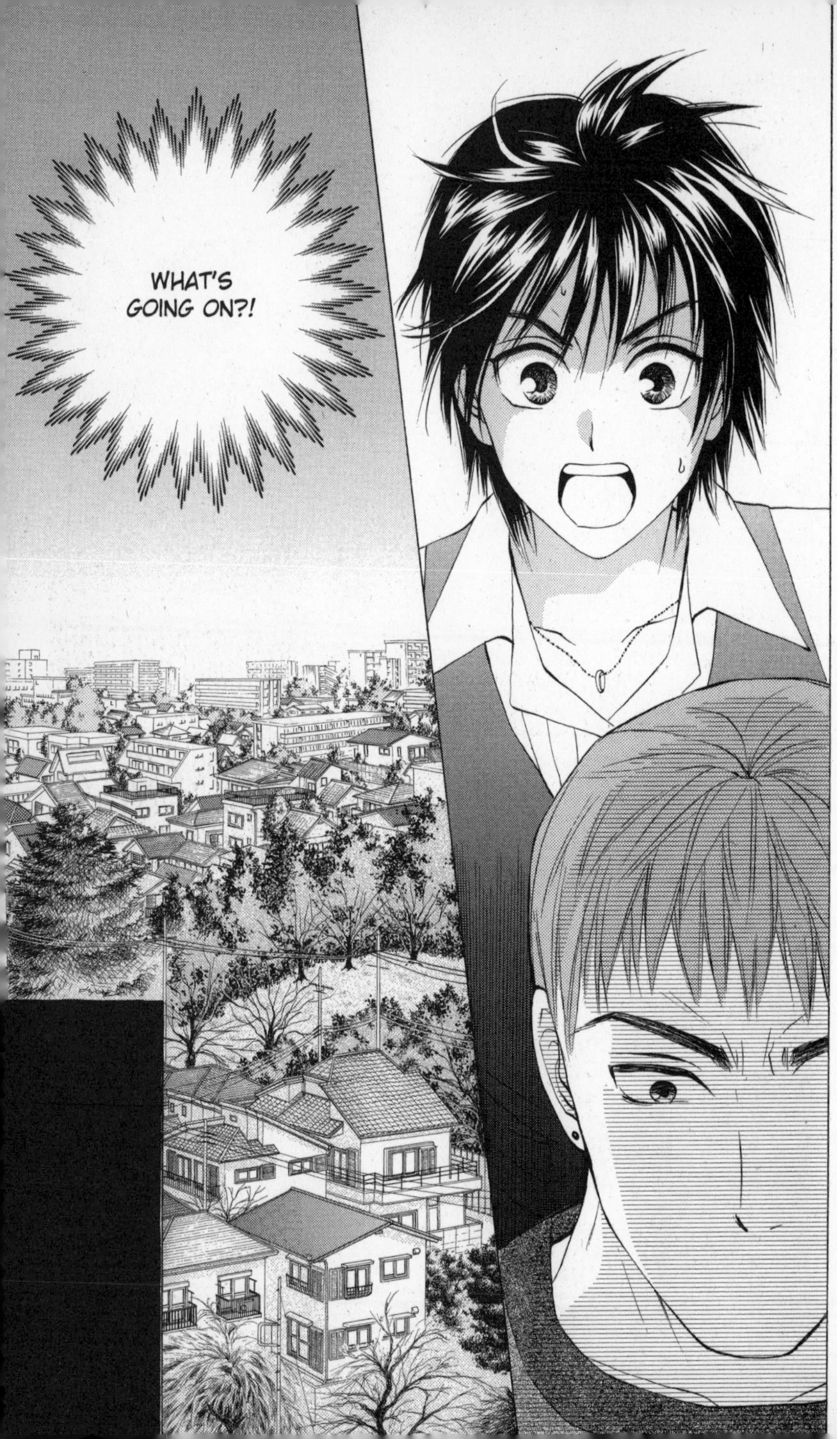
WHAT'S GOING ON?!

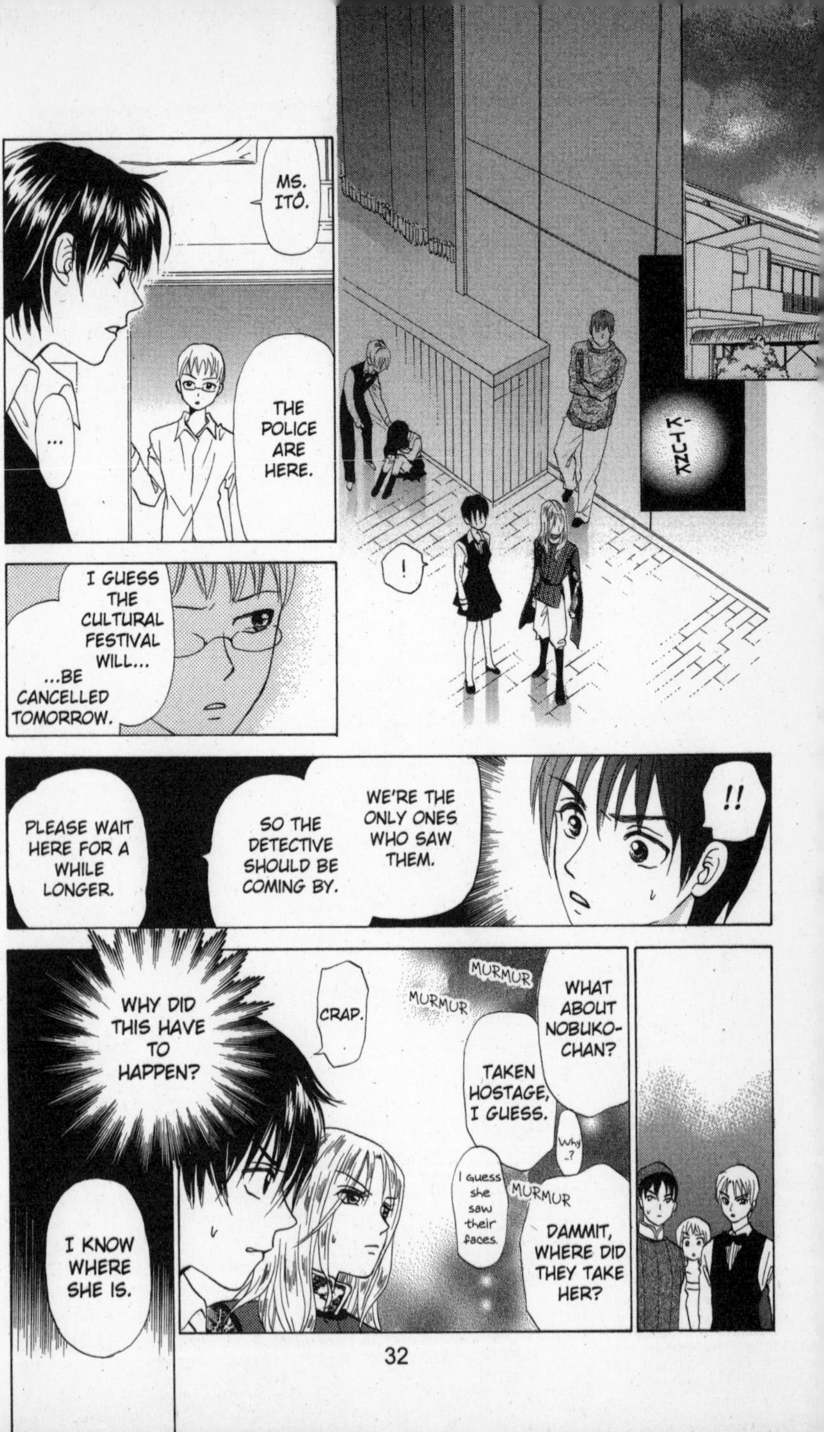
K-TUNK
!
MS. ITŌ.
THE POLICE ARE HERE.
...
I GUESS THE CULTURAL FESTIVAL WILL...
...BE CANCELLED TOMORROW.
!!
WE'RE THE ONLY ONES WHO SAW THEM.
SO THE DETECTIVE SHOULD BE COMING BY.
PLEASE WAIT HERE FOR A WHILE LONGER.
MURMUR
MURMUR
WHAT ABOUT NOBUKO-CHAN?
TAKEN HOSTAGE, I GUESS.
Why ..?
I guess she saw their faces.
MURMUR
DAMMIT, WHERE DID THEY TAKE HER?
CRAP.
WHY DID THIS HAVE TO HAPPEN?
I KNOW WHERE SHE IS.

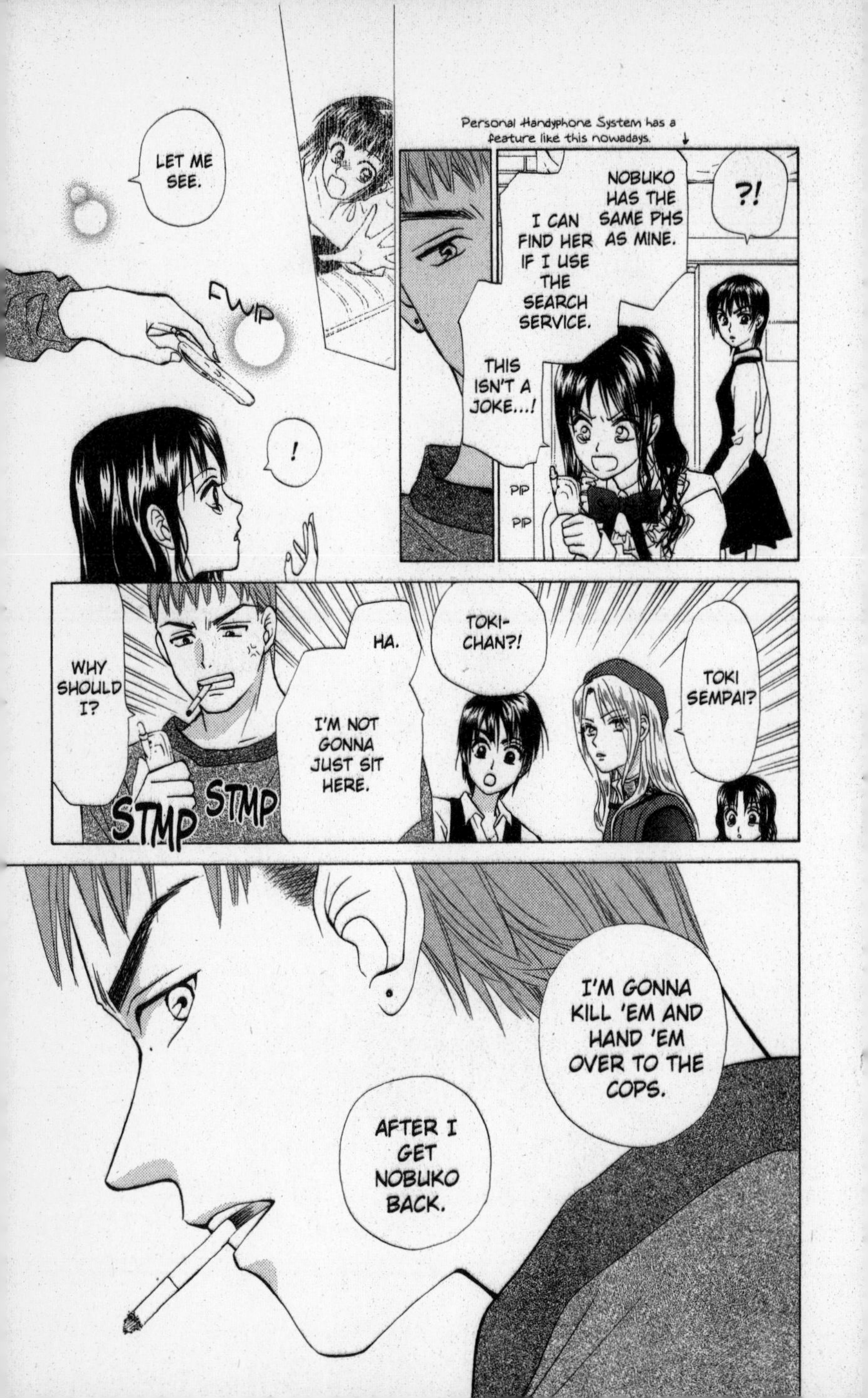
Personal Handyphone System has a feature like this nowadays.
?!
NOBUKO HAS THE SAME PHS AS MINE.
I CAN FIND HER IF I USE THE SEARCH SERVICE.
THIS ISN'T A JOKE...!
PIP
PIP
LET ME SEE.
FWIP
!
TOKI SEMPAI?
TOKI-CHAN?!
HA.
I'M NOT GONNA JUST SIT HERE.
WHY SHOULD I?
STMP
STMP
I'M GONNA KILL 'EM AND HAND 'EM OVER TO THE COPS.
AFTER I GET NOBUKO BACK.

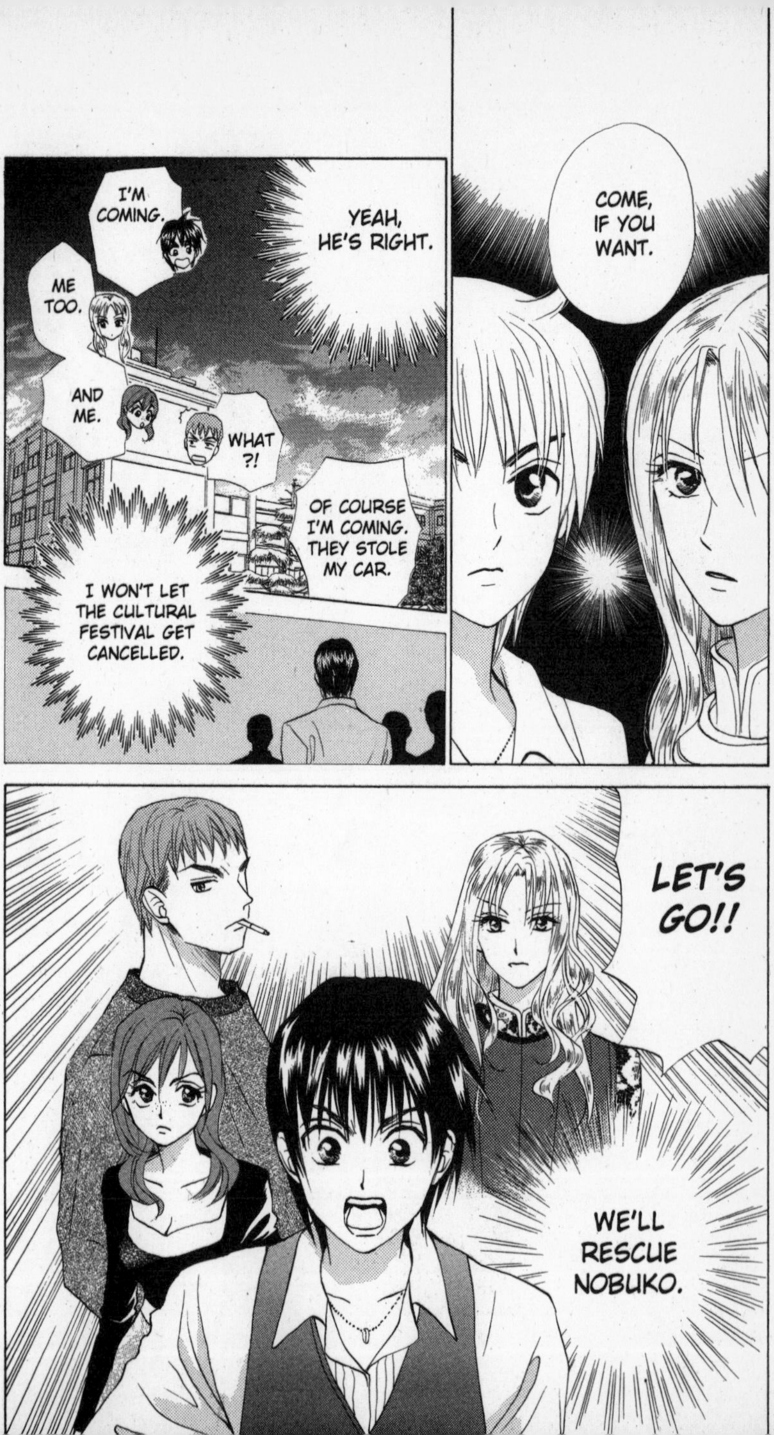
COME, IF YOU WANT.
YEAH, HE'S RIGHT.
I'M COMING.
ME TOO.
AND ME.
WHAT?!
OF COURSE I'M COMING. THEY STOLE MY CAR.
I WON'T LET THE CULTURAL FESTIVAL GET CANCELLED.
LET'S GO!!
WE'LL RESCUE NOBUKO.

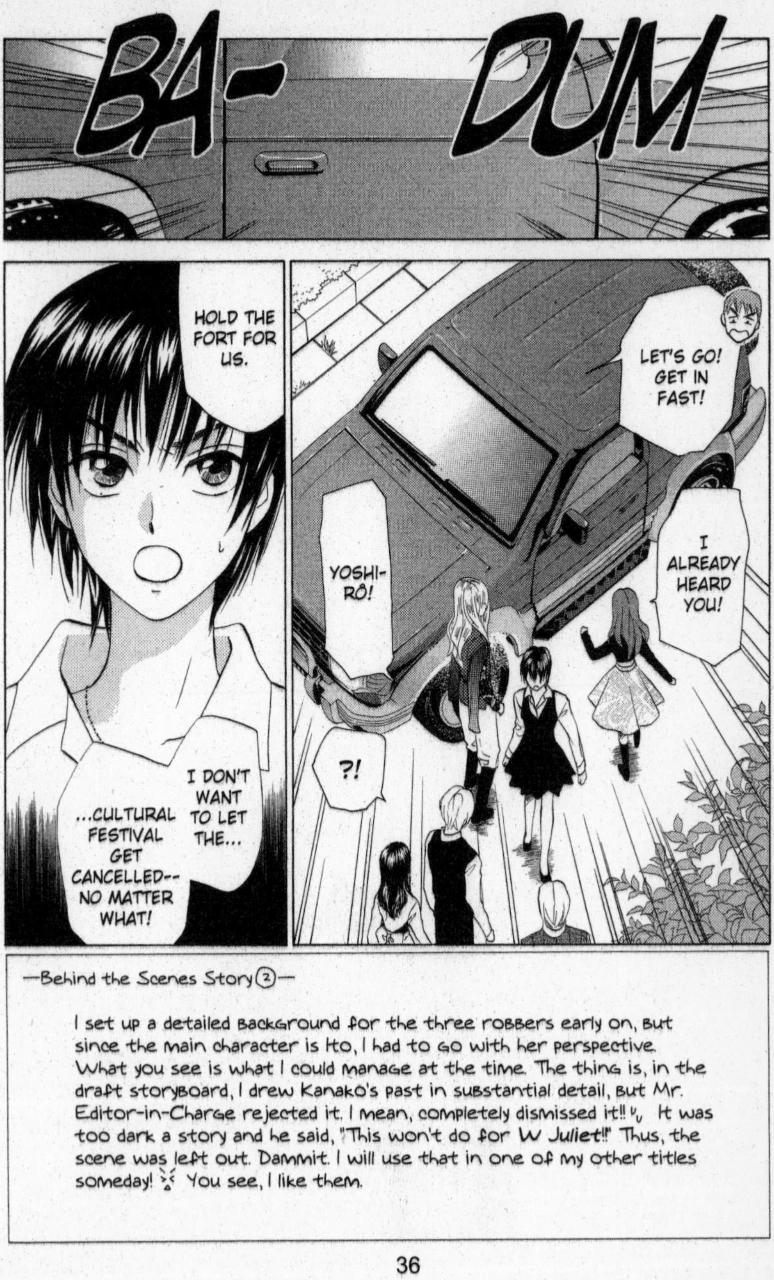
BA- DUM
LET'S GO! GET IN FAST!
I ALREADY HEARD YOU!
YOSHI-RÔ!
?!
HOLD THE FORT FOR US.
I DON'T WANT TO LET THE...
...CULTURAL FESTIVAL GET CANCELLED--NO MATTER WHAT!

—Behind the Scenes Story ②—

I set up a detailed background for the three robbers early on, but since the main character is Ito, I had to go with her perspective. What you see is what I could manage at the time. The thing is, in the draft storyboard, I drew Kanako's past in substantial detail, but Mr. Editor-in-Charge rejected it. I mean, completely dismissed it!! It was too dark a story and he said, "This won't do for *W Juliet*!!" Thus, the scene was left out. Dammit. I will use that in one of my other titles someday! You see, I like them.

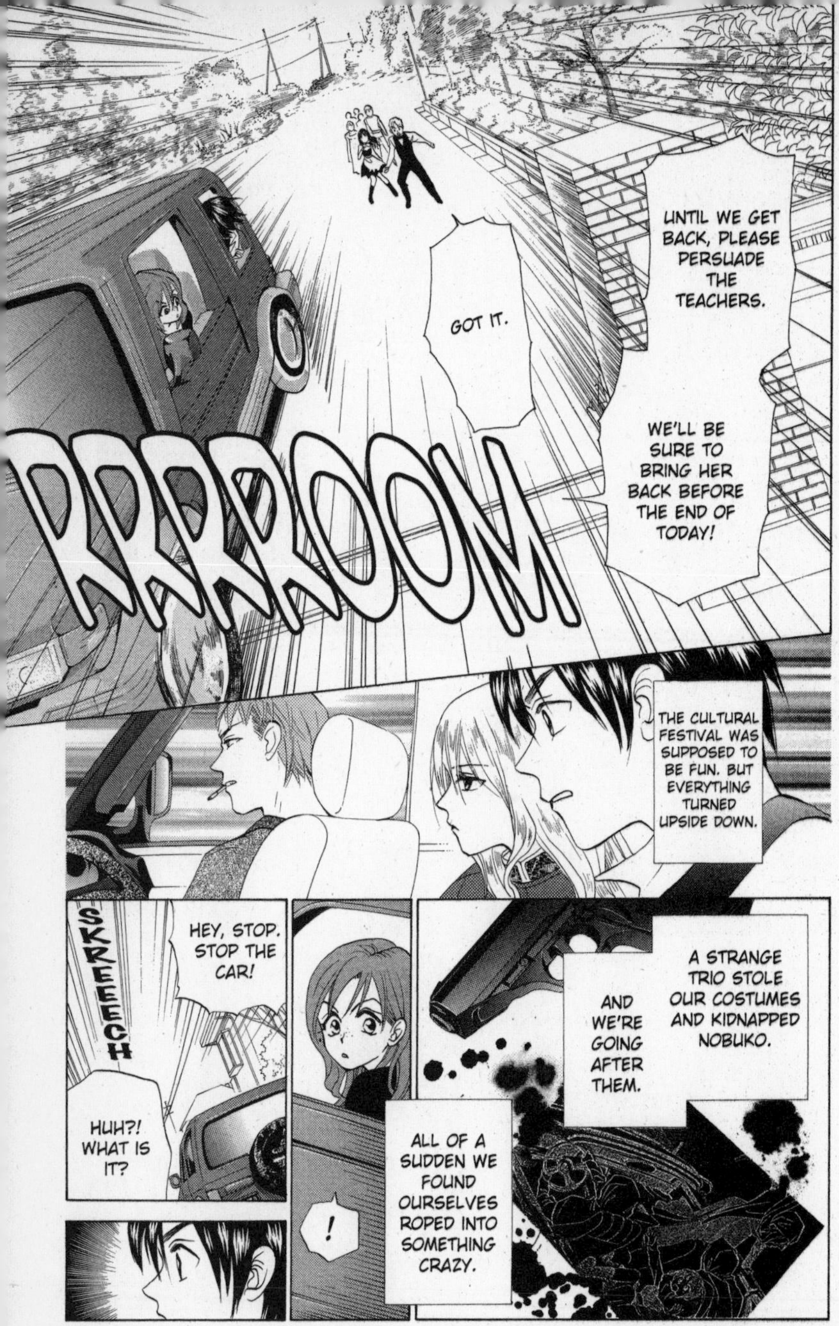
UNTIL WE GET BACK, PLEASE PERSUADE THE TEACHERS.
GOT IT.
WE'LL BE SURE TO BRING HER BACK BEFORE THE END OF TODAY!
RRRROOM
THE CULTURAL FESTIVAL WAS SUPPOSED TO BE FUN. BUT EVERYTHING TURNED UPSIDE DOWN.
A STRANGE TRIO STOLE OUR COSTUMES AND KIDNAPPED NOBUKO.
AND WE'RE GOING AFTER THEM.
ALL OF A SUDDEN WE FOUND OURSELVES ROPED INTO SOMETHING CRAZY.
!
HEY, STOP. STOP THE CAR!
SKREEEECH
HUH?! WHAT IS IT?

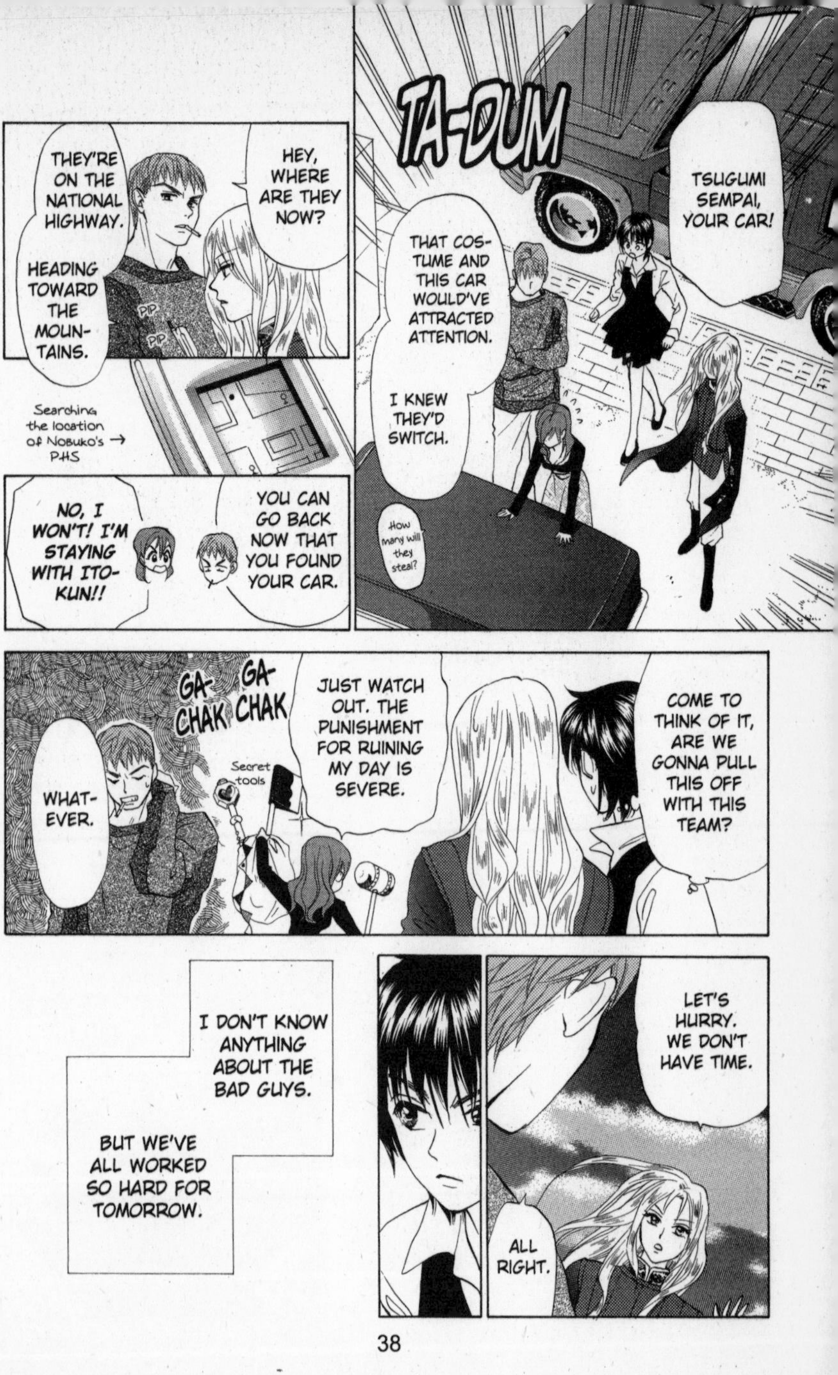
TA-DUM
TSUGUMI SEMPAI, YOUR CAR!
THAT COSTUME AND THIS CAR WOULD'VE ATTRACTED ATTENTION.
I KNEW THEY'D SWITCH.
How many will they steal?
HEY, WHERE ARE THEY NOW?
THEY'RE ON THE NATIONAL HIGHWAY.
HEADING TOWARD THE MOUNTAINS.
PIP
PIP
Searching the location of Nobuko's → PHS
YOU CAN GO BACK NOW THAT YOU FOUND YOUR CAR.
NO, I WON'T! I'M STAYING WITH ITO-KUN!!
COME TO THINK OF IT, ARE WE GONNA PULL THIS OFF WITH THIS TEAM?
JUST WATCH OUT. THE PUNISHMENT FOR RUINING MY DAY IS SEVERE.
GA-CHAK GA-CHAK
Secret tools
WHATEVER.
LET'S HURRY. WE DON'T HAVE TIME.
ALL RIGHT.
I DON'T KNOW ANYTHING ABOUT THE BAD GUYS.
BUT WE'VE ALL WORKED SO HARD FOR TOMORROW.

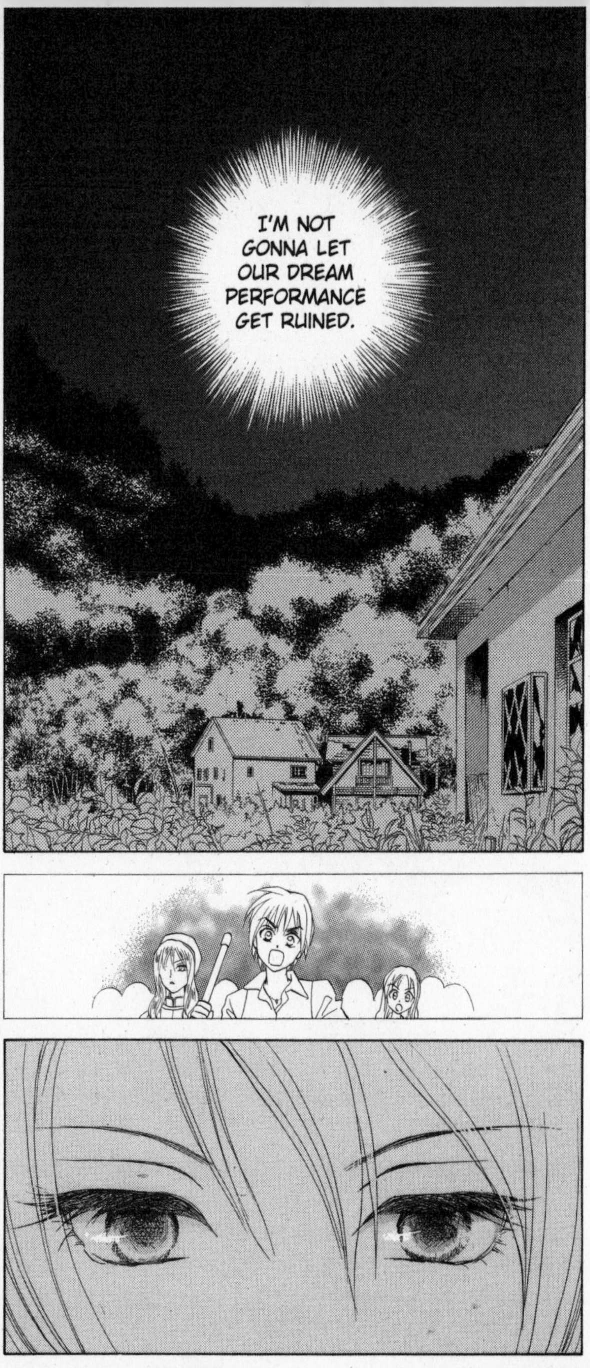
I'M NOT GONNA LET OUR DREAM PERFORMANCE GET RUINED.

STRANGE EVENTS

It's been more than a year since we moved from the previous office, but for some reason, now that a year went by, strange things are happening.

In the Volume-Ending Afterward Manga of volume 3, I talked a bit about my sister getting a paralyzed feeling. The fact is, after that, I also started to have the same thing happen to me. Because I slept at the office, I experienced the paralyzing feeling twice a week.

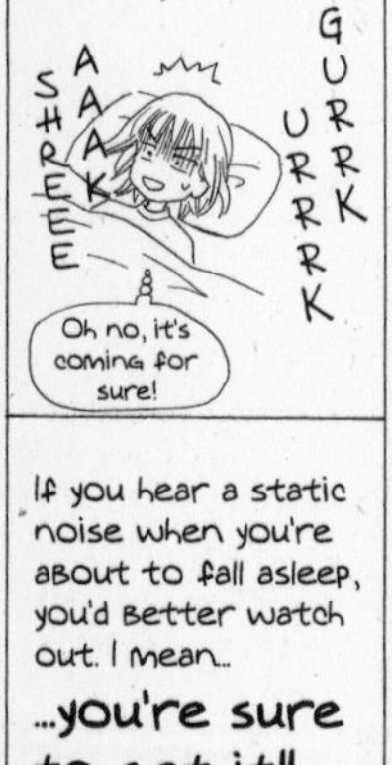
GURRK
URRRK
AAAAK
SHREEEE
Oh no, it's coming for sure!

If you hear a static noise when you're about to fall asleep, you'd better watch out. I mean...

...you're sure to get it!!

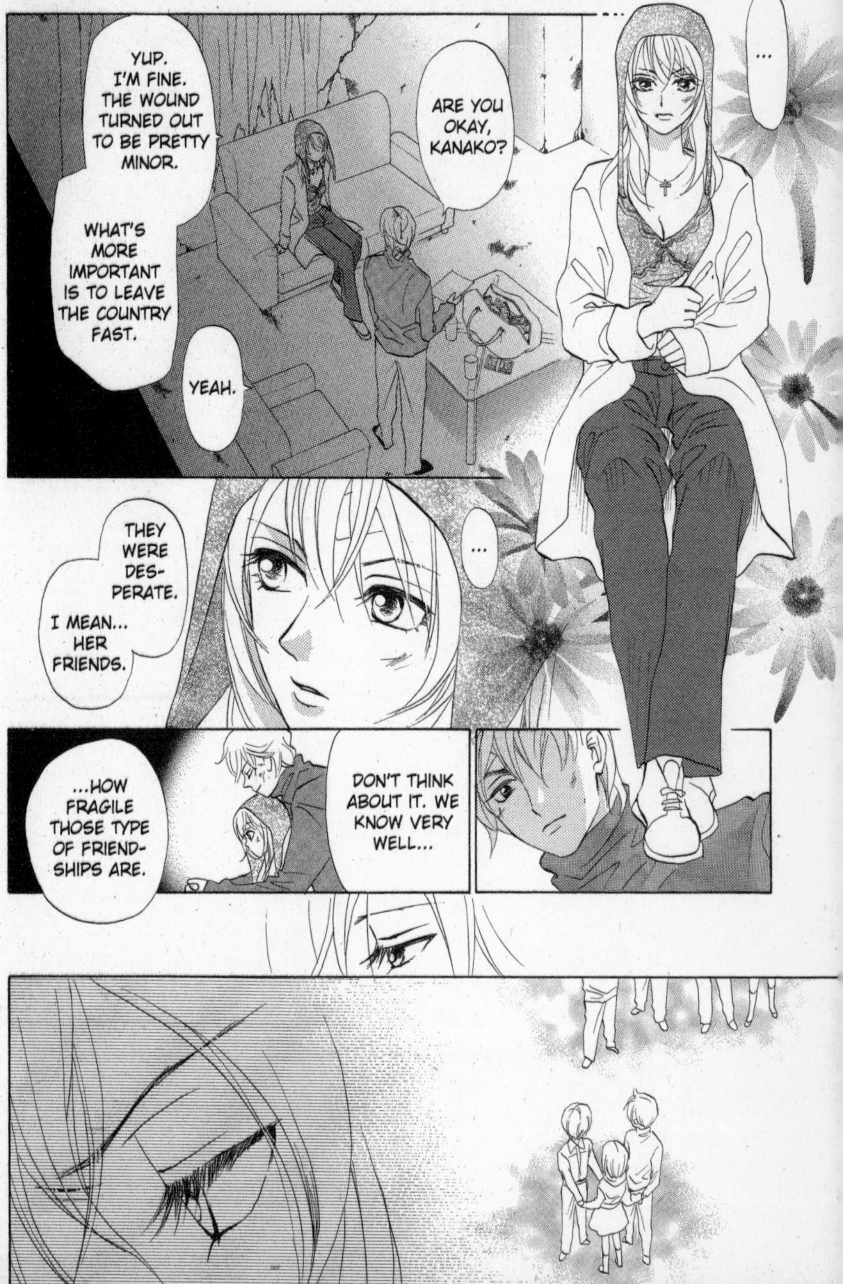
...
ARE YOU OKAY, KANAKO?
YUP. I'M FINE. THE WOUND TURNED OUT TO BE PRETTY MINOR.
WHAT'S MORE IMPORTANT IS TO LEAVE THE COUNTRY FAST.
YEAH.
...
THEY WERE DES-PERATE.
I MEAN... HER FRIENDS.
DON'T THINK ABOUT IT. WE KNOW VERY WELL...
...HOW FRAGILE THOSE TYPE OF FRIEND-SHIPS ARE.

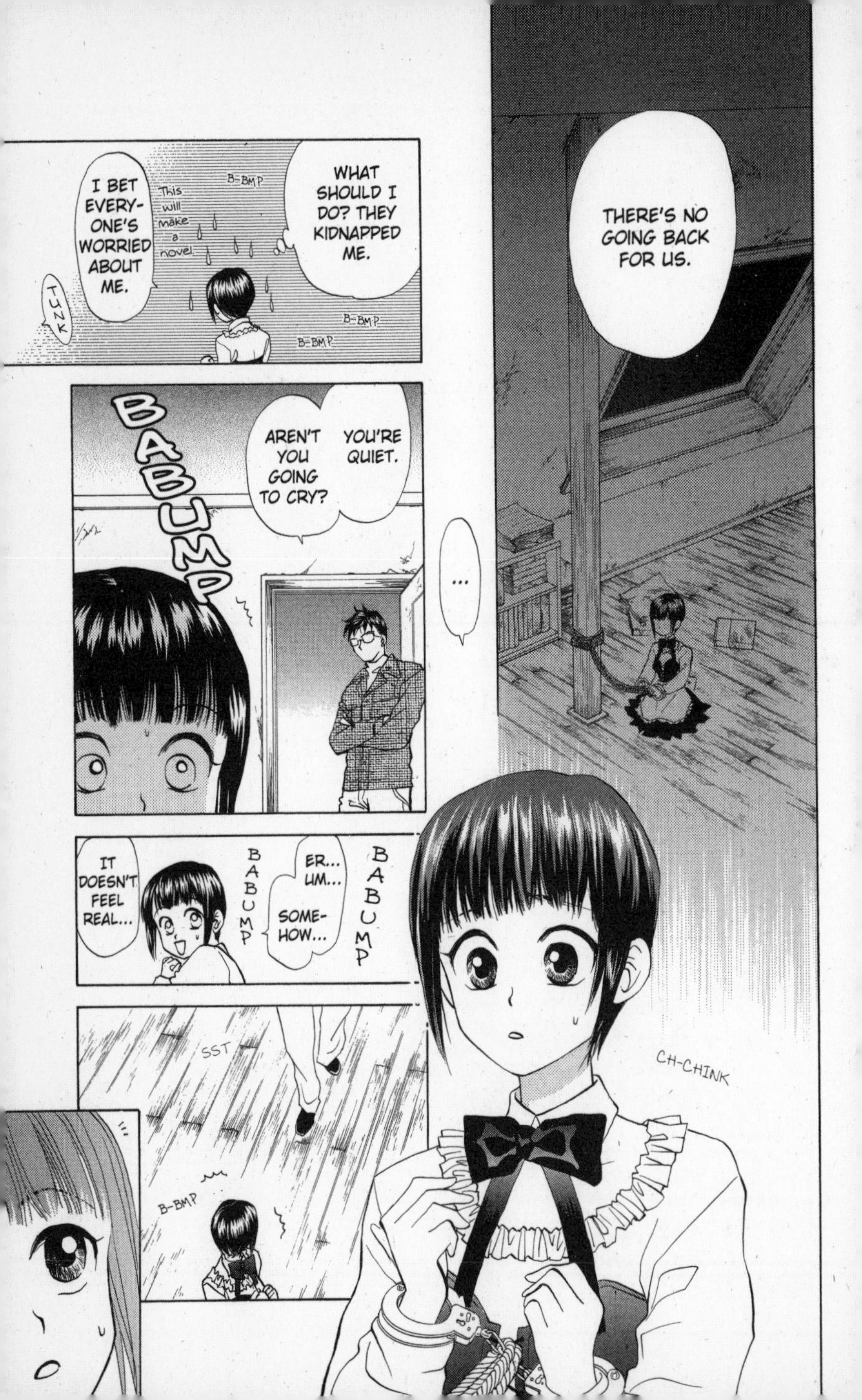
THERE'S NO GOING BACK FOR US.
...
CH-CHINK
WHAT SHOULD I DO? THEY KIDNAPPED ME.
B-BMP
I BET EVERYONE'S WORRIED ABOUT ME.
This will make a novel.
B-BMP
B-BMP
TUNK
YOU'RE QUIET.
AREN'T YOU GOING TO CRY?
BABUMP
BABUMP
ER... UM...
SOMEHOW...
BABUMP
IT DOESN'T FEEL REAL...
SST
B-BMP

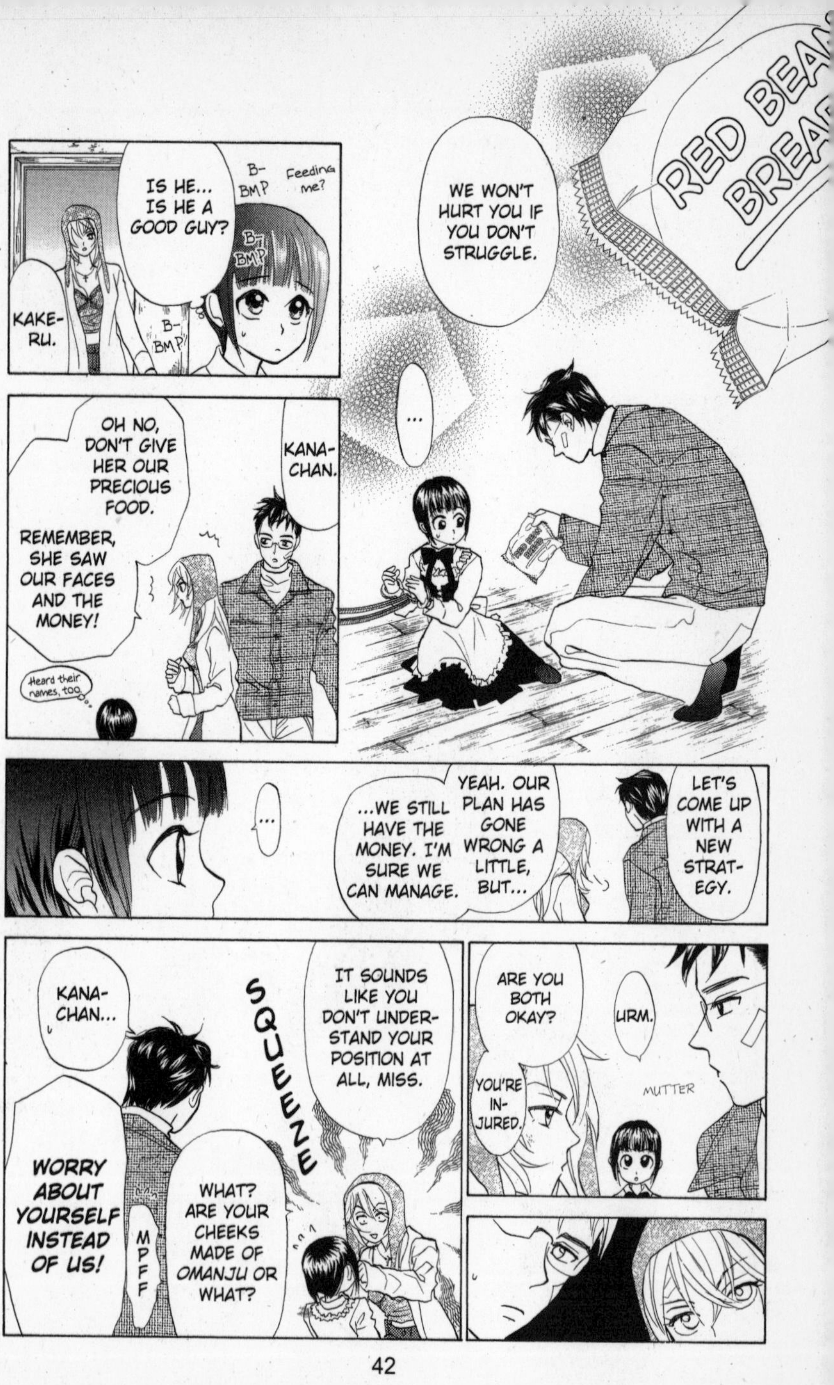
RED BEA
BREA
WE WON'T HURT YOU IF YOU DON'T STRUGGLE.
...
Feeding me?
B-BMP
IS HE... IS HE A GOOD GUY?
B-BMP
B-BMP
KAKE-RU.
KANA-CHAN.
OH NO, DON'T GIVE HER OUR PRECIOUS FOOD.
REMEMBER, SHE SAW OUR FACES AND THE MONEY!
Heard their names, too.
LET'S COME UP WITH A NEW STRATEGY.
YEAH. OUR PLAN HAS GONE WRONG A LITTLE, BUT...
...WE STILL HAVE THE MONEY. I'M SURE WE CAN MANAGE.
...
URM.
ARE YOU BOTH OKAY?
MUTTER
YOU'RE IN-JURED.
IT SOUNDS LIKE YOU DON'T UNDER-STAND YOUR POSITION AT ALL, MISS.
SQUEEZE
KANA-CHAN...
WHAT? ARE YOUR CHEEKS MADE OF OMANJU OR WHAT?
MPFF
WORRY ABOUT YOURSELF INSTEAD OF US!

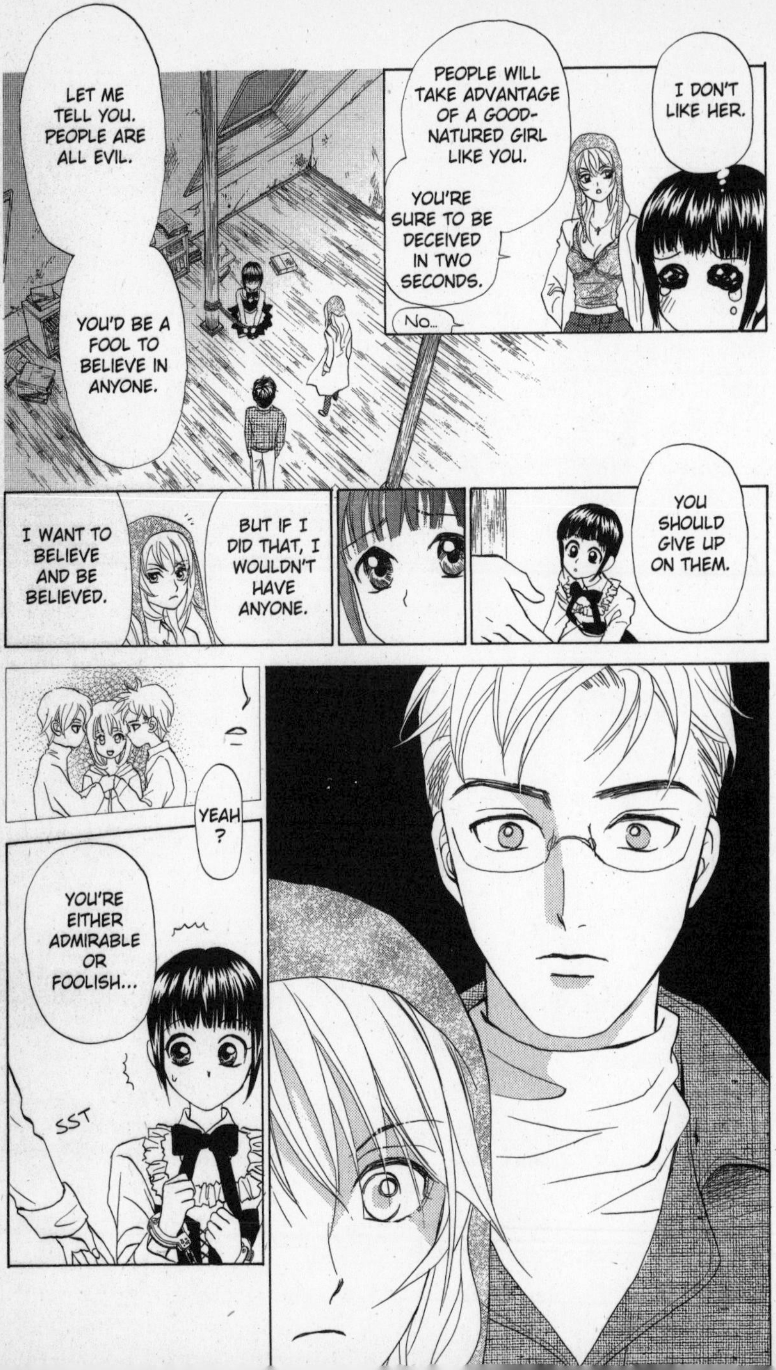
I DON'T LIKE HER.
PEOPLE WILL TAKE ADVANTAGE OF A GOOD-NATURED GIRL LIKE YOU.
YOU'RE SURE TO BE DECEIVED IN TWO SECONDS.
No...
LET ME TELL YOU. PEOPLE ARE ALL EVIL.
YOU'D BE A FOOL TO BELIEVE IN ANYONE.
YOU SHOULD GIVE UP ON THEM.
BUT IF I DID THAT, I WOULDN'T HAVE ANYONE.
I WANT TO BELIEVE AND BE BELIEVED.
YEAH?
YOU'RE EITHER ADMIRABLE OR FOOLISH...
SST

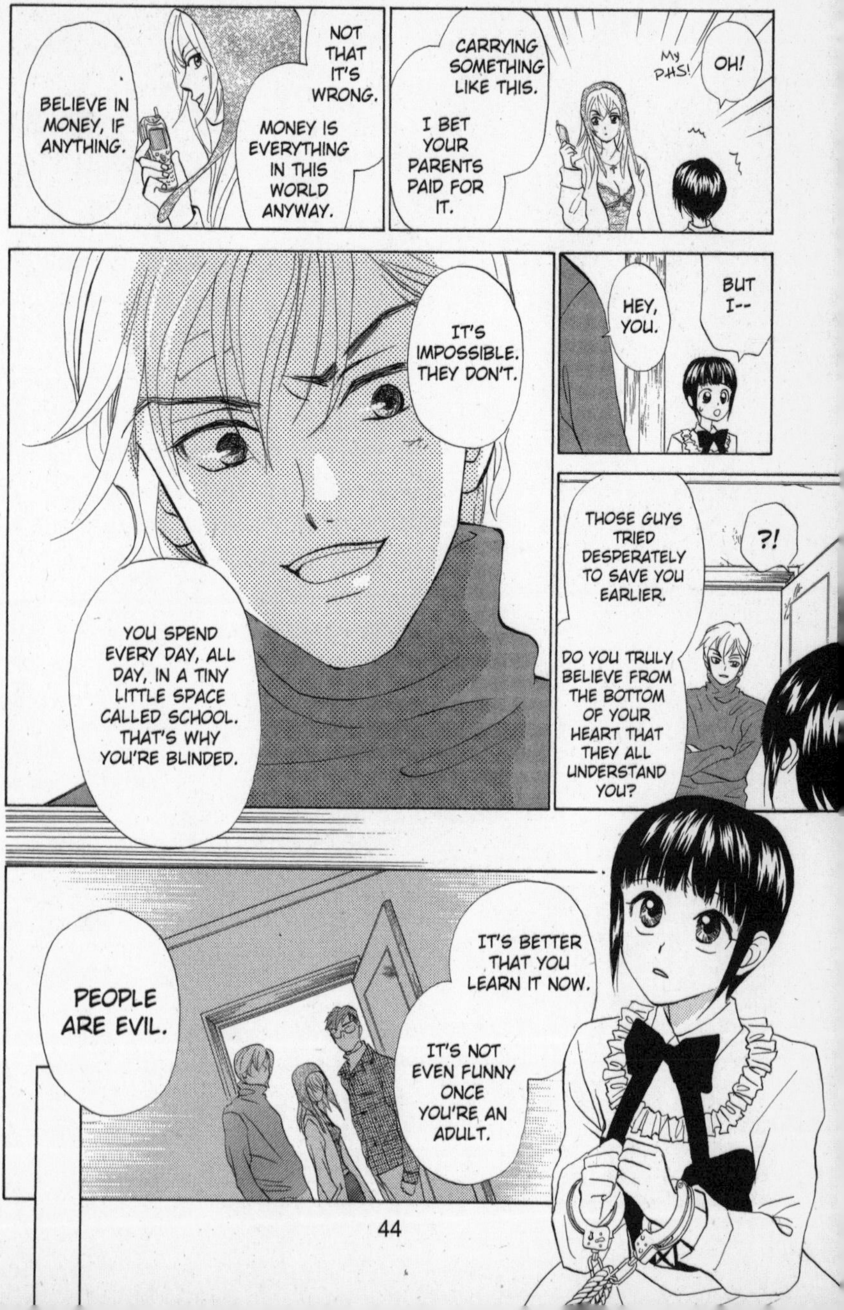
OH!
My PHS!
CARRYING SOMETHING LIKE THIS.
I BET YOUR PARENTS PAID FOR IT.
NOT THAT IT'S WRONG.
MONEY IS EVERYTHING IN THIS WORLD ANYWAY.
BELIEVE IN MONEY, IF ANYTHING.
BUT I--
HEY, YOU.
?!
THOSE GUYS TRIED DESPERATELY TO SAVE YOU EARLIER.
DO YOU TRULY BELIEVE FROM THE BOTTOM OF YOUR HEART THAT THEY ALL UNDERSTAND YOU?
IT'S IMPOSSIBLE. THEY DON'T.
YOU SPEND EVERY DAY, ALL DAY, IN A TINY LITTLE SPACE CALLED SCHOOL. THAT'S WHY YOU'RE BLINDED.
IT'S BETTER THAT YOU LEARN IT NOW.
IT'S NOT EVEN FUNNY ONCE YOU'RE AN ADULT.
PEOPLE ARE EVIL.

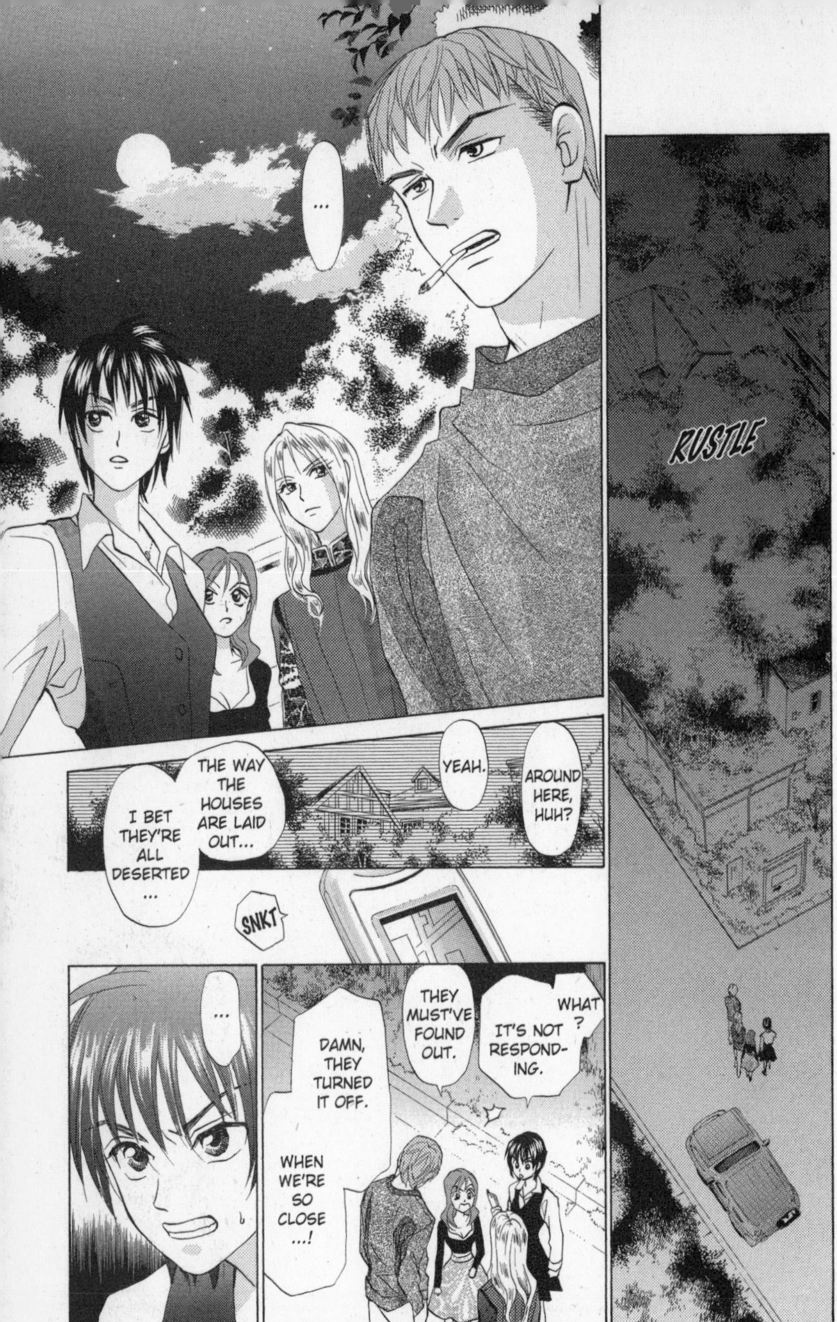
RUSTLE
...
AROUND HERE, HUH?
YEAH.
THE WAY THE HOUSES ARE LAID OUT...
I BET THEY'RE ALL DESERTED...
SNKT
WHAT?
IT'S NOT RESPONDING.
THEY MUST'VE FOUND OUT.
DAMN, THEY TURNED IT OFF.
WHEN WE'RE SO CLOSE...!
...

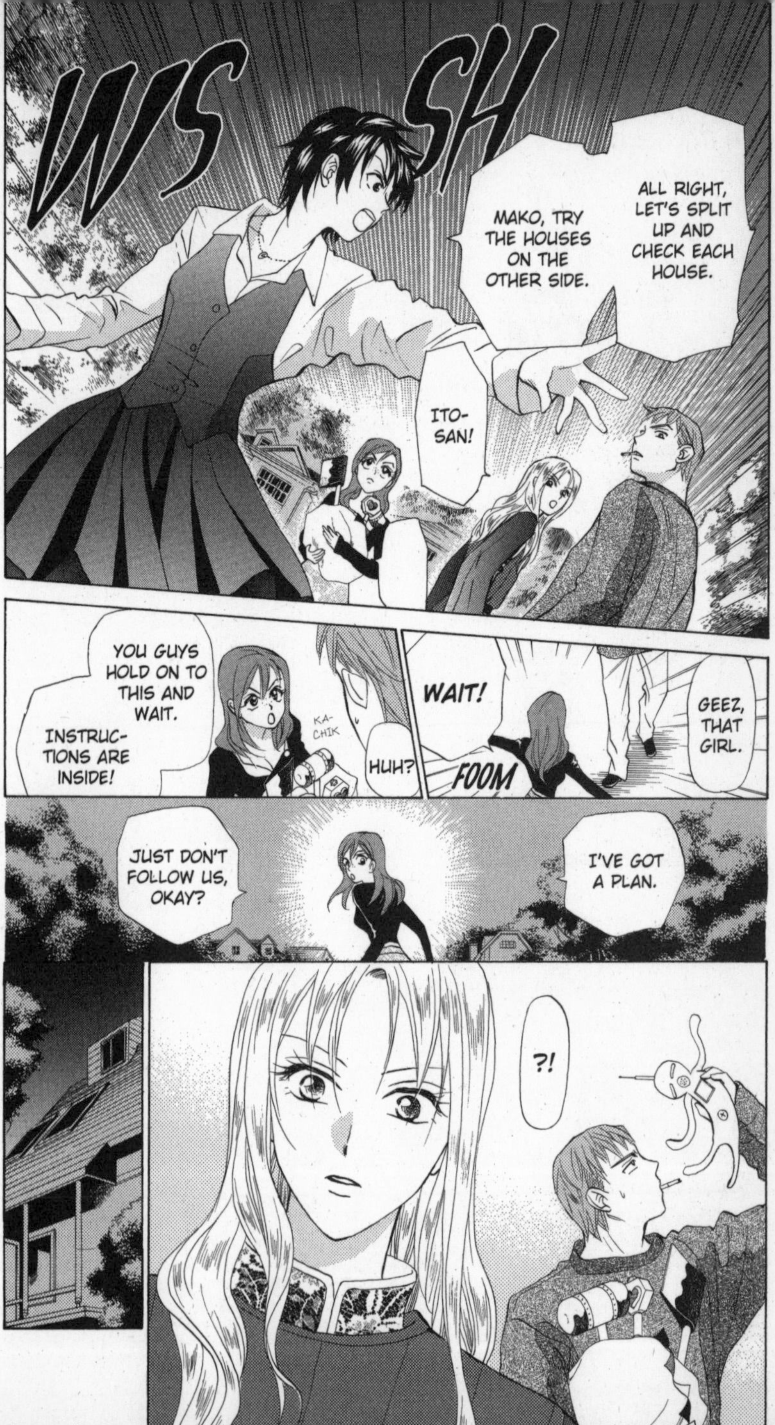
WSSH
ALL RIGHT, LET'S SPLIT UP AND CHECK EACH HOUSE.
MAKO, TRY THE HOUSES ON THE OTHER SIDE.
ITO-SAN!
GEEZ, THAT GIRL.
WAIT!
FOOM
YOU GUYS HOLD ON TO THIS AND WAIT.
INSTRUCTIONS ARE INSIDE!
KA-CHIK
HUH?
I'VE GOT A PLAN.
JUST DON'T FOLLOW US, OKAY?
?!

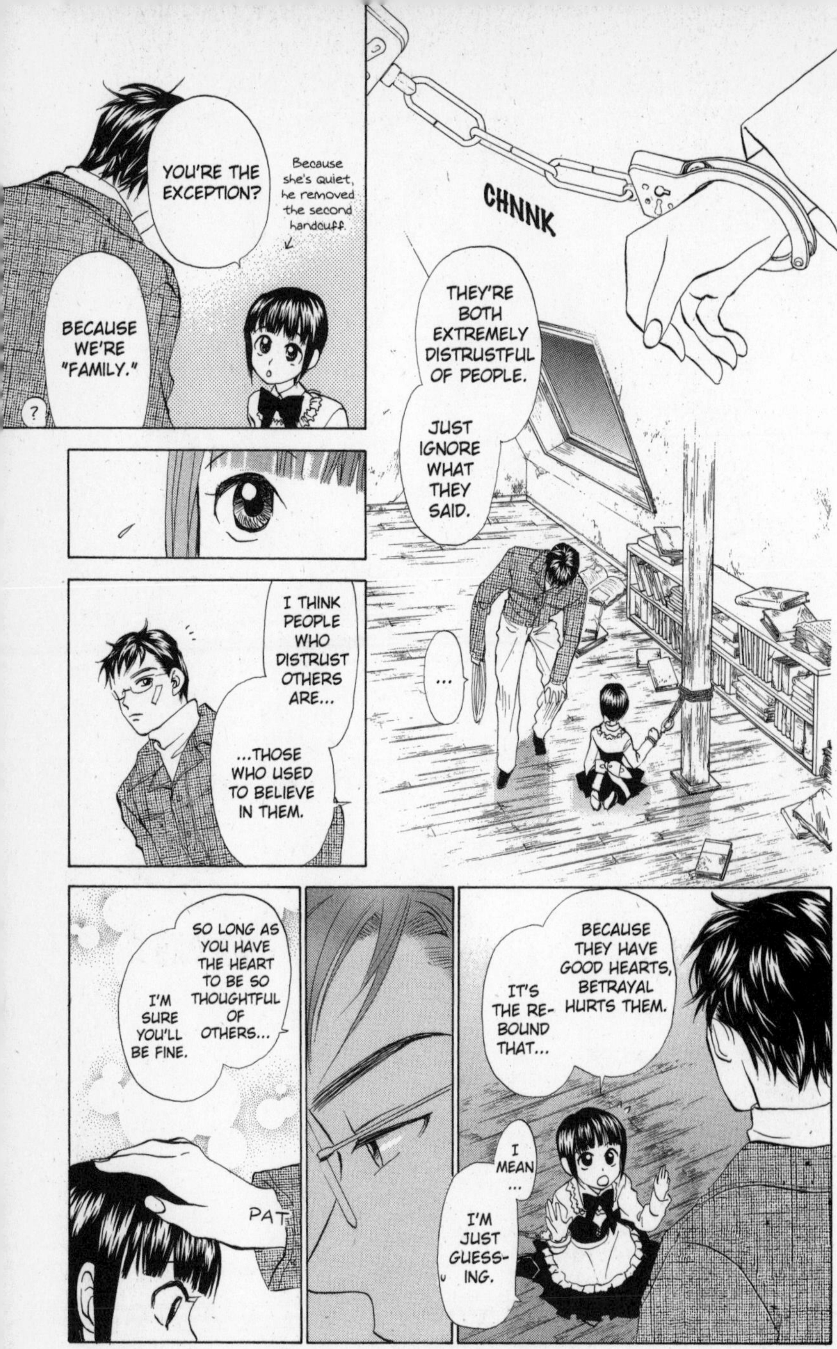
CHNNK
THEY'RE BOTH EXTREMELY DISTRUSTFUL OF PEOPLE.
JUST IGNORE WHAT THEY SAID.
...
YOU'RE THE EXCEPTION?
Because she's quiet, he removed the second handcuff.
BECAUSE WE'RE "FAMILY."
?
I THINK PEOPLE WHO DISTRUST OTHERS ARE...
...THOSE WHO USED TO BELIEVE IN THEM.
BECAUSE THEY HAVE GOOD HEARTS, BETRAYAL HURTS THEM.
IT'S THE RE-BOUND THAT...
I MEAN...
I'M JUST GUESS-ING.
SO LONG AS YOU HAVE THE HEART TO BE SO THOUGHTFUL OF OTHERS...
I'M SURE YOU'LL BE FINE.
PAT

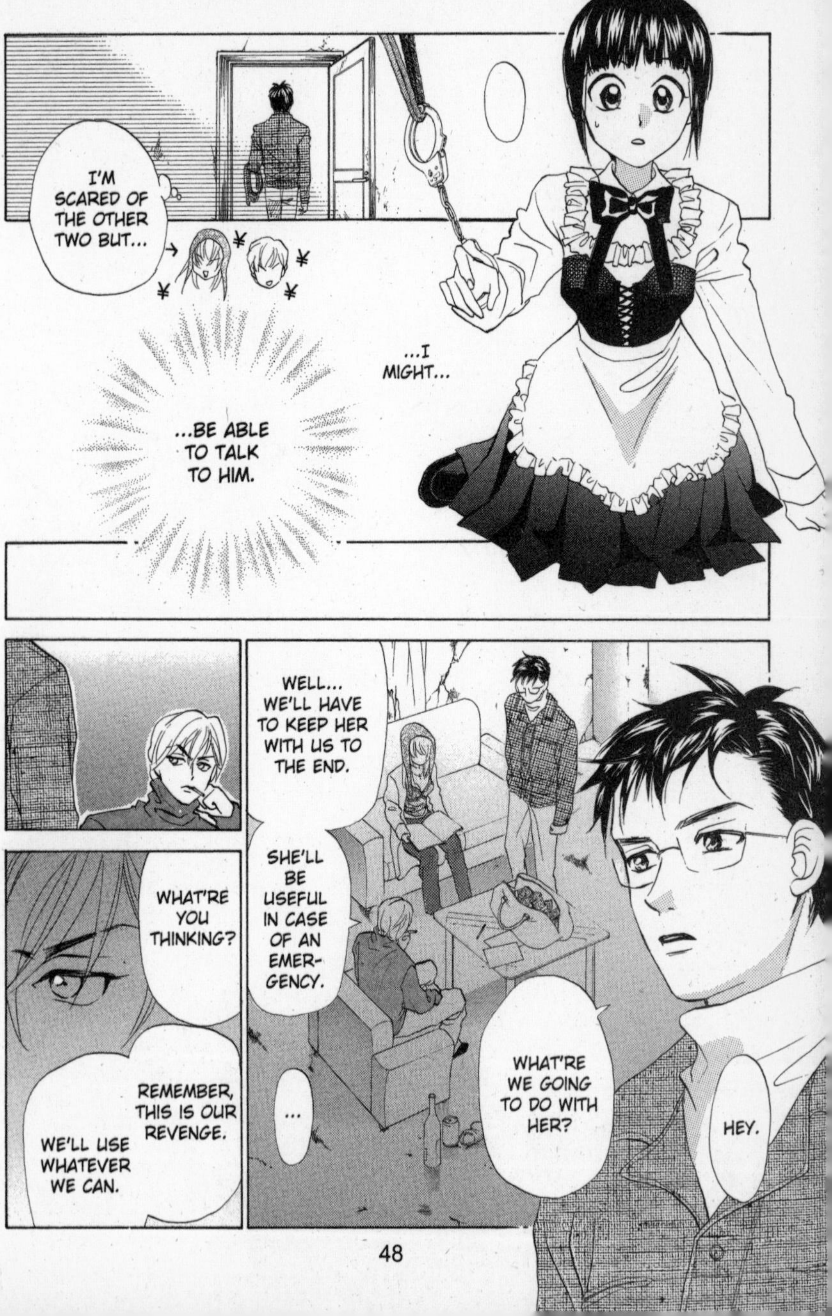
I'M SCARED OF THE OTHER TWO BUT...
...I MIGHT...
...BE ABLE TO TALK TO HIM.
HEY.
WHAT'RE WE GOING TO DO WITH HER?
...
WELL... WE'LL HAVE TO KEEP HER WITH US TO THE END.
SHE'LL BE USEFUL IN CASE OF AN EMERGENCY.
WHAT'RE YOU THINKING?
REMEMBER, THIS IS OUR REVENGE.
WE'LL USE WHATEVER WE CAN.

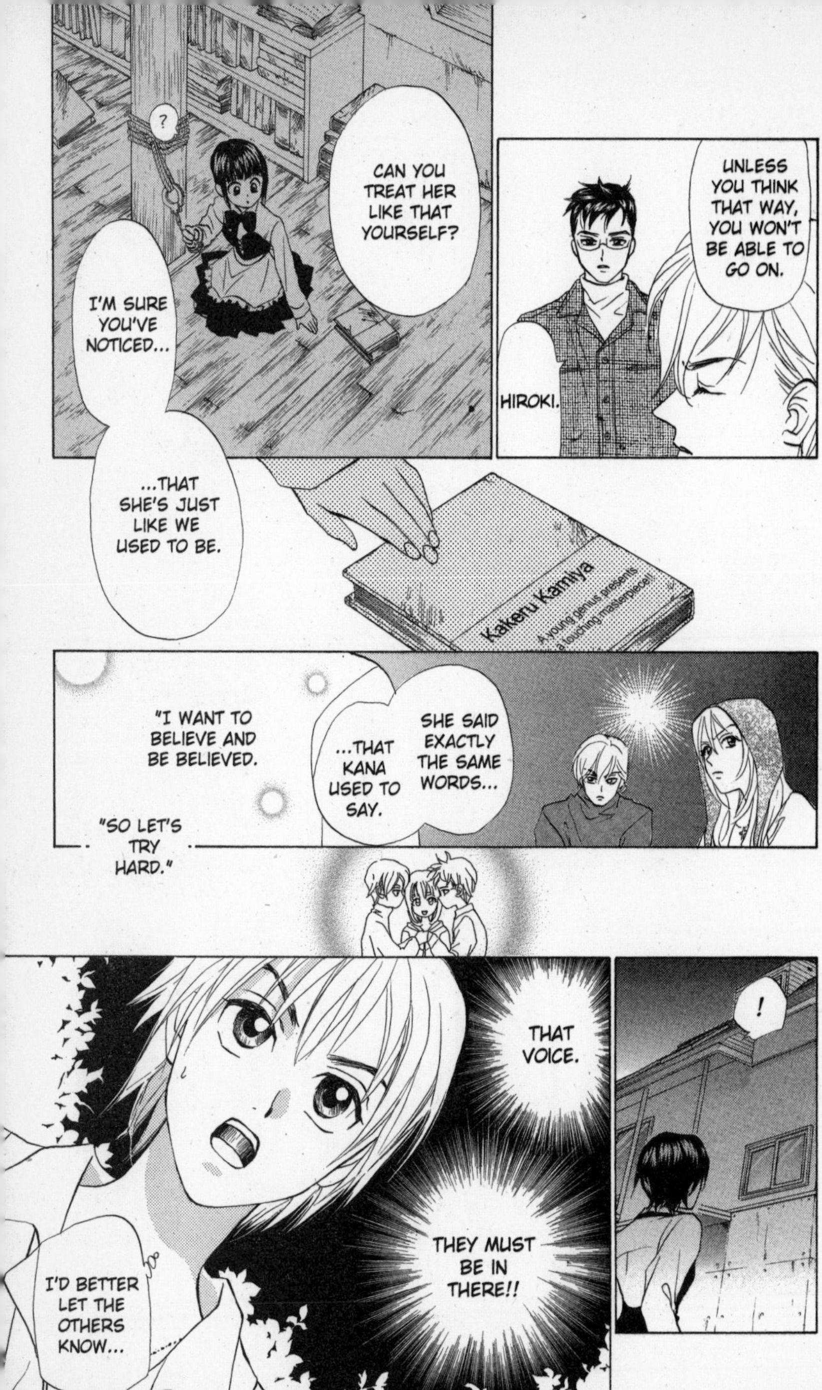
UNLESS YOU THINK THAT WAY, YOU WON'T BE ABLE TO GO ON.
HIROKI.
?
CAN YOU TREAT HER LIKE THAT YOURSELF?
I'M SURE YOU'VE NOTICED...
...THAT SHE'S JUST LIKE WE USED TO BE.
Kakeru Kamiya
A young genius presents a touching masterpiece!!
SHE SAID EXACTLY THE SAME WORDS...
...THAT KANA USED TO SAY.
"I WANT TO BELIEVE AND BE BELIEVED.
"SO LET'S TRY HARD."
!
THAT VOICE.
THEY MUST BE IN THERE!!
I'D BETTER LET THE OTHERS KNOW...

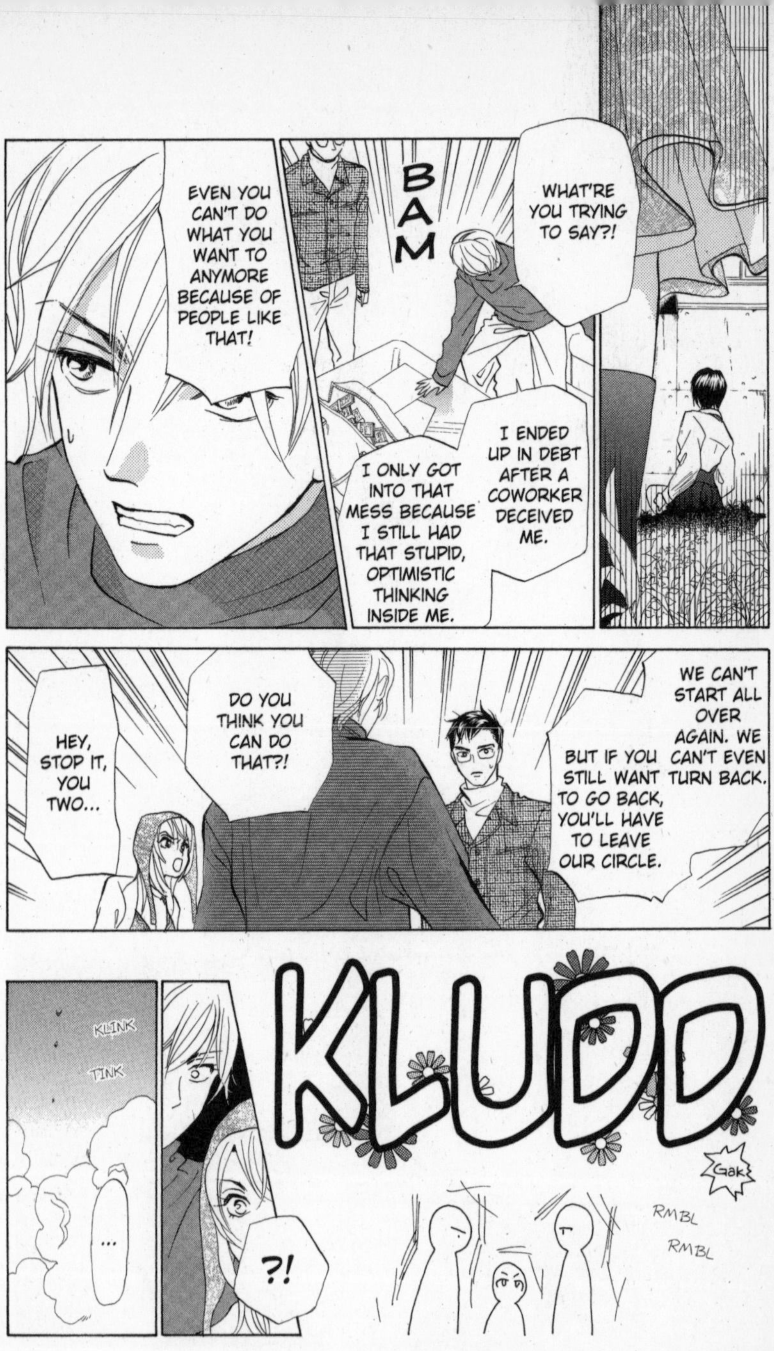
WHAT'RE YOU TRYING TO SAY?!
BAM
I ENDED UP IN DEBT AFTER A COWORKER DECEIVED ME.
I ONLY GOT INTO THAT MESS BECAUSE I STILL HAD THAT STUPID, OPTIMISTIC THINKING INSIDE ME.
EVEN YOU CAN'T DO WHAT YOU WANT TO ANYMORE BECAUSE OF PEOPLE LIKE THAT!
WE CAN'T START ALL OVER AGAIN. WE CAN'T EVEN TURN BACK.
BUT IF YOU STILL WANT TO GO BACK, YOU'LL HAVE TO LEAVE OUR CIRCLE.
DO YOU THINK YOU CAN DO THAT?!
HEY, STOP IT, YOU TWO...
KLUDD
Gak
RMBL
RMBL
?!
KLINK
TINK
...

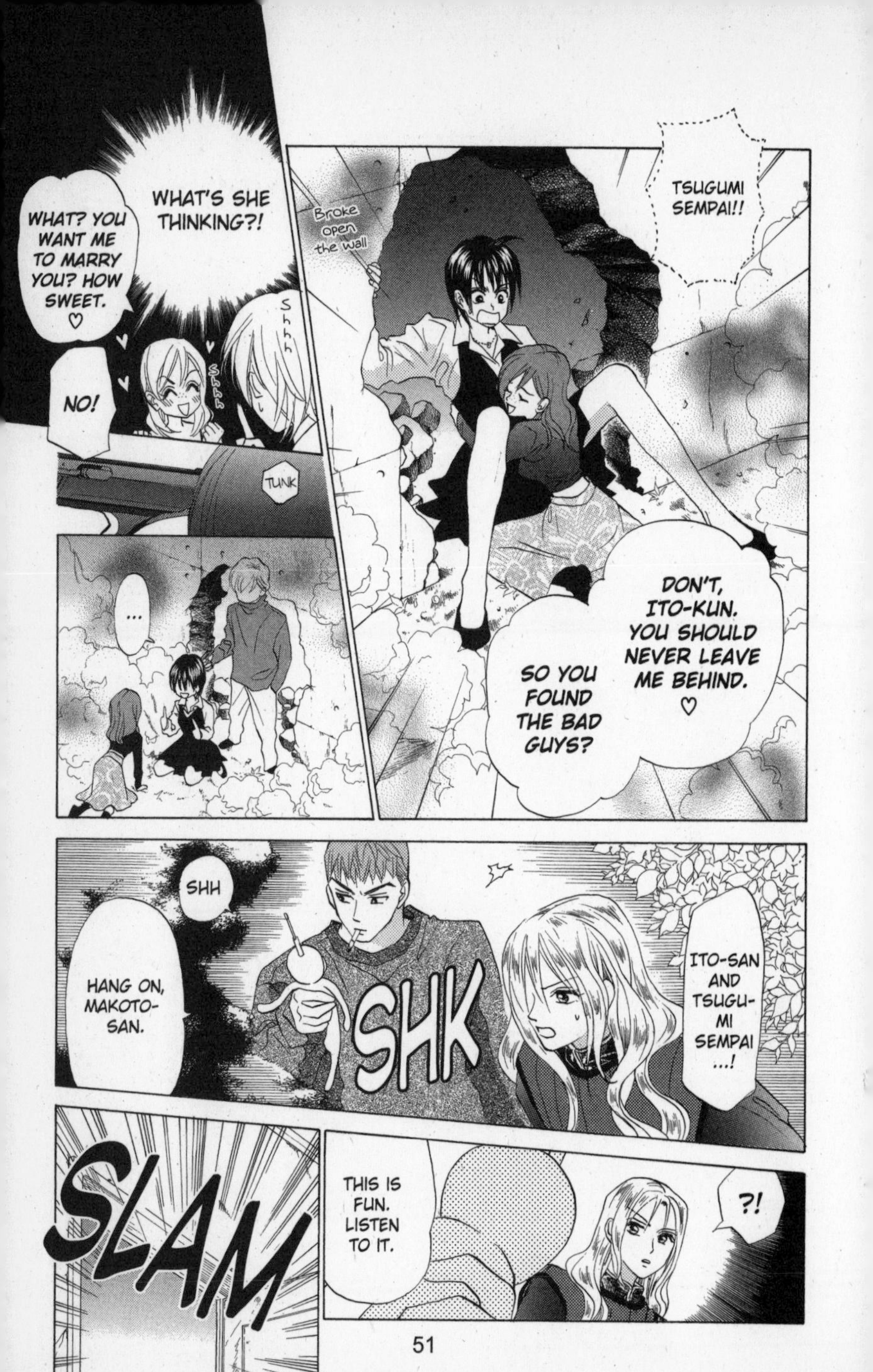
TSUGUMI SEMPAI!!
Broke open the wall
DON'T, ITO-KUN. YOU SHOULD NEVER LEAVE ME BEHIND. ♡
SO YOU FOUND THE BAD GUYS?
WHAT'S SHE THINKING?!
WHAT? YOU WANT ME TO MARRY YOU? HOW SWEET. ♡
Shhh
Shhh
NO!
TUNK
...
ITO-SAN AND TSUGU-MI SEMPAI ...!
SHH
SHK
HANG ON, MAKOTO-SAN.
?!
THIS IS FUN. LISTEN TO IT.
SLAM

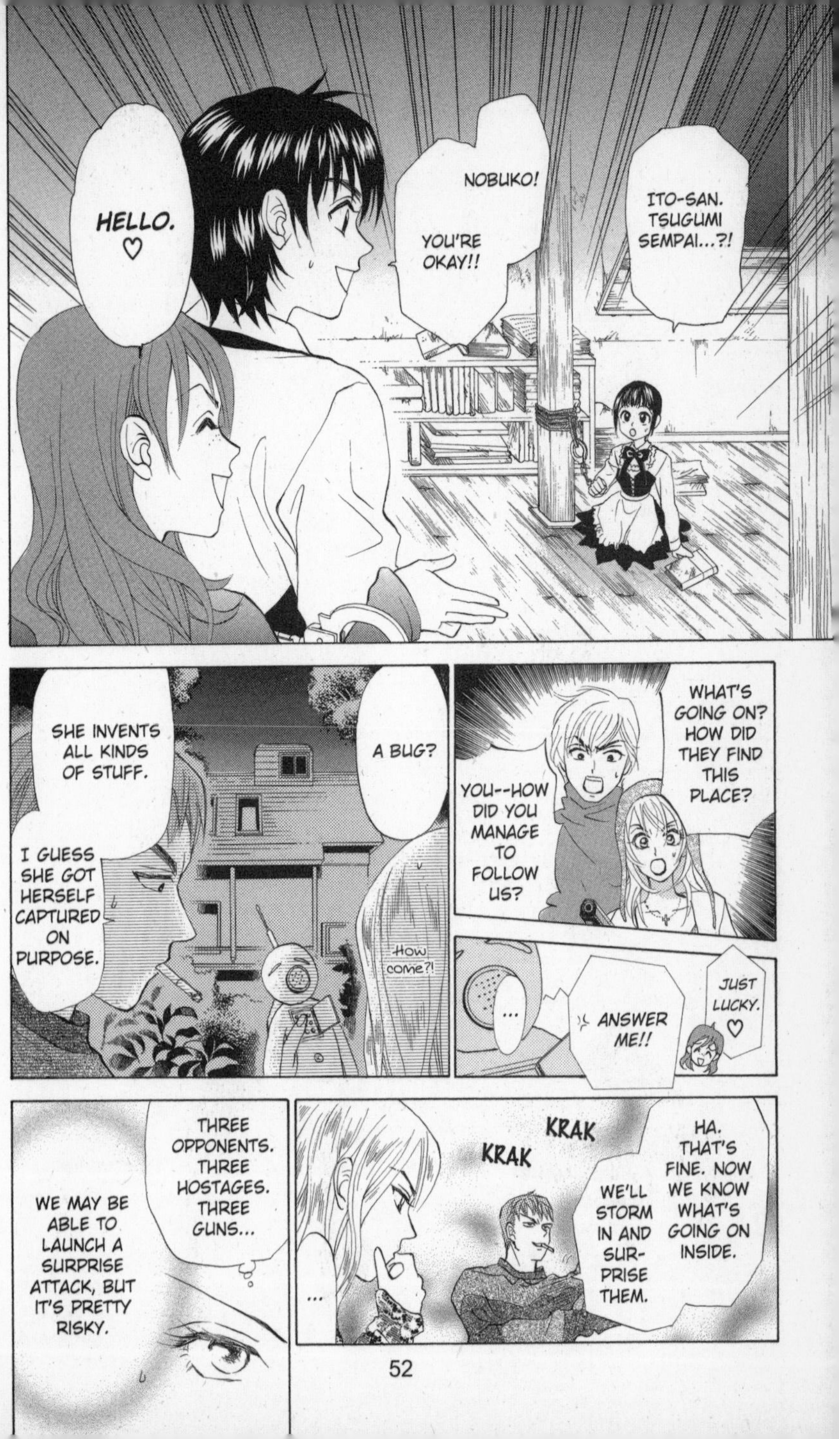
ITO-SAN. TSUGUMI SEMPAI...?!
NOBUKO! YOU'RE OKAY!!
HELLO. ♡
WHAT'S GOING ON? HOW DID THEY FIND THIS PLACE?
YOU--HOW DID YOU MANAGE TO FOLLOW US?
JUST LUCKY. ♡
ANSWER ME!!
...
A BUG?
How come?!
SHE INVENTS ALL KINDS OF STUFF.
I GUESS SHE GOT HERSELF CAPTURED ON PURPOSE.
HA. THAT'S FINE. NOW WE KNOW WHAT'S GOING ON INSIDE.
WE'LL STORM IN AND SUR-PRISE THEM.
KRAK
KRAK
...
THREE OPPONENTS. THREE HOSTAGES. THREE GUNS...
WE MAY BE ABLE TO LAUNCH A SURPRISE ATTACK, BUT IT'S PRETTY RISKY.

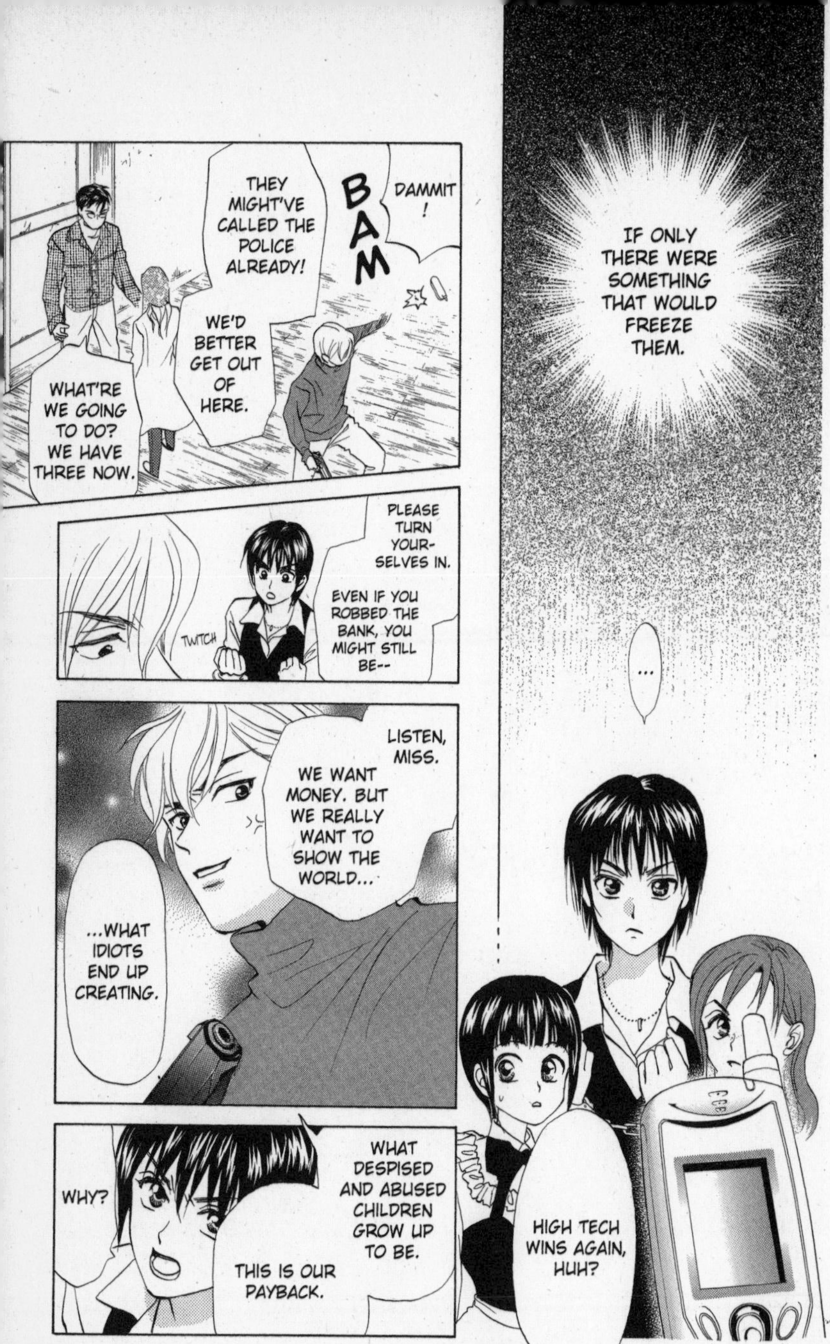
IF ONLY THERE WERE SOMETHING THAT WOULD FREEZE THEM.
...
HIGH TECH WINS AGAIN, HUH?
DAMMIT!
BAM
THEY MIGHT'VE CALLED THE POLICE ALREADY!
WE'D BETTER GET OUT OF HERE.
WHAT'RE WE GOING TO DO? WE HAVE THREE NOW.
PLEASE TURN YOUR-SELVES IN.
EVEN IF YOU ROBBED THE BANK, YOU MIGHT STILL BE--
TWITCH
LISTEN, MISS.
WE WANT MONEY. BUT WE REALLY WANT TO SHOW THE WORLD...
...WHAT IDIOTS END UP CREATING.
WHAT DESPISED AND ABUSED CHILDREN GROW UP TO BE.
THIS IS OUR PAYBACK.
WHY?

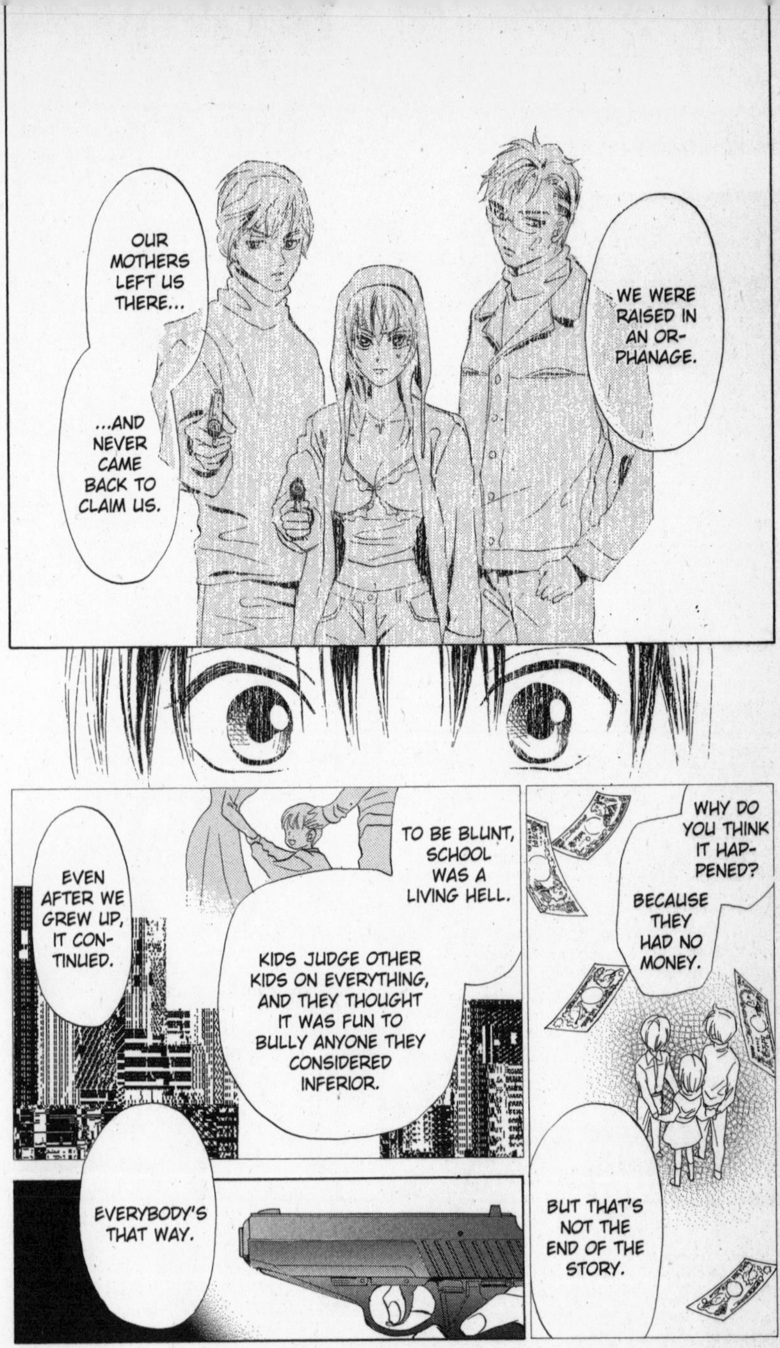
WE WERE RAISED IN AN OR-PHANAGE.
OUR MOTHERS LEFT US THERE...
...AND NEVER CAME BACK TO CLAIM US.
WHY DO YOU THINK IT HAP-PENED?
BECAUSE THEY HAD NO MONEY.
BUT THAT'S NOT THE END OF THE STORY.
TO BE BLUNT, SCHOOL WAS A LIVING HELL.
KIDS JUDGE OTHER KIDS ON EVERYTHING, AND THEY THOUGHT IT WAS FUN TO BULLY ANYONE THEY CONSIDERED INFERIOR.
EVEN AFTER WE GREW UP, IT CONTINUED.
EVERYBODY'S THAT WAY.

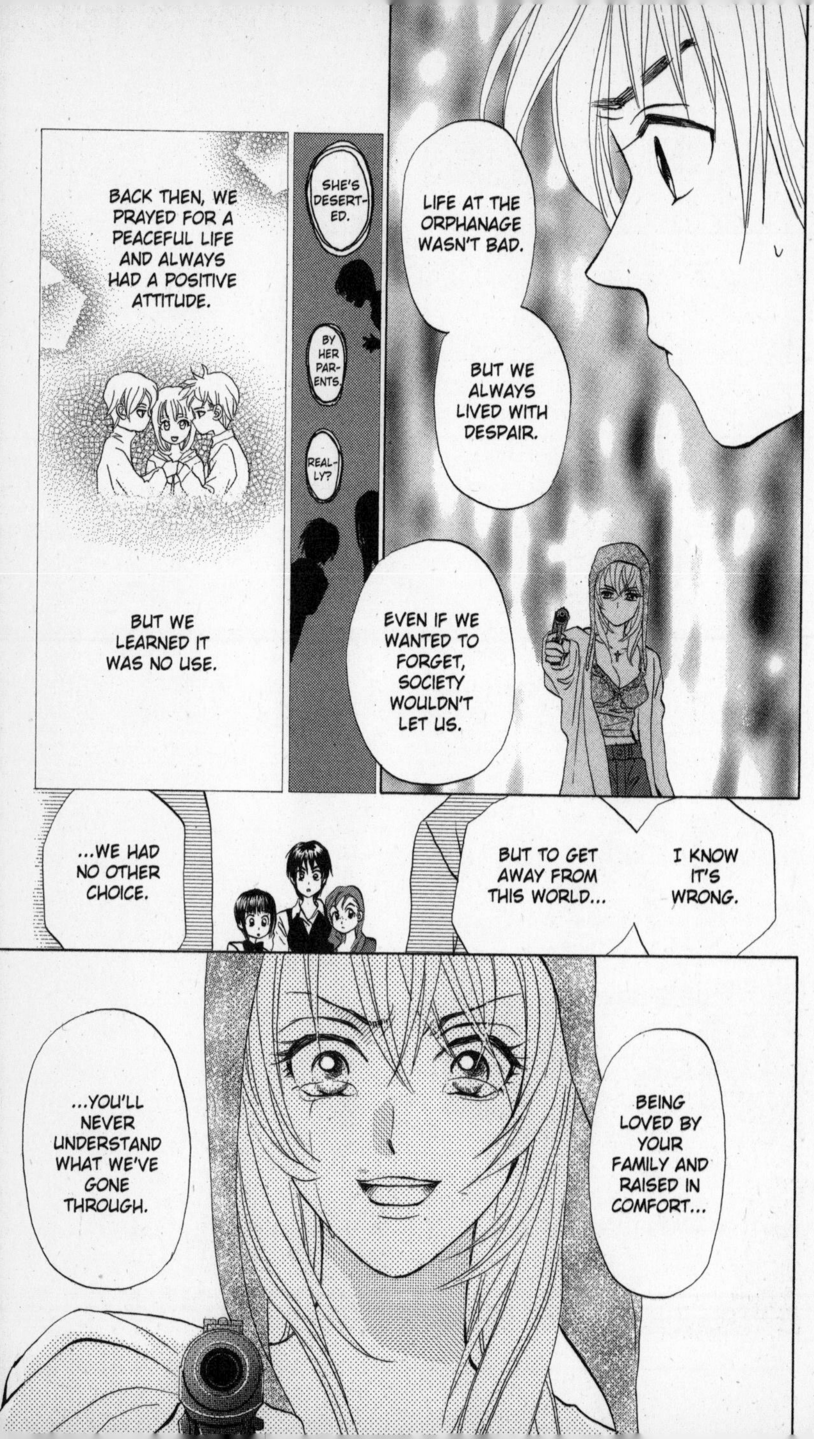
LIFE AT THE ORPHANAGE WASN'T BAD.
BUT WE ALWAYS LIVED WITH DESPAIR.
EVEN IF WE WANTED TO FORGET, SOCIETY WOULDN'T LET US.
SHE'S DESERT-ED.
BY HER PAR-ENTS.
REAL-LY?
BACK THEN, WE PRAYED FOR A PEACEFUL LIFE AND ALWAYS HAD A POSITIVE ATTITUDE.
BUT WE LEARNED IT WAS NO USE.
I KNOW IT'S WRONG.
BUT TO GET AWAY FROM THIS WORLD...
...WE HAD NO OTHER CHOICE.
BEING LOVED BY YOUR FAMILY AND RAISED IN COMFORT...
...YOU'LL NEVER UNDERSTAND WHAT WE'VE GONE THROUGH.

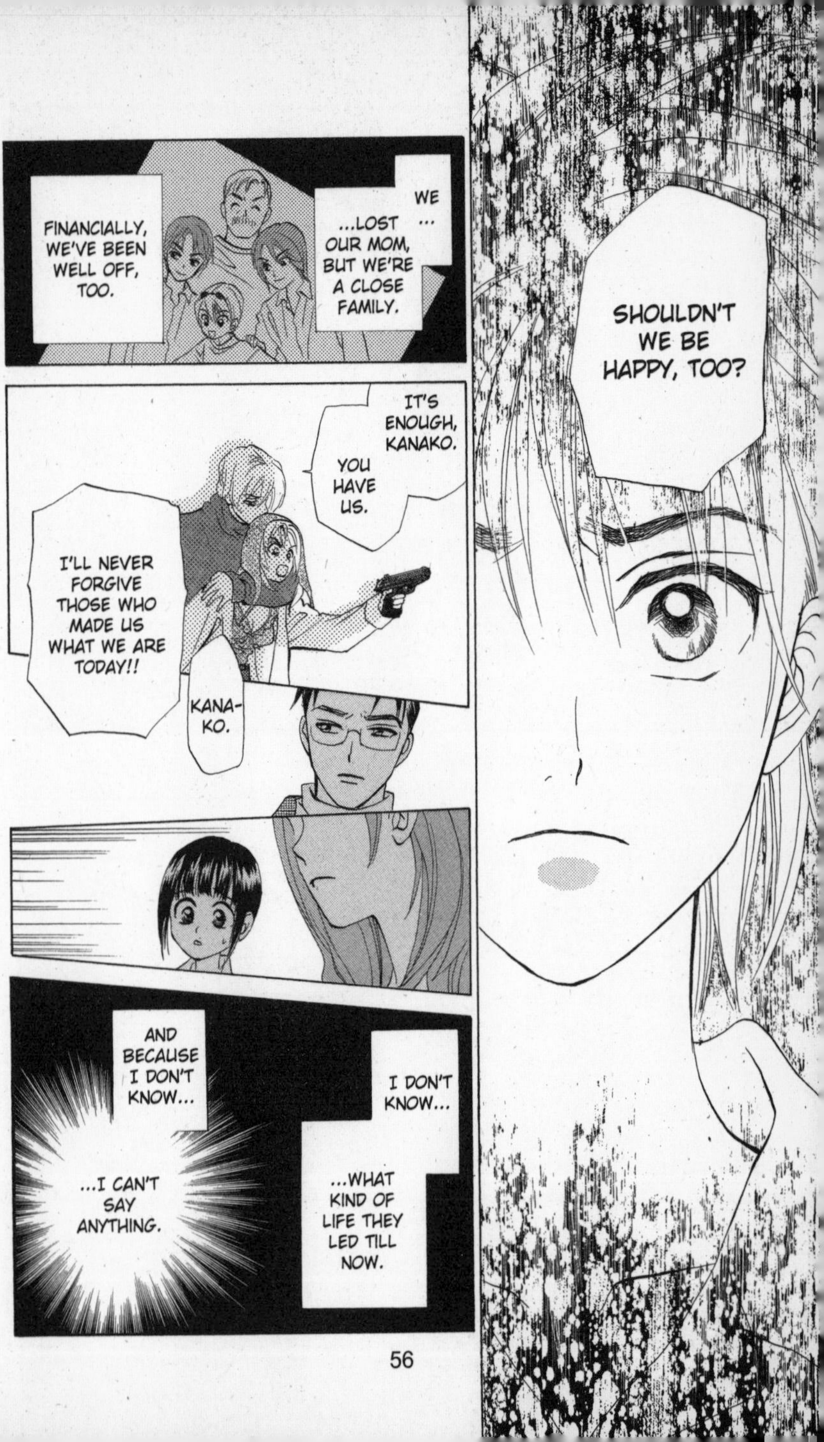
SHOULDN'T WE BE HAPPY, TOO?
WE ...
...LOST OUR MOM, BUT WE'RE A CLOSE FAMILY.
FINANCIALLY, WE'VE BEEN WELL OFF, TOO.
IT'S ENOUGH, KANAKO.
YOU HAVE US.
I'LL NEVER FORGIVE THOSE WHO MADE US WHAT WE ARE TODAY!!
KANA-KO.
I DON'T KNOW...
...WHAT KIND OF LIFE THEY LED TILL NOW.
AND BECAUSE I DON'T KNOW...
...I CAN'T SAY ANYTHING.

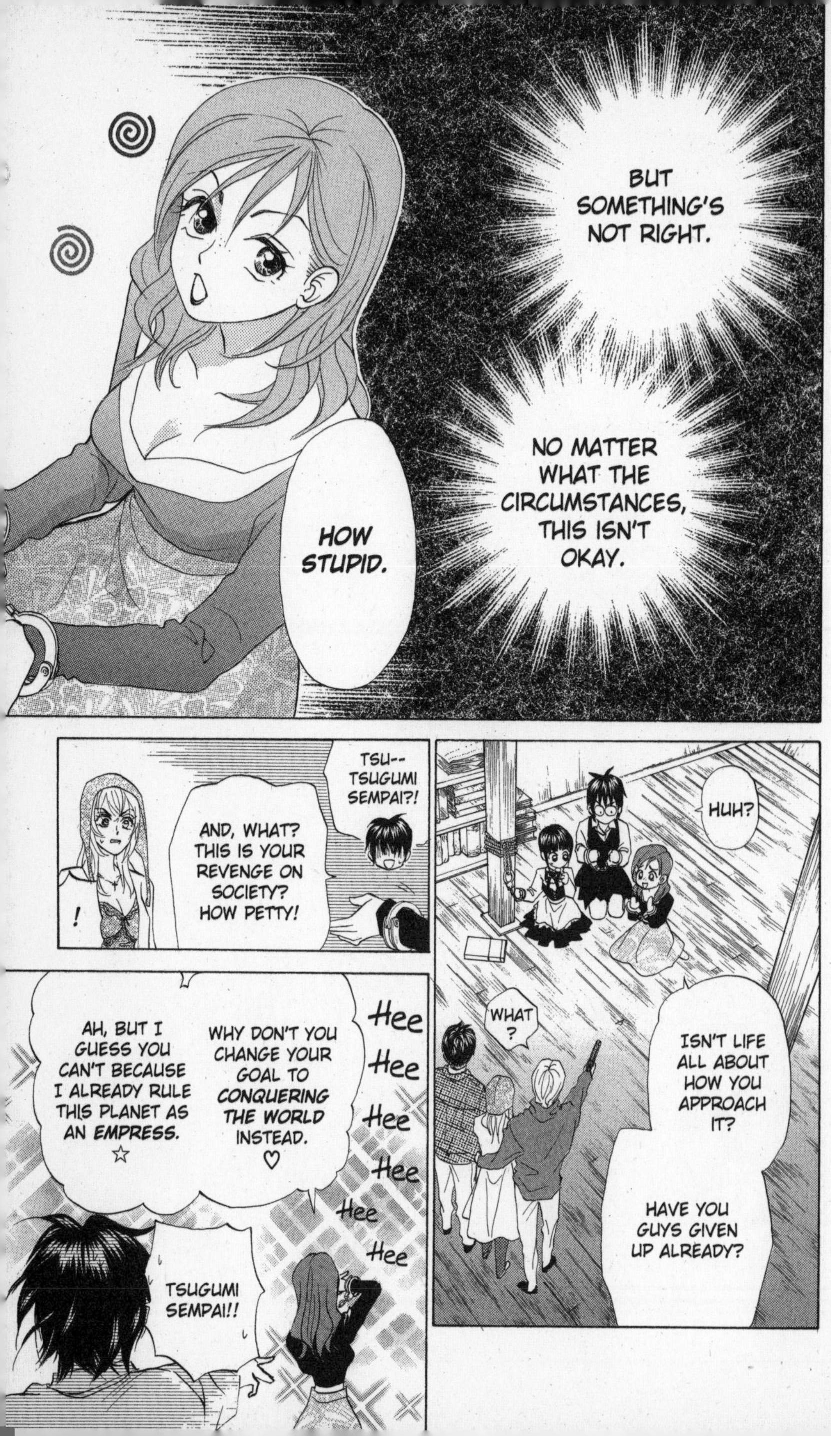
BUT SOMETHING'S NOT RIGHT.
NO MATTER WHAT THE CIRCUMSTANCES, THIS ISN'T OKAY.
HOW STUPID.
HUH?
WHAT?
ISN'T LIFE ALL ABOUT HOW YOU APPROACH IT?
HAVE YOU GUYS GIVEN UP ALREADY?
TSU-- TSUGUMI SEMPAI?!
AND, WHAT? THIS IS YOUR REVENGE ON SOCIETY? HOW PETTY!
!
Hee Hee Hee Hee Hee Hee
WHY DON'T YOU CHANGE YOUR GOAL TO CONQUERING THE WORLD INSTEAD. ♡
AH, BUT I GUESS YOU CAN'T BECAUSE I ALREADY RULE THIS PLANET AS AN EMPRESS. ☆
TSUGUMI SEMPAI!!

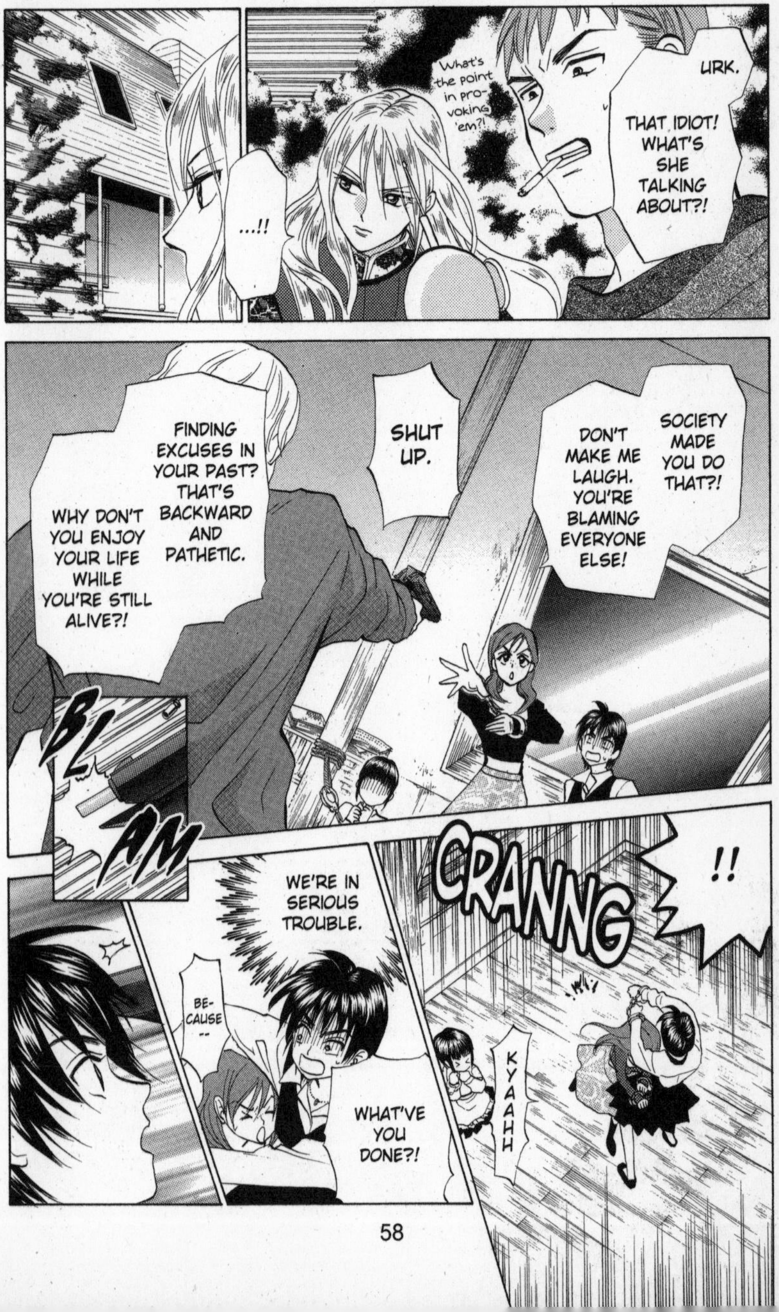
URK.
THAT IDIOT! WHAT'S SHE TALKING ABOUT?!
What's the point in provoking 'em?!
...!!
SOCIETY MADE YOU DO THAT?!
DON'T MAKE ME LAUGH. YOU'RE BLAMING EVERYONE ELSE!
SHUT UP.
FINDING EXCUSES IN YOUR PAST? THAT'S BACKWARD AND PATHETIC.
WHY DON'T YOU ENJOY YOUR LIFE WHILE YOU'RE STILL ALIVE?!
BLAM
CRANNG !!
KYAAHH
WE'RE IN SERIOUS TROUBLE.
BE-CAUSE --
WHAT'VE YOU DONE?!

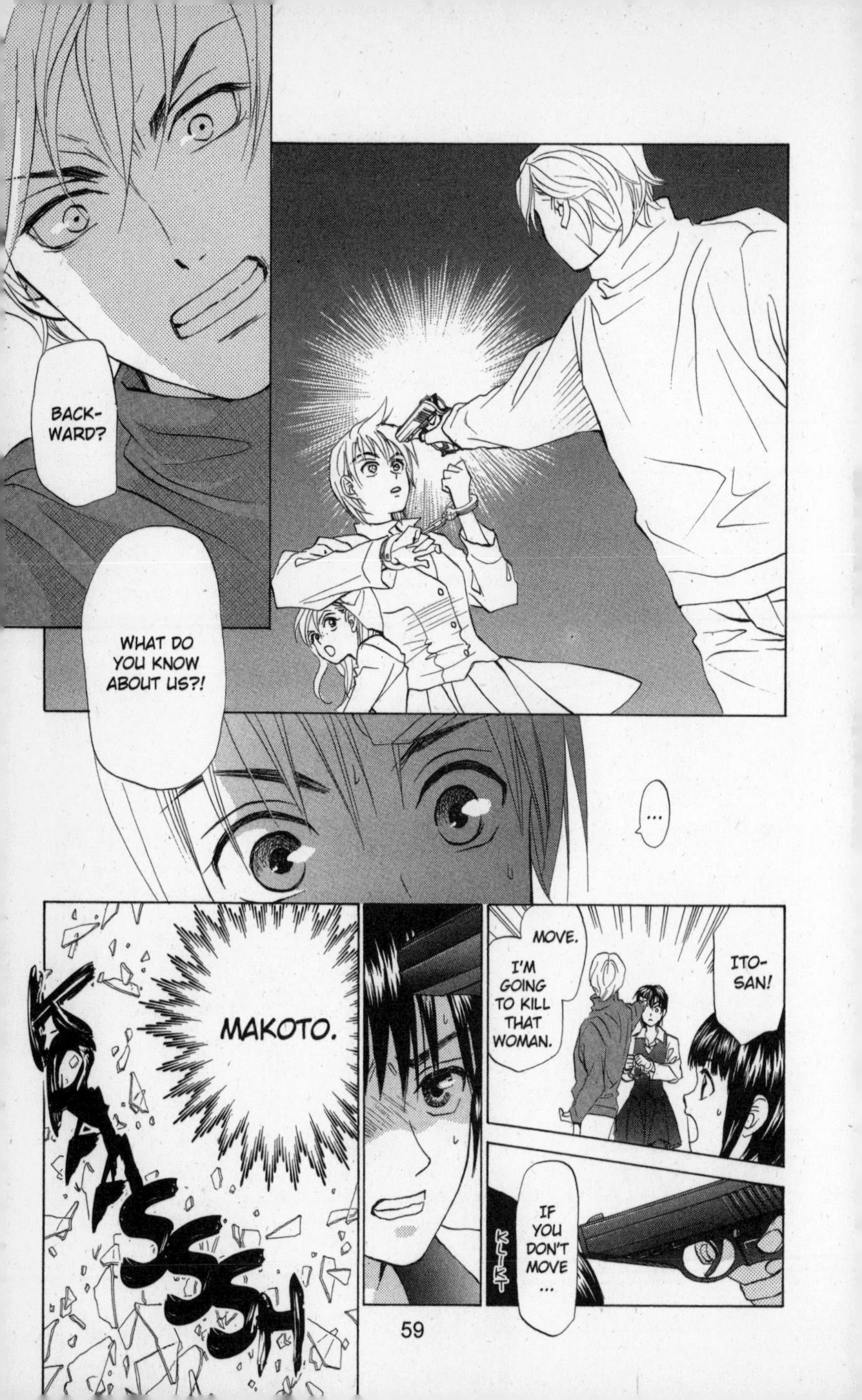
BACK-WARD?
WHAT DO YOU KNOW ABOUT US?!
...
ITO-SAN!
MOVE.
I'M GOING TO KILL THAT WOMAN.
KLIKT
IF YOU DON'T MOVE ...
MAKOTO.
SSS

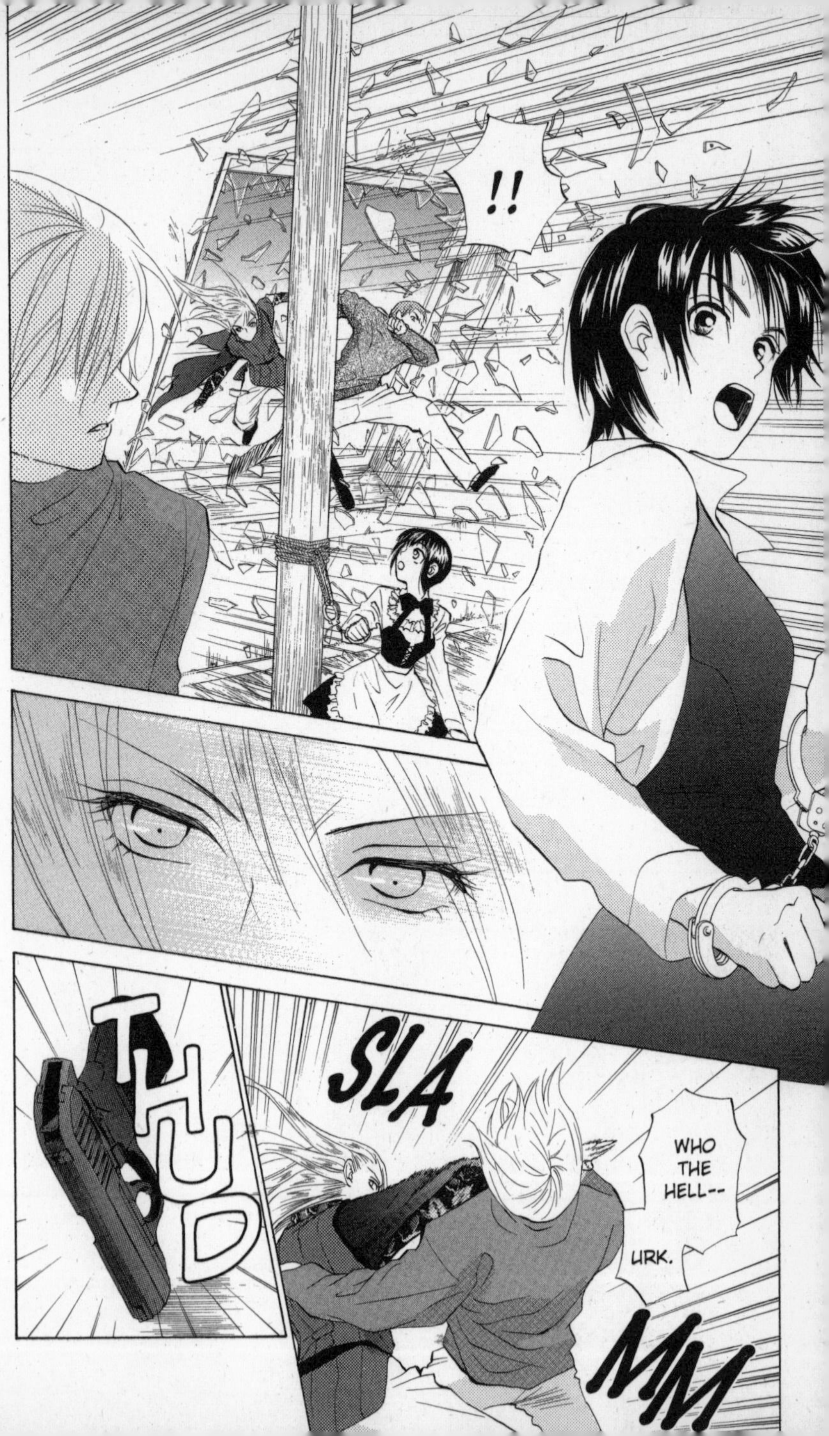
!!
SLA
WHO THE HELL--
URK.
MM
THUD

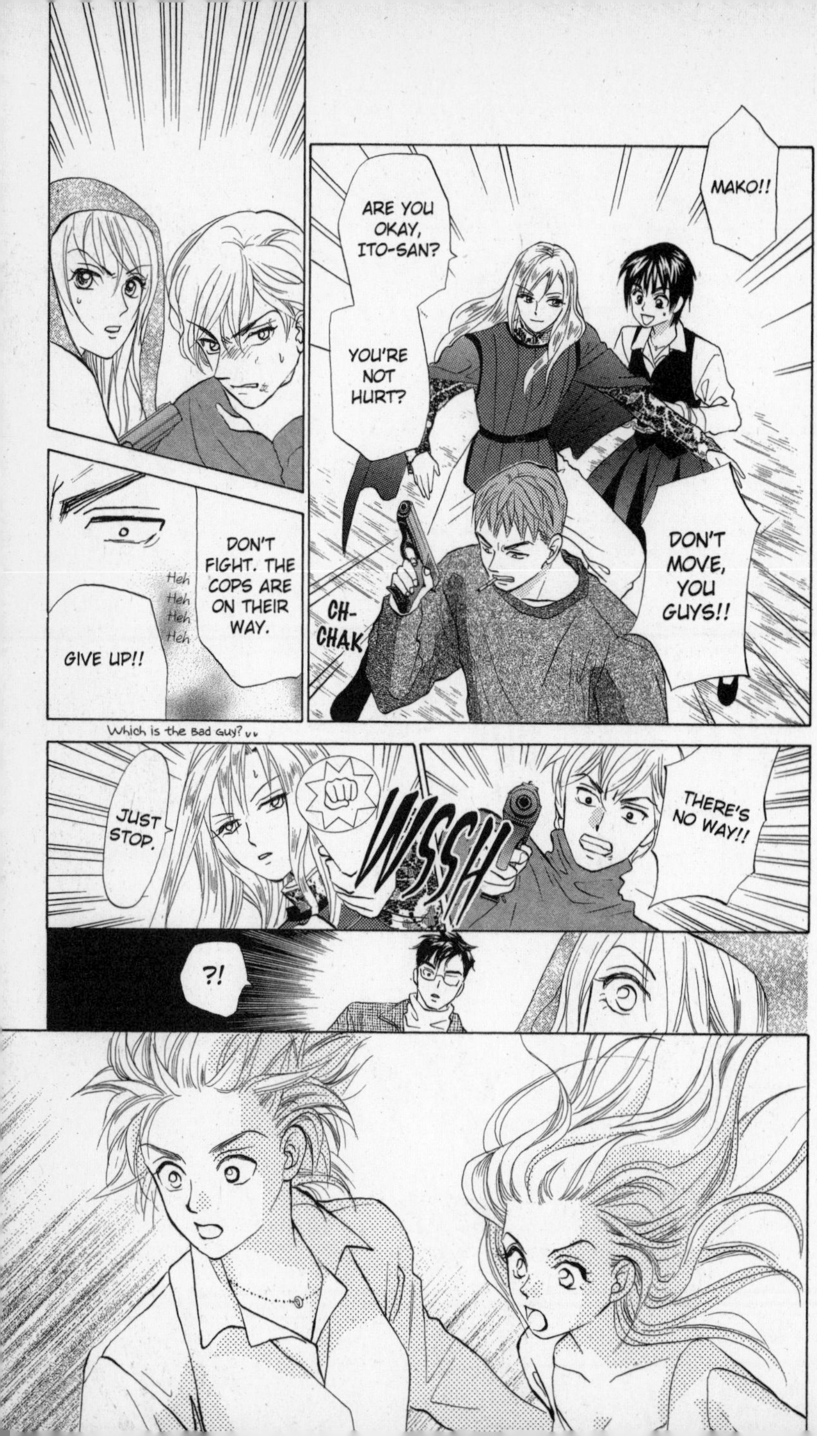
MAKO!!
ARE YOU OKAY, ITO-SAN?
YOU'RE NOT HURT?
DON'T MOVE, YOU GUYS!!
CH-CHAK
DON'T FIGHT. THE COPS ARE ON THEIR WAY.
Heh Heh Heh Heh
GIVE UP!!
Which is the Bad Guy?
THERE'S NO WAY!!
WSSH
JUST STOP.
?!

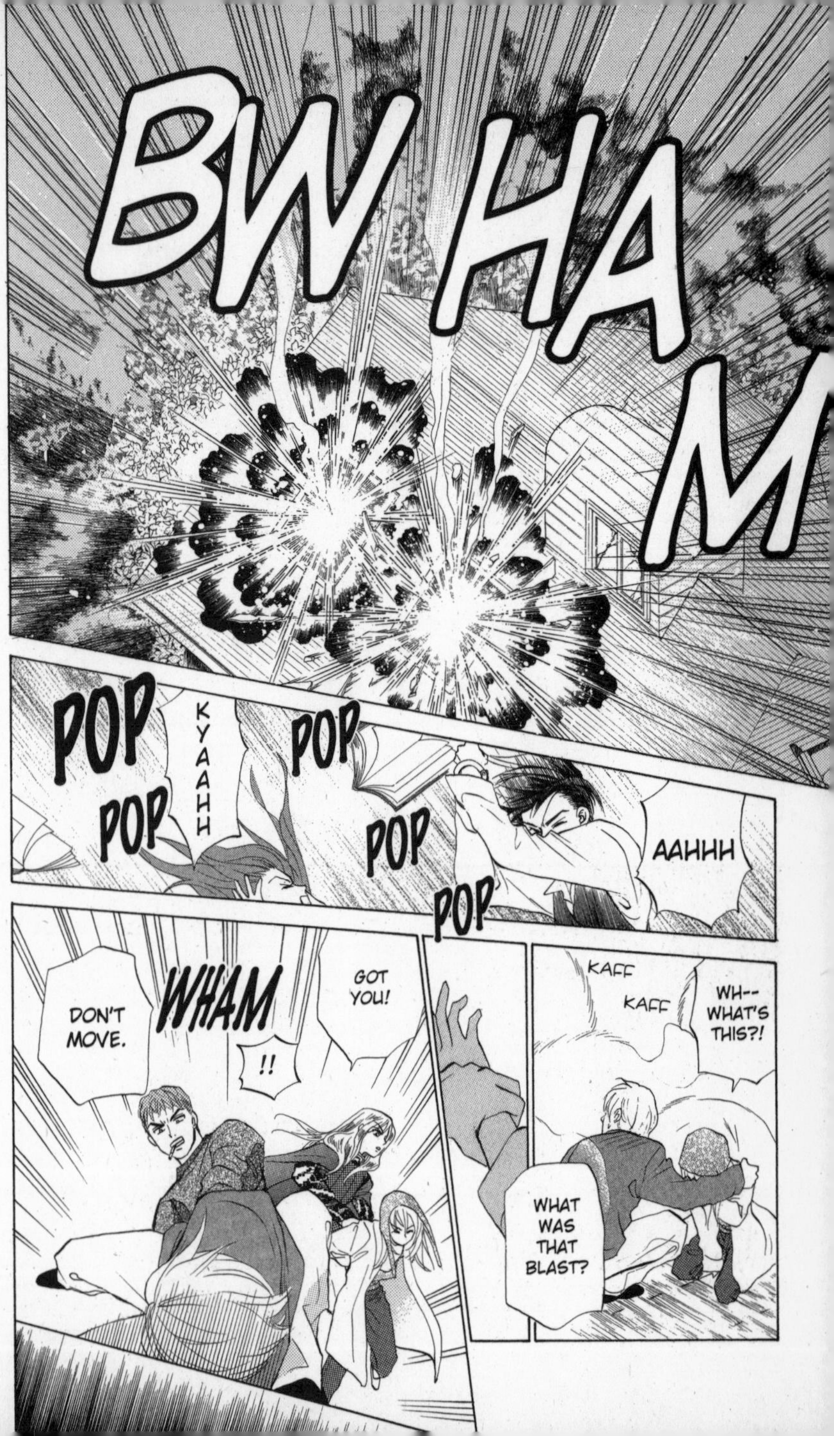
BWHAMM
AAHHH
POP
POP
POP
KYAAHH
POP
POP
WH-- WHAT'S THIS?!
KAFF
KAFF
WHAT WAS THAT BLAST?
GOT YOU!
!!
WHAM
DON'T MOVE.

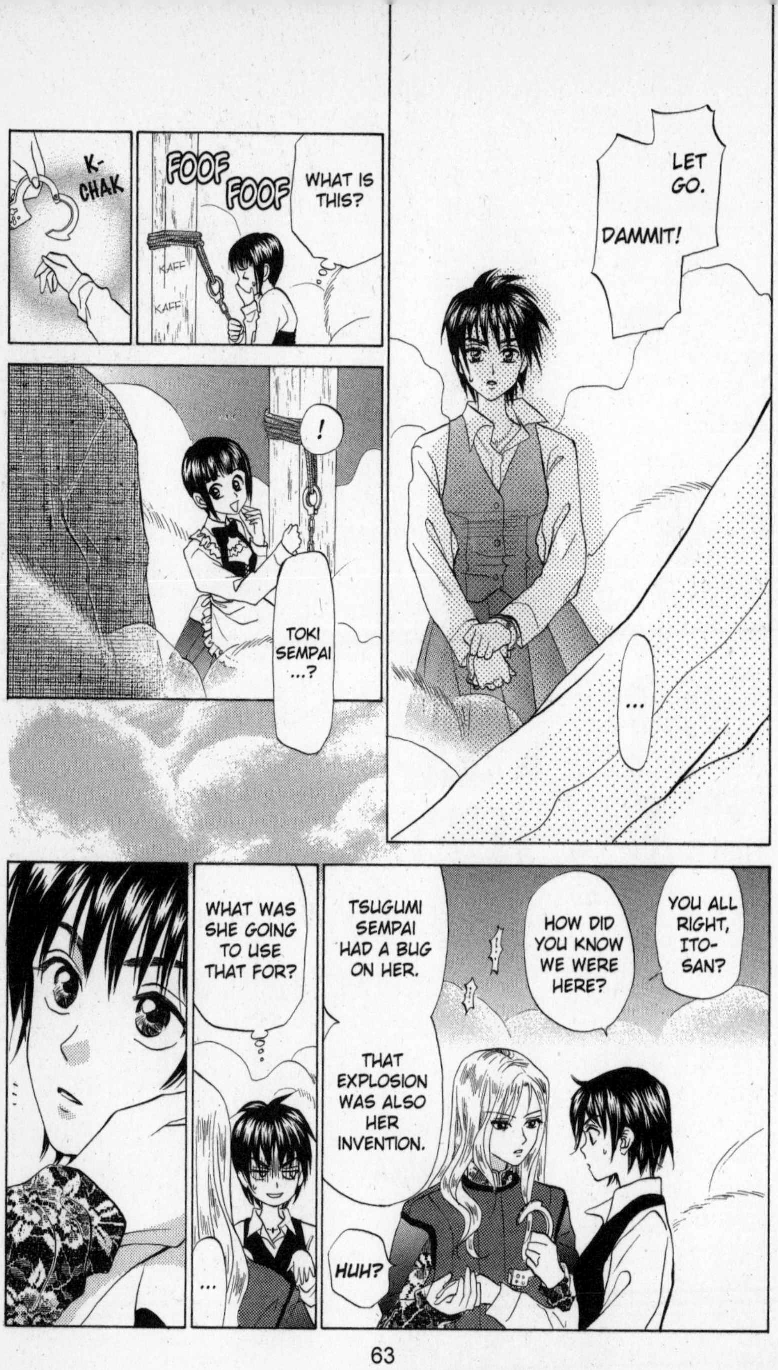
LET GO.
DAMMIT!
...
FOOF FOOF
WHAT IS THIS?
KAFF KAFF
K-CHAK
!
TOKI SEMPAI ...?
YOU ALL RIGHT, ITO-SAN?
HOW DID YOU KNOW WE WERE HERE?
TSUGUMI SEMPAI HAD A BUG ON HER.
THAT EXPLOSION WAS ALSO HER INVENTION.
HUH?
WHAT WAS SHE GOING TO USE THAT FOR?
...

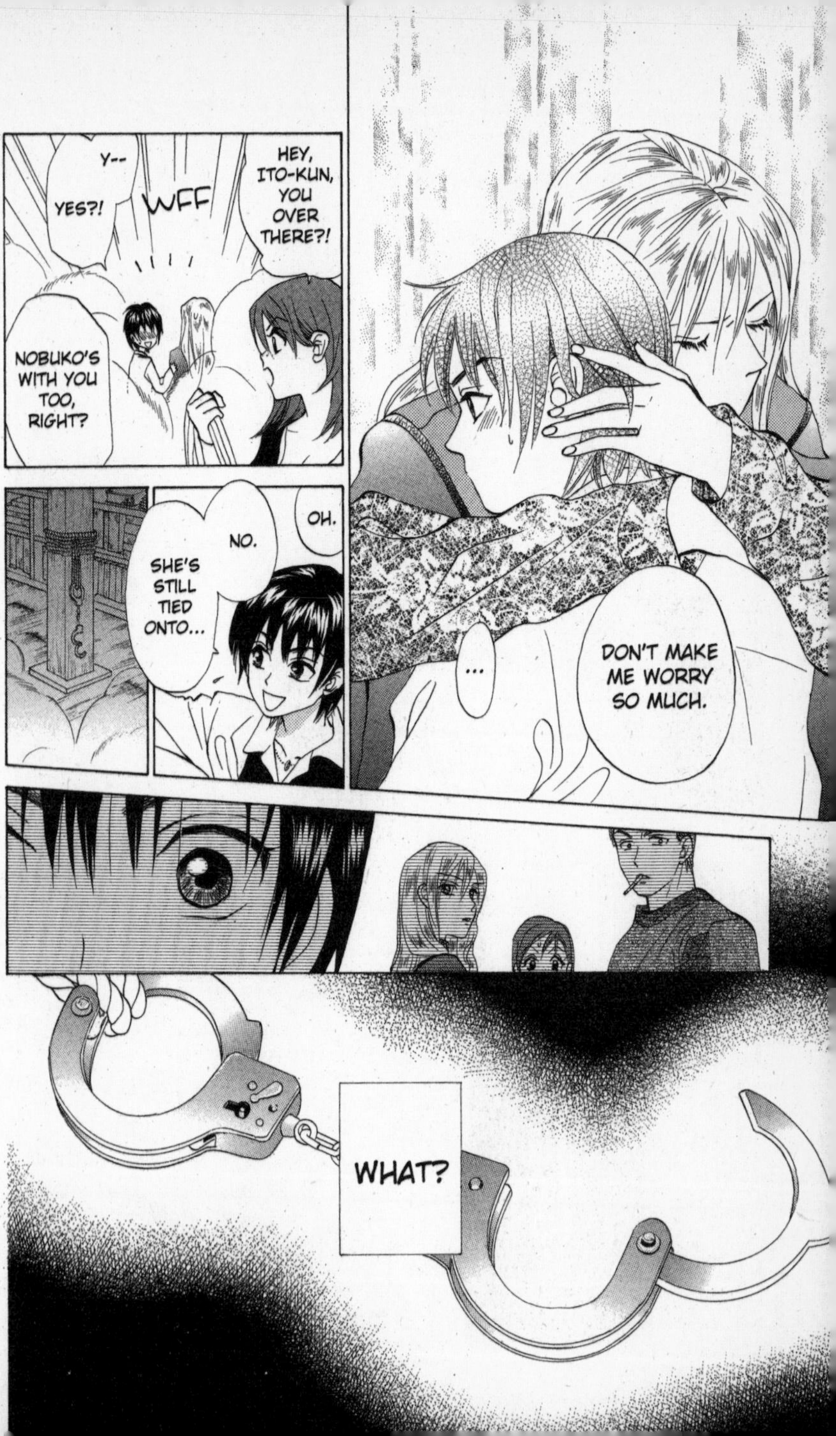
DON'T MAKE ME WORRY SO MUCH.
...
HEY, ITO-KUN, YOU OVER THERE?!
Y--
YES?!
WFF
NOBUKO'S WITH YOU TOO, RIGHT?
OH.
NO.
SHE'S STILL TIED ONTO...
WHAT?

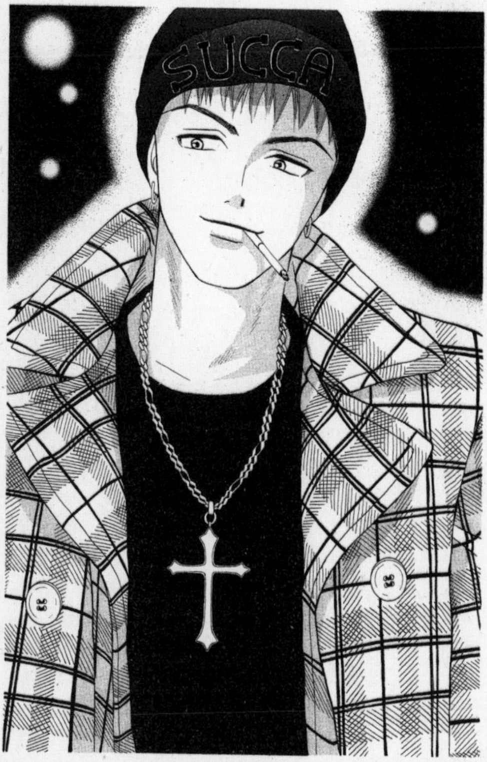
SUCCA

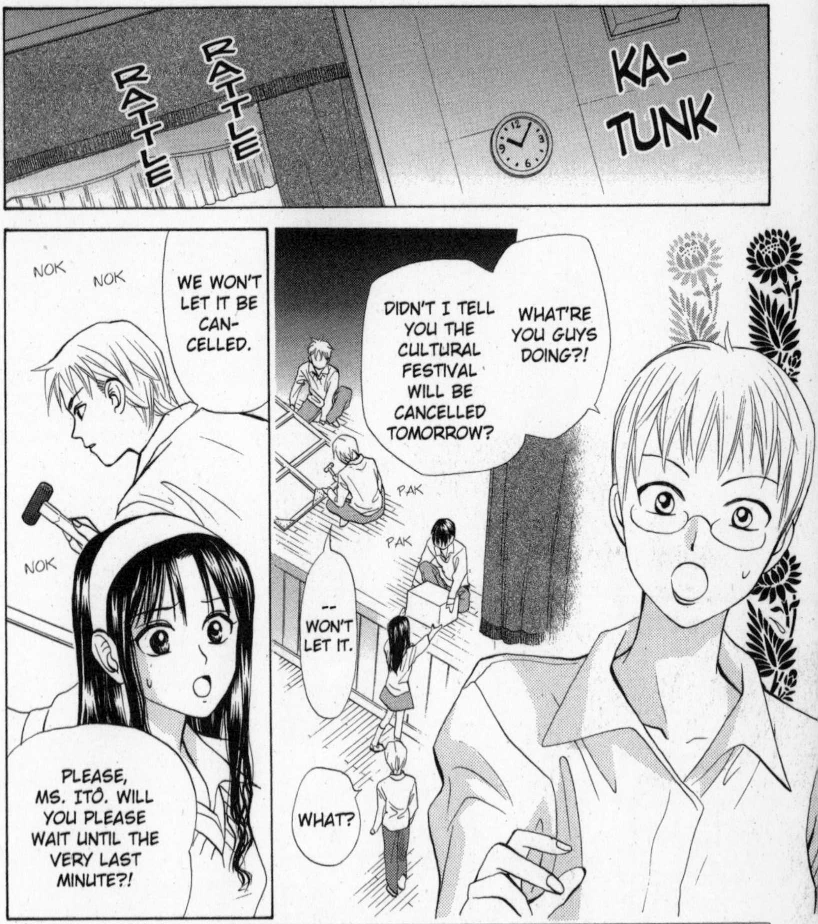
KA-TUNK
RATTLE RATTLE
WHAT'RE YOU GUYS DOING?!
DIDN'T I TELL YOU THE CULTURAL FESTIVAL WILL BE CANCELLED TOMORROW?
PAK
PAK
-- WON'T LET IT.
WHAT?
WE WON'T LET IT BE CAN-CELLED.
NOK NOK
NOK
PLEASE, MS. ITÔ. WILL YOU PLEASE WAIT UNTIL THE VERY LAST MINUTE?!

—Behind the Scenes Story ③—

I had fun drawing Toki-chan & Nobuko.
I might have intentionally put the story together so that I could draw the scene near the end where Toki-chan says, "You did your best" (page 90)...
I like creating stories about subcharacters. But of course, I enjoy the ones about Ito and Makoto, too. By the way, after I worked on Kakeru for some time, I came to think he looks like my older brother... It's not like I modeled him after him. Maybe the dark, short hair did it. My brother wears glasses, too.

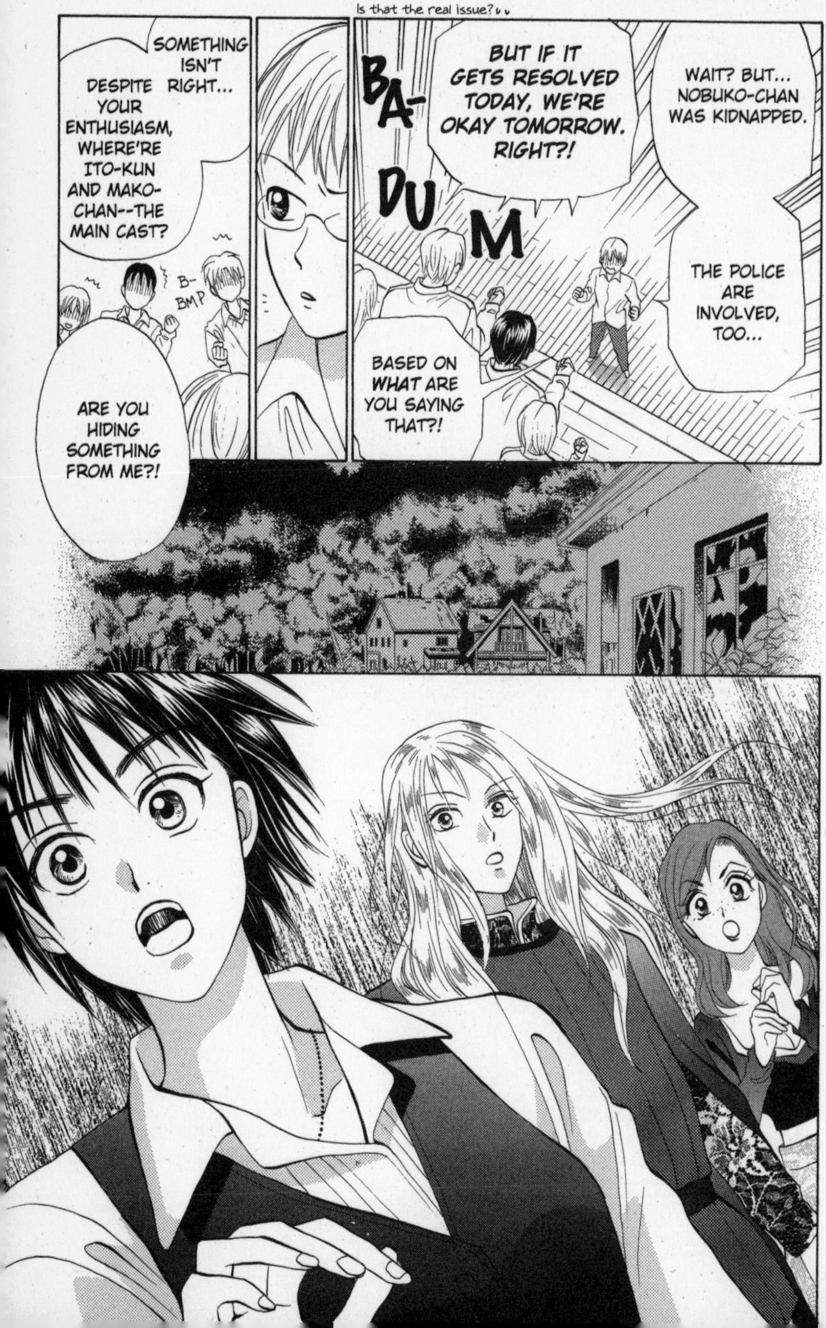
Is that the real issue?
WAIT? BUT... NOBUKO-CHAN WAS KIDNAPPED.
THE POLICE ARE INVOLVED, TOO...
BUT IF IT GETS RESOLVED TODAY, WE'RE OKAY TOMORROW. RIGHT?!
BA-DUM
BASED ON WHAT ARE YOU SAYING THAT?!
SOMETHING ISN'T RIGHT...
DESPITE YOUR ENTHUSIASM, WHERE'RE ITO-KUN AND MAKO-CHAN--THE MAIN CAST?
B-BMP
ARE YOU HIDING SOMETHING FROM ME?!

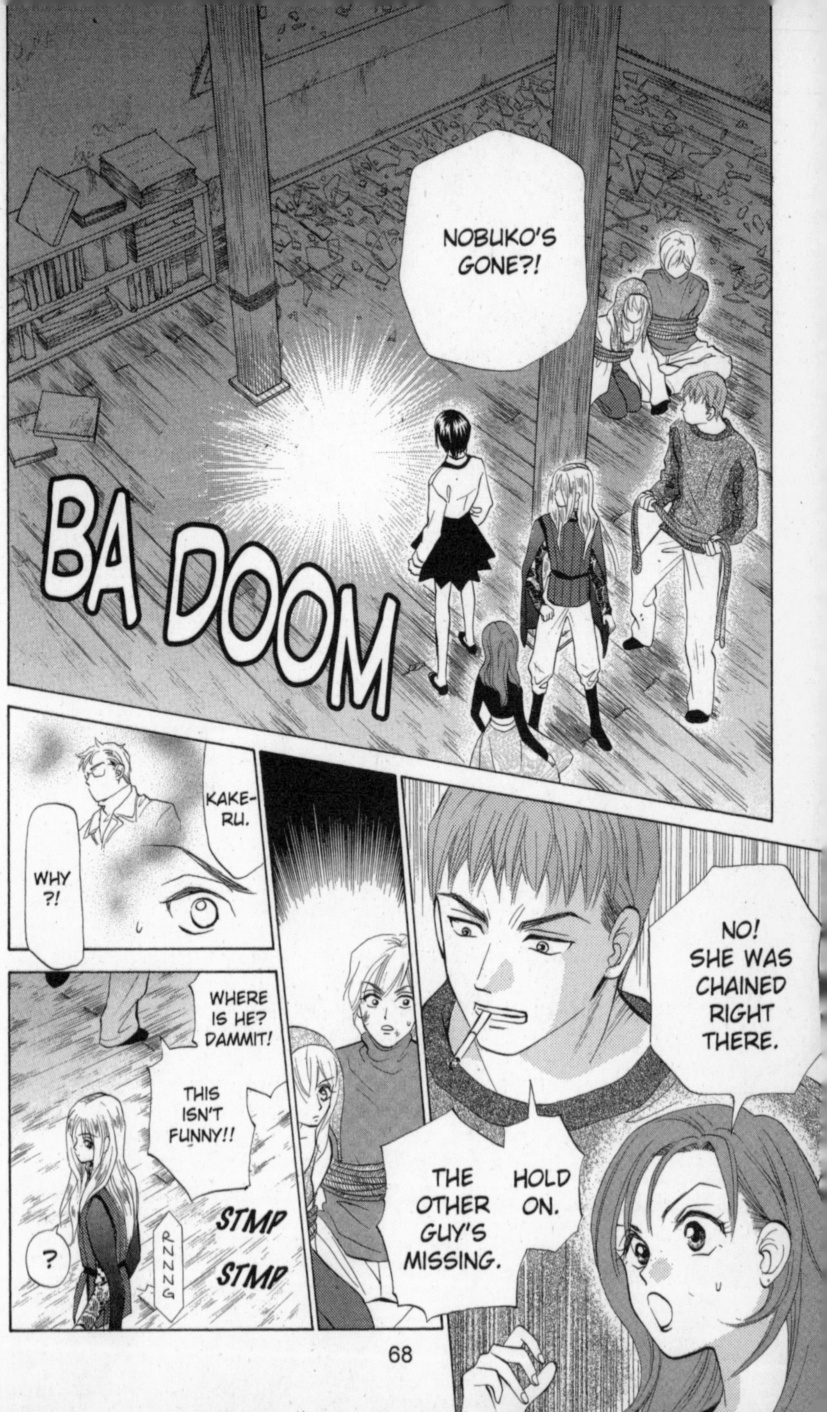
NOBUKO'S GONE?!
BA DOOM
NO! SHE WAS CHAINED RIGHT THERE.
HOLD ON.
THE OTHER GUY'S MISSING.
KAKE-RU.
WHY?!
WHERE IS HE? DAMMIT!
THIS ISN'T FUNNY!!
STMP
STMP
RNNNG
?

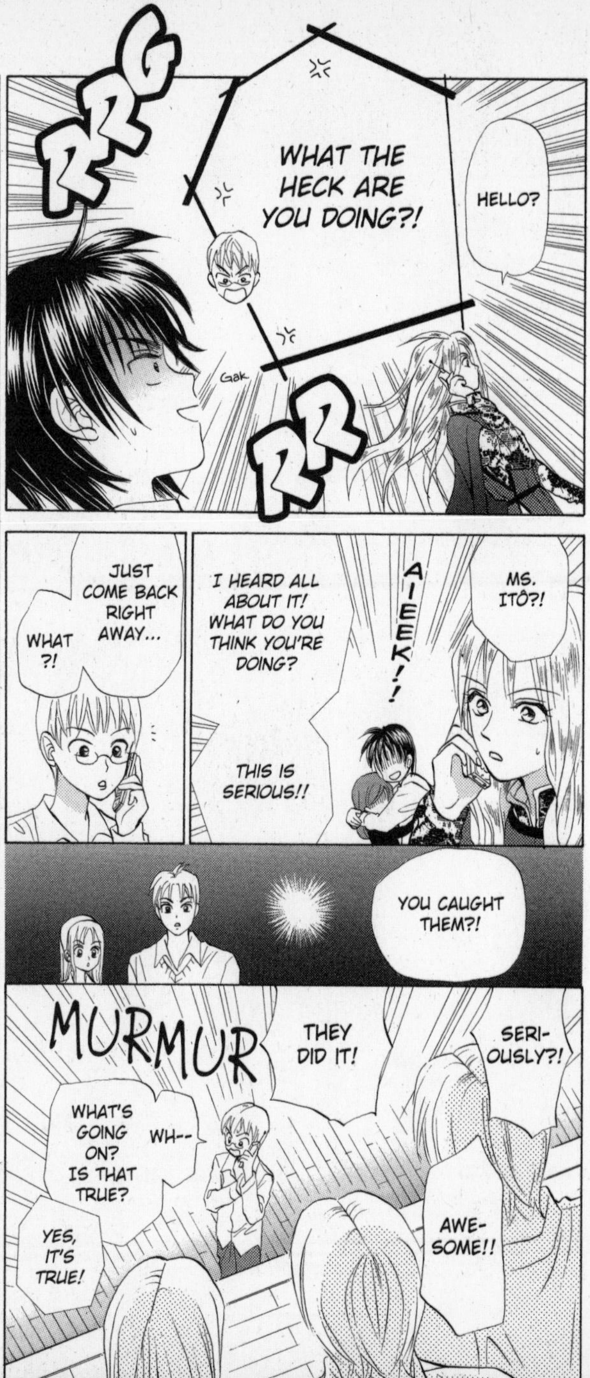
RRG
HELLO?
WHAT THE HECK ARE YOU DOING?!
Gak.
RR
MS. ITÔ?!
AIEEK!!
I HEARD ALL ABOUT IT! WHAT DO YOU THINK YOU'RE DOING?
THIS IS SERIOUS!!
JUST COME BACK RIGHT AWAY...
WHAT?!
YOU CAUGHT THEM?!
SERIOUSLY?!
THEY DID IT!
MURMUR
AWESOME!!
WH--
WHAT'S GOING ON? IS THAT TRUE?
YES, IT'S TRUE!

Apparently, my sister had the same "paralyzing feeling with the noise." But my other assistants experienced none. I'm jealous.

But we said goodbye to that office early last summer. After we moved, it stopped happening completely. ♪♪

However...

Exactly one year after we moved, my sister and I experienced the same paralyzing feeling again! This time, it happened suddenly without warning! Apparently, the same is true with my sister. What's going on?

When we talked about it with my family, it turned out that only the female family members had ever experienced it so far.

Could it be hereditary?!

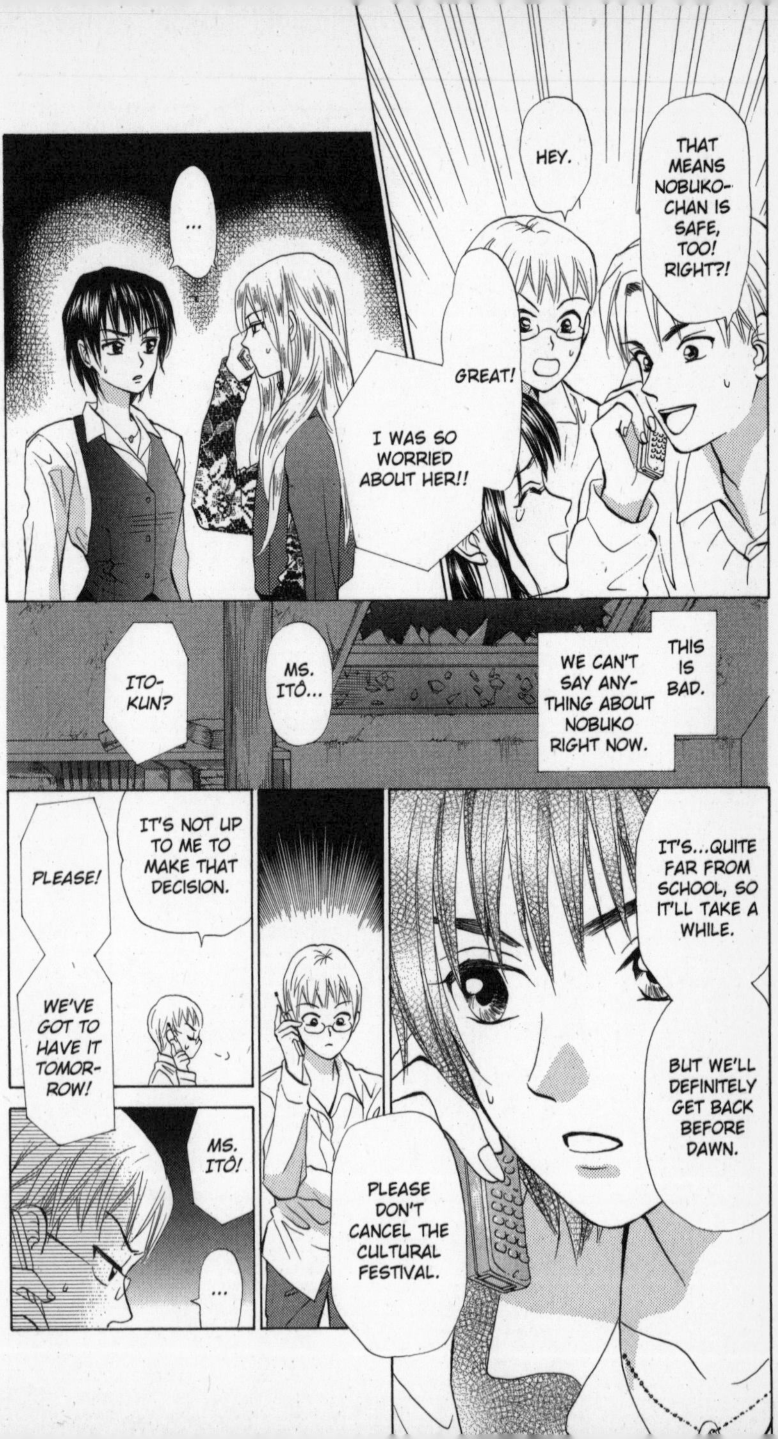
THAT MEANS NOBUKO-CHAN IS SAFE, TOO! RIGHT?!
HEY.
GREAT!
I WAS SO WORRIED ABOUT HER!!
...
THIS IS BAD.
WE CAN'T SAY ANYTHING ABOUT NOBUKO RIGHT NOW.
MS. ITÔ...
ITO-KUN?
IT'S...QUITE FAR FROM SCHOOL, SO IT'LL TAKE A WHILE.
BUT WE'LL DEFINITELY GET BACK BEFORE DAWN.
PLEASE DON'T CANCEL THE CULTURAL FESTIVAL.
IT'S NOT UP TO ME TO MAKE THAT DECISION.
PLEASE!
WE'VE GOT TO HAVE IT TOMORROW!
MS. ITÔ!
...

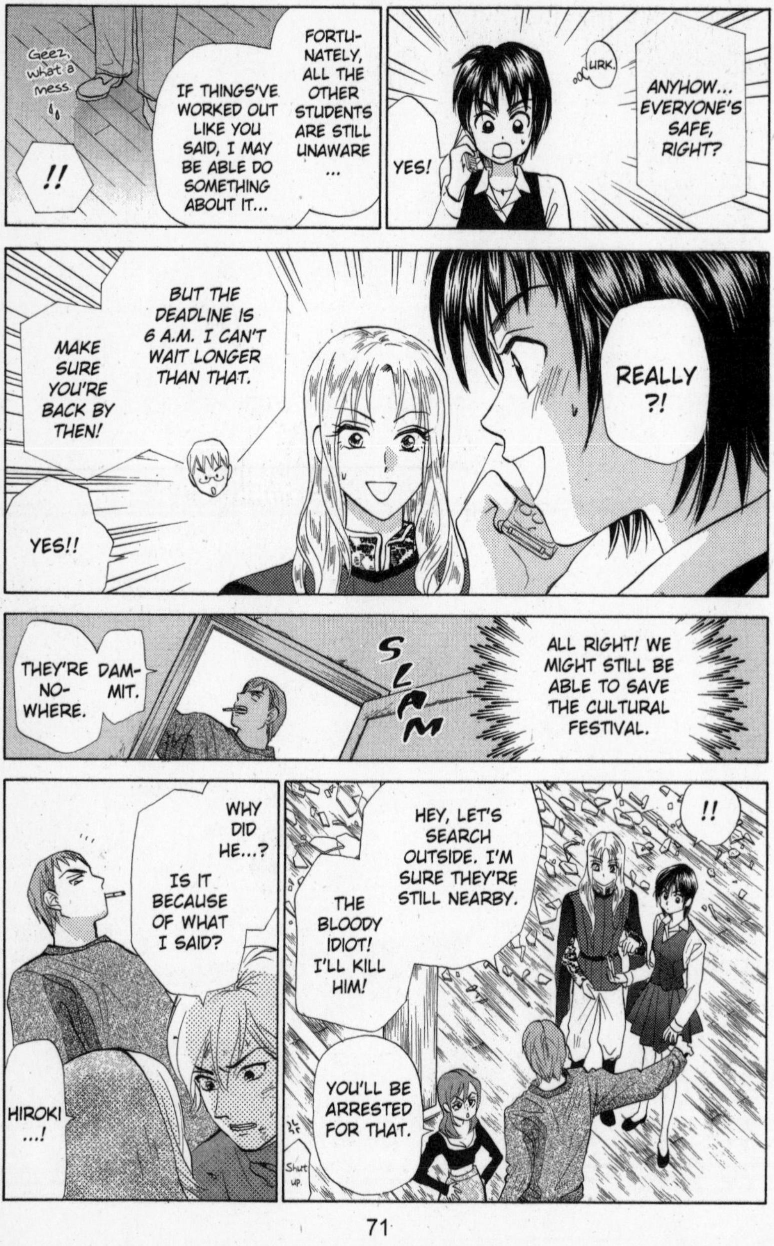
ANYHOW... EVERYONE'S SAFE, RIGHT?
URK.
YES!
FORTU-NATELY, ALL THE OTHER STUDENTS ARE STILL UNAWARE ...
IF THINGS'VE WORKED OUT LIKE YOU SAID, I MAY BE ABLE DO SOMETHING ABOUT IT...
Geez, what a mess.
!!
REALLY ?!
BUT THE DEADLINE IS 6 A.M. I CAN'T WAIT LONGER THAN THAT.
MAKE SURE YOU'RE BACK BY THEN!
YES!!
ALL RIGHT! WE MIGHT STILL BE ABLE TO SAVE THE CULTURAL FESTIVAL.
SLAM
DAM-MIT.
THEY'RE NO-WHERE.
!!
HEY, LET'S SEARCH OUTSIDE. I'M SURE THEY'RE STILL NEARBY.
THE BLOODY IDIOT! I'LL KILL HIM!
YOU'LL BE ARRESTED FOR THAT.
Shut up.
WHY DID HE...?
IS IT BECAUSE OF WHAT I SAID?
HIROKI ...!

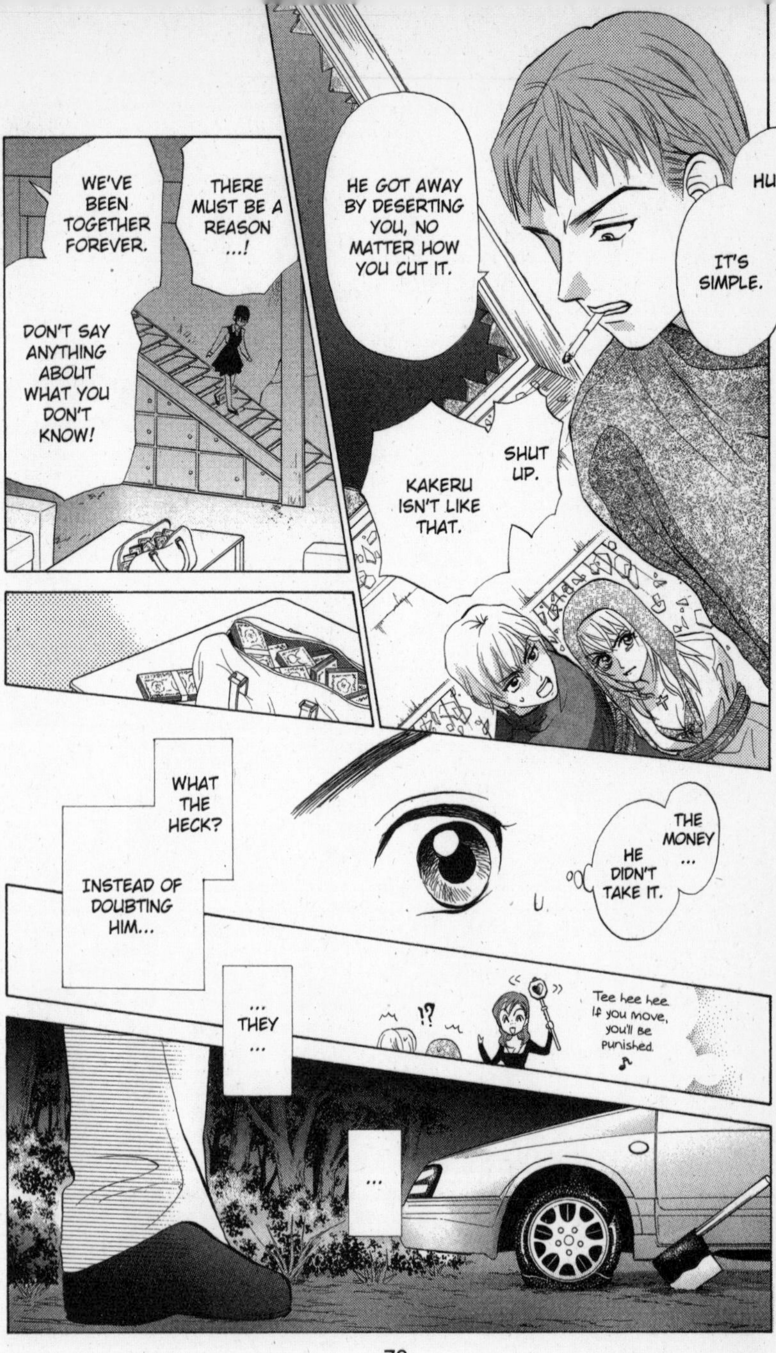
HUH?
IT'S SIMPLE.
HE GOT AWAY BY DESERTING YOU, NO MATTER HOW YOU CUT IT.
SHUT UP.
KAKERU ISN'T LIKE THAT.
THERE MUST BE A REASON ...!
WE'VE BEEN TOGETHER FOREVER.
DON'T SAY ANYTHING ABOUT WHAT YOU DON'T KNOW!
THE MONEY ...
HE DIDN'T TAKE IT.
WHAT THE HECK?
INSTEAD OF DOUBTING HIM...
Tee hee hee. If you move, you'll be punished. ♪
!?
... THEY ...
...

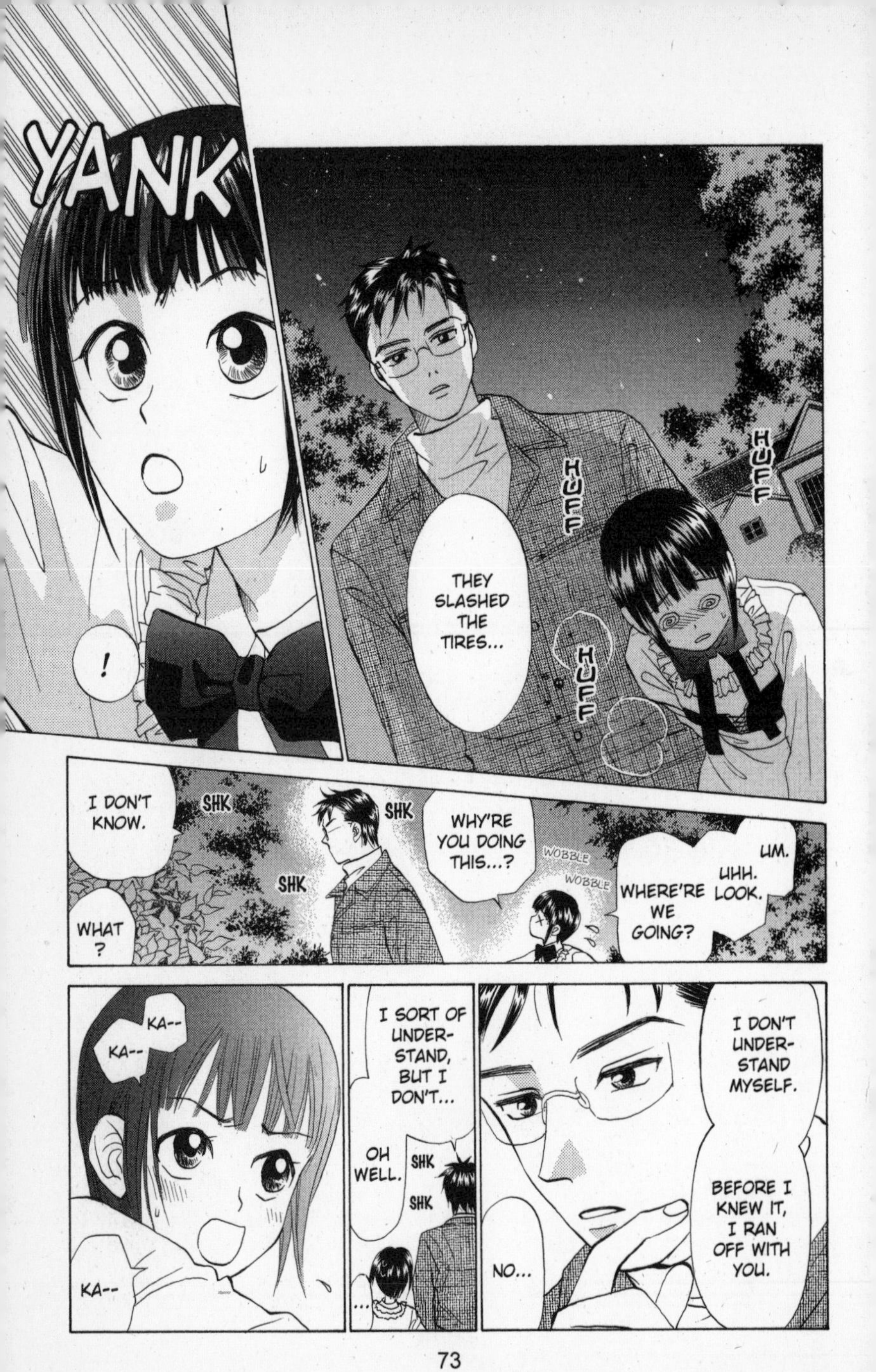
HUFF
HUFF
THEY SLASHED THE TIRES...
HUFF
YANK
!
UM.
UHH. LOOK.
WHERE'RE WE GOING?
WOBBLE
WOBBLE
WHY'RE YOU DOING THIS...?
SHK
SHK
SHK
I DON'T KNOW.
WHAT?
I DON'T UNDER-STAND MYSELF.
BEFORE I KNEW IT, I RAN OFF WITH YOU.
NO...
I SORT OF UNDER-STAND, BUT I DON'T...
SHK
SHK
OH WELL.
...
KA--
KA--
KA--

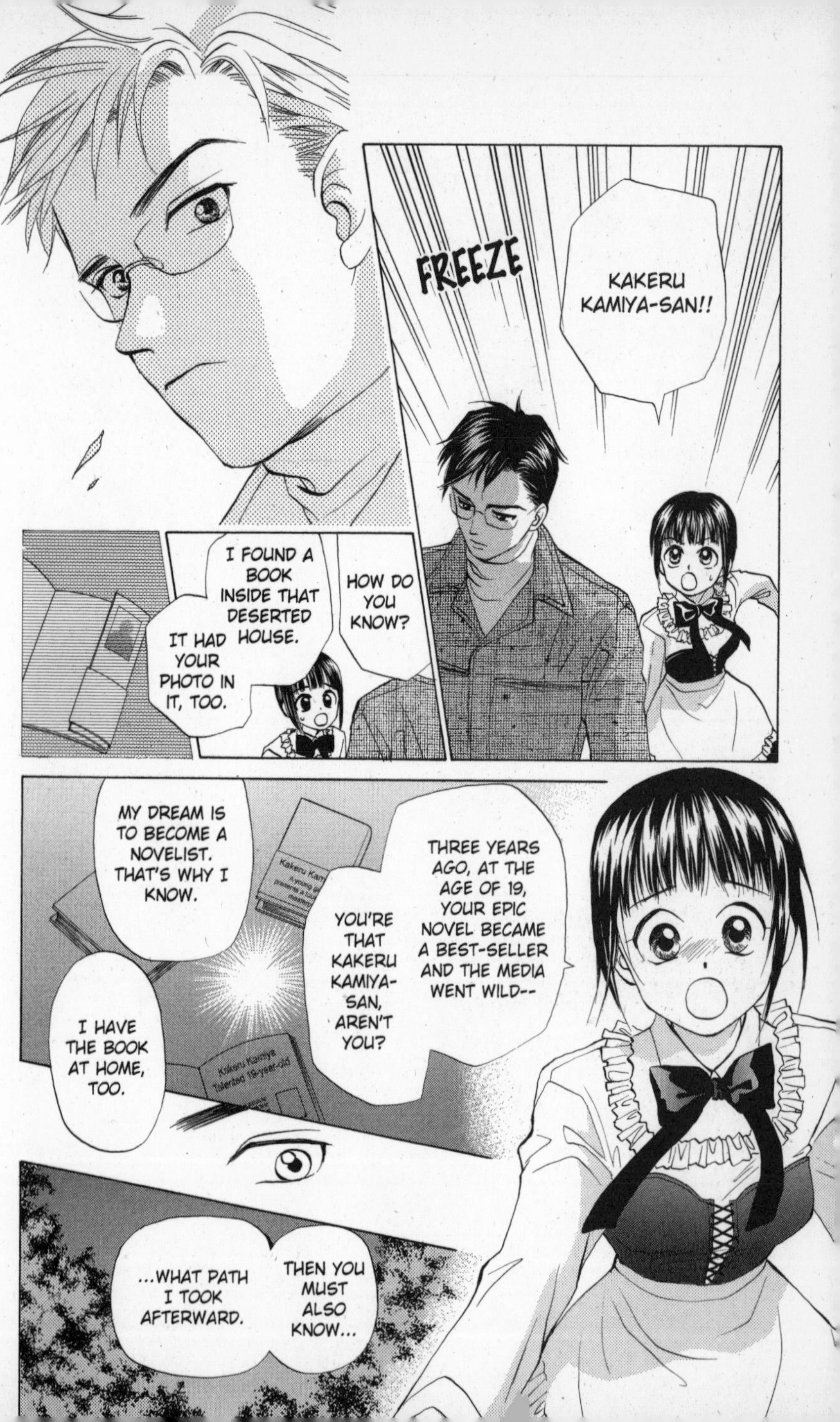
FREEZE
KAKERU KAMIYA-SAN!!
HOW DO YOU KNOW?
I FOUND A BOOK INSIDE THAT DESERTED HOUSE.
IT HAD YOUR PHOTO IN IT, TOO.
THREE YEARS AGO, AT THE AGE OF 19, YOUR EPIC NOVEL BECAME A BEST-SELLER AND THE MEDIA WENT WILD--
YOU'RE THAT KAKERU KAMIYA-SAN, AREN'T YOU?
MY DREAM IS TO BECOME A NOVELIST. THAT'S WHY I KNOW.
I HAVE THE BOOK AT HOME, TOO.
Kakeru Kamiya
Talented 19-year-old
THEN YOU MUST ALSO KNOW...
...WHAT PATH I TOOK AFTERWARD.

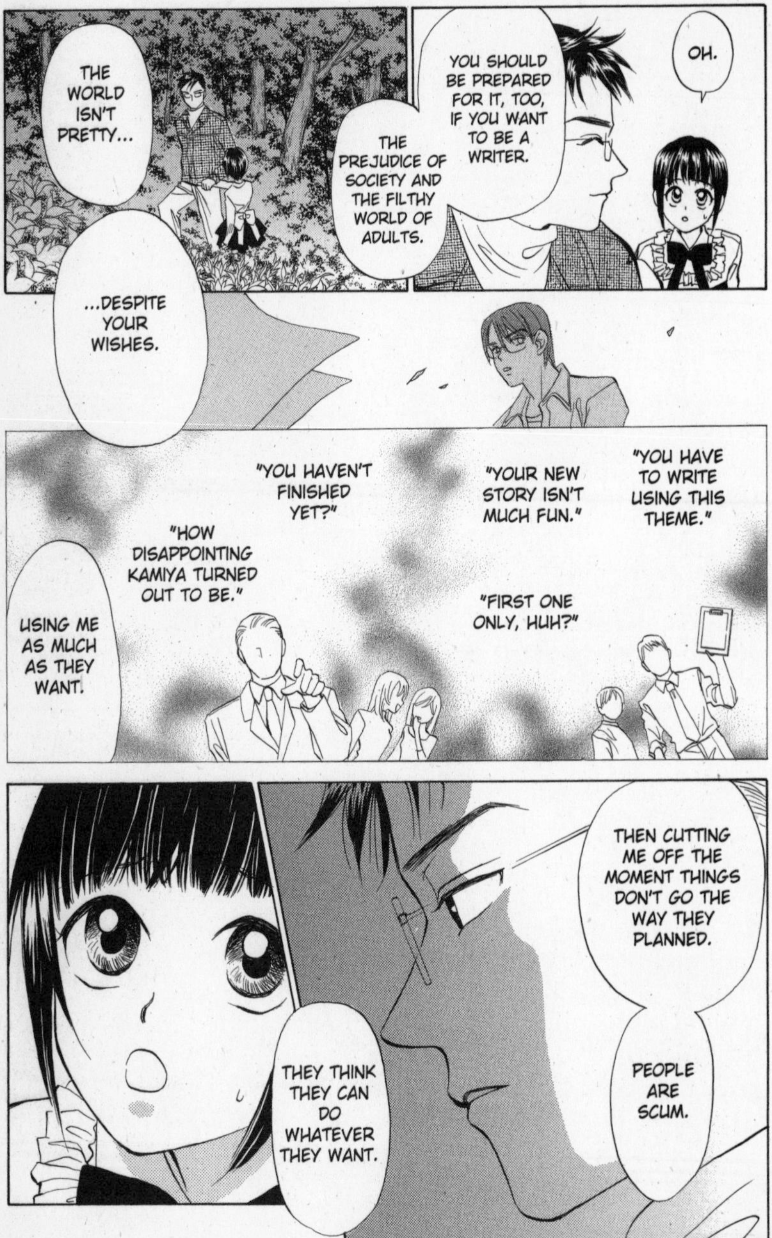
OH.
YOU SHOULD BE PREPARED FOR IT, TOO, IF YOU WANT TO BE A WRITER.
THE PREJUDICE OF SOCIETY AND THE FILTHY WORLD OF ADULTS.
THE WORLD ISN'T PRETTY...
...DESPITE YOUR WISHES.
"YOU HAVE TO WRITE USING THIS THEME."
"YOUR NEW STORY ISN'T MUCH FUN."
"FIRST ONE ONLY, HUH?"
"YOU HAVEN'T FINISHED YET?"
"HOW DISAPPOINTING KAMIYA TURNED OUT TO BE."
USING ME AS MUCH AS THEY WANT.
THEN CUTTING ME OFF THE MOMENT THINGS DON'T GO THE WAY THEY PLANNED.
PEOPLE ARE SCUM.
THEY THINK THEY CAN DO WHATEVER THEY WANT.

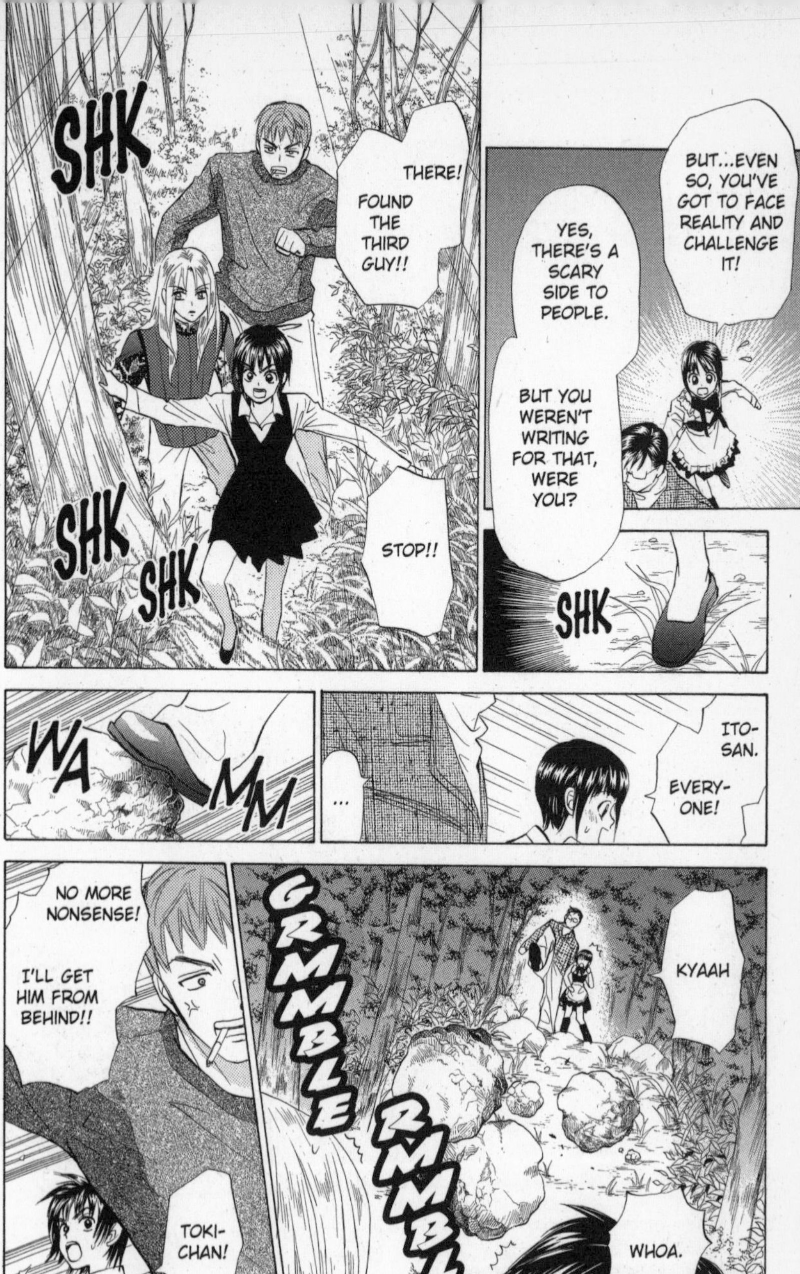
BUT...EVEN SO, YOU'VE GOT TO FACE REALITY AND CHALLENGE IT!
YES, THERE'S A SCARY SIDE TO PEOPLE.
BUT YOU WEREN'T WRITING FOR THAT, WERE YOU?
SHK
SHK
THERE!
FOUND THE THIRD GUY!!
STOP!!
SHK
SHK
ITO-SAN.
EVERY-ONE!
...
WAMM
KYAAH
WHOA.
GRMMBLE
RMMBLE
NO MORE NONSENSE!
I'LL GET HIM FROM BEHIND!!
TOKI-CHAN!

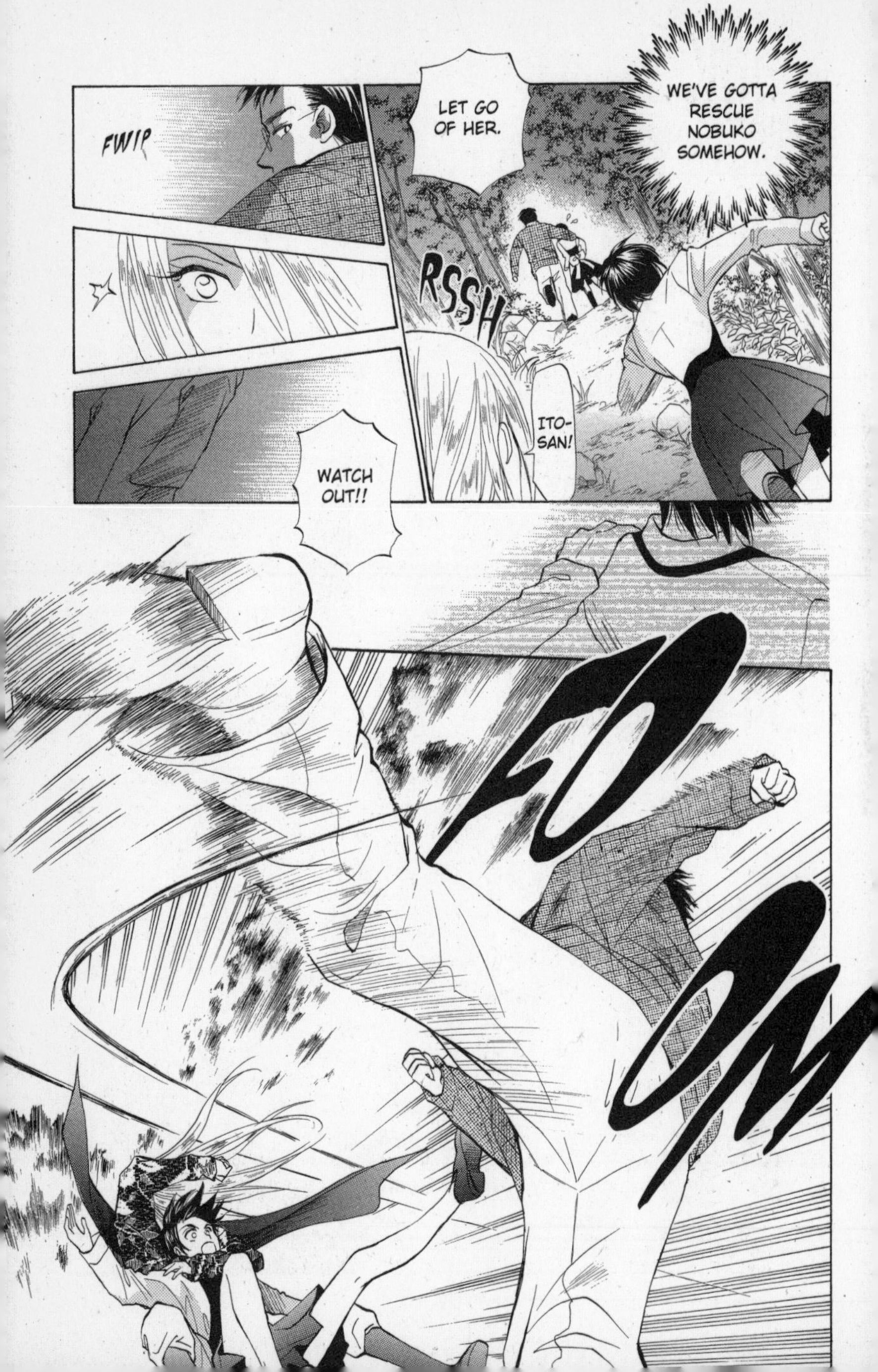
WE'VE GOTTA RESCUE NOBUKO SOMEHOW.
LET GO OF HER.
RSSH
ITO-SAN!
FWIP
WATCH OUT!!
FOOM

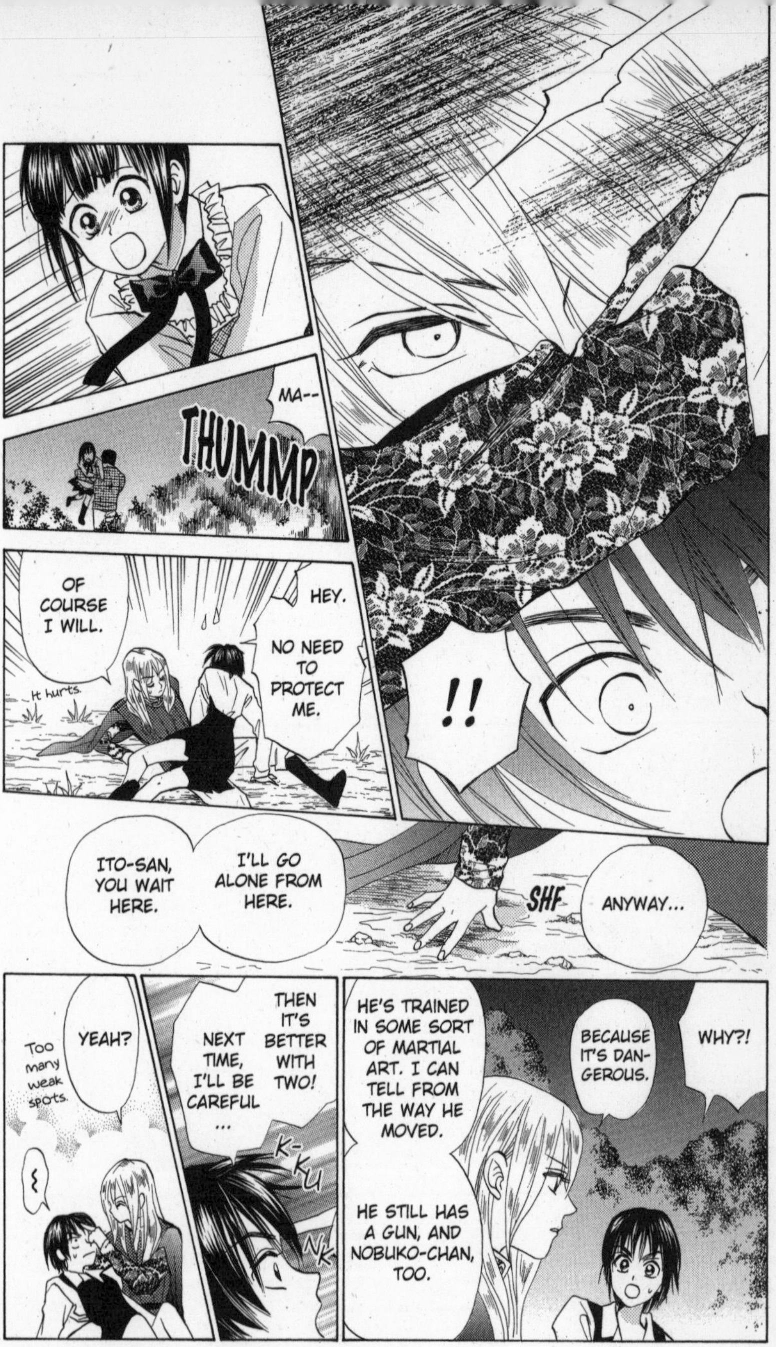
!!
MA--
THUMMP
HEY.
NO NEED TO PROTECT ME.
OF COURSE I WILL.
It hurts.
ANYWAY...
SHF
I'LL GO ALONE FROM HERE.
ITO-SAN, YOU WAIT HERE.
WHY?!
BECAUSE IT'S DANGEROUS.
HE'S TRAINED IN SOME SORT OF MARTIAL ART. I CAN TELL FROM THE WAY HE MOVED.
HE STILL HAS A GUN, AND NOBUKO-CHAN, TOO.
THEN IT'S BETTER WITH TWO!
NEXT TIME, I'LL BE CAREFUL...
K-KU
NK
YEAH?
Too many weak spots.

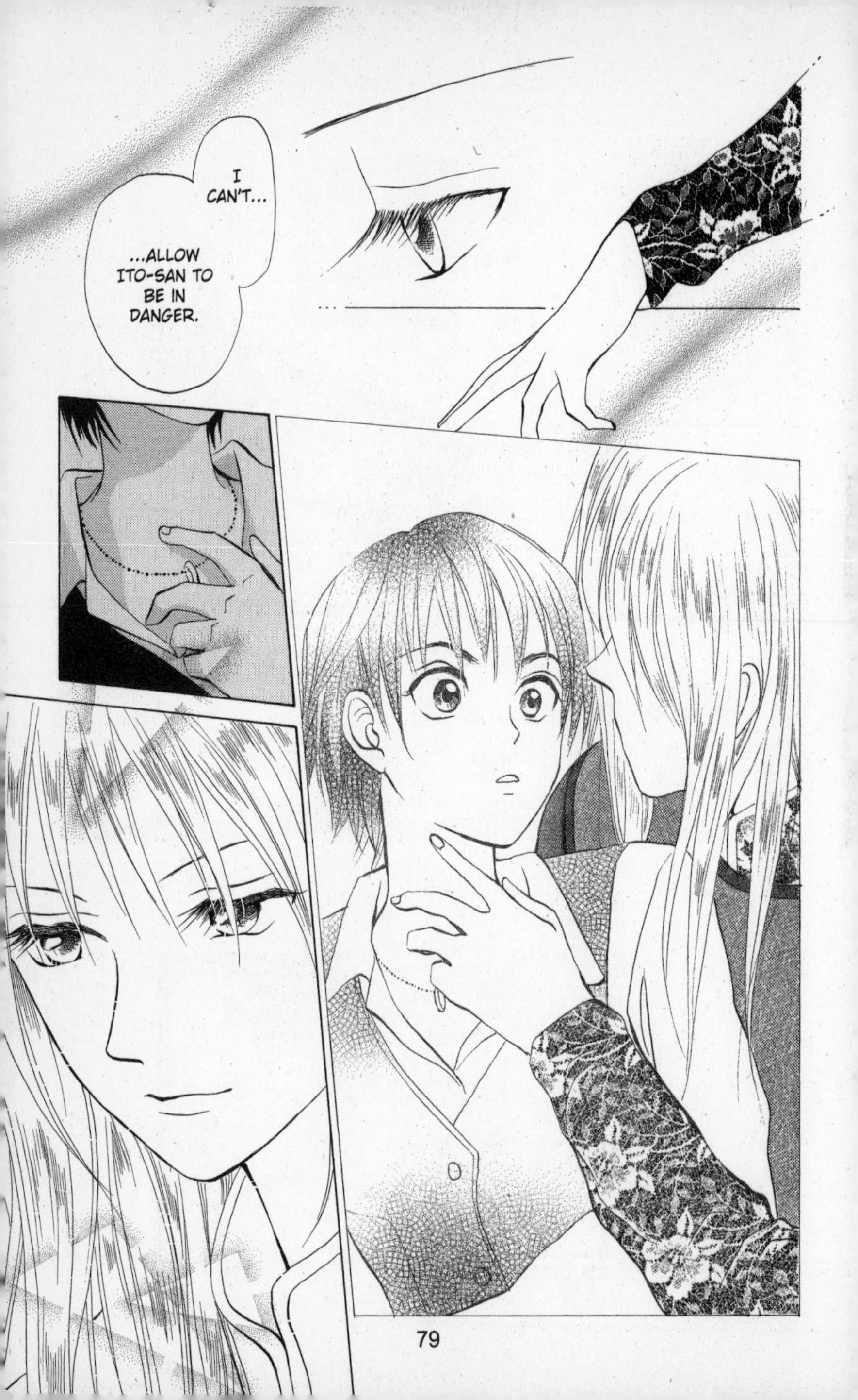
I CAN'T...
...ALLOW ITO-SAN TO BE IN DANGER.

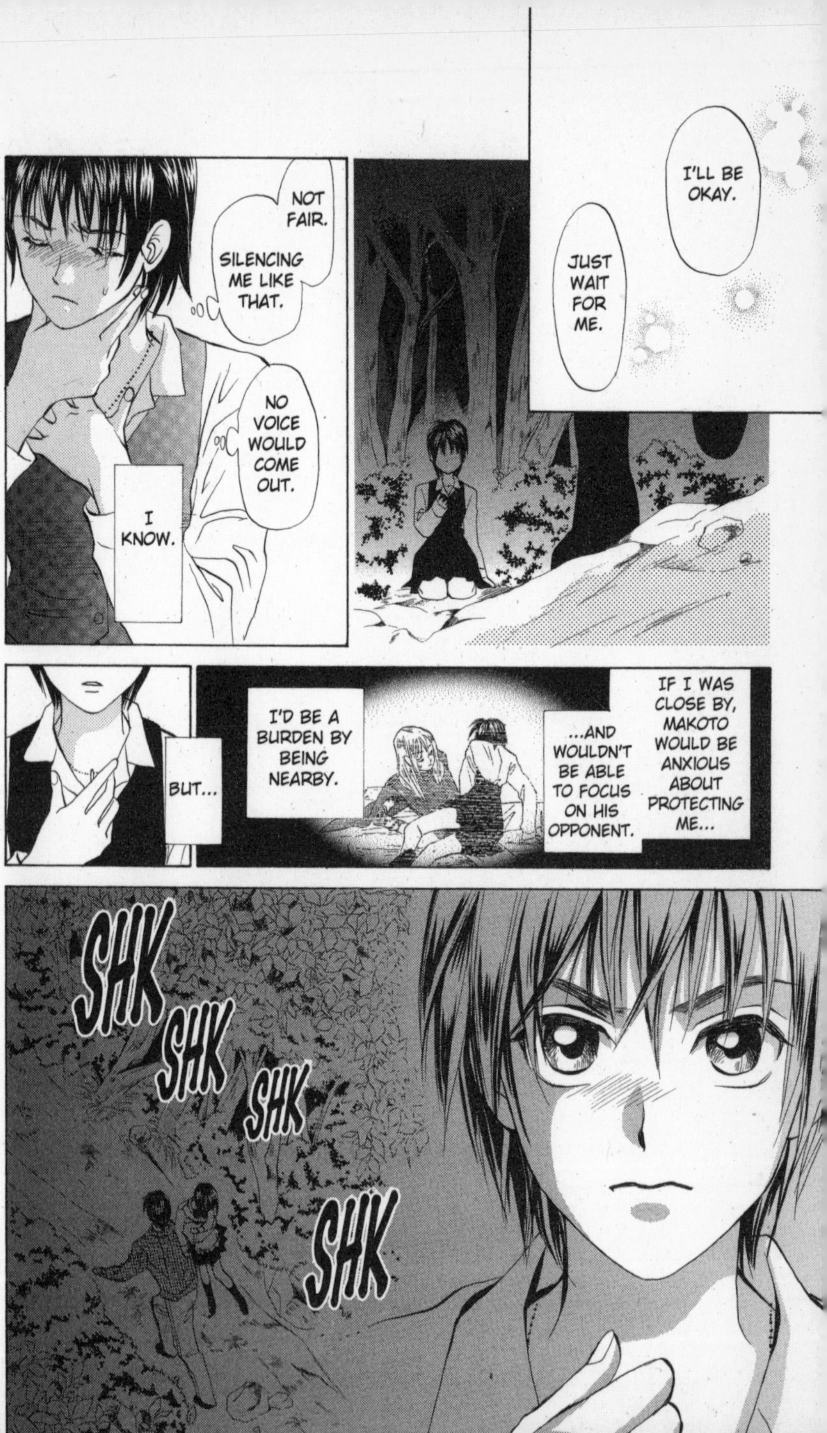
I'LL BE OKAY.
JUST WAIT FOR ME.
NOT FAIR.
SILENCING ME LIKE THAT.
NO VOICE WOULD COME OUT.
I KNOW.
IF I WAS CLOSE BY, MAKOTO WOULD BE ANXIOUS ABOUT PROTECTING ME...
...AND WOULDN'T BE ABLE TO FOCUS ON HIS OPPONENT.
I'D BE A BURDEN BY BEING NEARBY.
BUT...
SHK
SHK
SHK
SHK

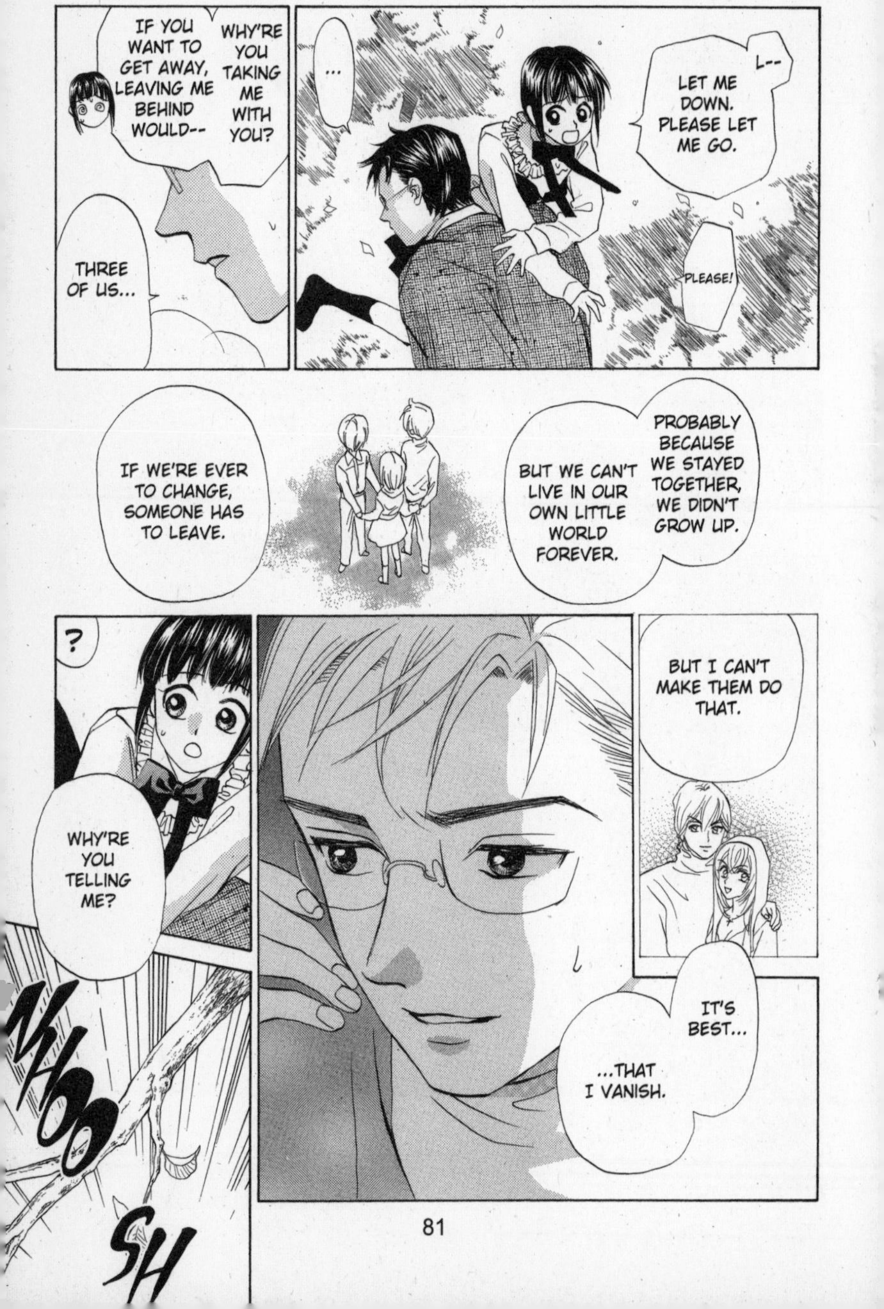
L--
LET ME DOWN. PLEASE LET ME GO.
PLEASE!
...
WHY'RE YOU TAKING ME WITH YOU?
IF YOU WANT TO GET AWAY, LEAVING ME BEHIND WOULD--
THREE OF US...
PROBABLY BECAUSE WE STAYED TOGETHER, WE DIDN'T GROW UP.
BUT WE CAN'T LIVE IN OUR OWN LITTLE WORLD FOREVER.
IF WE'RE EVER TO CHANGE, SOMEONE HAS TO LEAVE.
BUT I CAN'T MAKE THEM DO THAT.
IT'S BEST...
...THAT I VANISH.
?
WHY'RE YOU TELLING ME?
WHOOSH

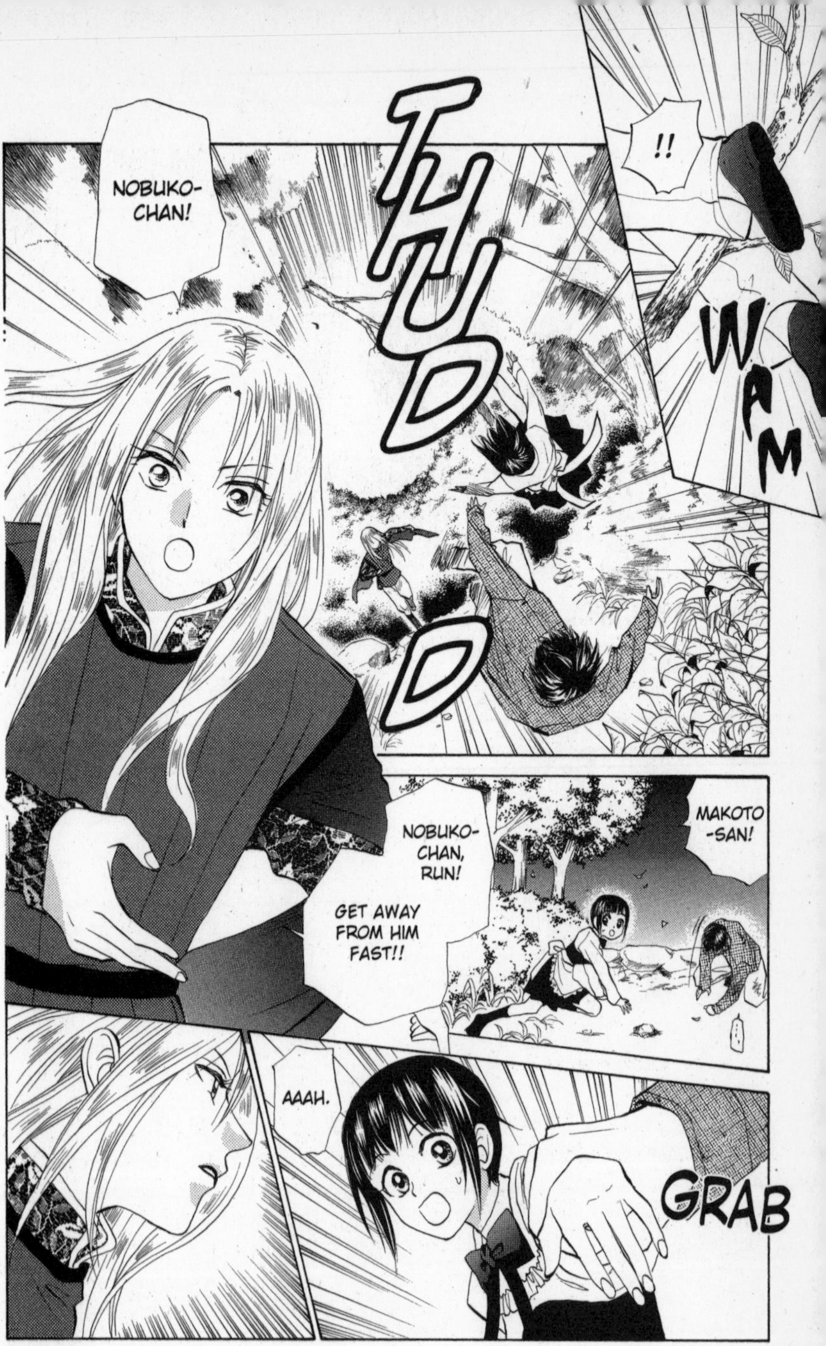
!!
WAM
THUD
NOBUKO-CHAN!
MAKOTO-SAN!
NOBUKO-CHAN, RUN!
GET AWAY FROM HIM FAST!!
GRAB
AAAH.

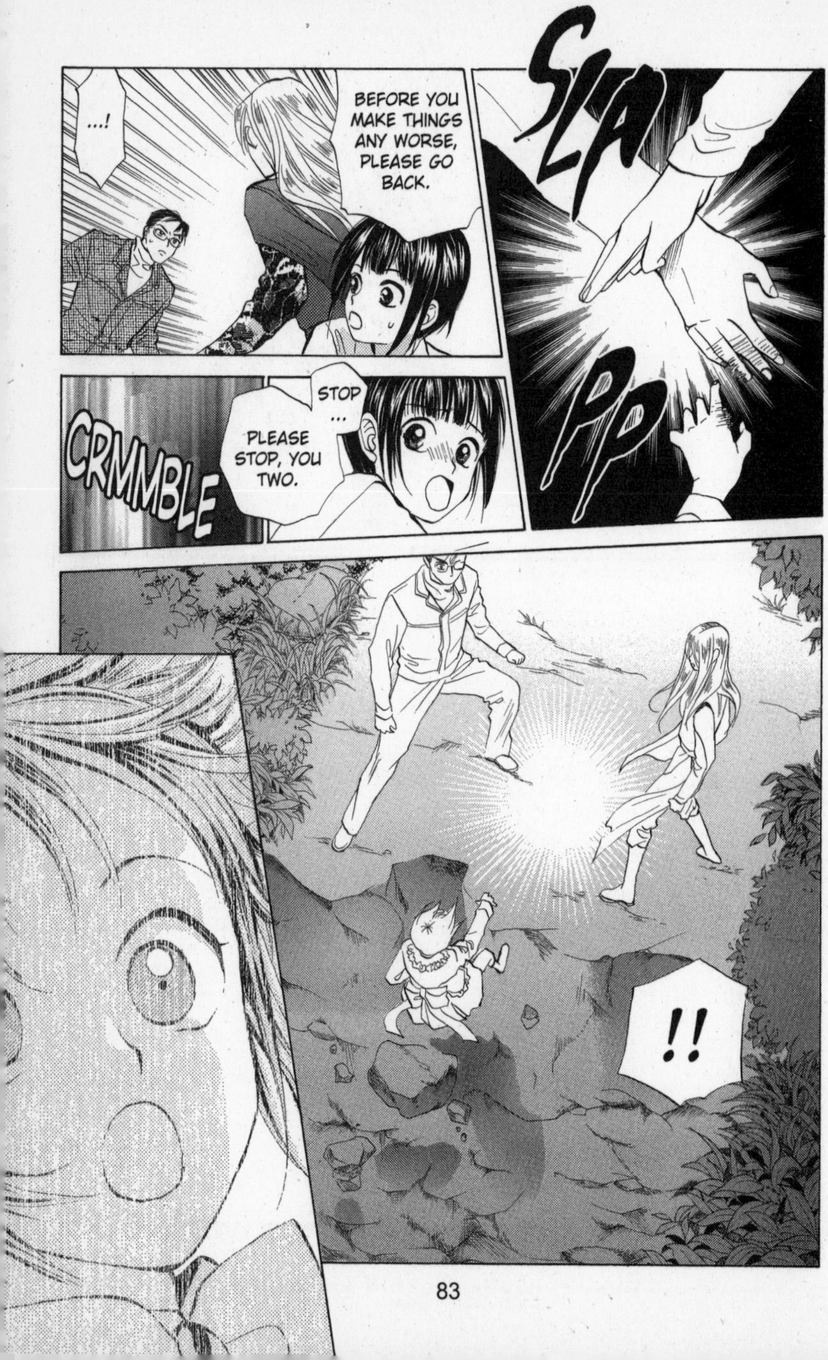
SLAPP
BEFORE YOU MAKE THINGS ANY WORSE, PLEASE GO BACK.
...!
STOP ... PLEASE STOP, YOU TWO.
CRMMBLE
!!

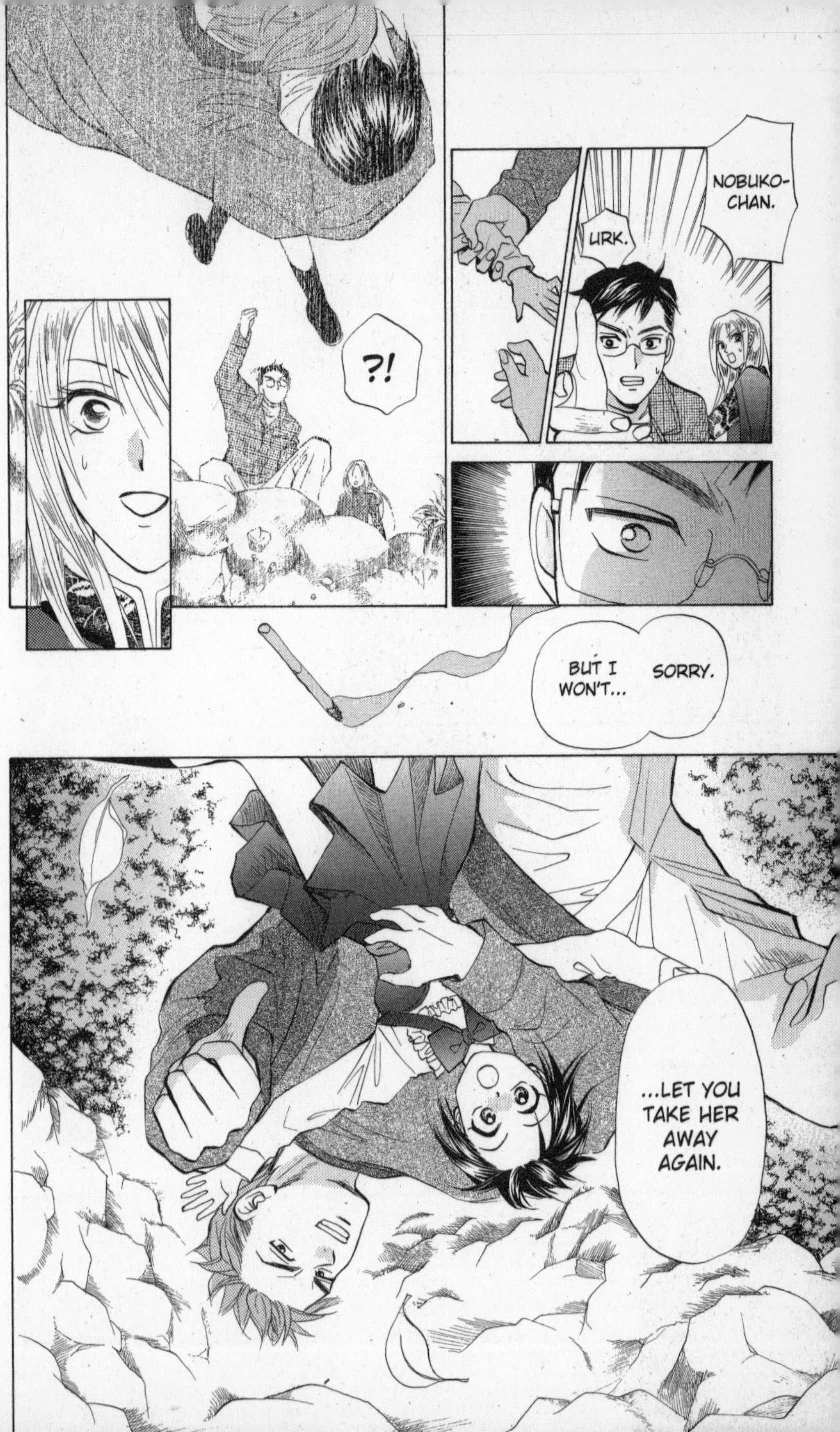
NOBUKO-CHAN.
URK.
?!
SORRY.
BUT I WON'T...
...LET YOU TAKE HER AWAY AGAIN.

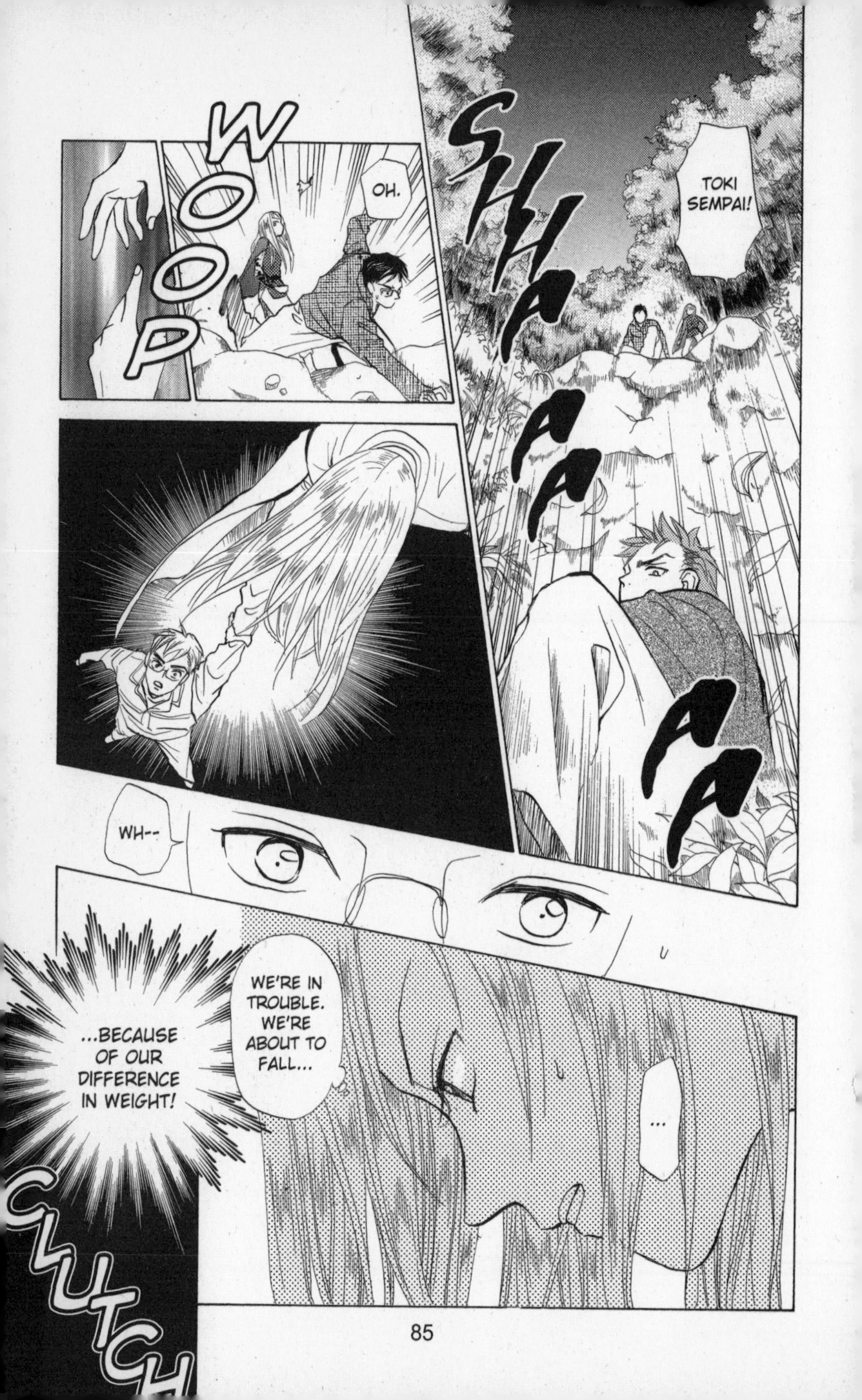
TOKI SEMPAI!
SHAPAPAPAPA
WOOOP
OH.
WH--
...
WE'RE IN TROUBLE. WE'RE ABOUT TO FALL...
...BECAUSE OF OUR DIFFERENCE IN WEIGHT!
CLUTCH

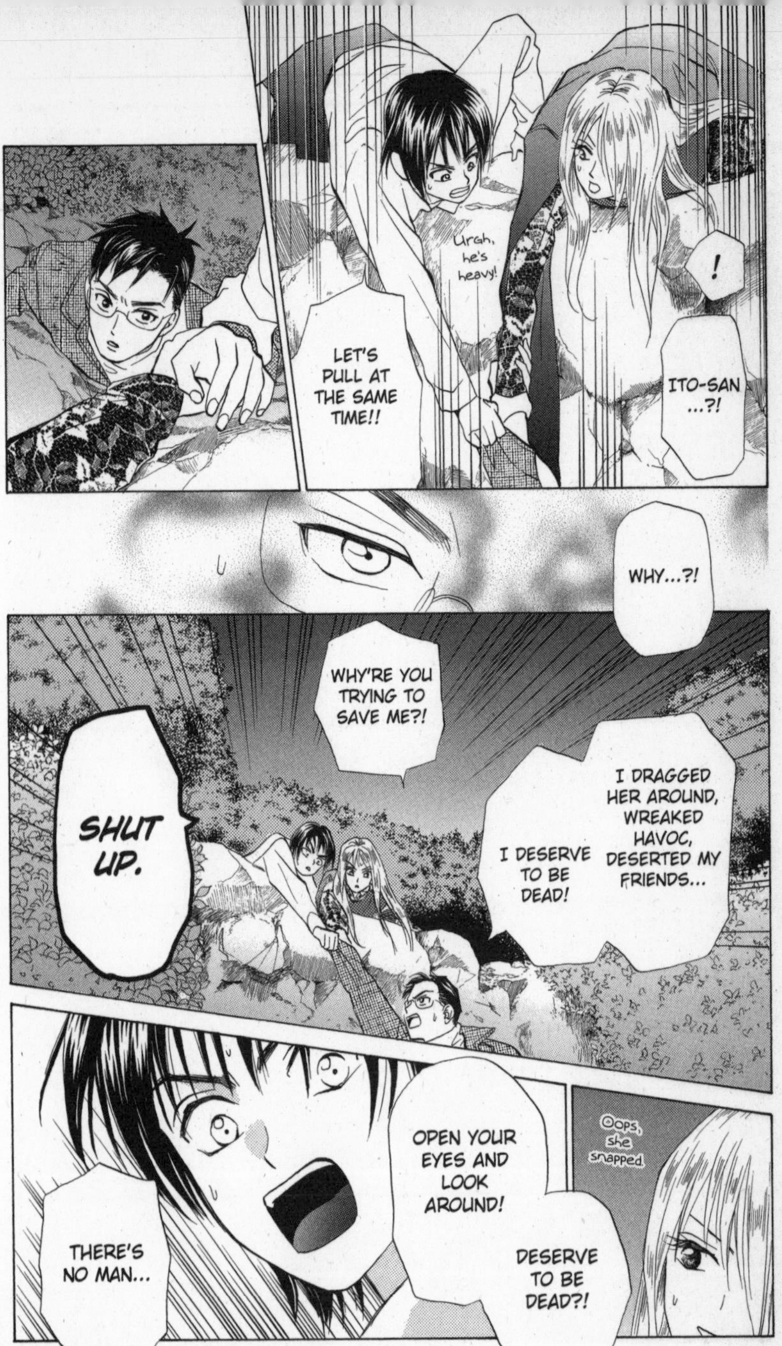
!
ITO-SAN ...?!
Urgh, he's heavy!
LET'S PULL AT THE SAME TIME!!
WHY...?!
WHY'RE YOU TRYING TO SAVE ME?!
I DRAGGED HER AROUND, WREAKED HAVOC, DESERTED MY FRIENDS...
I DESERVE TO BE DEAD!
SHUT UP.
Oops, she snapped.
DESERVE TO BE DEAD?!
OPEN YOUR EYES AND LOOK AROUND!
THERE'S NO MAN...

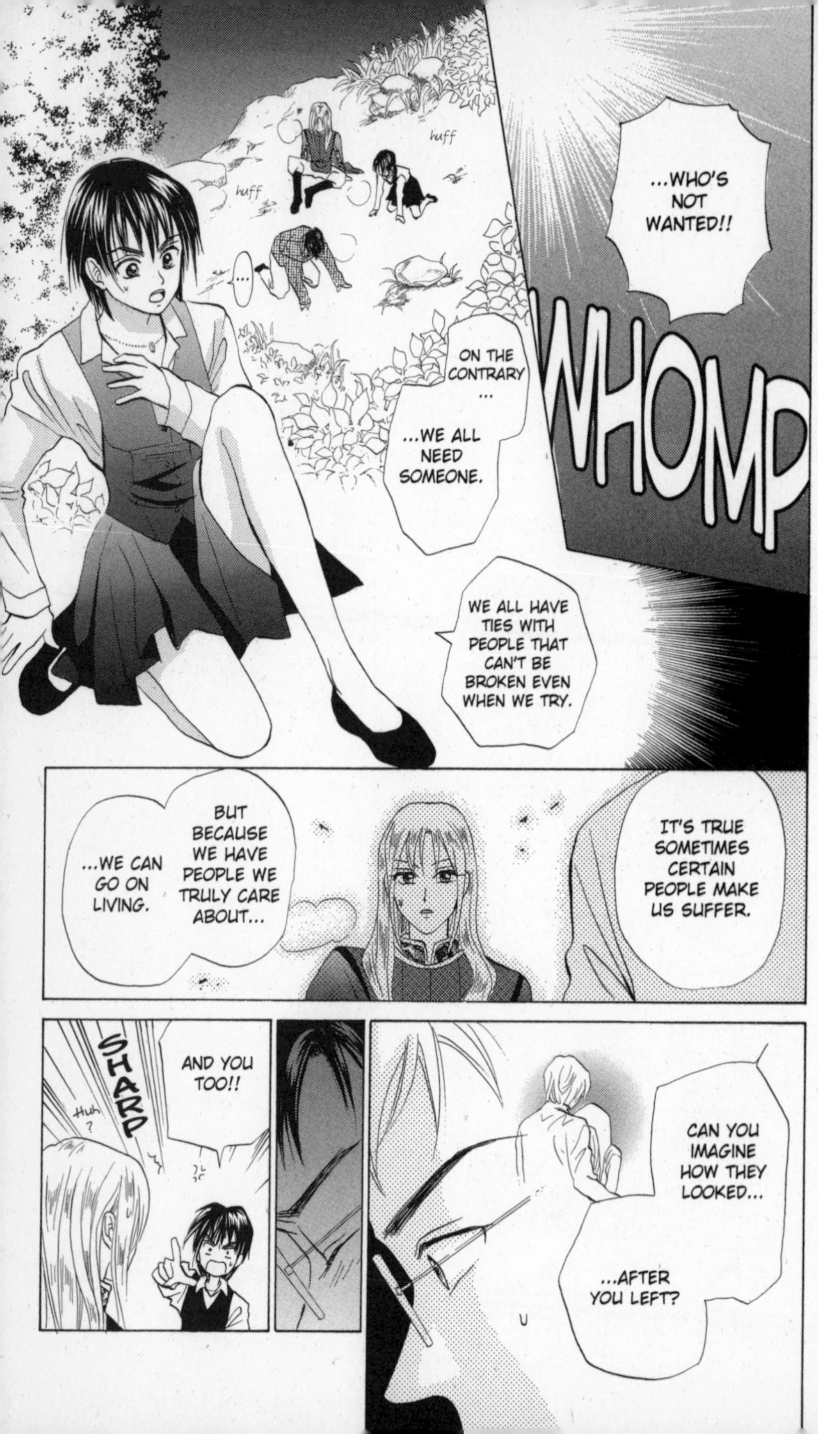
...WHO'S NOT WANTED!!
WHOMP
huff
huff
...
ON THE CONTRARY...
...WE ALL NEED SOMEONE.
WE ALL HAVE TIES WITH PEOPLE THAT CAN'T BE BROKEN EVEN WHEN WE TRY.
IT'S TRUE SOMETIMES CERTAIN PEOPLE MAKE US SUFFER.
BUT BECAUSE WE HAVE PEOPLE WE TRULY CARE ABOUT...
...WE CAN GO ON LIVING.
CAN YOU IMAGINE HOW THEY LOOKED...
...AFTER YOU LEFT?
SHARP
AND YOU TOO!!
Huh?

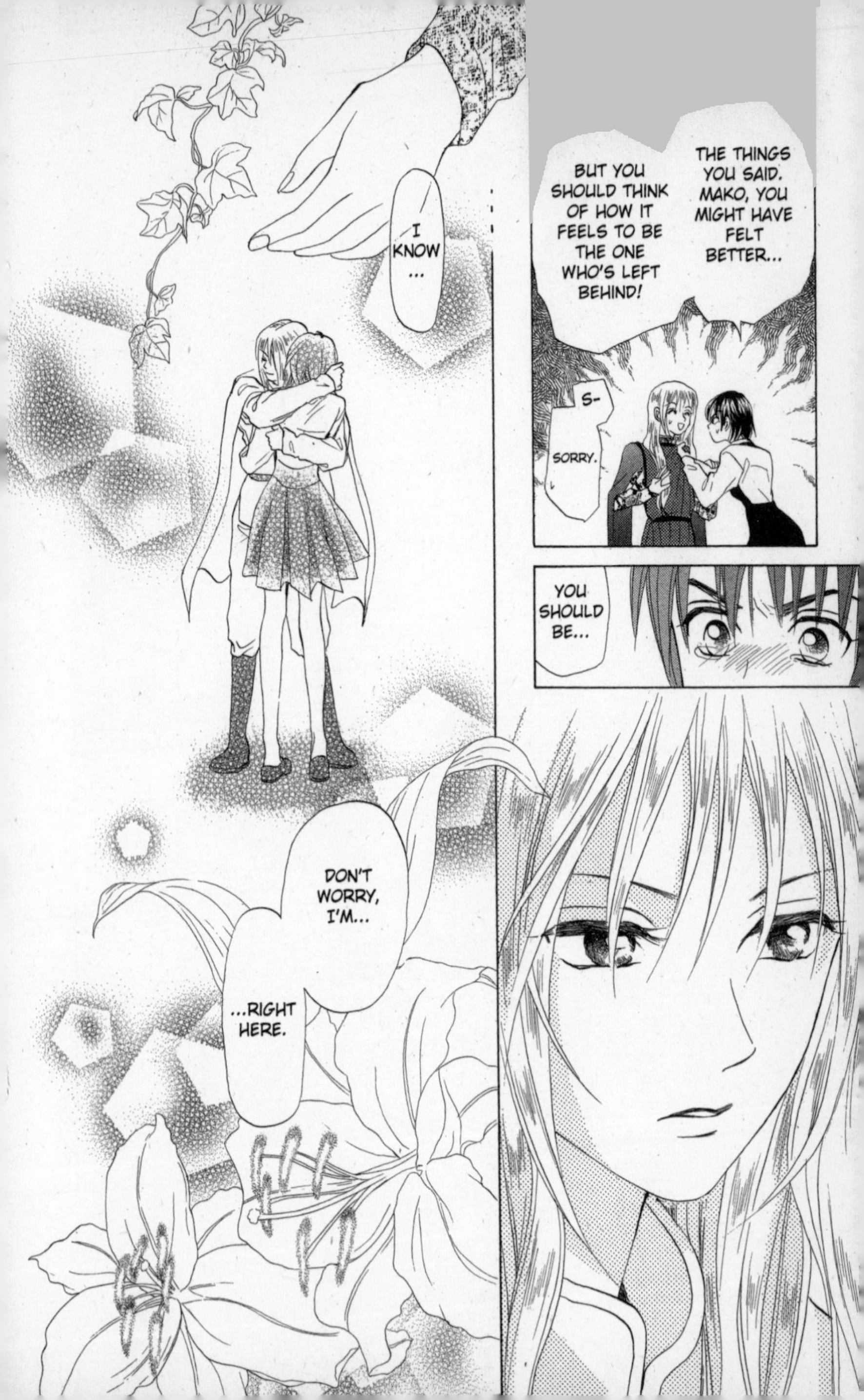
THE THINGS YOU SAID. MAKO, YOU MIGHT HAVE FELT BETTER...
BUT YOU SHOULD THINK OF HOW IT FEELS TO BE THE ONE WHO'S LEFT BEHIND!
S-
SORRY.
YOU SHOULD BE...
I KNOW...
DON'T WORRY, I'M...
...RIGHT HERE.

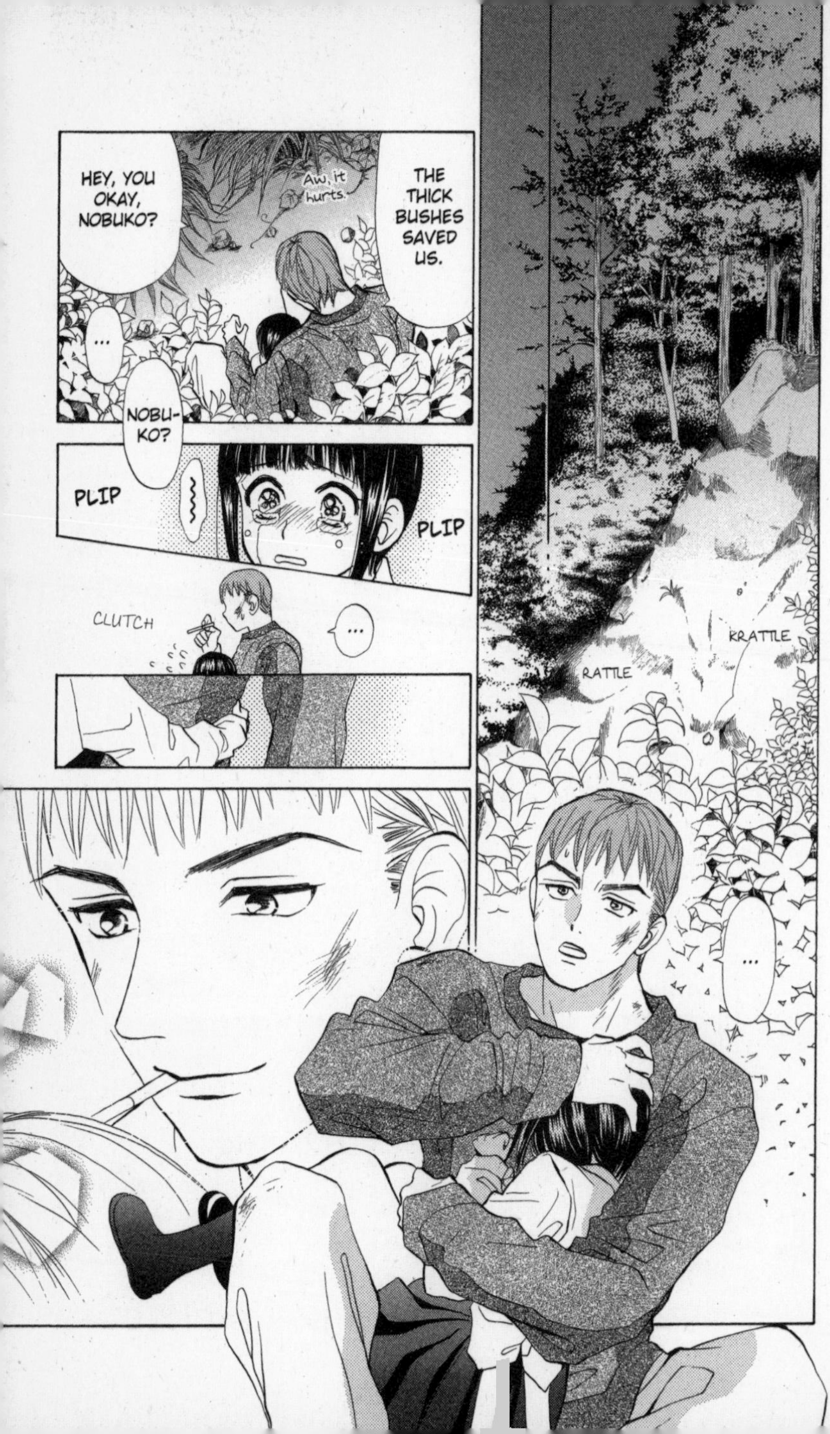
KRATTLE
RATTLE
...
THE THICK BUSHES SAVED US.
Aw, it hurts.
HEY, YOU OKAY, NOBUKO?
...
NOBU-KO?
PLIP
PLIP
...
CLUTCH

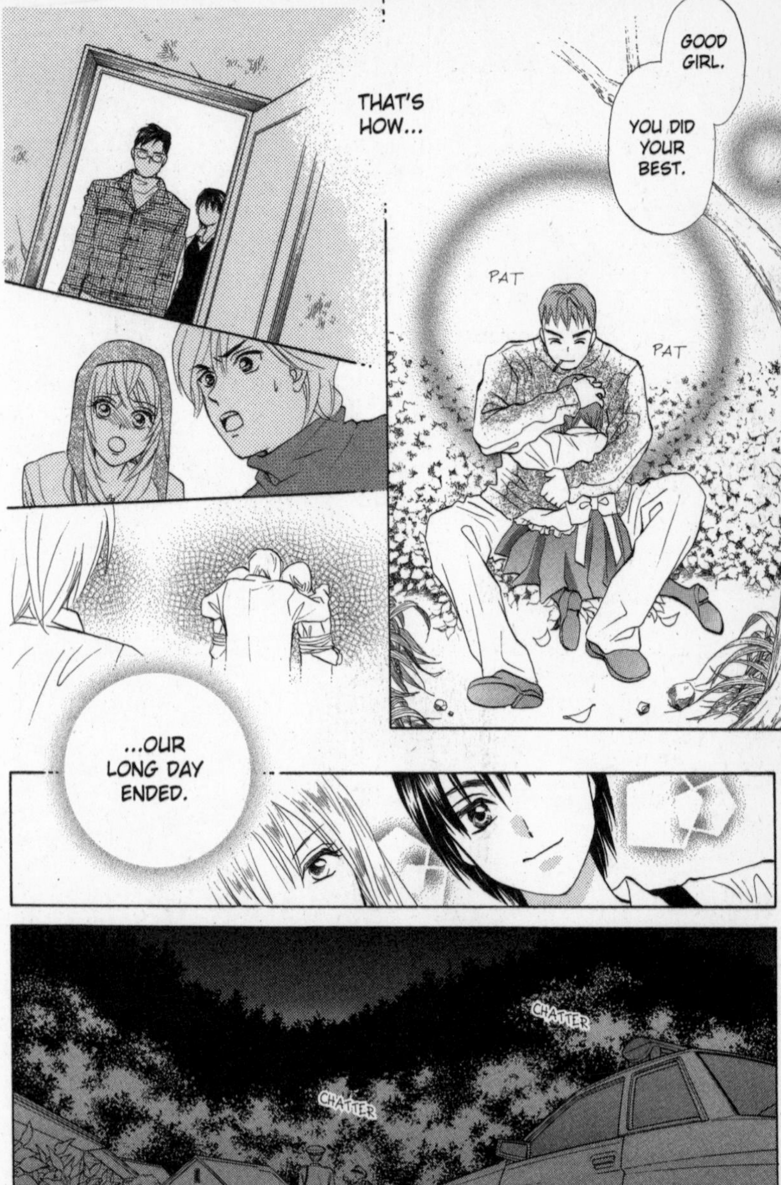
GOOD GIRL.
YOU DID YOUR BEST.
PAT
PAT
THAT'S HOW...
...OUR LONG DAY ENDED.
CHATTER
CHATTER

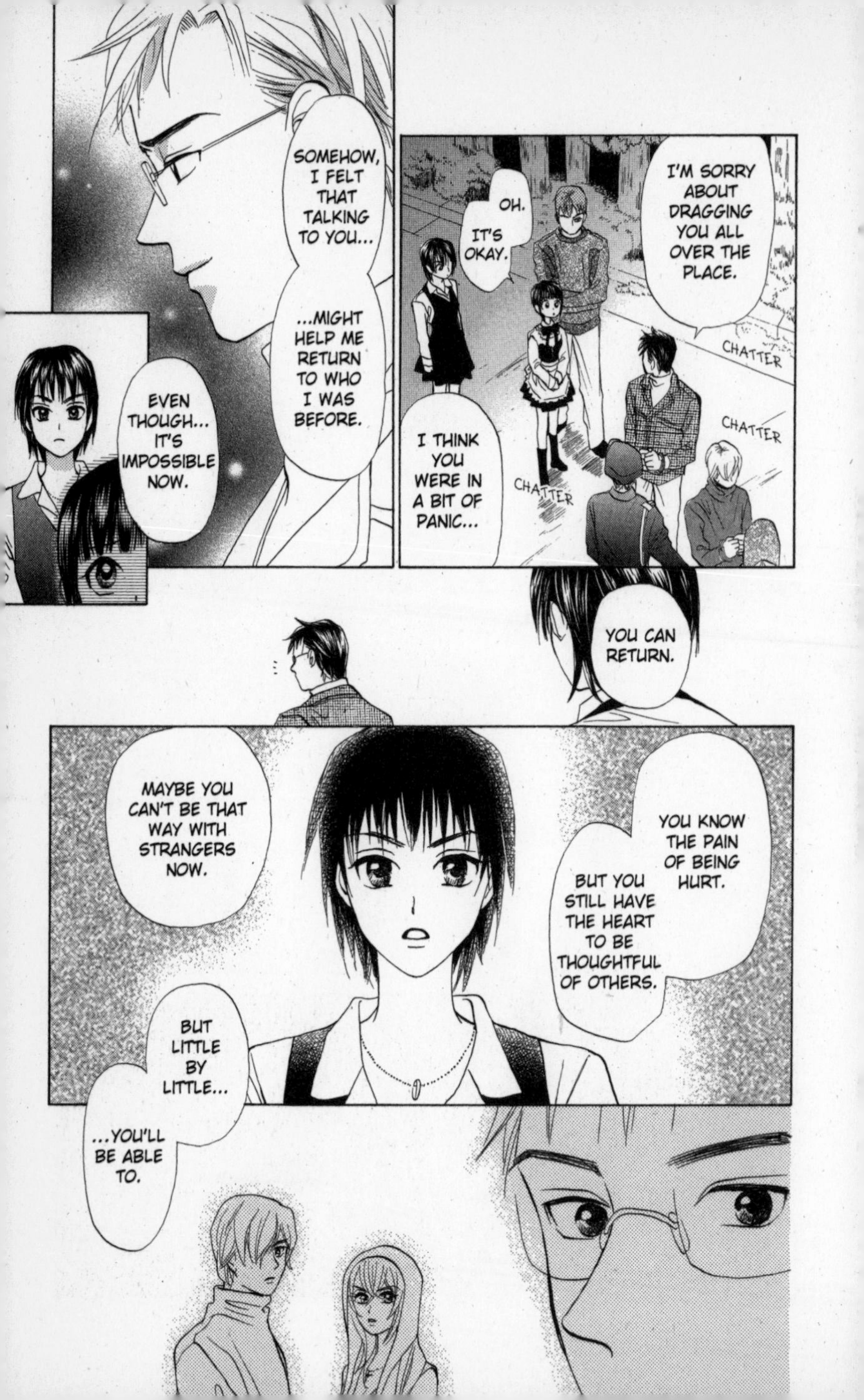
I'M SORRY ABOUT DRAGGING YOU ALL OVER THE PLACE.
OH. IT'S OKAY.
CHATTER
CHATTER
I THINK YOU WERE IN A BIT OF PANIC...
CHATTER
SOMEHOW, I FELT THAT TALKING TO YOU...
...MIGHT HELP ME RETURN TO WHO I WAS BEFORE.
EVEN THOUGH... IT'S IMPOSSIBLE NOW.
YOU CAN RETURN.
YOU KNOW THE PAIN OF BEING HURT.
BUT YOU STILL HAVE THE HEART TO BE THOUGHTFUL OF OTHERS.
MAYBE YOU CAN'T BE THAT WAY WITH STRANGERS NOW.
BUT LITTLE BY LITTLE...
...YOU'LL BE ABLE TO.

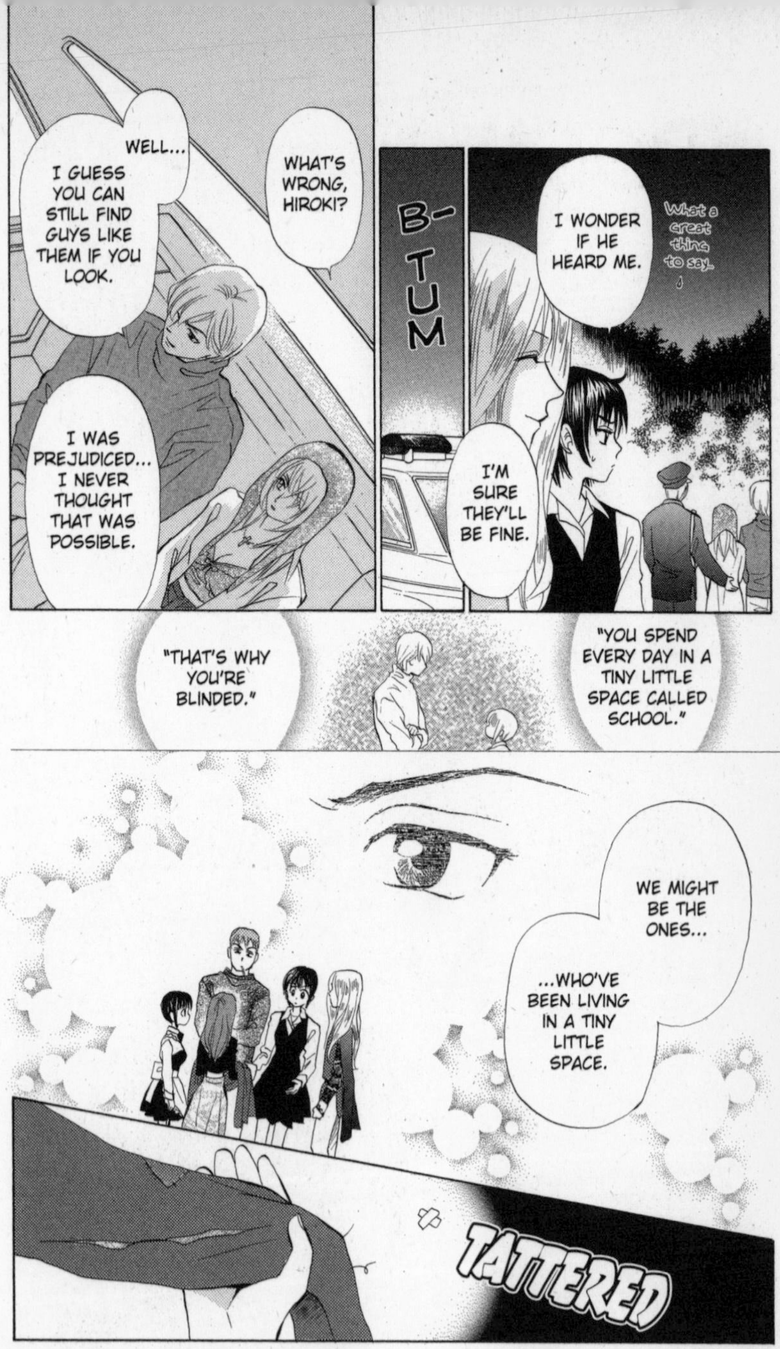

I WONDER IF HE HEARD ME.
What a great thing to say...
I'M SURE THEY'LL BE FINE.
B-TUM
WHAT'S WRONG, HIROKI?
WELL... I GUESS YOU CAN STILL FIND GUYS LIKE THEM IF YOU LOOK.
I WAS PREJUDICED... I NEVER THOUGHT THAT WAS POSSIBLE.
"YOU SPEND EVERY DAY IN A TINY LITTLE SPACE CALLED SCHOOL."
"THAT'S WHY YOU'RE BLINDED."
WE MIGHT BE THE ONES...
...WHO'VE BEEN LIVING IN A TINY LITTLE SPACE.
TATTERED

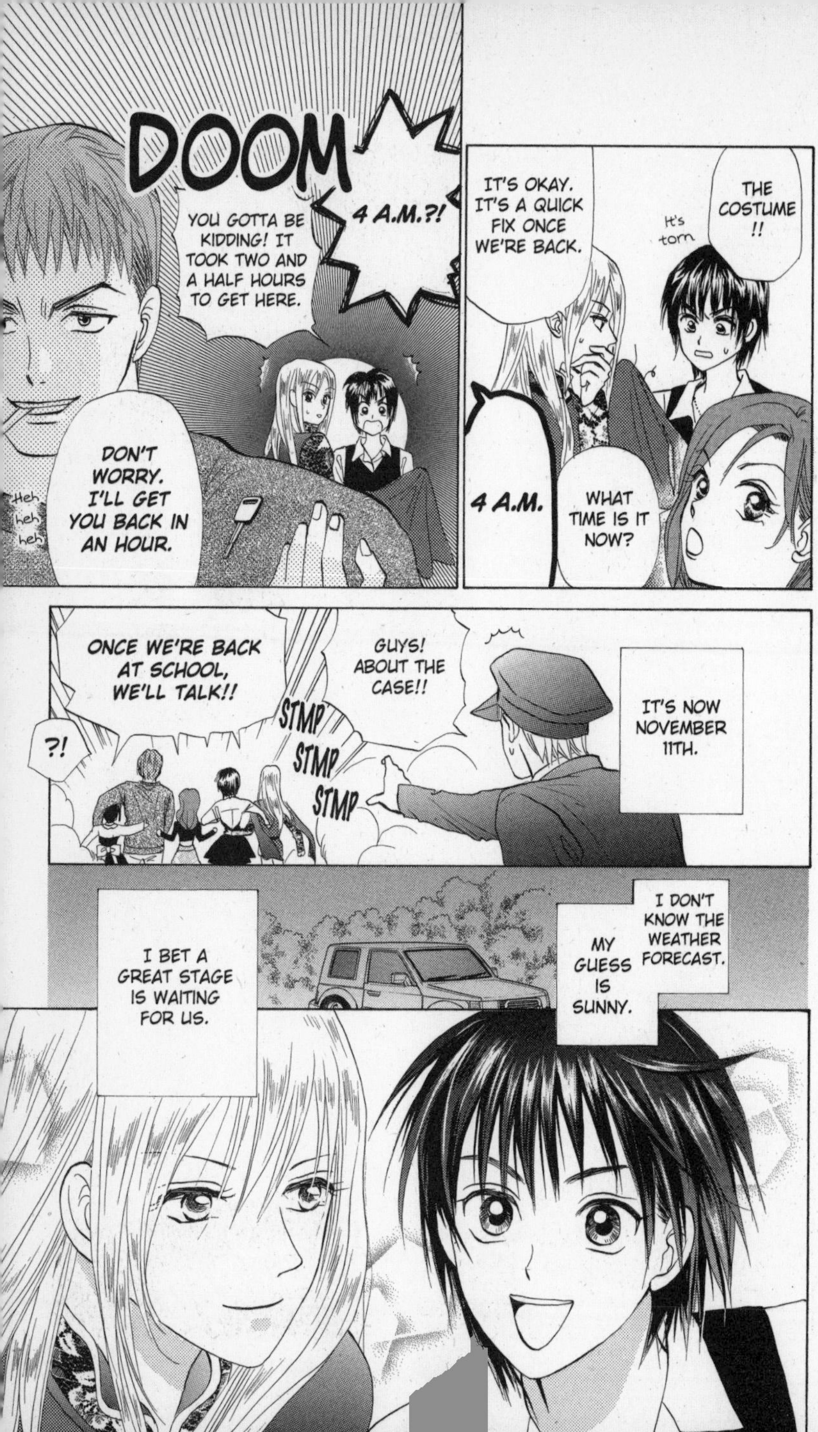
THE COSTUME !!
It's torn
IT'S OKAY. IT'S A QUICK FIX ONCE WE'RE BACK.
WHAT TIME IS IT NOW?
4 A.M.
DOOM
4 A.M.?!
YOU GOTTA BE KIDDING! IT TOOK TWO AND A HALF HOURS TO GET HERE.
DON'T WORRY. I'LL GET YOU BACK IN AN HOUR.
Heh heh heh
IT'S NOW NOVEMBER 11TH.
GUYS! ABOUT THE CASE!!
ONCE WE'RE BACK AT SCHOOL, WE'LL TALK!!
STMP STMP STMP
?!
I DON'T KNOW THE WEATHER FORECAST.
MY GUESS IS SUNNY.
I BET A GREAT STAGE IS WAITING FOR US.

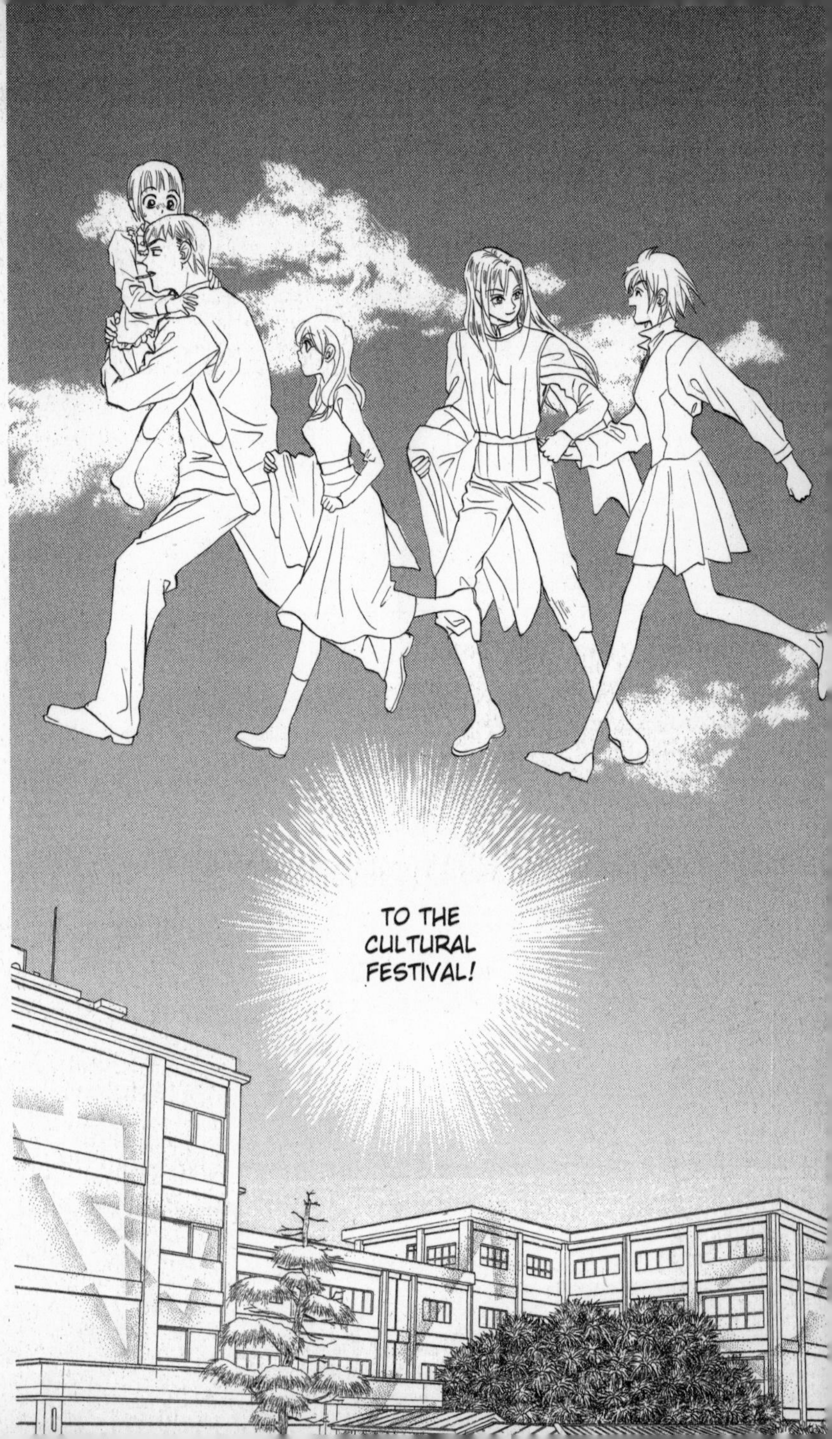
TO THE CULTURAL FESTIVAL!

2002
← W Juliet Character Book
cover art (draft B4 size)

2002 Zensa phone card
↓

2002 HCD "W Juliet II"
et "Bottom"
↓

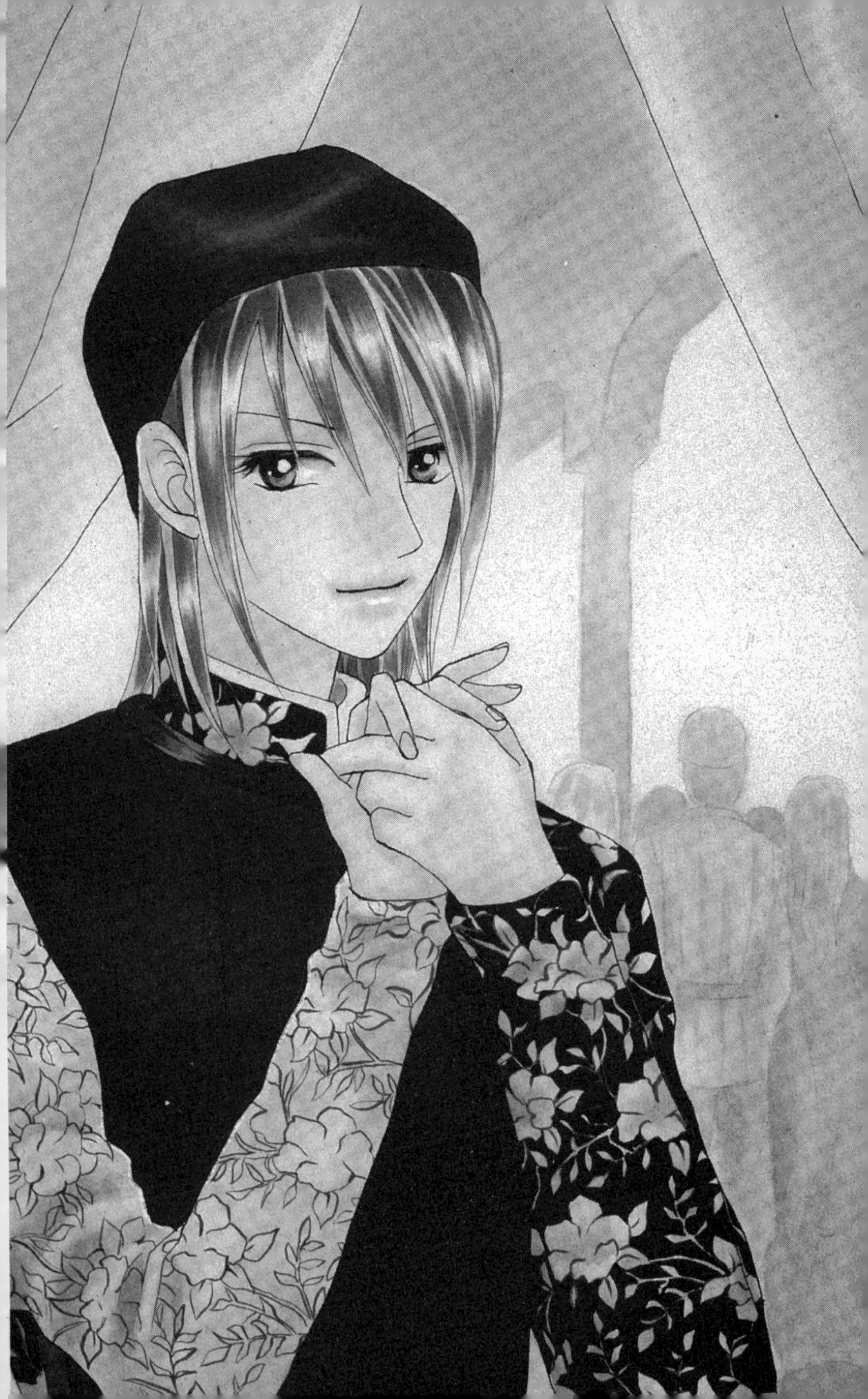

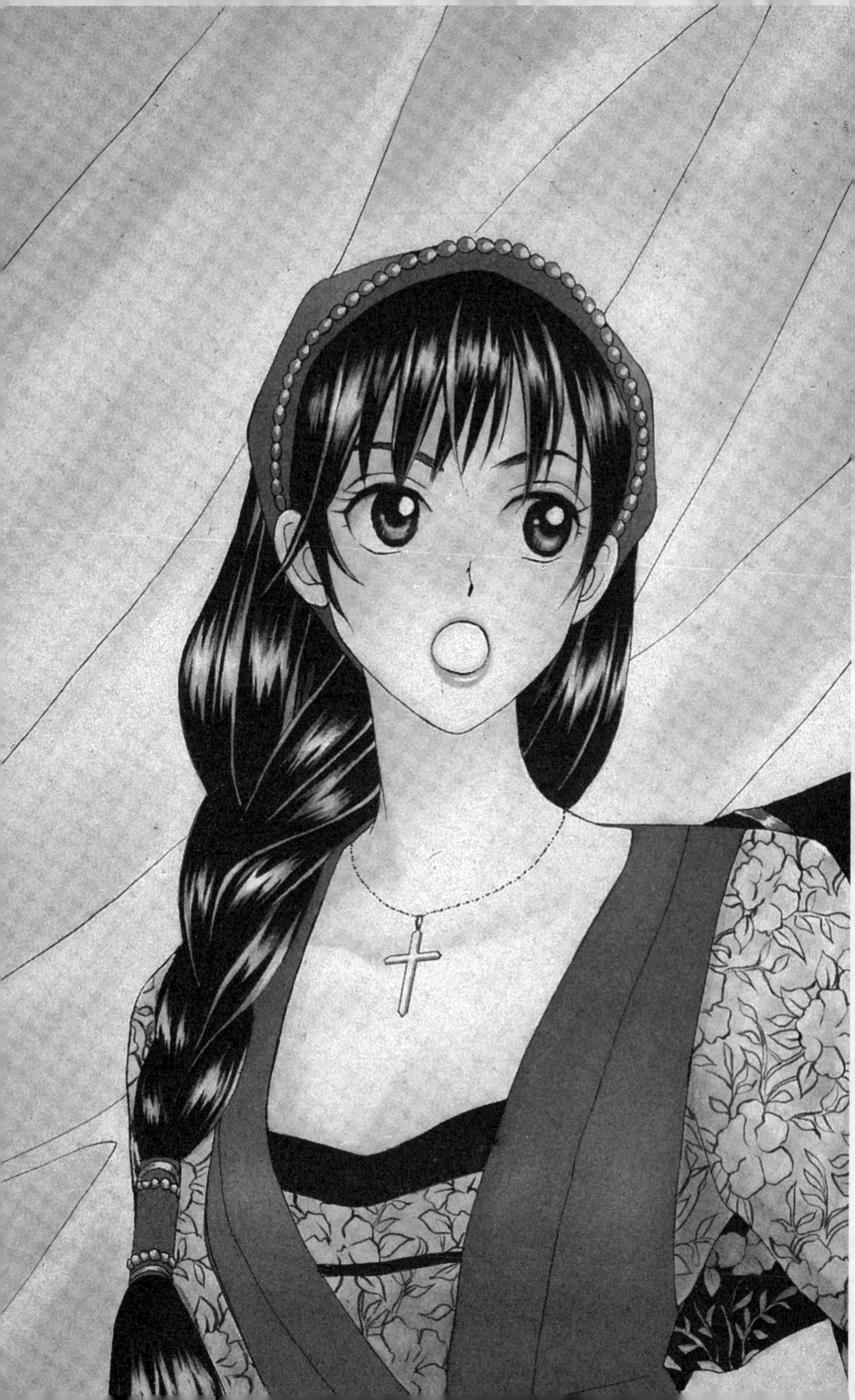

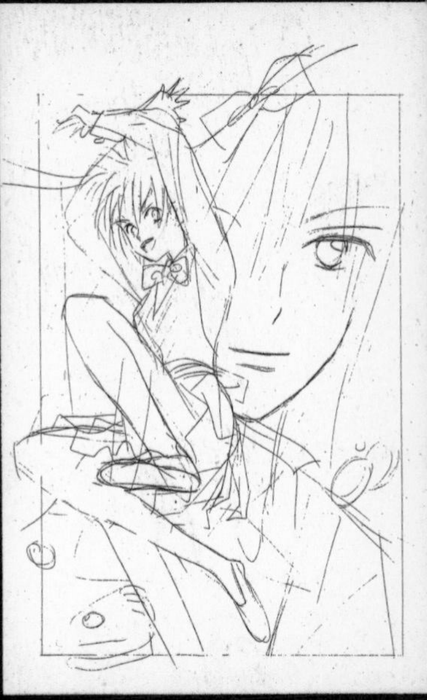

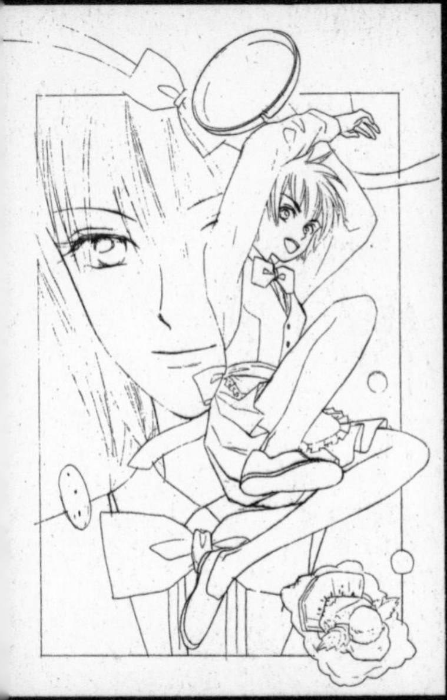

2002 Hana to Yume No. 5 cover ↑ draft ↑ Rough draft

2002 HCD "W Juliet II" CD jacket draft ↓

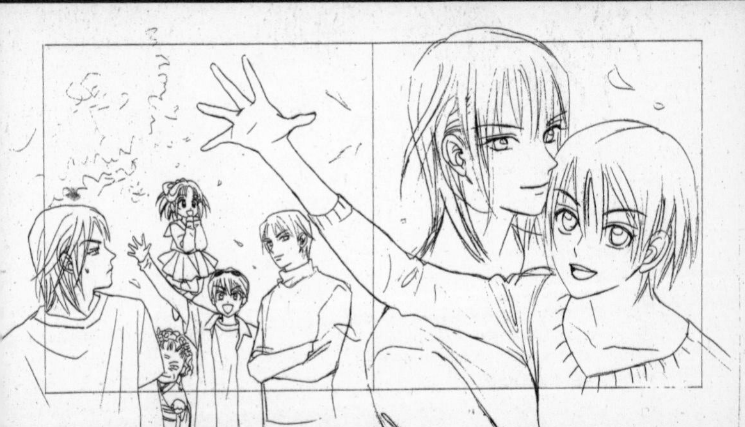

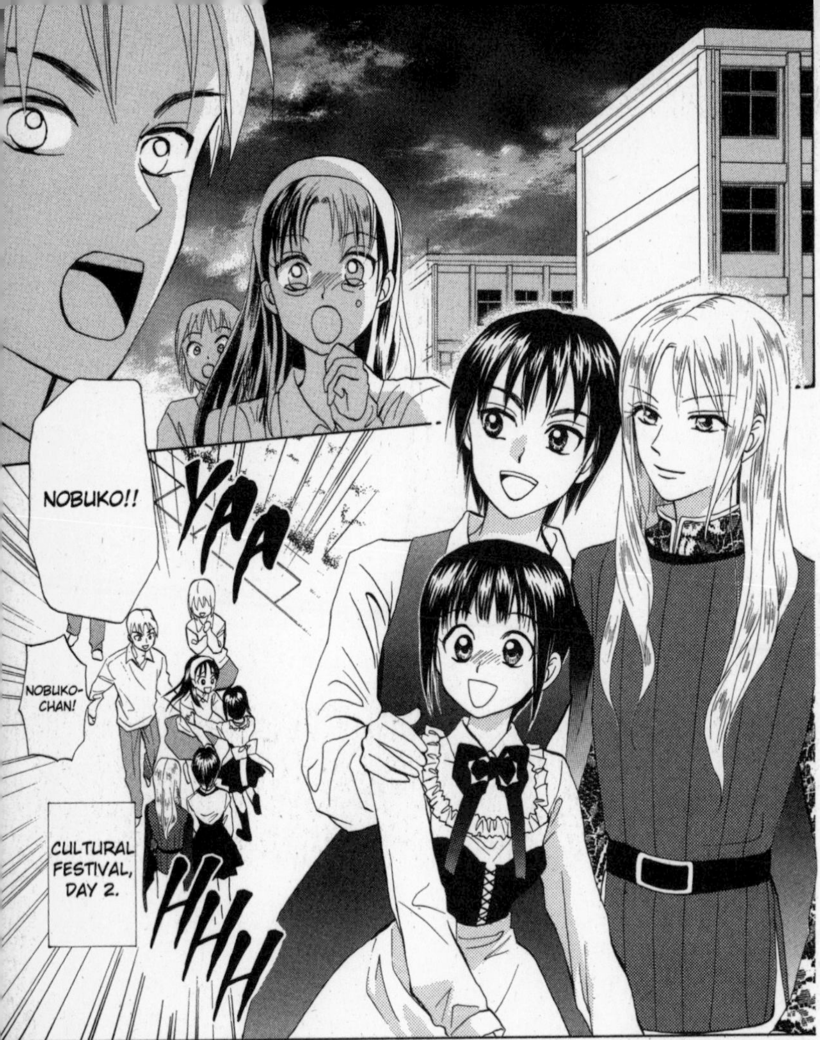
NOBUKO!!
YAAHHH
NOBUKO-CHAN!
CULTURAL FESTIVAL, DAY 2.

—Behind the Scenes Story ④.⑤—

Romeo and Juliet is to be performed on stage at last. But it was hard to draw this one... Once again, I couldn't leave "Ito's perspective" or "Mako's father's perspective" so I couldn't make a complete drama-within-a-drama type play. Even if I tried, due to my lack of skill, it would've confused the readers, I guess. Ito's costume is different from the one in volume 8, though... Well, it's only the color that's changed for various reasons. This one's simpler and better, right?

I would've liked to change Makoto's, too, if I could have...

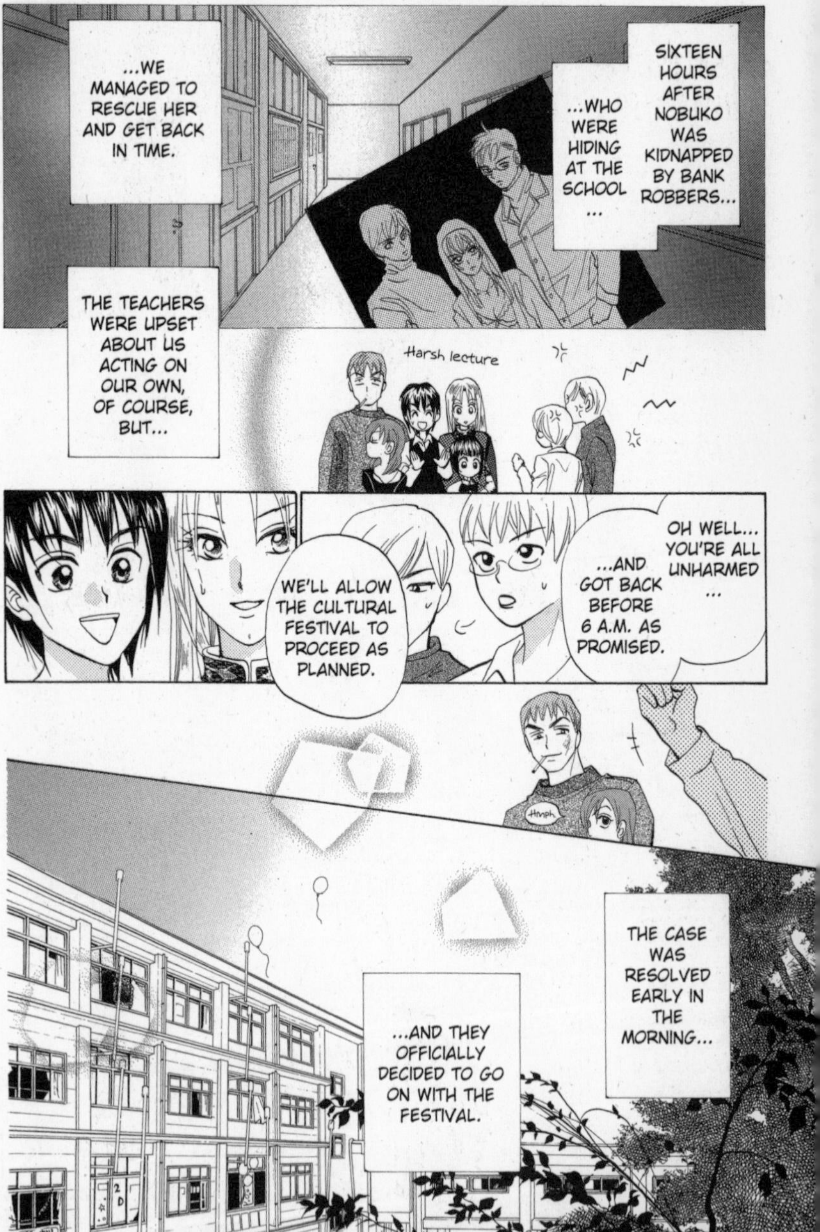
SIXTEEN HOURS AFTER NOBUKO WAS KIDNAPPED BY BANK ROBBERS...
...WHO WERE HIDING AT THE SCHOOL...
...WE MANAGED TO RESCUE HER AND GET BACK IN TIME.
THE TEACHERS WERE UPSET ABOUT US ACTING ON OUR OWN, OF COURSE, BUT...
Harsh lecture
OH WELL... YOU'RE ALL UNHARMED...
...AND GOT BACK BEFORE 6 A.M. AS PROMISED.
WE'LL ALLOW THE CULTURAL FESTIVAL TO PROCEED AS PLANNED.
Hmph
THE CASE WAS RESOLVED EARLY IN THE MORNING...
...AND THEY OFFICIALLY DECIDED TO GO ON WITH THE FESTIVAL.

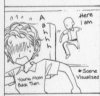

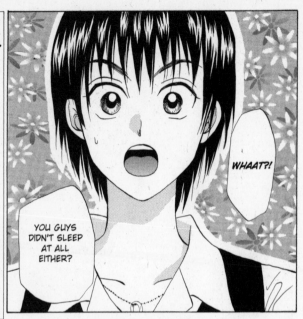

WHAAT?!
YOU GUYS DIDN'T SLEEP AT ALL EITHER?
WHAT DO YOU THINK?! HOW COULD WE SLEEP WHEN YOU GUYS WERE IN TROUBLE?
RSSSH
OH NO, THE COSTUME'S TORN!
FIX IT FAST!
FOUR MORE HOURS BEFORE CURTAIN.
I hope we can keep our energy up.
WE STILL HAVE A LOT TO PREPARE.
STMP
STMP
STMP
WE'VE GOT NO TIME TO NAP...
ITO-SAN, HURRY AND GET CHANGED.
MAKOTO-SAN, YOUR SISTER'S HERE!
!

DO YOU BELIEVE IN SPIRITS?

If it were only the paralyzed feelings, I could've reasoned that "I just imagined it" or "I was exhausted." But seeing makes it impossible. Not that I wouldn't believe its existence without seeing. But I'd be happier not to see something like that!

Scary story from Mother-Daughter Conference (?) The No. 1 was my mom's!

Aahhh
Here I am.
*Scene Visualized
Young Mom Back Then

Spirits and paralyzing feelings were everyday experiences for her.

Apparently, some 20 years ago, a faceless skinhead used to pass through the wall always at same time and roam about the house.

Ah, it's scary!

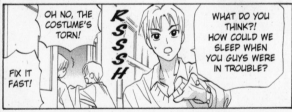

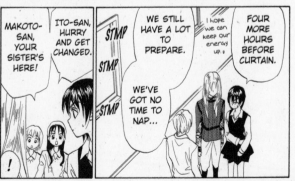

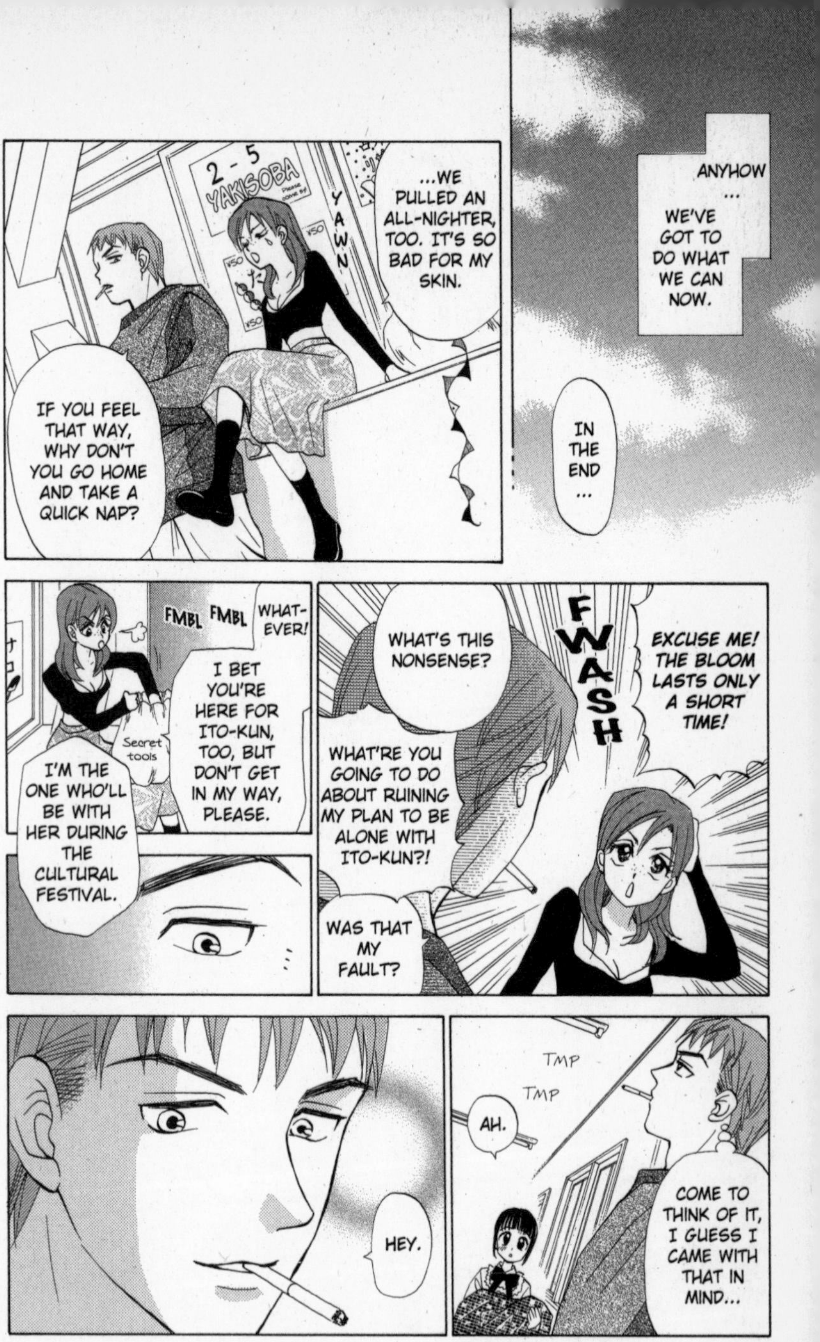
ANYHOW ... WE'VE GOT TO DO WHAT WE CAN NOW.
IN THE END ...
2-5
YAKISOBA
...WE PULLED AN ALL-NIGHTER, TOO. IT'S SO BAD FOR MY SKIN.
YAWN
IF YOU FEEL THAT WAY, WHY DON'T YOU GO HOME AND TAKE A QUICK NAP?
EXCUSE ME! THE BLOOM LASTS ONLY A SHORT TIME!
FWASH
WHAT'S THIS NONSENSE?
WHAT'RE YOU GOING TO DO ABOUT RUINING MY PLAN TO BE ALONE WITH ITO-KUN?!
WAS THAT MY FAULT?
WHAT-EVER!
FMBL FMBL
I BET YOU'RE HERE FOR ITO-KUN, TOO, BUT DON'T GET IN MY WAY, PLEASE.
Secret tools
I'M THE ONE WHO'LL BE WITH HER DURING THE CULTURAL FESTIVAL.
TMP
TMP
AH.
COME TO THINK OF IT, I GUESS I CAME WITH THAT IN MIND...
HEY.

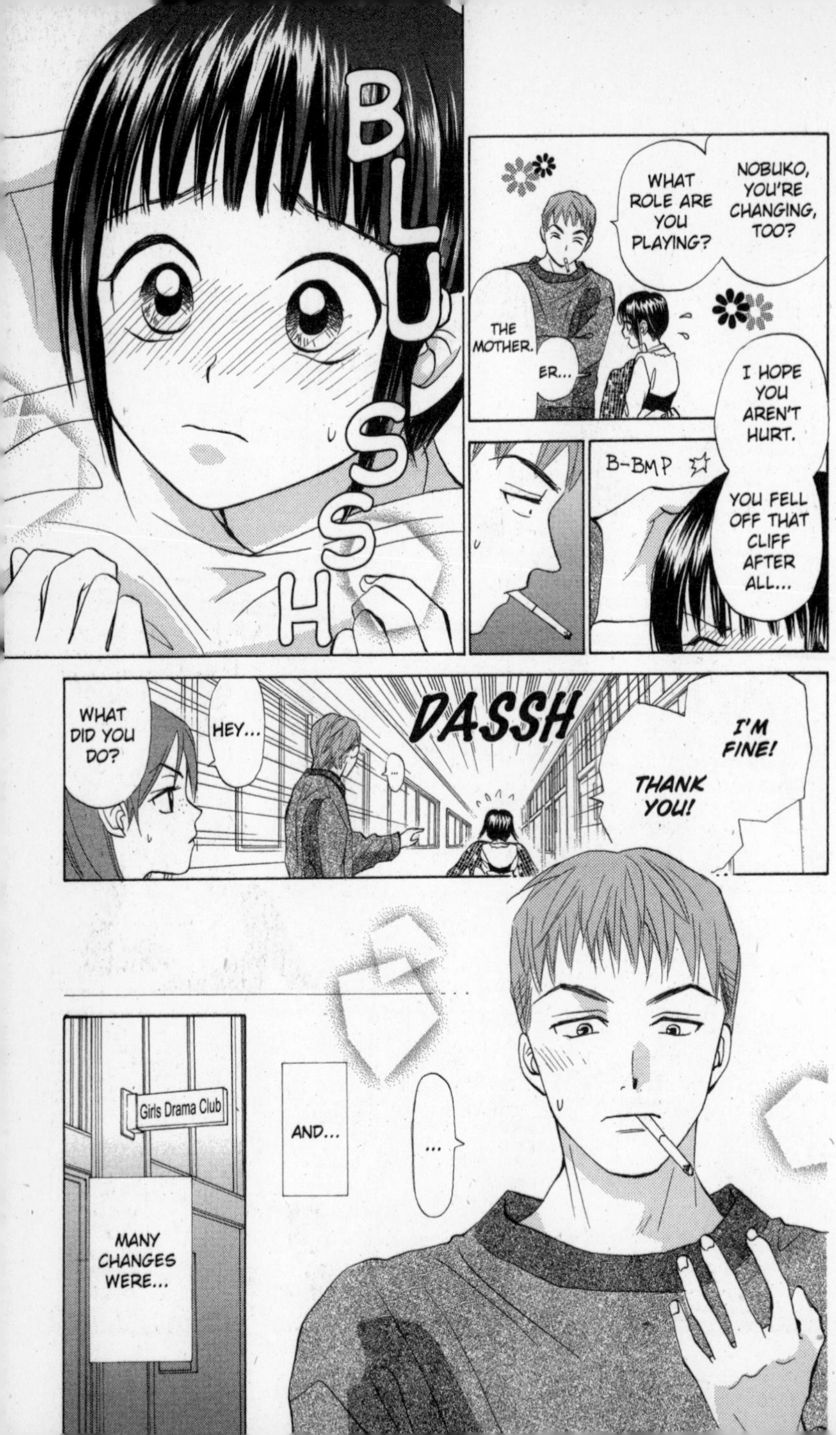
NOBUKO, YOU'RE CHANGING, TOO?
WHAT ROLE ARE YOU PLAYING?
ER...
THE MOTHER.
I HOPE YOU AREN'T HURT.
B-BMP
YOU FELL OFF THAT CLIFF AFTER ALL...
BLUSH
I'M FINE!
THANK YOU!
DASSH
...
HEY...
WHAT DID YOU DO?
...
AND...
Girls Drama Club
MANY CHANGES WERE...

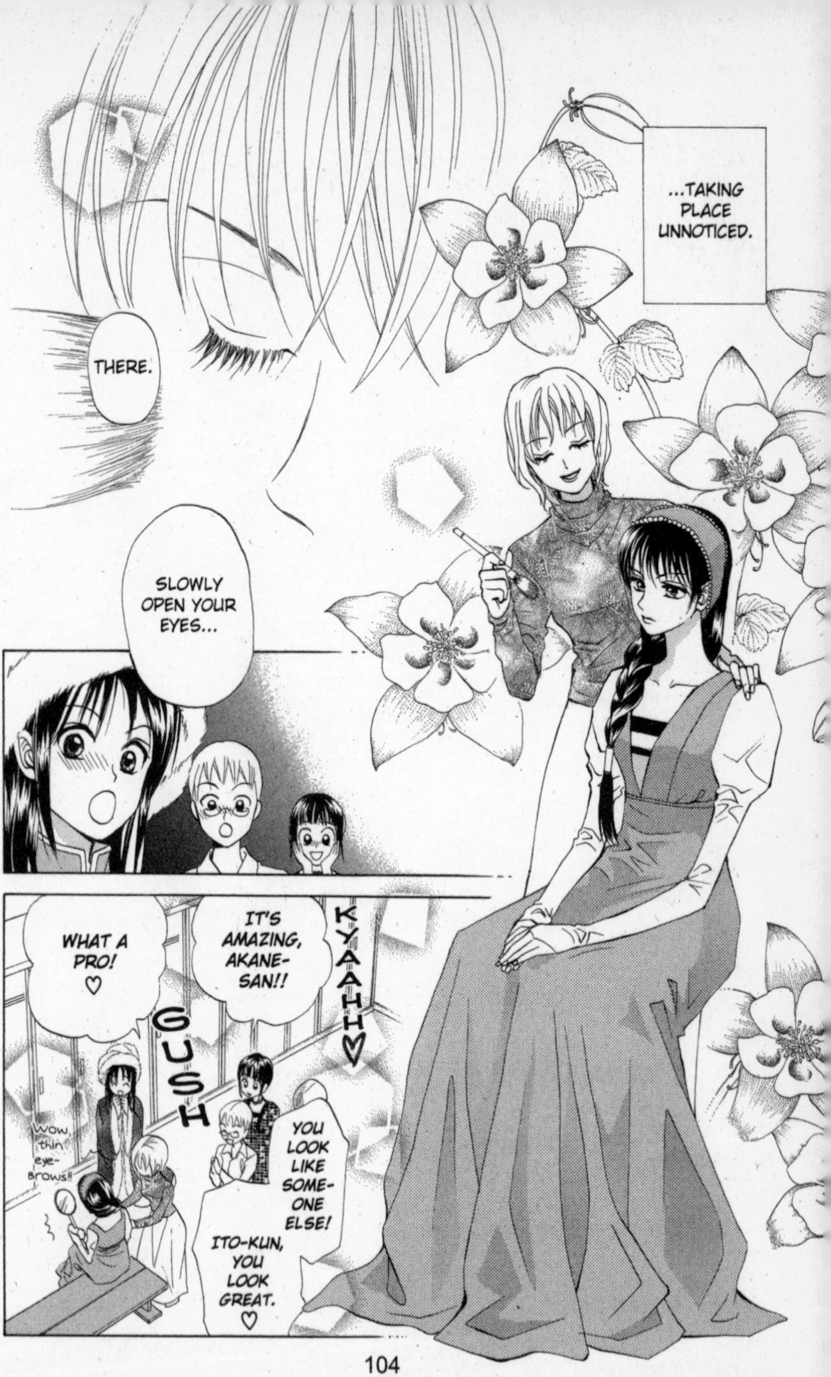
...TAKING PLACE UNNOTICED.
THERE.
SLOWLY OPEN YOUR EYES...
KYAAAHH♡
IT'S AMAZING, AKANE-SAN!!
WHAT A PRO! ♡
GUSH
YOU LOOK LIKE SOME-ONE ELSE!
ITO-KUN, YOU LOOK GREAT. ♡
Wow, thin eye-brows!!

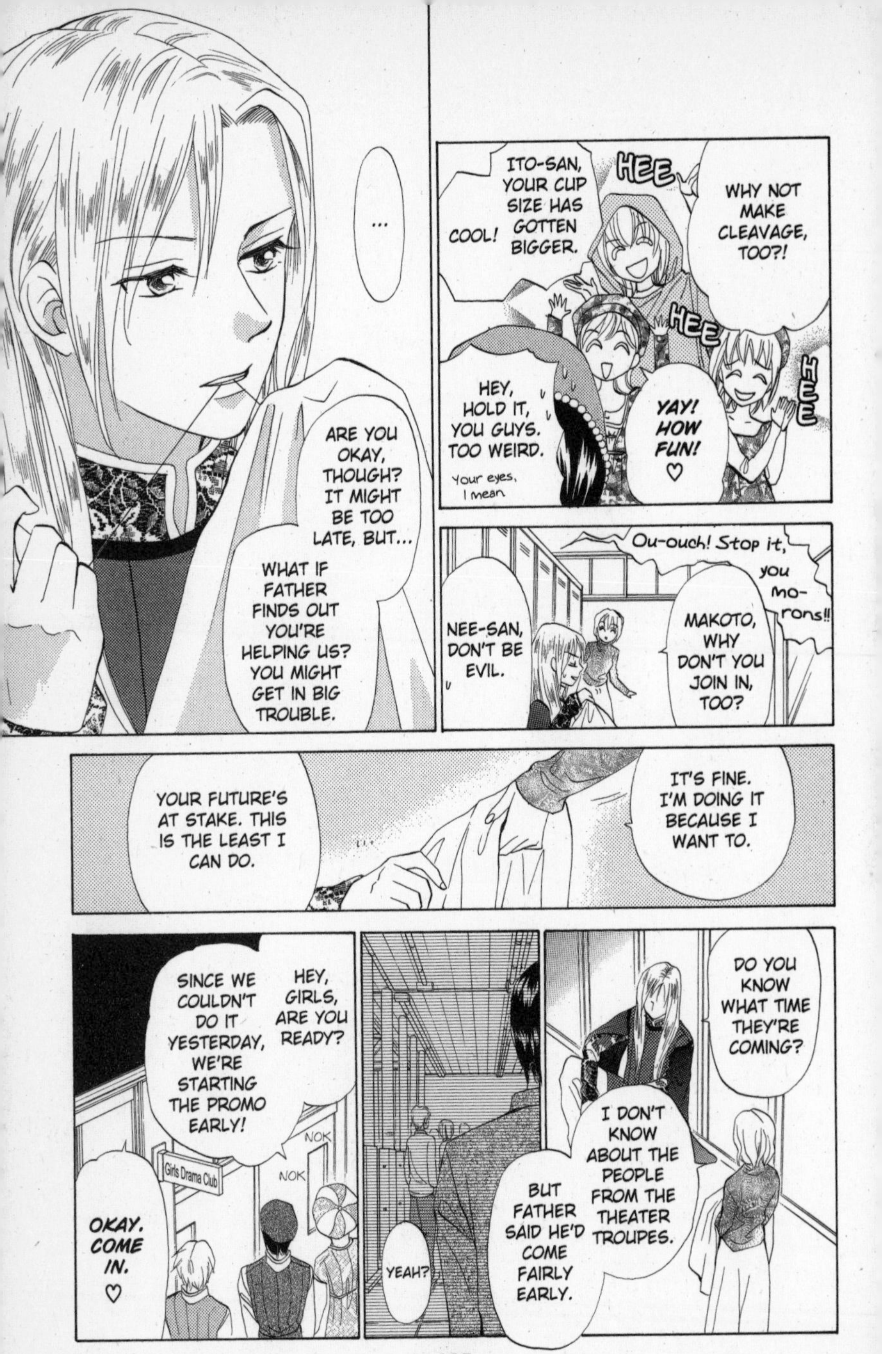
WHY NOT MAKE CLEAVAGE, TOO?!
HEE
ITO-SAN, YOUR CUP SIZE HAS GOTTEN BIGGER.
COOL!
HEE
HEE
YAY! HOW FUN! ♡
HEY, HOLD IT, YOU GUYS. TOO WEIRD.
Your eyes, I mean
Ou-ouch! Stop it, you mo-rons!!
MAKOTO, WHY DON'T YOU JOIN IN, TOO?
NEE-SAN, DON'T BE EVIL.
...
ARE YOU OKAY, THOUGH? IT MIGHT BE TOO LATE, BUT...
WHAT IF FATHER FINDS OUT YOU'RE HELPING US? YOU MIGHT GET IN BIG TROUBLE.
IT'S FINE. I'M DOING IT BECAUSE I WANT TO.
YOUR FUTURE'S AT STAKE. THIS IS THE LEAST I CAN DO.
DO YOU KNOW WHAT TIME THEY'RE COMING?
I DON'T KNOW ABOUT THE PEOPLE FROM THE THEATER TROUPES.
BUT FATHER SAID HE'D COME FAIRLY EARLY.
YEAH?
HEY, GIRLS, ARE YOU READY?
SINCE WE COULDN'T DO IT YESTERDAY, WE'RE STARTING THE PROMO EARLY!
NOK
NOK
Girls Drama Club
OKAY. COME IN. ♡

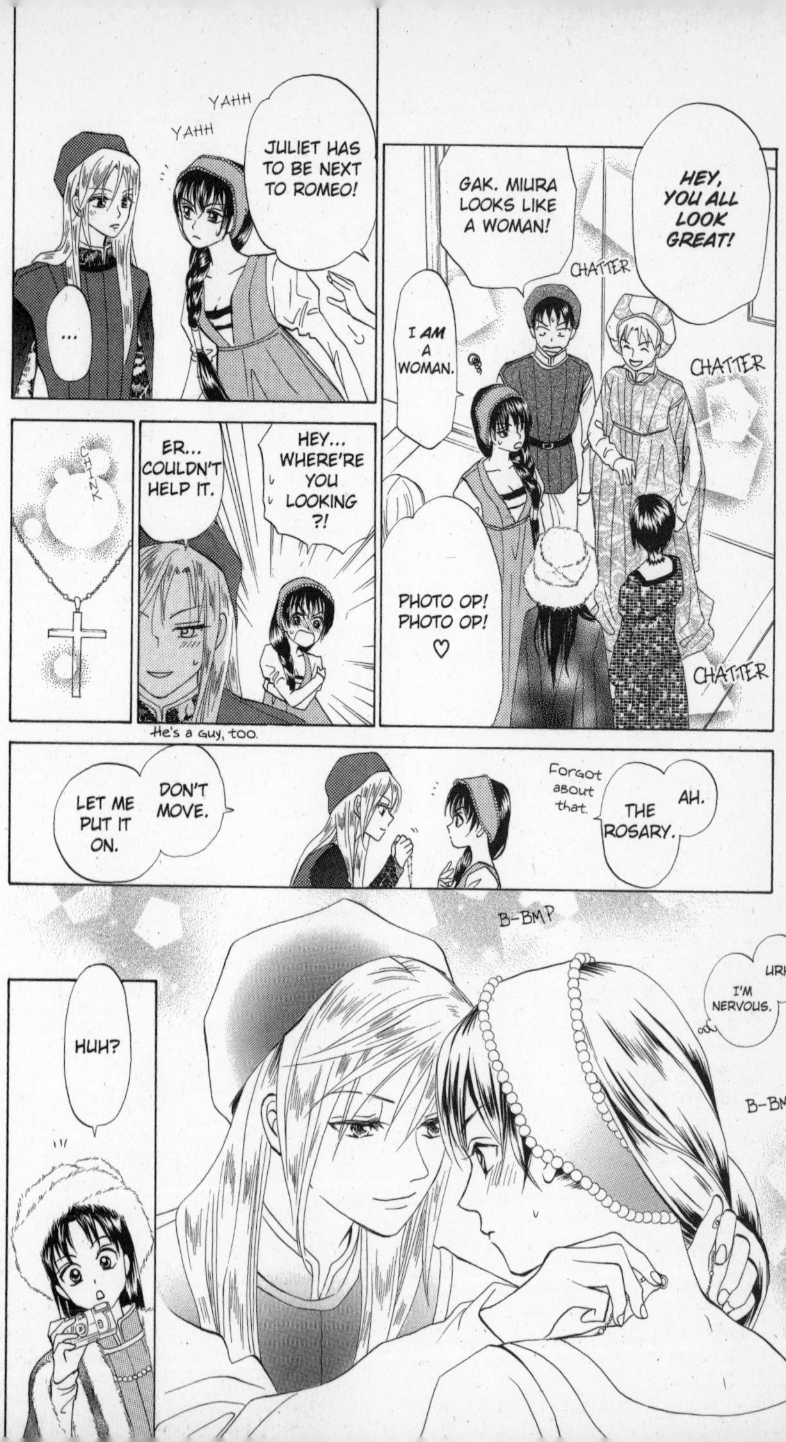
HEY, YOU ALL LOOK GREAT!
GAK. MIURA LOOKS LIKE A WOMAN!
CHATTER
CHATTER
I AM A WOMAN.
PHOTO OP! PHOTO OP! ♡
CHATTER
YAHH
YAHH
JULIET HAS TO BE NEXT TO ROMEO!
...
HEY... WHERE'RE YOU LOOKING ?!
ER... COULDN'T HELP IT.
He's a guy, too.
CHINK
AH.
THE ROSARY.
Forgot about that.
DON'T MOVE.
LET ME PUT IT ON.
B-BMP
URK. I'M NERVOUS.
B-BMP
HUH?

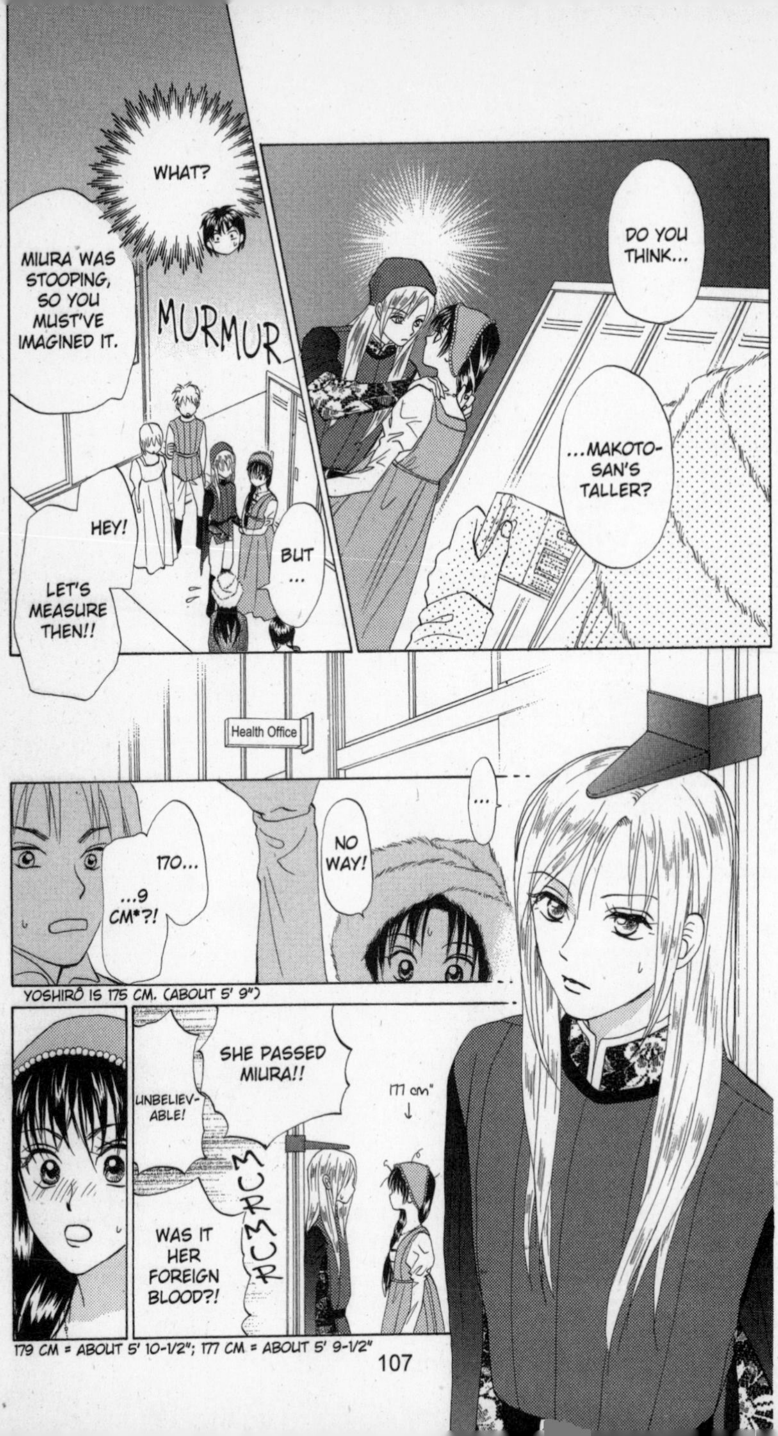
DO YOU THINK...
...MAKOTO-SAN'S TALLER?
WHAT?
MIURA WAS STOOPING, SO YOU MUST'VE IMAGINED IT.
MURMUR
BUT ...
HEY!
LET'S MEASURE THEN!!
Health Office
...
NO WAY!
170...
...9 CM*?!
SHE PASSED MIURA!!
177 cm"
UNBELIEV-ABLE!
MURMUR
WAS IT HER FOREIGN BLOOD?!

YOSHIRÔ IS 175 CM. (ABOUT 5' 9")

179 CM = ABOUT 5' 10-1/2"; 177 CM = ABOUT 5' 9-1/2"

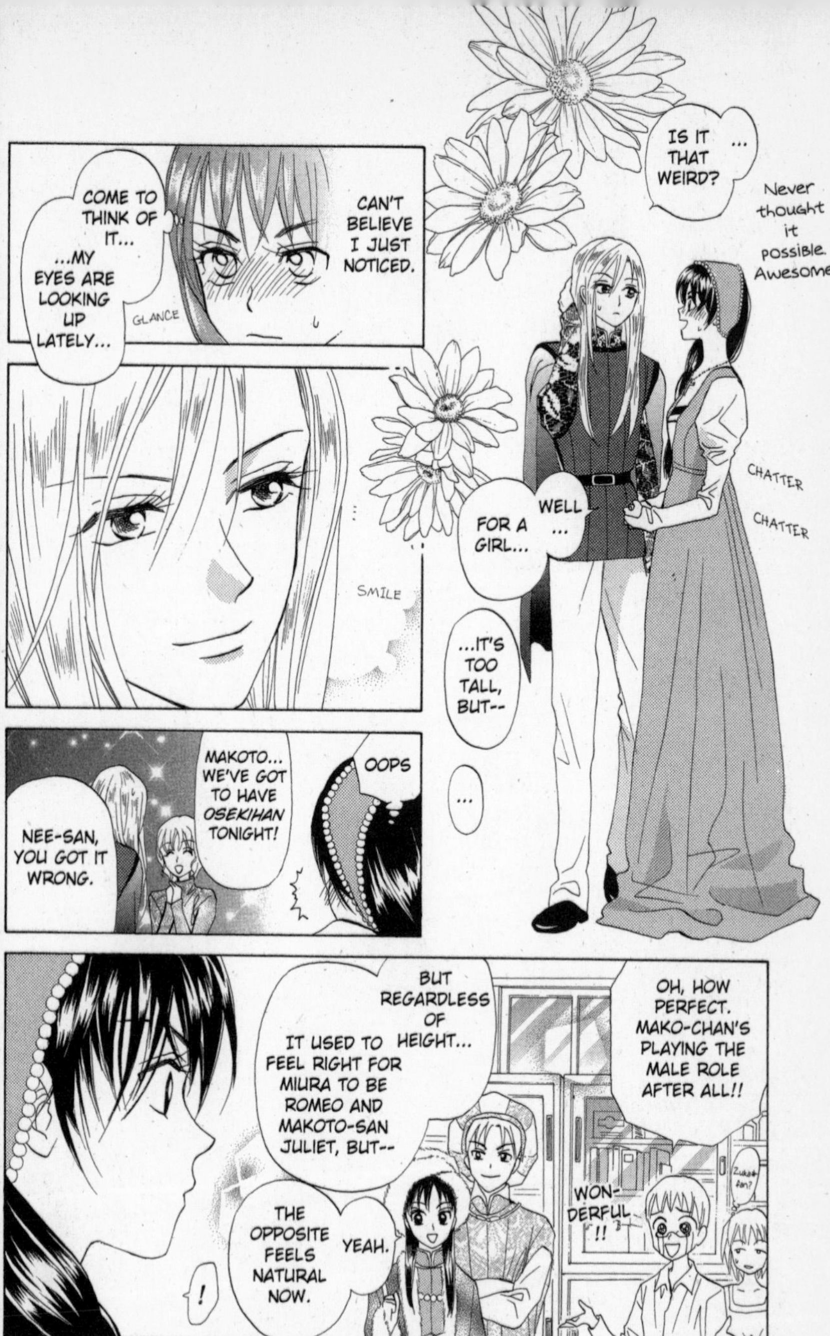
IS IT THAT WEIRD?
...
Never thought it possible. Awesome!
CHATTER
CHATTER
WELL ...
FOR A GIRL...
...IT'S TOO TALL, BUT--
...
CAN'T BELIEVE I JUST NOTICED.
COME TO THINK OF IT... ...MY EYES ARE LOOKING UP LATELY...
GLANCE
SMILE
...
OOPS
MAKOTO... WE'VE GOT TO HAVE OSEKIHAN TONIGHT!
NEE-SAN, YOU GOT IT WRONG.
OH, HOW PERFECT. MAKO-CHAN'S PLAYING THE MALE ROLE AFTER ALL!!
Zuka* fan?
WONDERFUL!!
BUT REGARDLESS OF HEIGHT...
IT USED TO FEEL RIGHT FOR MIURA TO BE ROMEO AND MAKOTO-SAN JULIET, BUT--
THE OPPOSITE FEELS NATURAL NOW.
YEAH.
!

*TAKARAZUKA, A FAMOUS ALL-FEMALE THEATER TROUPE

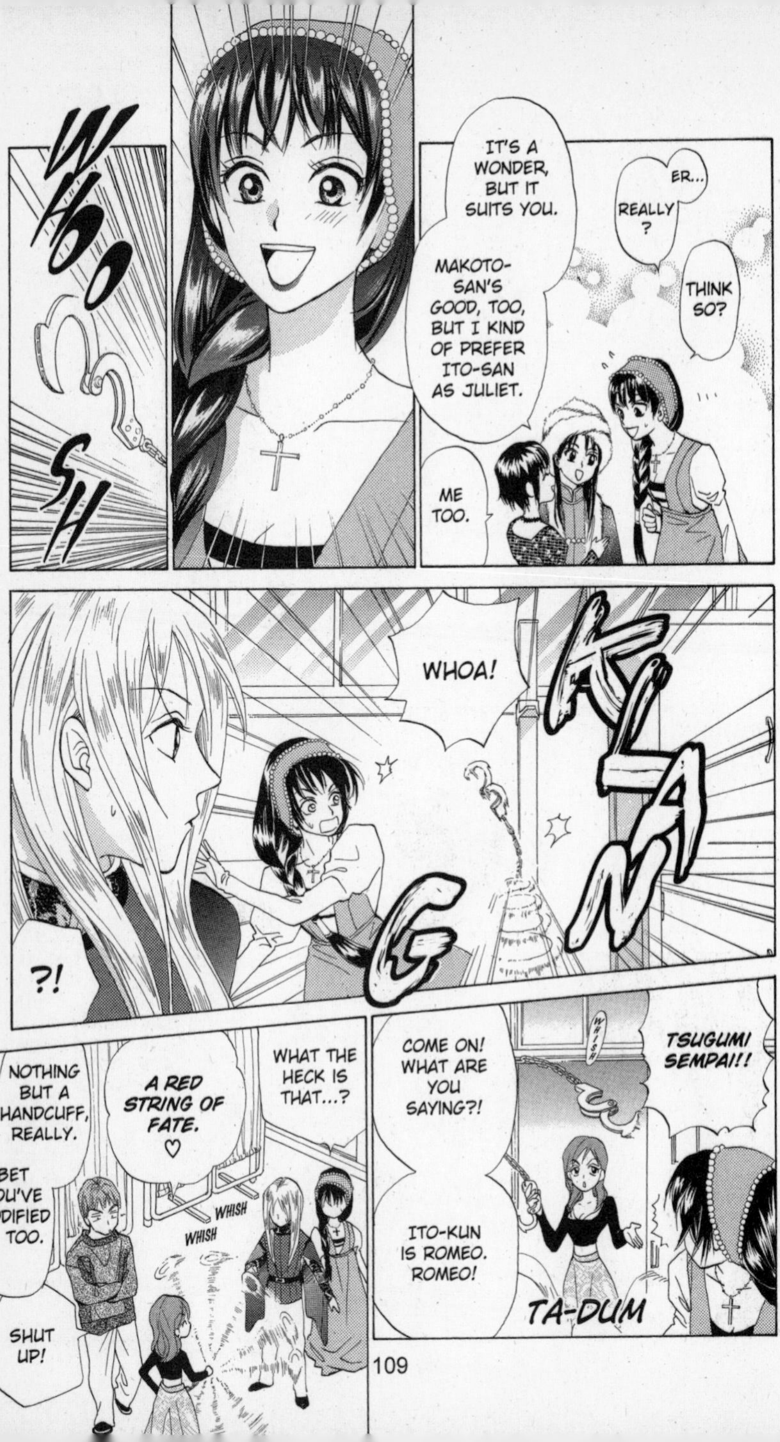
ER... REALLY?
THINK SO?
IT'S A WONDER, BUT IT SUITS YOU.
MAKOTO-SAN'S GOOD, TOO, BUT I KIND OF PREFER ITO-SAN AS JULIET.
ME TOO.
WHOOSH
KLANG
WHOA!
?!
TSUGUMI SEMPAI!!
WHISH
COME ON! WHAT ARE YOU SAYING?!
ITO-KUN IS ROMEO. ROMEO!
TA-DUM
WHAT THE HECK IS THAT...?
A RED STRING OF FATE. ♡
NOTHING BUT A HANDCUFF, REALLY.
BET YOU'VE MODIFIED IT, TOO.
WHISH
WHISH
SHUT UP!

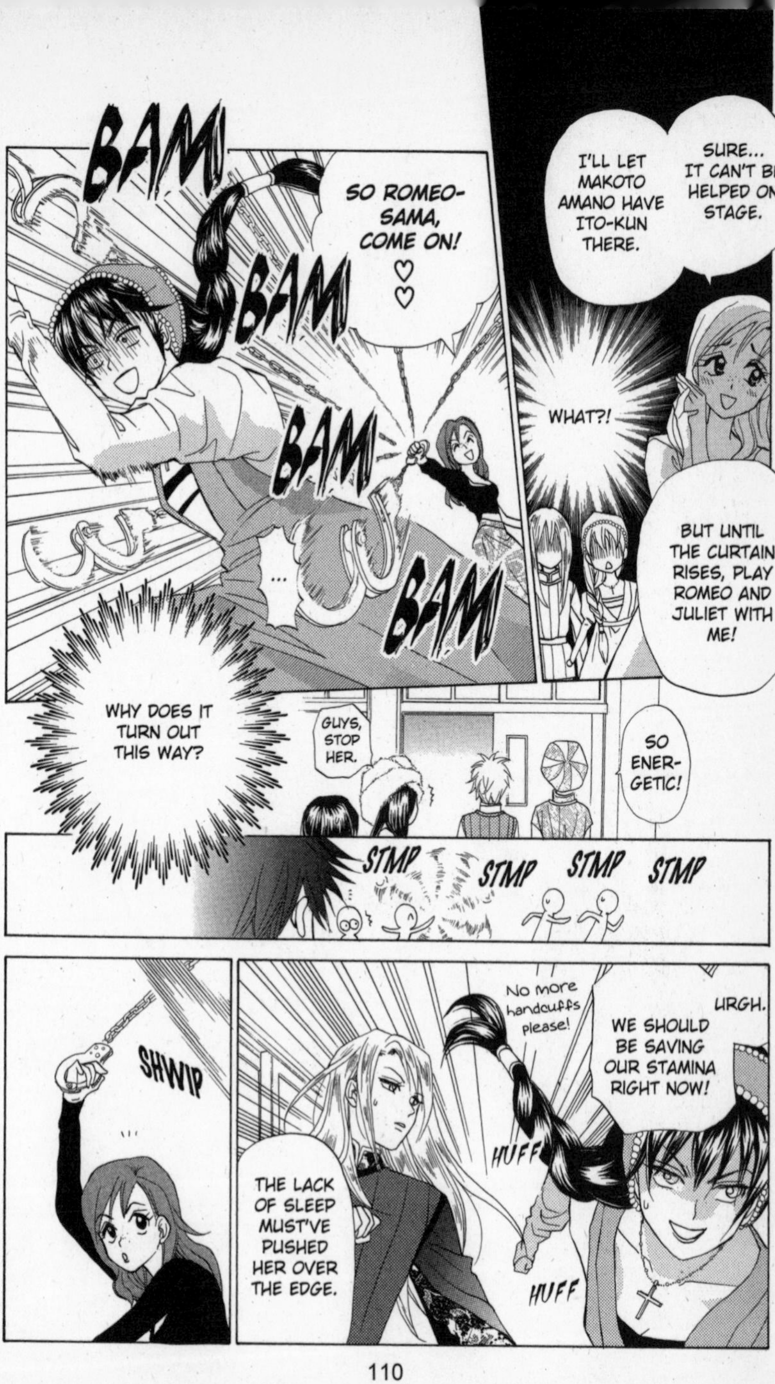
SURE... IT CAN'T BE HELPED ON STAGE.
I'LL LET MAKOTO AMANO HAVE ITO-KUN THERE.
WHAT?!
BUT UNTIL THE CURTAIN RISES, PLAY ROMEO AND JULIET WITH ME!
SO ROMEO-SAMA, COME ON! ♡ ♡
BAM
BAM
BAM
BAM
...
WHY DOES IT TURN OUT THIS WAY?
SO ENER-GETIC!
GUYS, STOP HER.
STMP
STMP
STMP
STMP
URGH.
WE SHOULD BE SAVING OUR STAMINA RIGHT NOW!
No more handcuffs please!
HUFF
HUFF
THE LACK OF SLEEP MUST'VE PUSHED HER OVER THE EDGE.
SHWIP

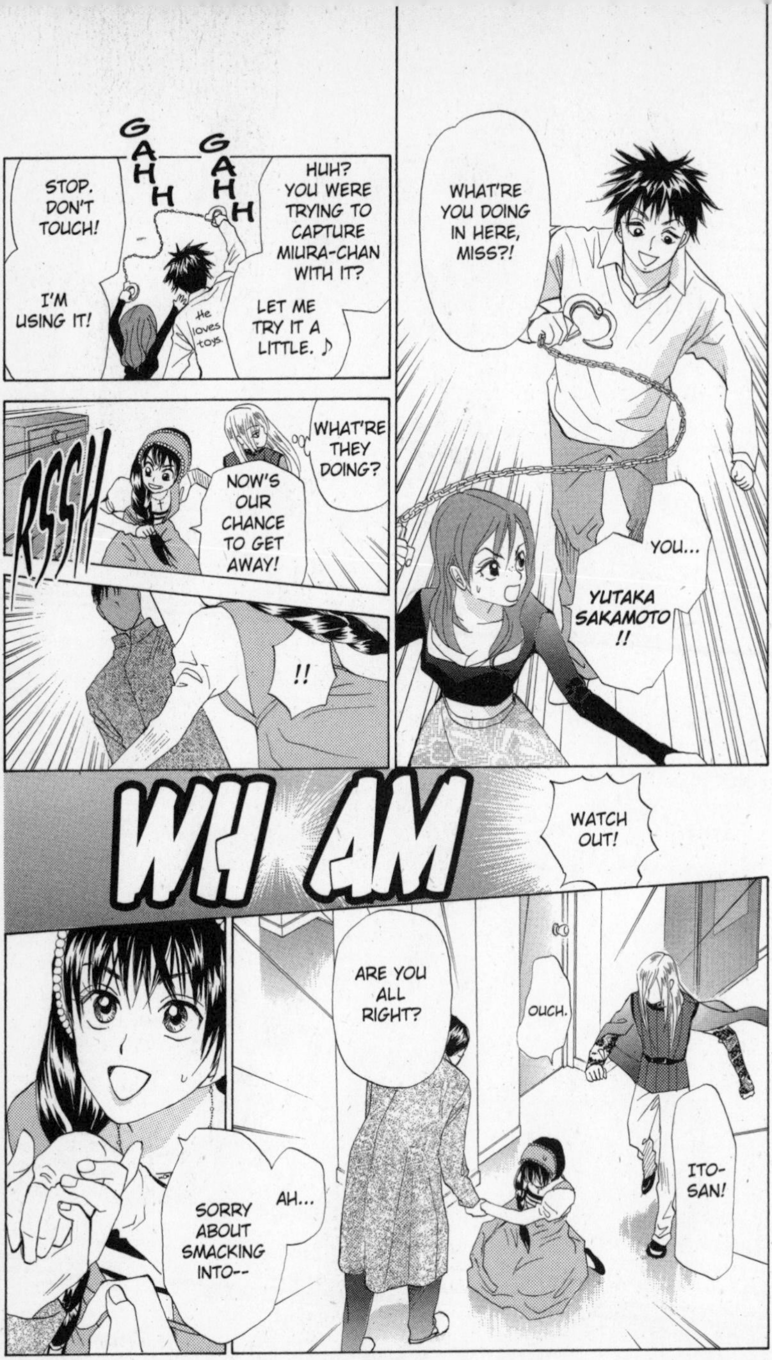
WHAT'RE YOU DOING IN HERE, MISS?!
YOU...
YUTAKA SAKAMOTO!!
HUH? YOU WERE TRYING TO CAPTURE MIURA-CHAN WITH IT?
GAHH GAHH
STOP. DON'T TOUCH!
LET ME TRY IT A LITTLE. ♪
He loves toys.
I'M USING IT!
WHAT'RE THEY DOING?
NOW'S OUR CHANCE TO GET AWAY!
RSSH
!!
WATCH OUT!
WH AM
ARE YOU ALL RIGHT?
OUCH.
ITO-SAN!
AH...
SORRY ABOUT SMACKING INTO--

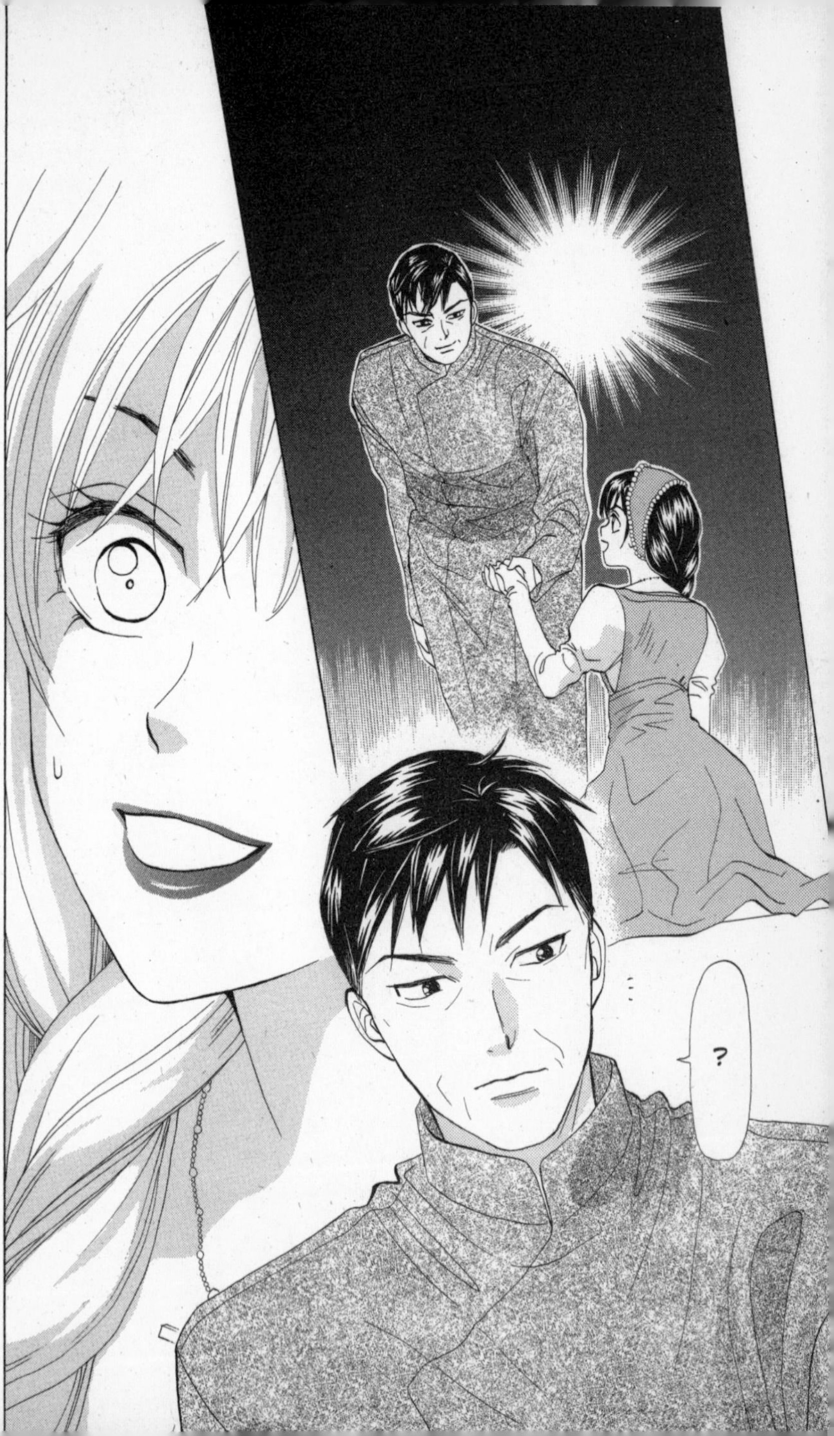
...?

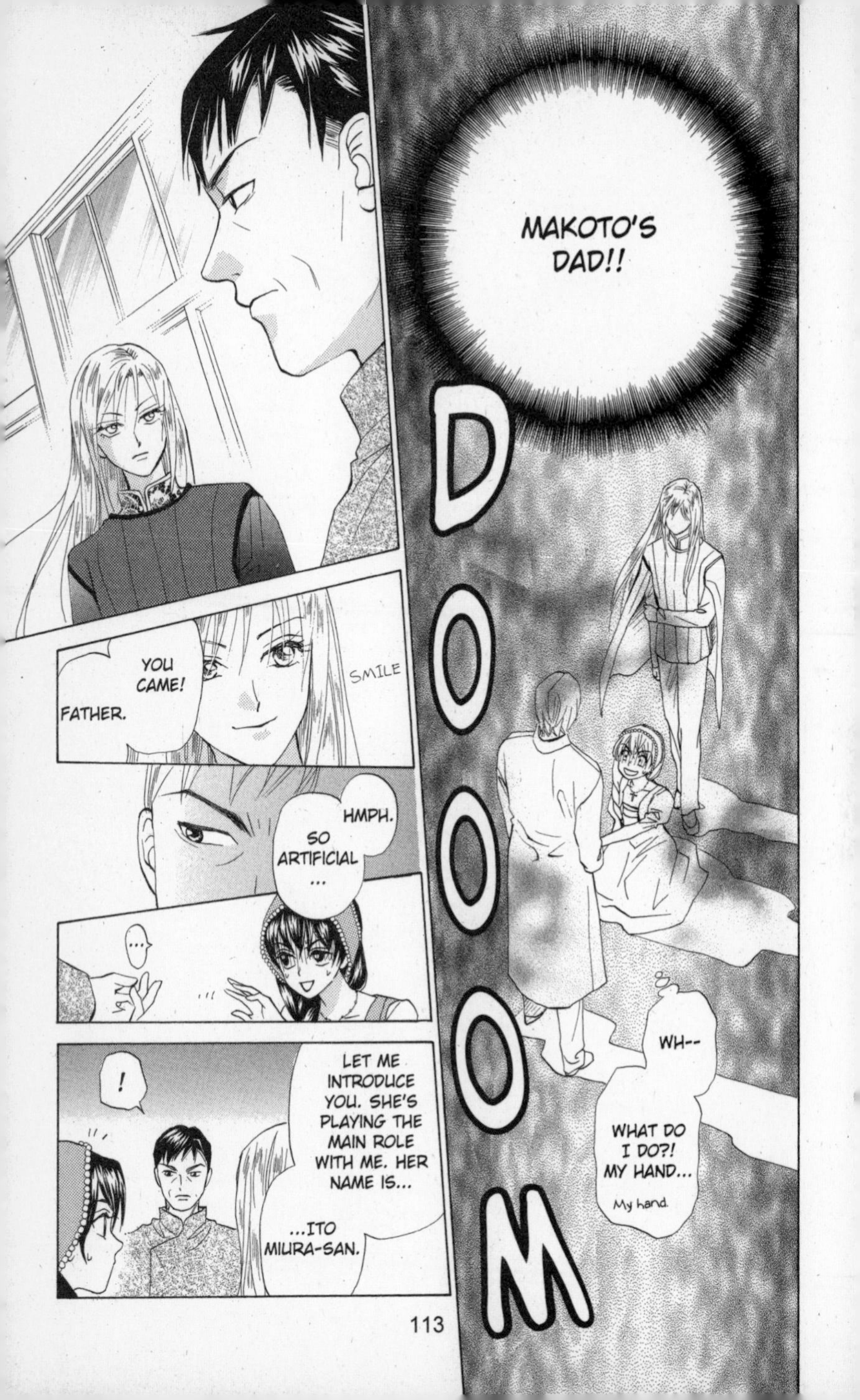
MAKOTO'S DAD!!
DOOOOM
WH--
WHAT DO I DO?! MY HAND...
My hand.
YOU CAME! FATHER.
SMILE
HMPH.
SO ARTIFICIAL...
...
!
LET ME INTRODUCE YOU. SHE'S PLAYING THE MAIN ROLE WITH ME. HER NAME IS...
...ITO MIURA-SAN.

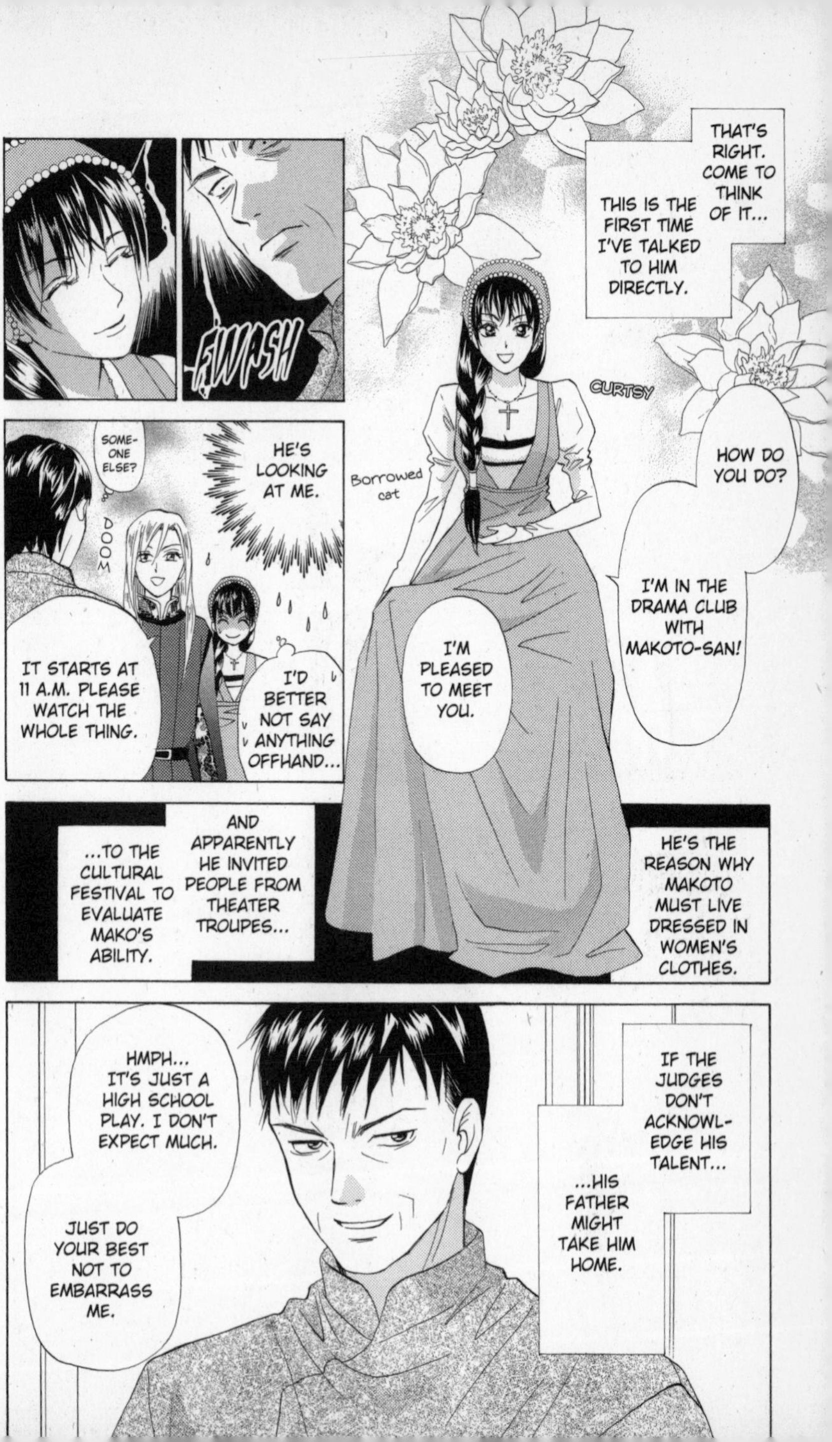
THAT'S RIGHT. COME TO THINK OF IT...
THIS IS THE FIRST TIME I'VE TALKED TO HIM DIRECTLY.
CURTSY
HOW DO YOU DO?
I'M IN THE DRAMA CLUB WITH MAKOTO-SAN!
I'M PLEASED TO MEET YOU.
Borrowed cat
FWASH
HE'S LOOKING AT ME.
SOME-ONE ELSE?
DOOM
I'D BETTER NOT SAY ANYTHING OFFHAND...
IT STARTS AT 11 A.M. PLEASE WATCH THE WHOLE THING.
HE'S THE REASON WHY MAKOTO MUST LIVE DRESSED IN WOMEN'S CLOTHES.
AND APPARENTLY HE INVITED PEOPLE FROM THEATER TROUPES...
...TO THE CULTURAL FESTIVAL TO EVALUATE MAKO'S ABILITY.
IF THE JUDGES DON'T ACKNOWL-EDGE HIS TALENT...
...HIS FATHER MIGHT TAKE HIM HOME.
HMPH... IT'S JUST A HIGH SCHOOL PLAY. I DON'T EXPECT MUCH.
JUST DO YOUR BEST NOT TO EMBARRASS ME.

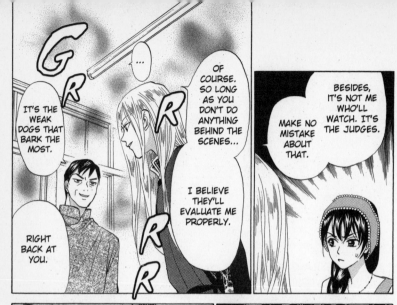

BESIDES, IT'S NOT ME WHO'LL WATCH. IT'S THE JUDGES.
MAKE NO MISTAKE ABOUT THAT.
...
OF COURSE. SO LONG AS YOU DON'T DO ANYTHING BEHIND THE SCENES...
I BELIEVE THEY'LL EVALUATE ME PROPERLY.
GRRRR
IT'S THE WEAK DOGS THAT BARK THE MOST.
RIGHT BACK AT YOU.
BUT REALLY, IT'S NOT THE PLACE...
...TO HAVE THAT KINDA CONVER-SATION!
BAM
UM.
EVERYONE WORKED VERY HARD FOR THIS DAY!

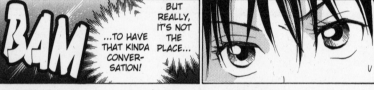

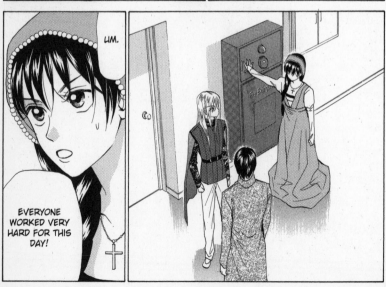

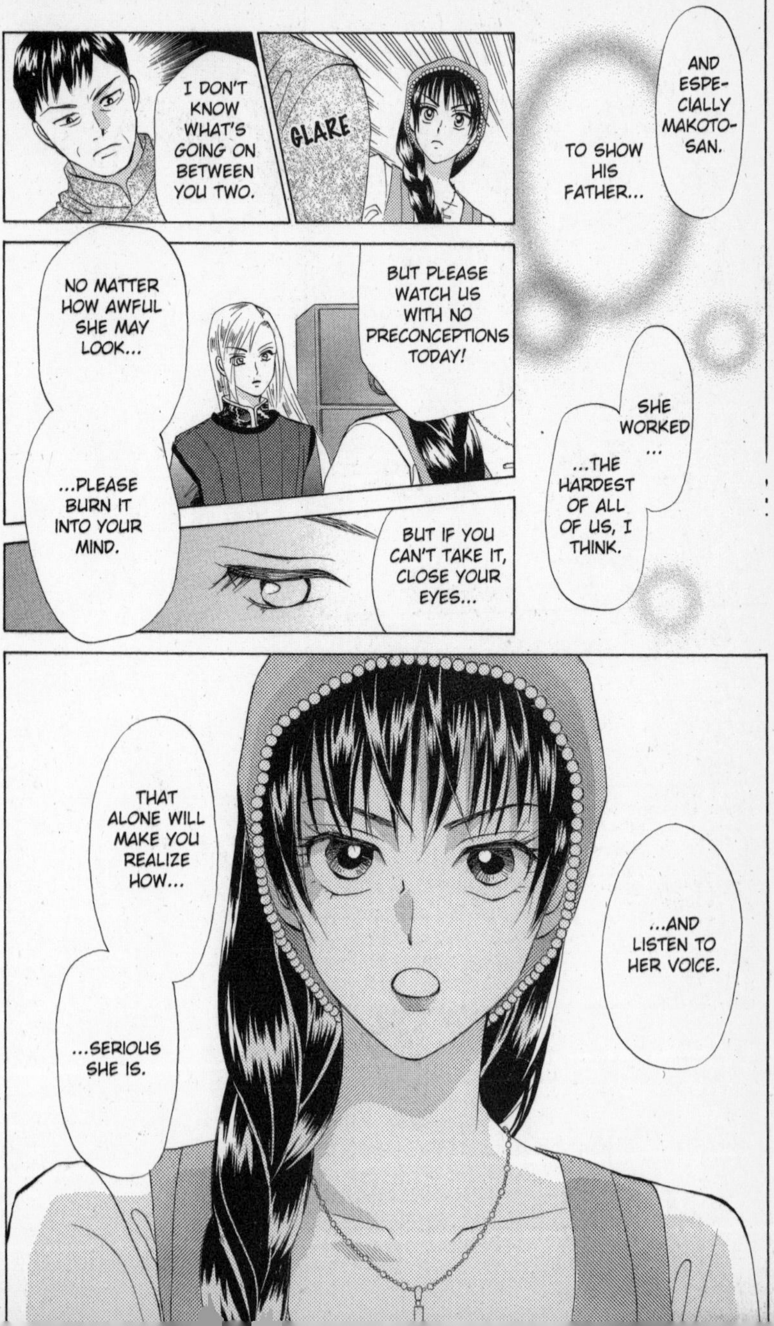
AND ESPECIALLY MAKOTO-SAN.
TO SHOW HIS FATHER...
GLARE
I DON'T KNOW WHAT'S GOING ON BETWEEN YOU TWO.
SHE WORKED ... ...THE HARDEST OF ALL OF US, I THINK.
BUT PLEASE WATCH US WITH NO PRECONCEPTIONS TODAY!
NO MATTER HOW AWFUL SHE MAY LOOK...
...PLEASE BURN IT INTO YOUR MIND.
BUT IF YOU CAN'T TAKE IT, CLOSE YOUR EYES...
...AND LISTEN TO HER VOICE.
THAT ALONE WILL MAKE YOU REALIZE HOW...
...SERIOUS SHE IS.

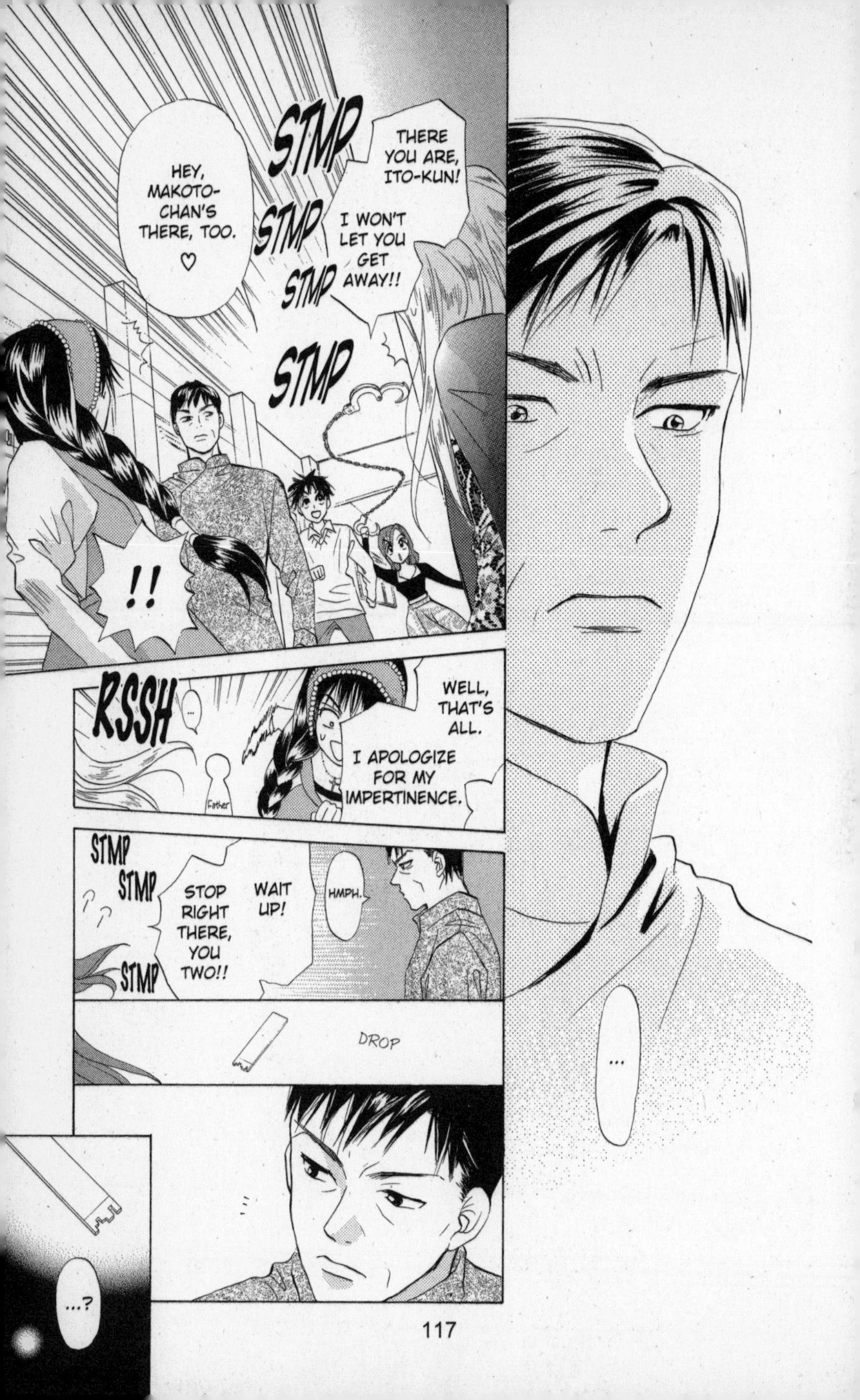
...
THERE YOU ARE, ITO-KUN!
I WON'T LET YOU GET AWAY!!
STMP STMP STMP STMP
HEY, MAKOTO-CHAN'S THERE, TOO. ♡
!!
WELL, THAT'S ALL.
I APOLOGIZE FOR MY IMPERTINENCE.
...
RSSH
Father
HMPH.
WAIT UP!
STOP RIGHT THERE, YOU TWO!!
STMP STMP STMP
DROP
...?

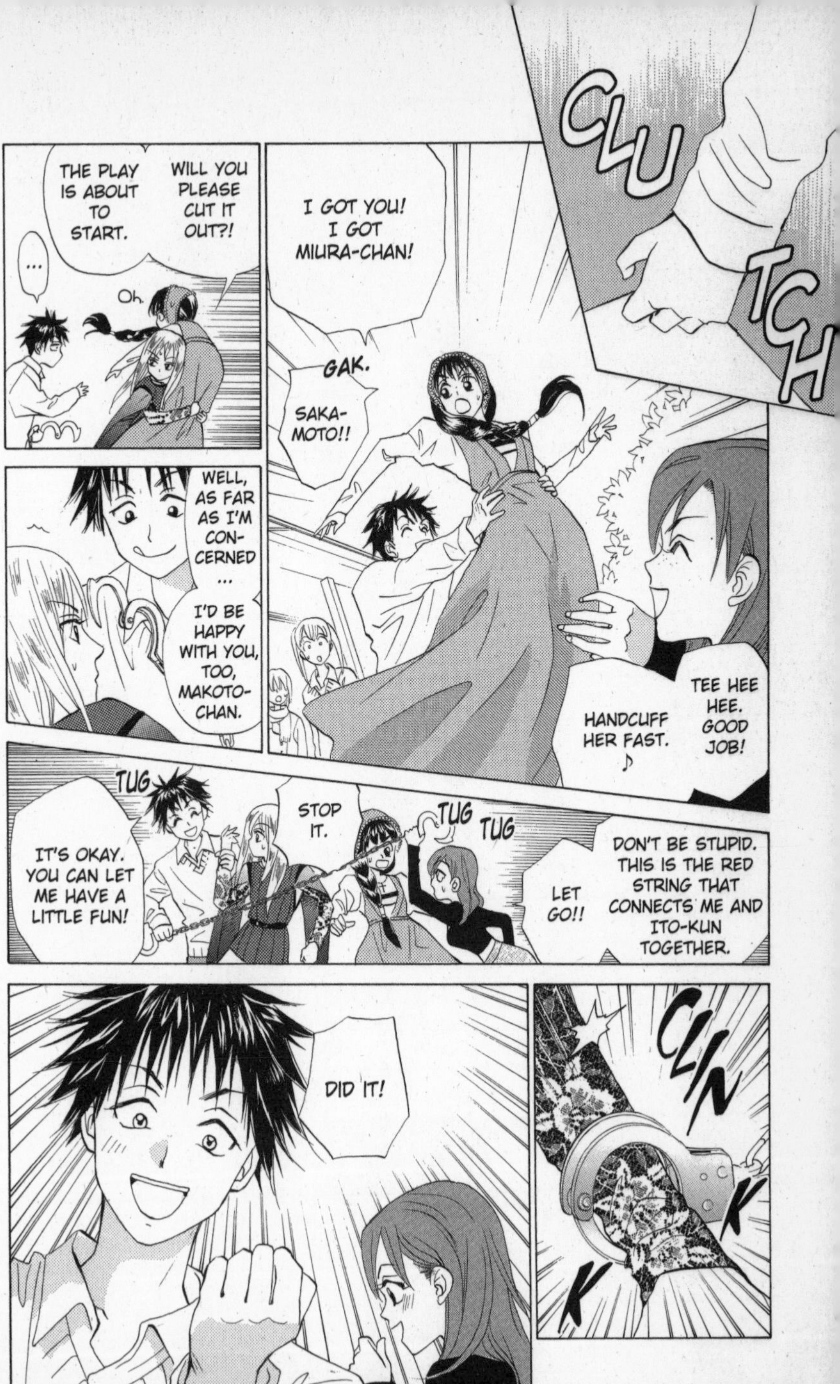
CLUTCH
I GOT YOU! I GOT MIURA-CHAN!
GAK.
SAKAMOTO!!
TEE HEE HEE. GOOD JOB!
HANDCUFF HER FAST. ♪
WILL YOU PLEASE CUT IT OUT?!
THE PLAY IS ABOUT TO START.
...
Oh.
WELL, AS FAR AS I'M CONCERNED...
I'D BE HAPPY WITH YOU, TOO, MAKOTO-CHAN.
DON'T BE STUPID. THIS IS THE RED STRING THAT CONNECTS ME AND ITO-KUN TOGETHER.
LET GO!!
TUG TUG
STOP IT.
TUG
IT'S OKAY. YOU CAN LET ME HAVE A LITTLE FUN!
CLINK
K
K
DID IT!

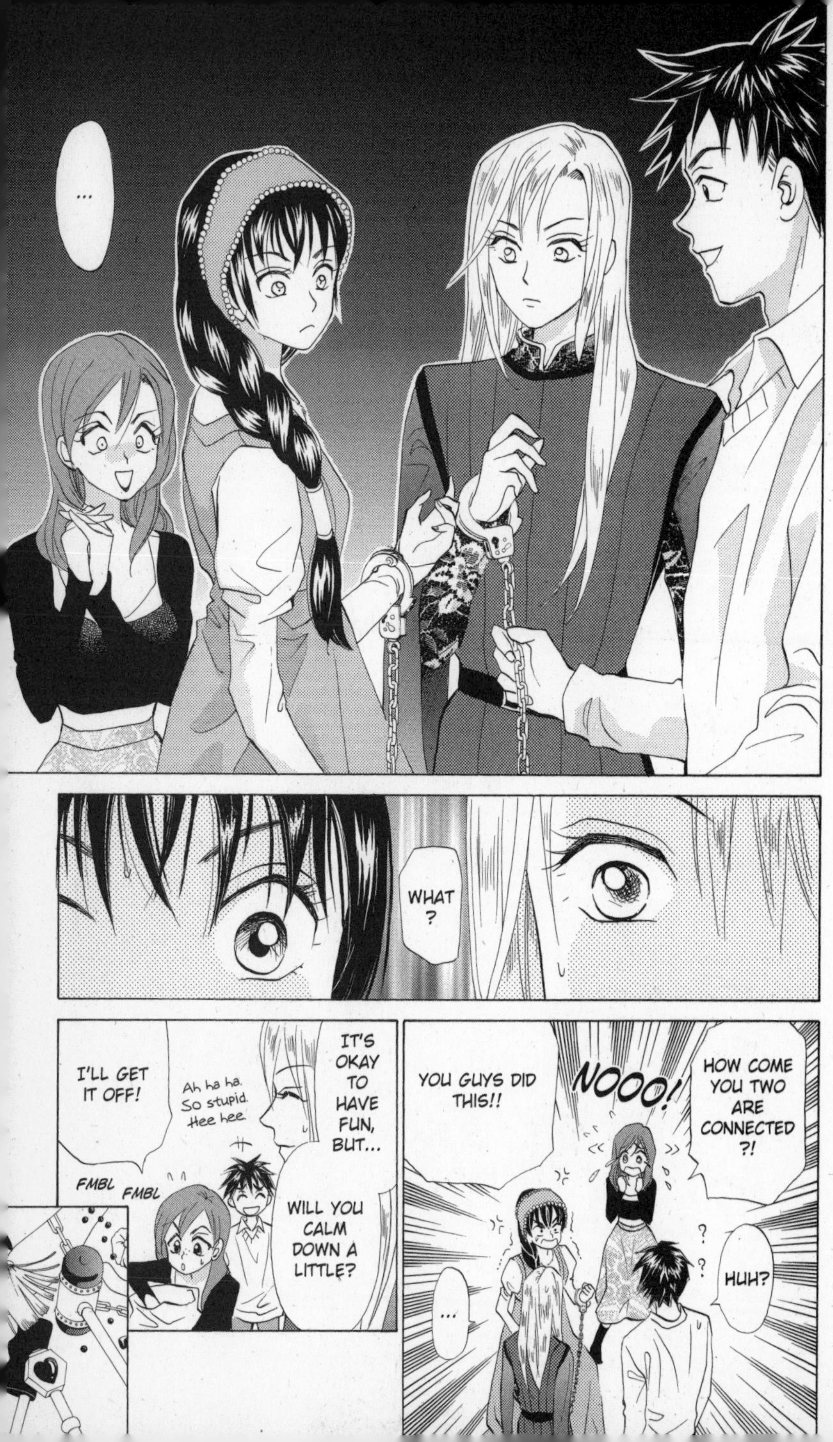
...
WHAT?
HOW COME YOU TWO ARE CONNECTED?!
NOOO!
YOU GUYS DID THIS!!
HUH?
...
IT'S OKAY TO HAVE FUN, BUT...
WILL YOU CALM DOWN A LITTLE?
Ah ha ha. So stupid. Hee hee
I'LL GET IT OFF!
FMBL FMBL

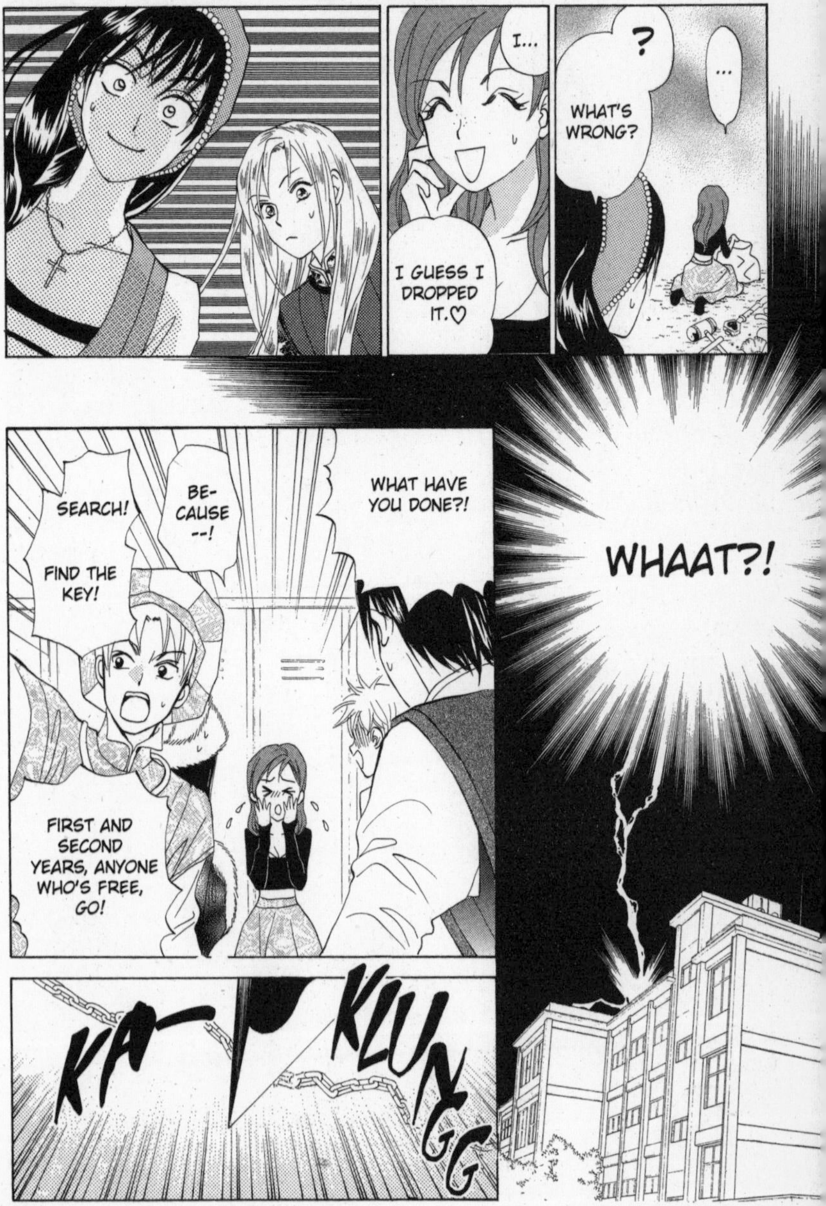

...
?
WHAT'S WRONG?
I...
I GUESS I DROPPED IT.♡
WHAAT?!
WHAT HAVE YOU DONE?!
BE-CAUSE --!
SEARCH!
FIND THE KEY!
FIRST AND SECOND YEARS, ANYONE WHO'S FREE, GO!
KA-KLUNGG

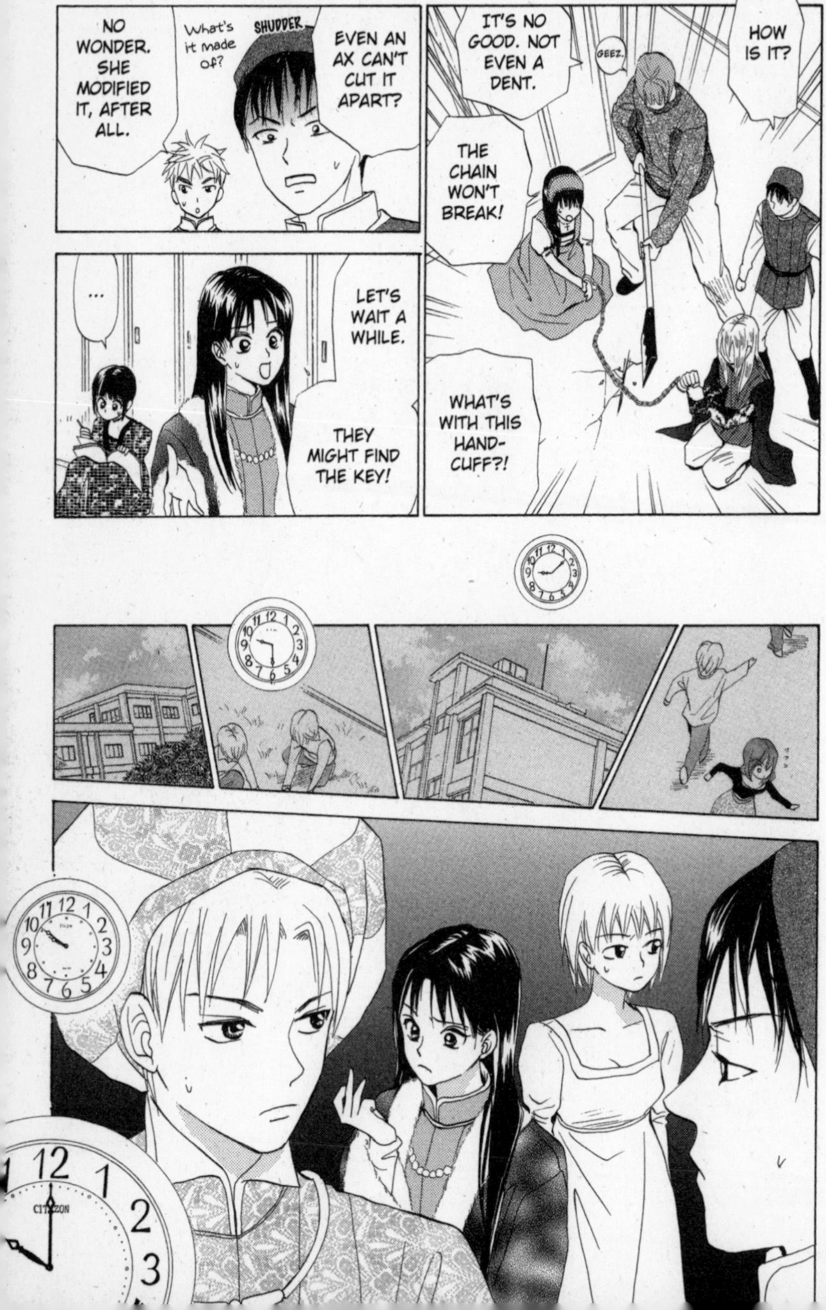
HOW IS IT?
IT'S NO GOOD. NOT EVEN A DENT.
GEEZ.
THE CHAIN WON'T BREAK!
WHAT'S WITH THIS HAND-CUFF?!
EVEN AN AX CAN'T CUT IT APART?
SHUDDER
What's it made of?
NO WONDER. SHE MODIFIED IT, AFTER ALL.
LET'S WAIT A WHILE.
THEY MIGHT FIND THE KEY!
...

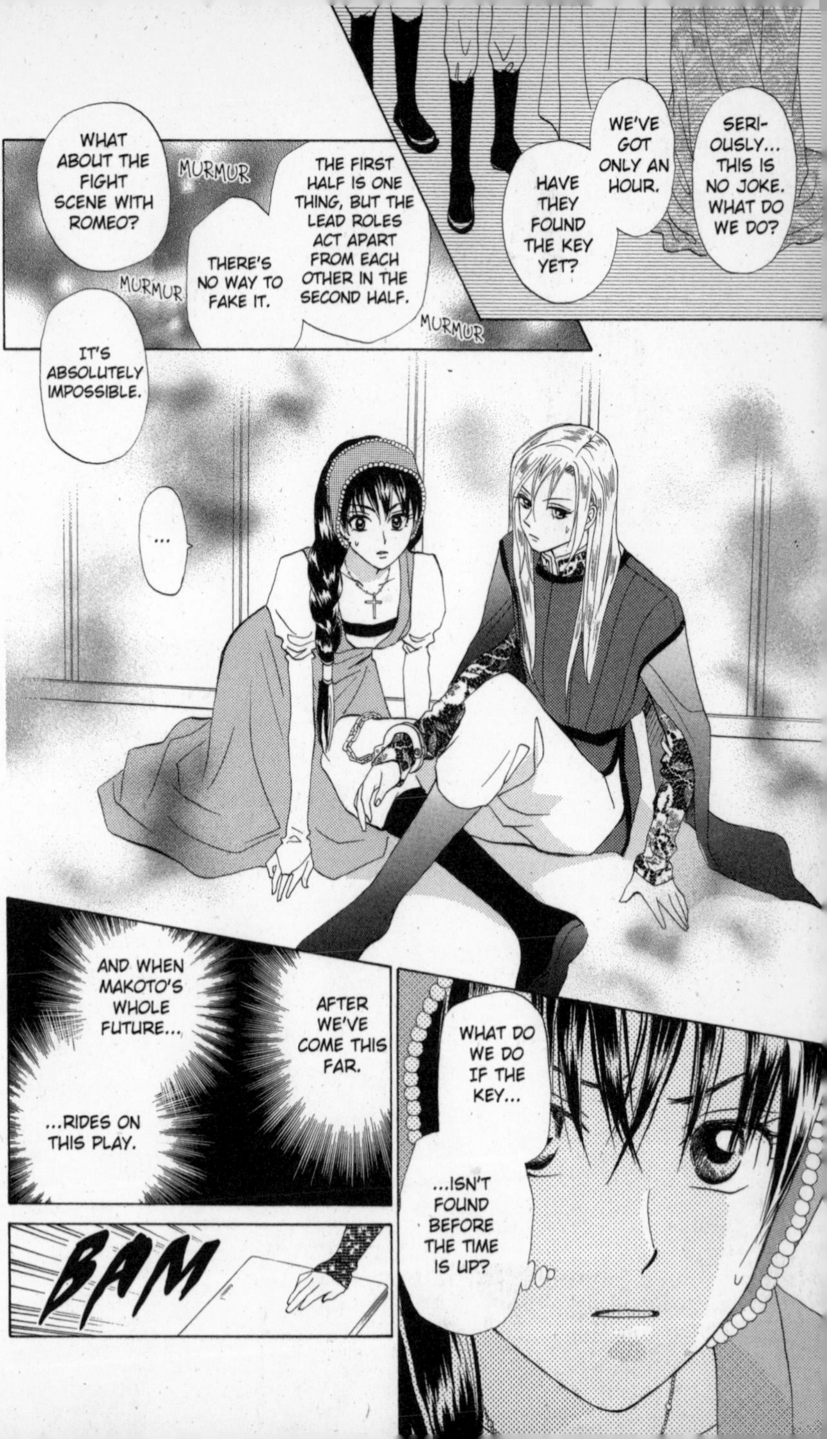
SERI-OUSLY... THIS IS NO JOKE. WHAT DO WE DO?
WE'VE GOT ONLY AN HOUR.
HAVE THEY FOUND THE KEY YET?
MURMUR
THE FIRST HALF IS ONE THING, BUT THE LEAD ROLES ACT APART FROM EACH OTHER IN THE SECOND HALF.
THERE'S NO WAY TO FAKE IT.
MURMUR
WHAT ABOUT THE FIGHT SCENE WITH ROMEO?
MURMUR
IT'S ABSOLUTELY IMPOSSIBLE.
...
WHAT DO WE DO IF THE KEY...
...ISN'T FOUND BEFORE THE TIME IS UP?
AFTER WE'VE COME THIS FAR.
AND WHEN MAKOTO'S WHOLE FUTURE...
...RIDES ON THIS PLAY.
BAM

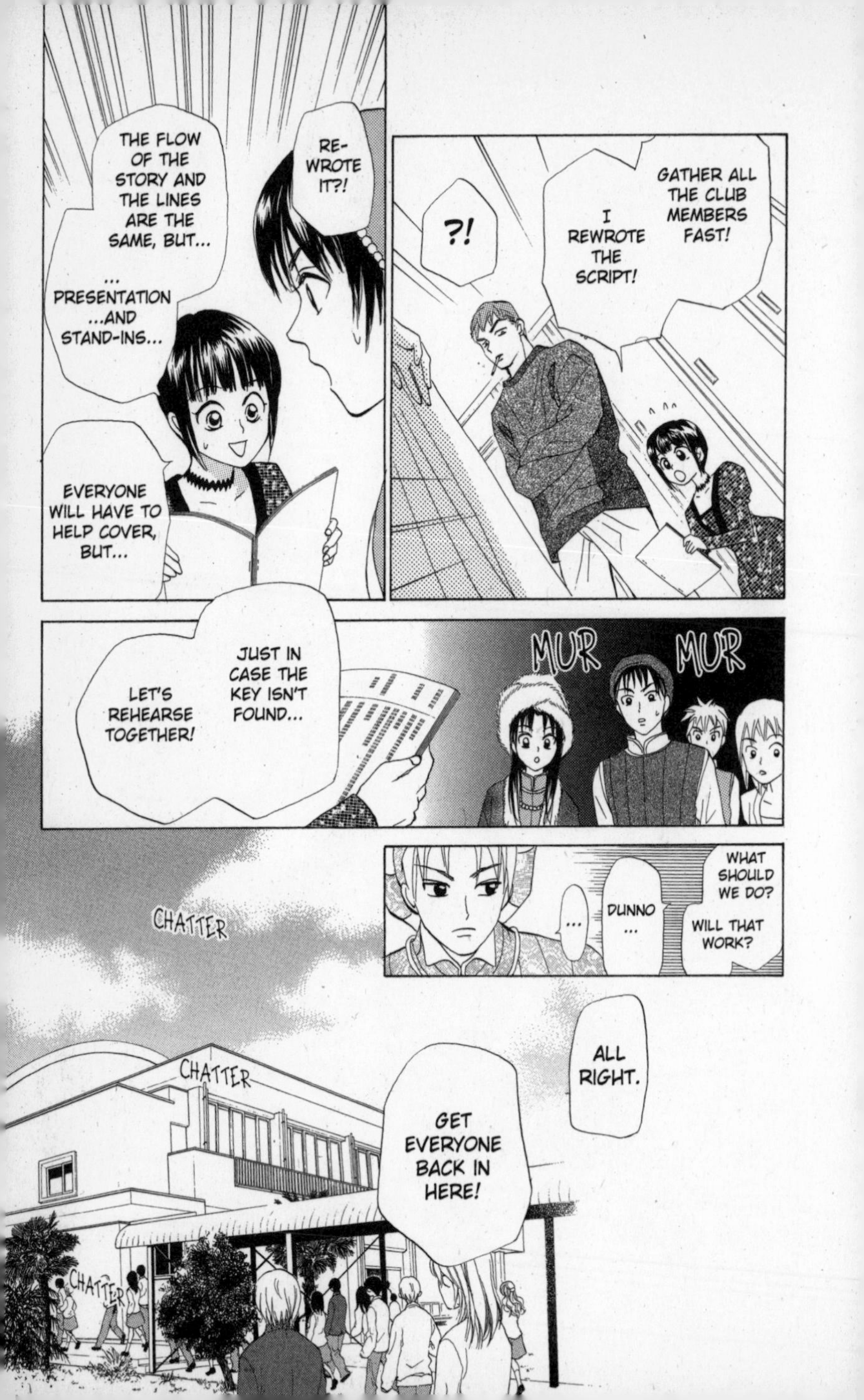
GATHER ALL THE CLUB MEMBERS FAST!
I REWROTE THE SCRIPT!
?!
RE-WROTE IT?!
THE FLOW OF THE STORY AND THE LINES ARE THE SAME, BUT...
... PRESENTATION ...AND STAND-INS...
EVERYONE WILL HAVE TO HELP COVER, BUT...
MUR MUR
JUST IN CASE THE KEY ISN'T FOUND...
LET'S REHEARSE TOGETHER!
WHAT SHOULD WE DO?
WILL THAT WORK?
DUNNO ...
...
CHATTER
ALL RIGHT.
GET EVERYONE BACK IN HERE!
CHATTER
CHATTER

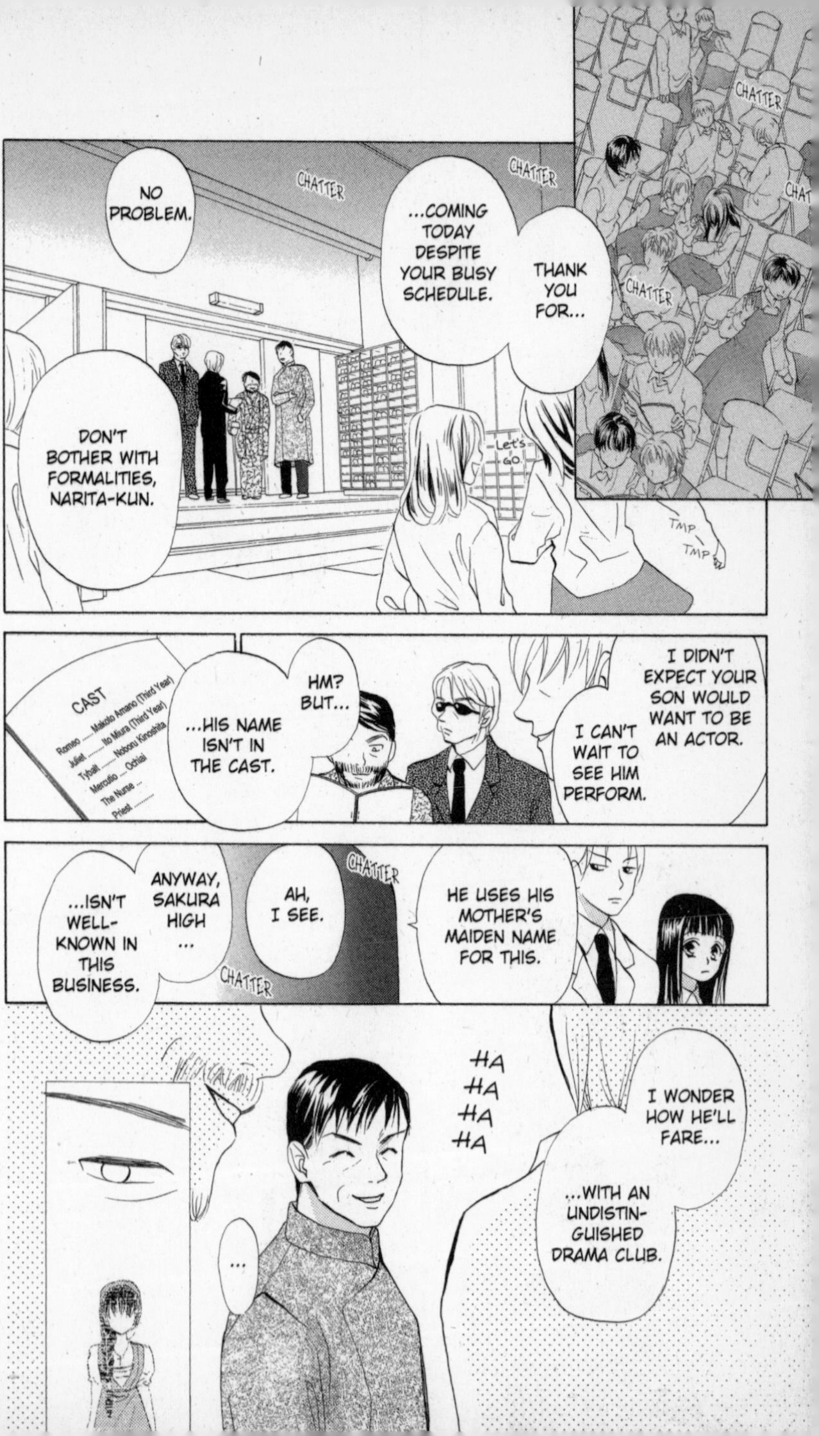
CHATTER
CHAT
CHATTER
THANK YOU FOR...
...COMING TODAY DESPITE YOUR BUSY SCHEDULE.
CHATTER
CHATTER
NO PROBLEM.
DON'T BOTHER WITH FORMALITIES, NARITA-KUN.
Let's go.
TMP
TMP
I DIDN'T EXPECT YOUR SON WOULD WANT TO BE AN ACTOR.
I CAN'T WAIT TO SEE HIM PERFORM.
HM? BUT...
...HIS NAME ISN'T IN THE CAST.
CAST
Romeo ...... Makoto Amano (Third Year)
Juliet ...... Ito Miura (Third Year)
Tybalt ...... Noboru Kinoshita
Mercutio ... Ochiai
The Nurse ...
Priest ....
HE USES HIS MOTHER'S MAIDEN NAME FOR THIS.
AH, I SEE.
CHATTER
ANYWAY, SAKURA HIGH ...
...ISN'T WELL-KNOWN IN THIS BUSINESS.
CHATTER
I WONDER HOW HE'LL FARE...
...WITH AN UNDISTIN-GUISHED DRAMA CLUB.
HA HA HA HA
...

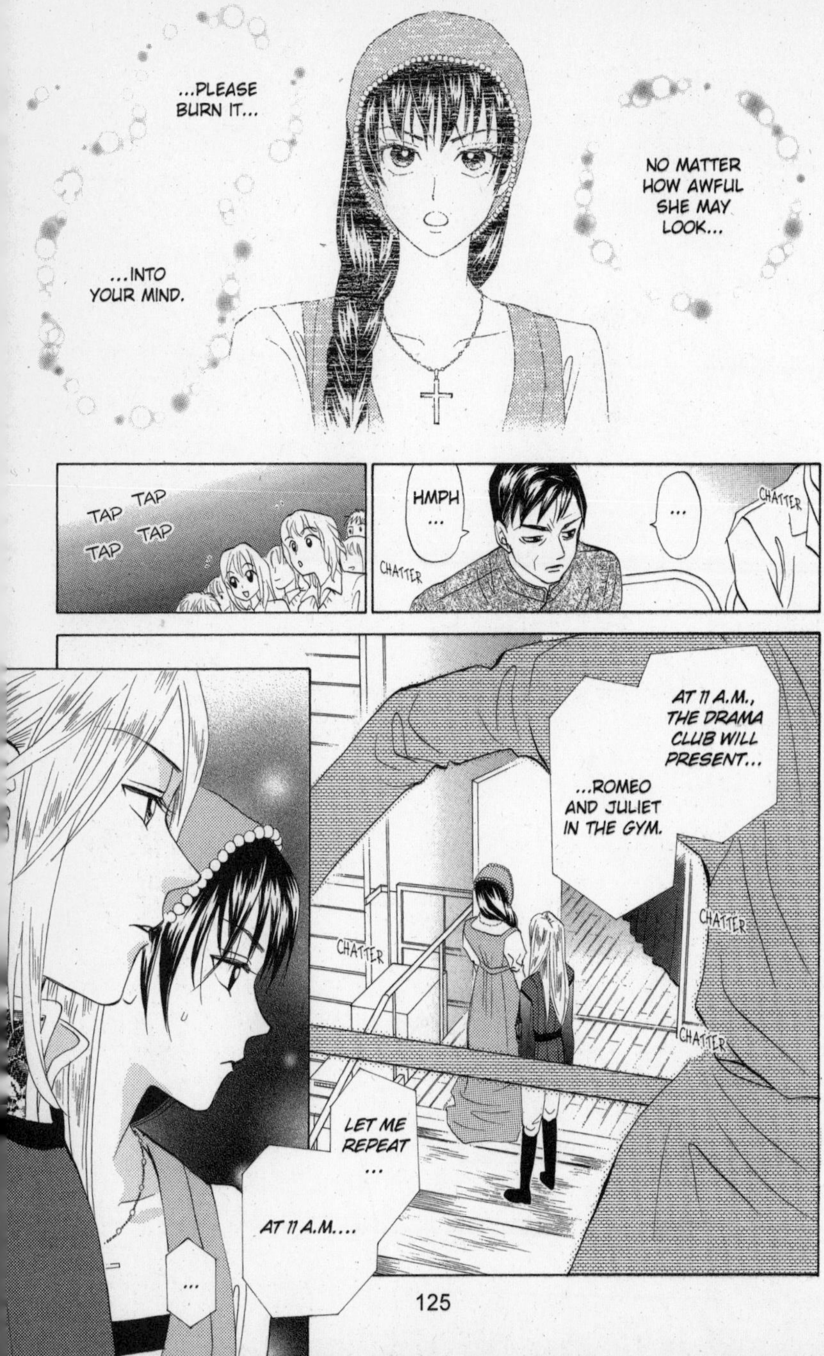
NO MATTER HOW AWFUL SHE MAY LOOK...
...PLEASE BURN IT...
...INTO YOUR MIND.
CHATTER
...
HMPH ...
CHATTER
TAP TAP
TAP TAP
AT 11 A.M., THE DRAMA CLUB WILL PRESENT...
...ROMEO AND JULIET IN THE GYM.
CHATTER
CHATTER
CHATTER
LET ME REPEAT ...
AT 11 A.M....
...

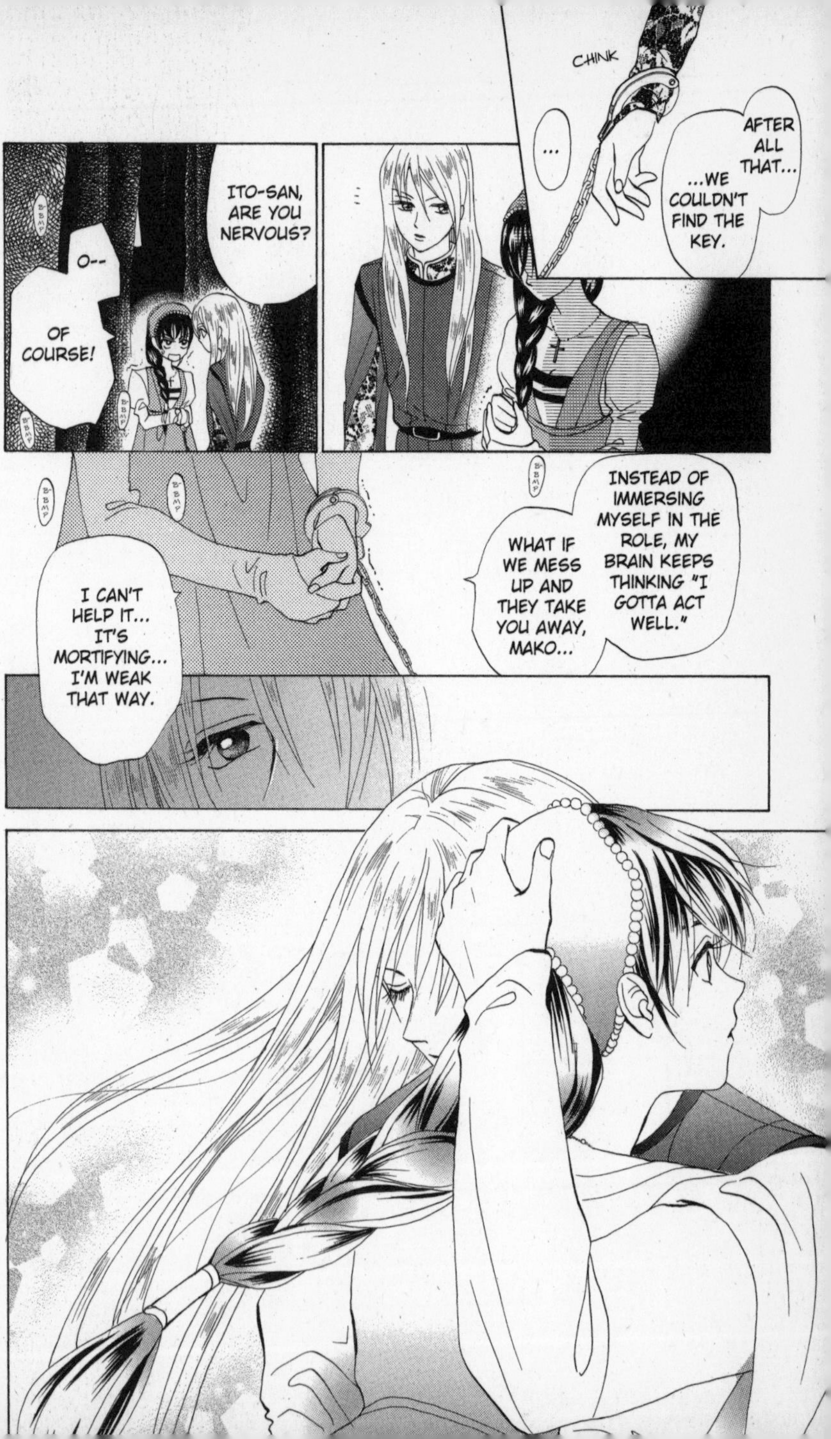
CHINK
AFTER ALL THAT...
...WE COULDN'T FIND THE KEY.
...
ITO-SAN, ARE YOU NERVOUS?
O--
OF COURSE!
B-BMP
B-BMP
B-BMP
B-BMP
B-BMP
B-BMP
INSTEAD OF IMMERSING MYSELF IN THE ROLE, MY BRAIN KEEPS THINKING "I GOTTA ACT WELL."
WHAT IF WE MESS UP AND THEY TAKE YOU AWAY, MAKO...
I CAN'T HELP IT... IT'S MORTIFYING... I'M WEAK THAT WAY.

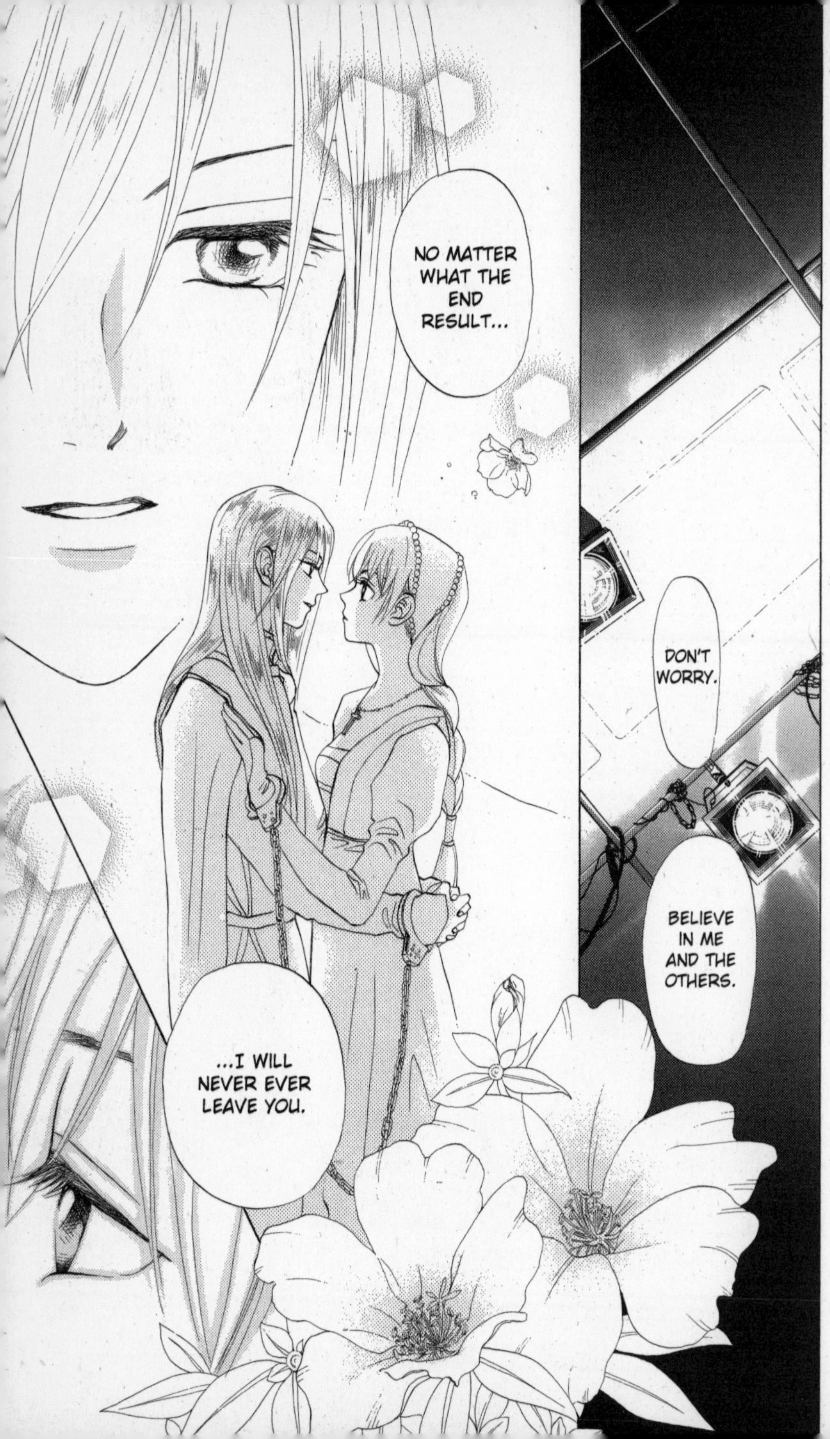
DON'T WORRY.
BELIEVE IN ME AND THE OTHERS.
NO MATTER WHAT THE END RESULT...
...I WILL NEVER EVER LEAVE YOU.

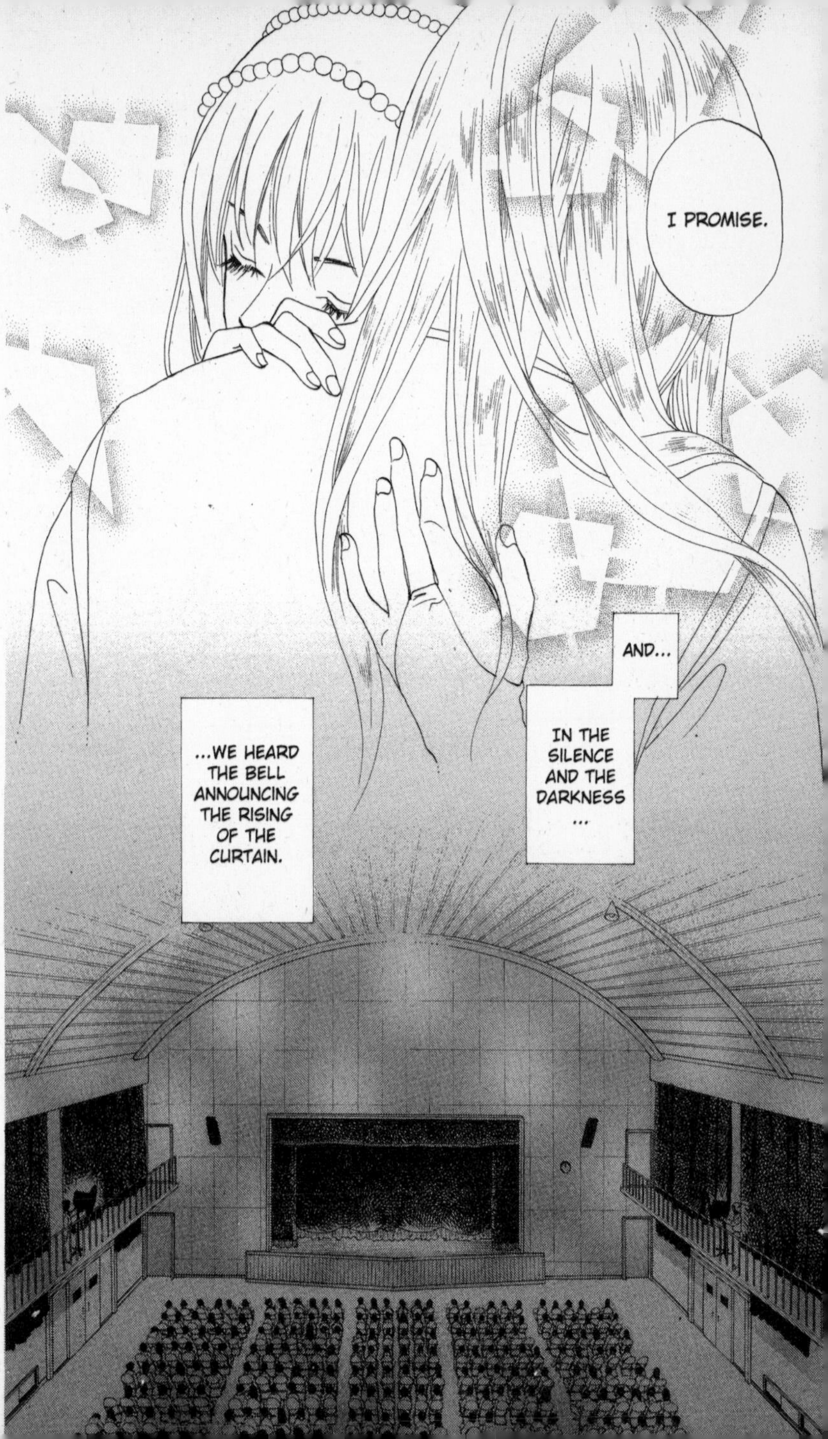
I PROMISE.
AND...
IN THE SILENCE AND THE DARKNESS ...
...WE HEARD THE BELL ANNOUNCING THE RISING OF THE CURTAIN.

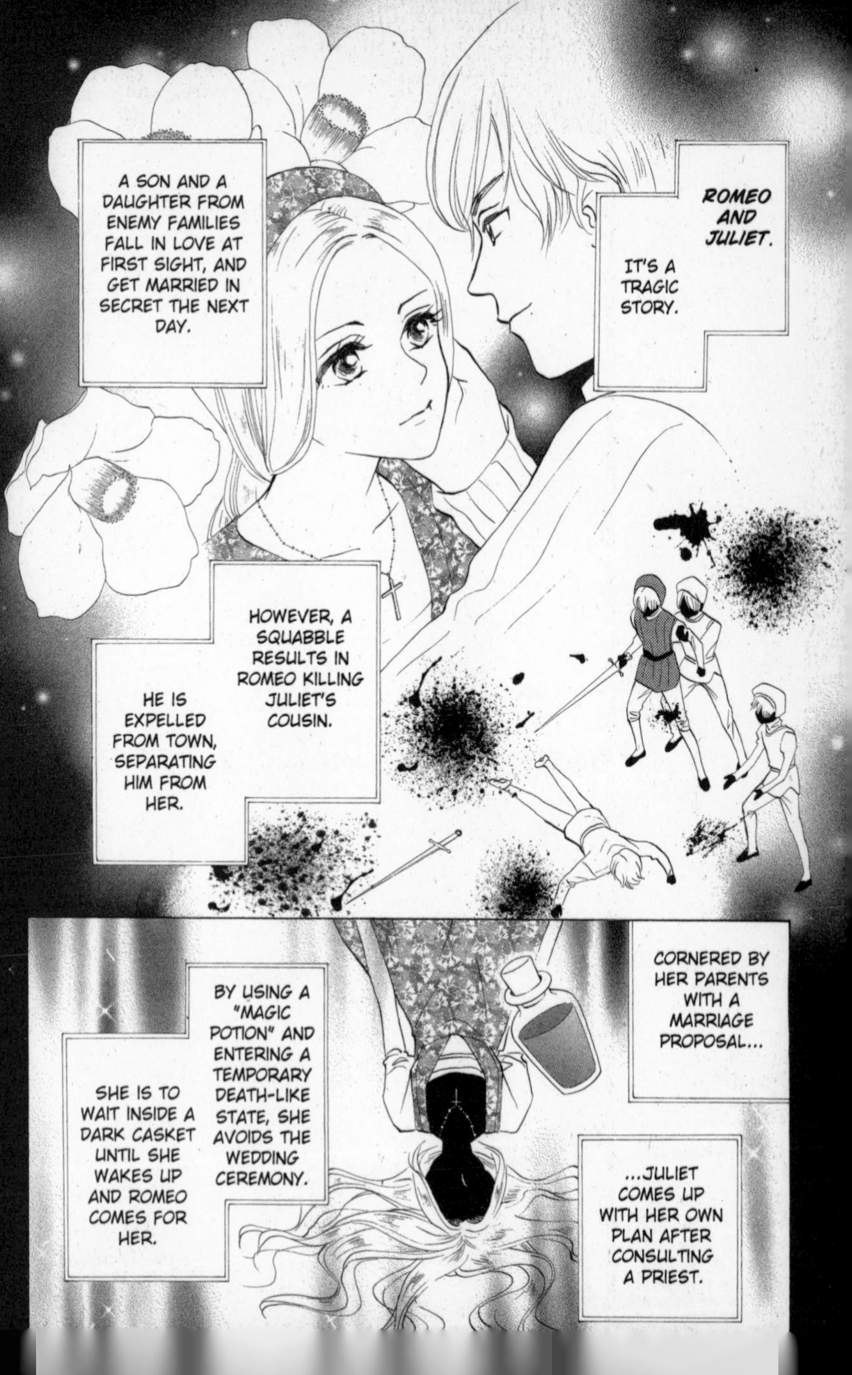
ROMEO AND JULIET.
IT'S A TRAGIC STORY.
A SON AND A DAUGHTER FROM ENEMY FAMILIES FALL IN LOVE AT FIRST SIGHT, AND GET MARRIED IN SECRET THE NEXT DAY.
HOWEVER, A SQUABBLE RESULTS IN ROMEO KILLING JULIET'S COUSIN.
HE IS EXPELLED FROM TOWN, SEPARATING HIM FROM HER.
CORNERED BY HER PARENTS WITH A MARRIAGE PROPOSAL...
...JULIET COMES UP WITH HER OWN PLAN AFTER CONSULTING A PRIEST.
BY USING A "MAGIC POTION" AND ENTERING A TEMPORARY DEATH-LIKE STATE, SHE AVOIDS THE WEDDING CEREMONY.
SHE IS TO WAIT INSIDE A DARK CASKET UNTIL SHE WAKES UP AND ROMEO COMES FOR HER.

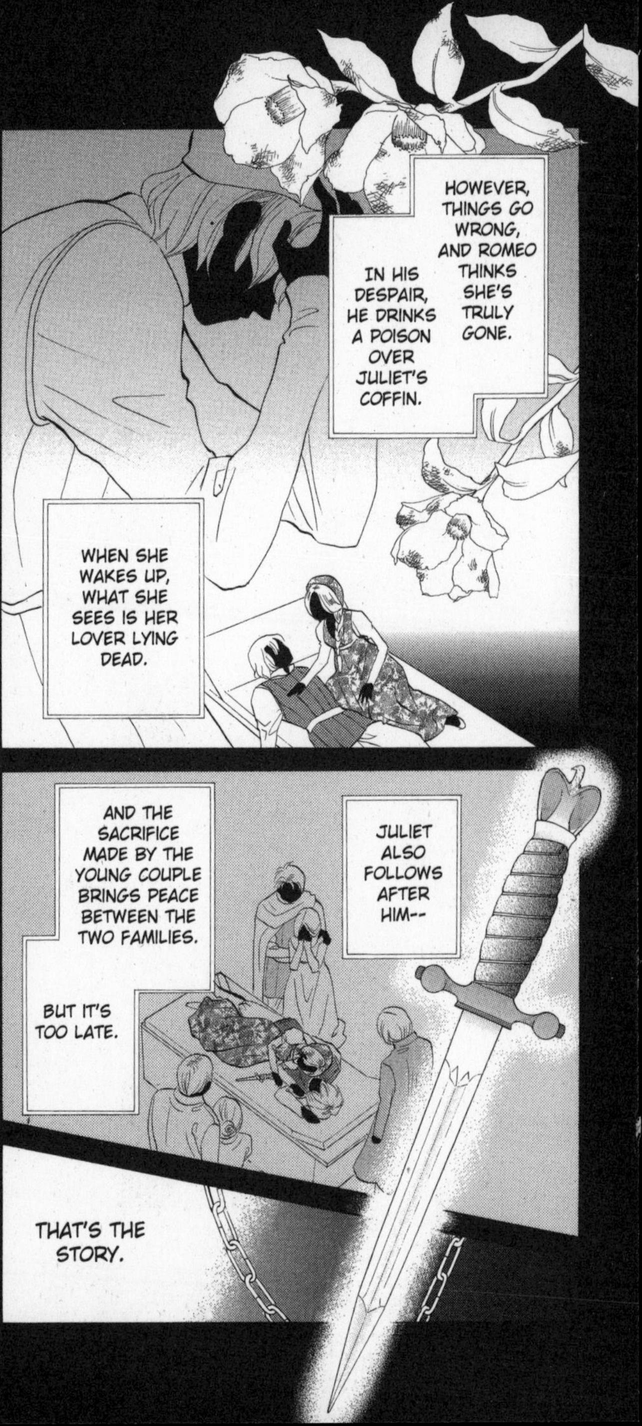
HOWEVER, THINGS GO WRONG, AND ROMEO THINKS SHE'S TRULY GONE.
IN HIS DESPAIR, HE DRINKS A POISON OVER JULIET'S COFFIN.
WHEN SHE WAKES UP, WHAT SHE SEES IS HER LOVER LYING DEAD.
JULIET ALSO FOLLOWS AFTER HIM--
AND THE SACRIFICE MADE BY THE YOUNG COUPLE BRINGS PEACE BETWEEN THE TWO FAMILIES.
BUT IT'S TOO LATE.
THAT'S THE STORY.

But somehow she managed to ignore him. I guess he thought it was boring, because he eventually stopped coming. Apparently, if you interact without thinking, he'd play tricks on you. Anyhow, my mom no longer experiences the paralyzing feeling, but (As expected) she's still exceptionally sensitive.

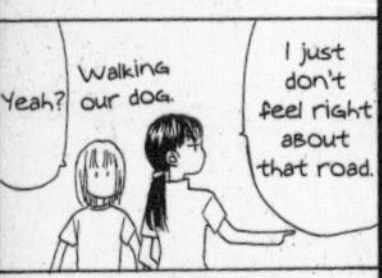
I just don't feel right about that road.
Walking our dog.
Yeah?

↓ Some Days Later ↓

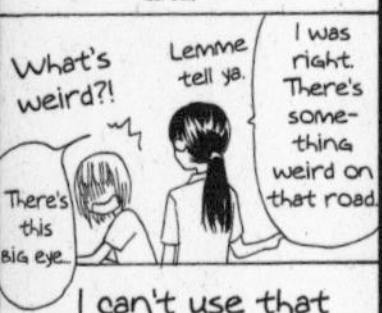
I was right. There's some-thing weird on that road.
Lemme tell ya.
What's weird?!
There's this big eye.

I can't use that road ever again. (SOB)

And scary story No. 2 is my Sis's!

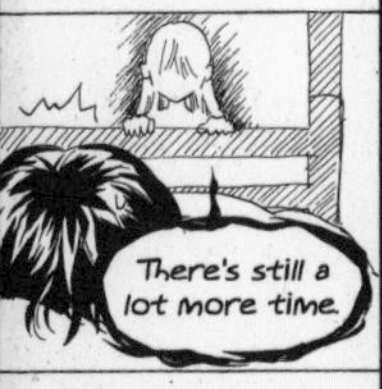
There's still a lot more time.

That's what a woman said who appeared in the gap in the bunk bed placed right next to the wall. What? You think this one's the scariest story??

It happened in our old office ♡

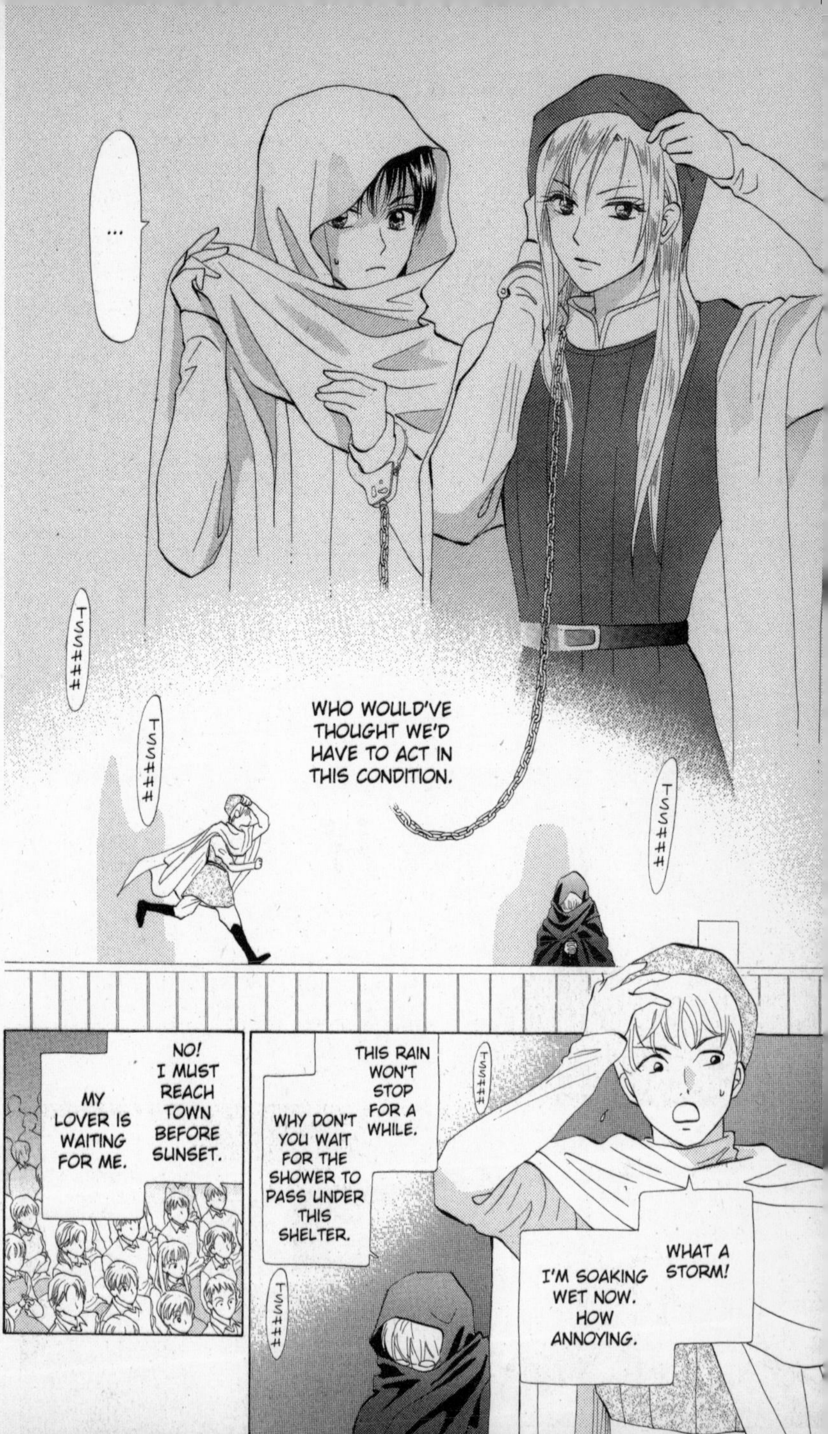
...
TSSHHH
TSSHHH
WHO WOULD'VE THOUGHT WE'D HAVE TO ACT IN THIS CONDITION.
TSSHHH
TSSHHH
WHAT A STORM!
I'M SOAKING WET NOW. HOW ANNOYING.
THIS RAIN WON'T STOP FOR A WHILE.
WHY DON'T YOU WAIT FOR THE SHOWER TO PASS UNDER THIS SHELTER.
TSSHHH
NO! I MUST REACH TOWN BEFORE SUNSET.
MY LOVER IS WAITING FOR ME.

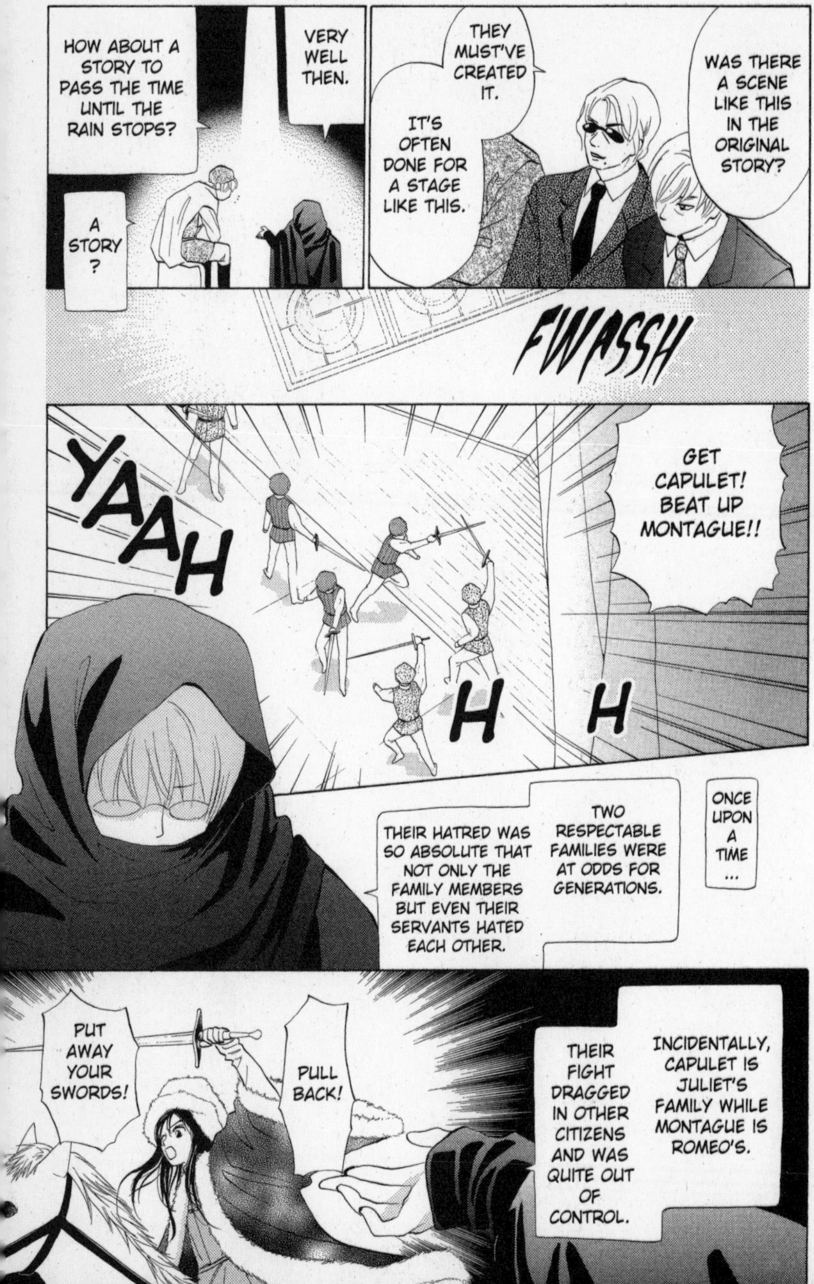
WAS THERE A SCENE LIKE THIS IN THE ORIGINAL STORY?
THEY MUST'VE CREATED IT.
IT'S OFTEN DONE FOR A STAGE LIKE THIS.
VERY WELL THEN.
HOW ABOUT A STORY TO PASS THE TIME UNTIL THE RAIN STOPS?
A STORY?
FWASSH
GET CAPULET! BEAT UP MONTAGUE!!
YAAH H H
ONCE UPON A TIME ...
TWO RESPECTABLE FAMILIES WERE AT ODDS FOR GENERATIONS.
THEIR HATRED WAS SO ABSOLUTE THAT NOT ONLY THE FAMILY MEMBERS BUT EVEN THEIR SERVANTS HATED EACH OTHER.
INCIDENTALLY, CAPULET IS JULIET'S FAMILY WHILE MONTAGUE IS ROMEO'S.
THEIR FIGHT DRAGGED IN OTHER CITIZENS AND WAS QUITE OUT OF CONTROL.
PULL BACK!
PUT AWAY YOUR SWORDS!

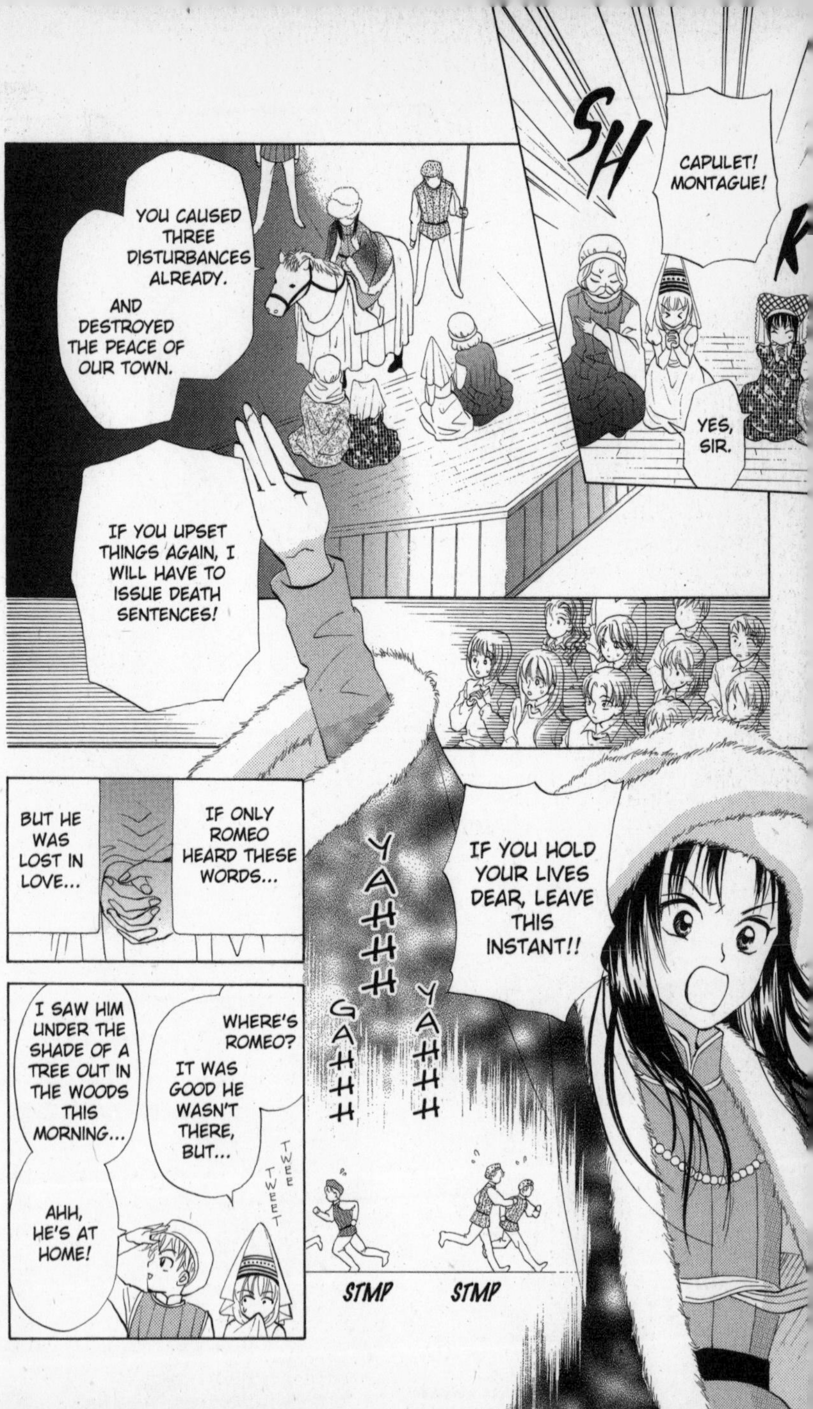
SH
K
CAPULET! MONTAGUE!
YES, SIR.
YOU CAUSED THREE DISTURBANCES ALREADY.
AND DESTROYED THE PEACE OF OUR TOWN.
IF YOU UPSET THINGS AGAIN, I WILL HAVE TO ISSUE DEATH SENTENCES!
IF YOU HOLD YOUR LIVES DEAR, LEAVE THIS INSTANT!!
YAHHHH
GAHHHH
YAHHHH
STMP
STMP
IF ONLY ROMEO HEARD THESE WORDS...
BUT HE WAS LOST IN LOVE...
WHERE'S ROMEO?
IT WAS GOOD HE WASN'T THERE, BUT...
I SAW HIM UNDER THE SHADE OF A TREE OUT IN THE WOODS THIS MORNING...
TWEE
TWEET
AHH, HE'S AT HOME!

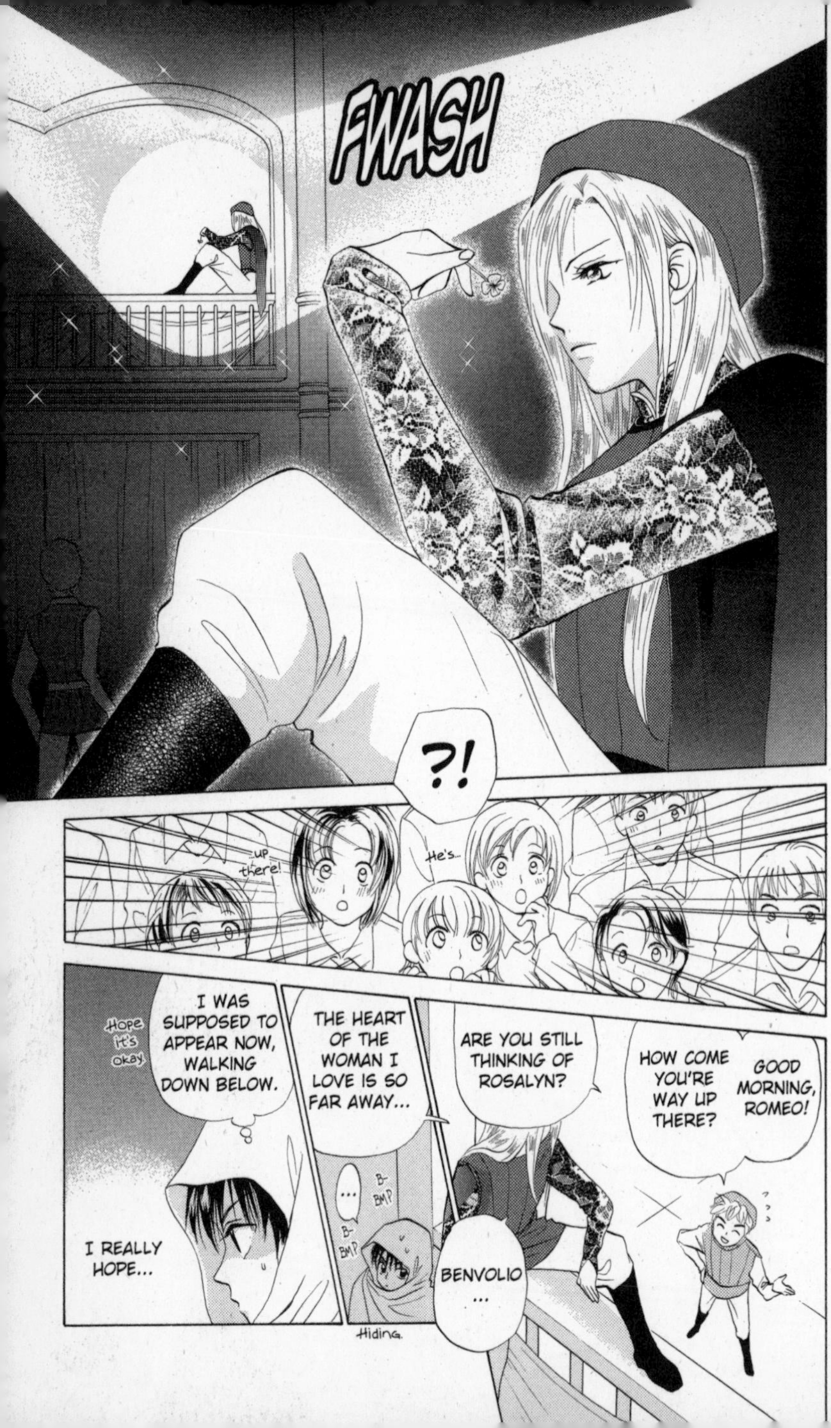
FWASH
?!
He's...
...up there!
GOOD MORNING, ROMEO!
HOW COME YOU'RE WAY UP THERE?
ARE YOU STILL THINKING OF ROSALYN?
THE HEART OF THE WOMAN I LOVE IS SO FAR AWAY...
BENVOLIO...
...
B-BMP
B-BMP
Hiding.
I WAS SUPPOSED TO APPEAR NOW, WALKING DOWN BELOW.
Hope it's okay.
I REALLY HOPE...

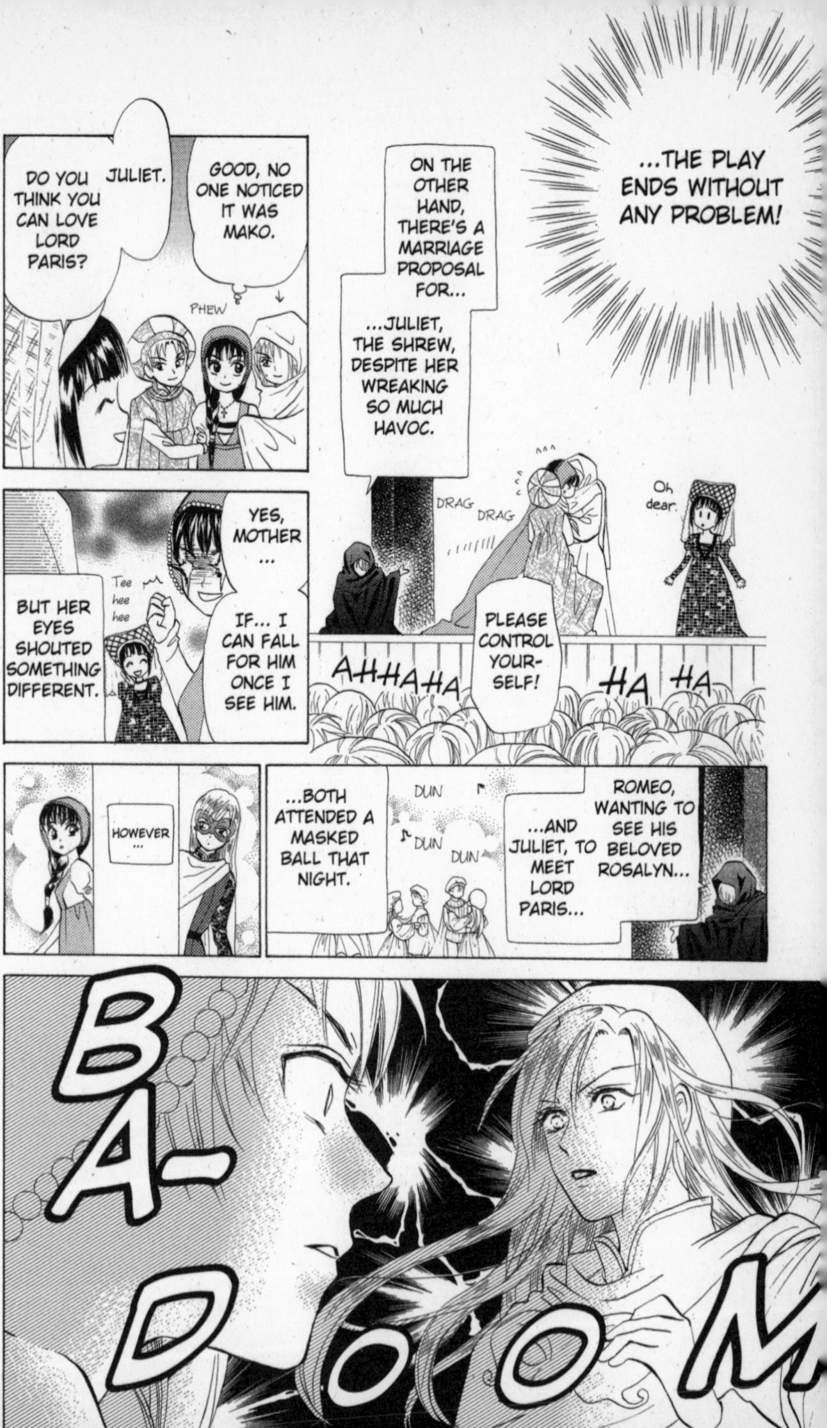
...THE PLAY ENDS WITHOUT ANY PROBLEM!
ON THE OTHER HAND, THERE'S A MARRIAGE PROPOSAL FOR...
...JULIET, THE SHREW, DESPITE HER WREAKING SO MUCH HAVOC.
DRAG DRAG
Oh dear.
PLEASE CONTROL YOUR-SELF!
AHHAHA
HA HA
JULIET.
DO YOU THINK YOU CAN LOVE LORD PARIS?
GOOD, NO ONE NOTICED IT WAS MAKO.
PHEW
YES, MOTHER ...
IF... I CAN FALL FOR HIM ONCE I SEE HIM.
Tee hee hee
BUT HER EYES SHOUTED SOMETHING DIFFERENT.
ROMEO, WANTING TO SEE HIS BELOVED ROSALYN...
...AND JULIET, TO MEET LORD PARIS...
DUN DUN DUN
...BOTH ATTENDED A MASKED BALL THAT NIGHT.
HOWEVER ...
BA-DOOOM

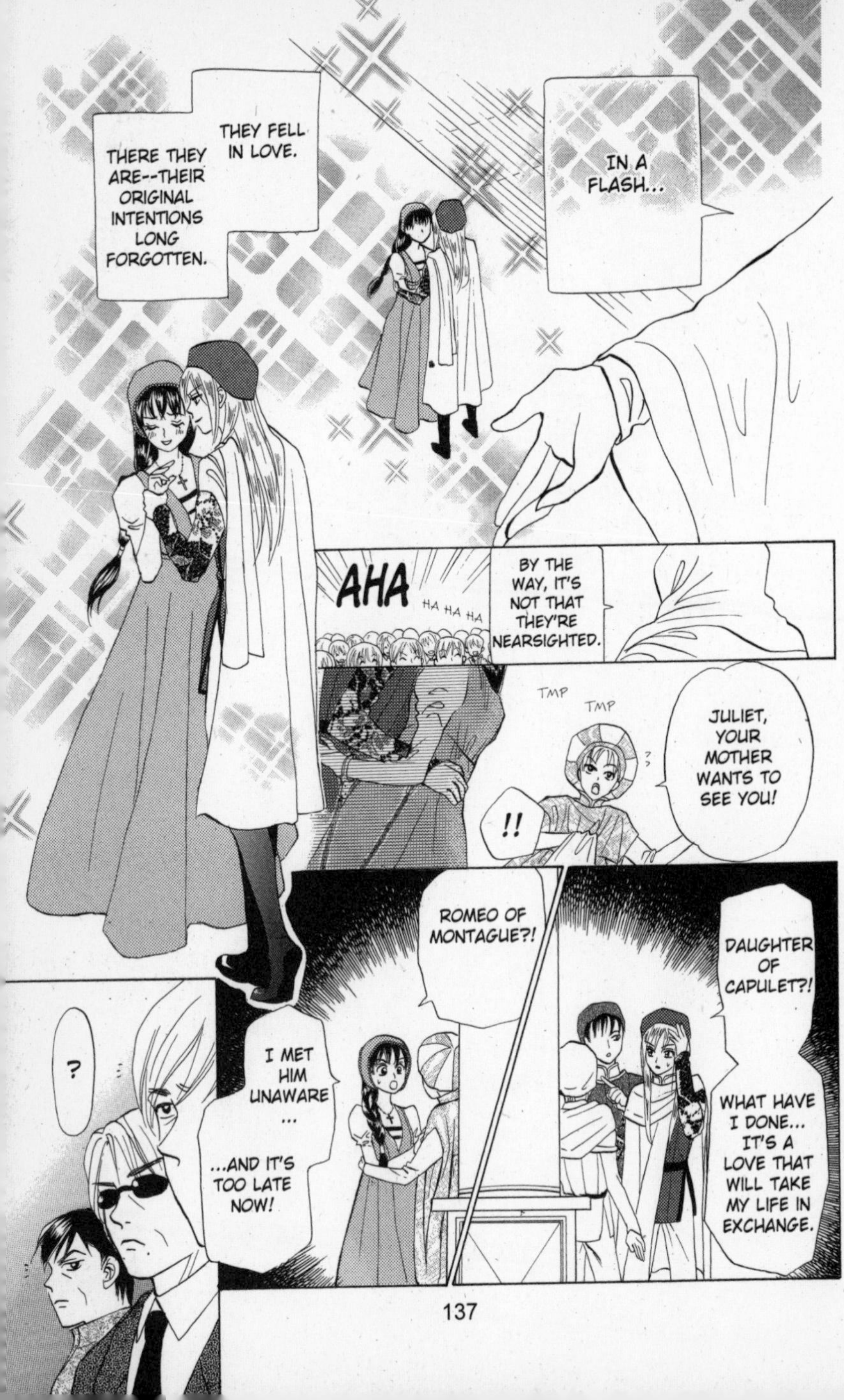
IN A FLASH...
THEY FELL IN LOVE.
THERE THEY ARE--THEIR ORIGINAL INTENTIONS LONG FORGOTTEN.
BY THE WAY, IT'S NOT THAT THEY'RE NEARSIGHTED.
AHA
HA HA HA
TMP
TMP
JULIET, YOUR MOTHER WANTS TO SEE YOU!
!!
DAUGHTER OF CAPULET?!
WHAT HAVE I DONE... IT'S A LOVE THAT WILL TAKE MY LIFE IN EXCHANGE.
ROMEO OF MONTAGUE?!
I MET HIM UNAWARE ...
...AND IT'S TOO LATE NOW!
?

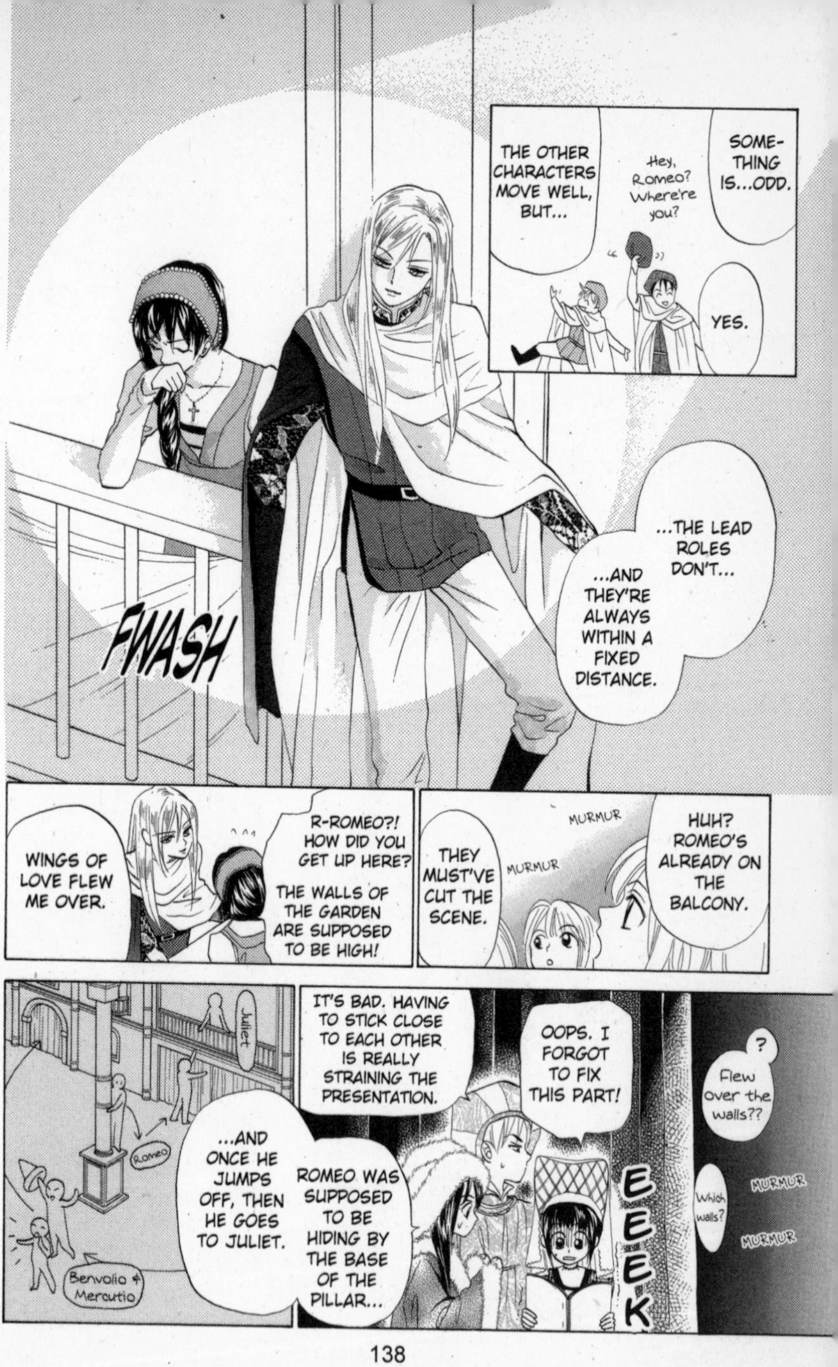
SOMETHING IS...ODD.
Hey, Romeo? Where're you?
THE OTHER CHARACTERS MOVE WELL, BUT...
YES.
...THE LEAD ROLES DON'T...
...AND THEY'RE ALWAYS WITHIN A FIXED DISTANCE.
FWASH
HUH? ROMEO'S ALREADY ON THE BALCONY.
MURMUR
MURMUR
THEY MUST'VE CUT THE SCENE.
R-ROMEO?! HOW DID YOU GET UP HERE?
THE WALLS OF THE GARDEN ARE SUPPOSED TO BE HIGH!
WINGS OF LOVE FLEW ME OVER.
?
Flew over the walls??
Which walls?
MURMUR
MURMUR
EEEK
OOPS. I FORGOT TO FIX THIS PART!
IT'S BAD. HAVING TO STICK CLOSE TO EACH OTHER IS REALLY STRAINING THE PRESENTATION.
ROMEO WAS SUPPOSED TO BE HIDING BY THE BASE OF THE PILLAR...
...AND ONCE HE JUMPS OFF, THEN HE GOES TO JULIET.
Juliet
Romeo
Benvolio & Mercutio

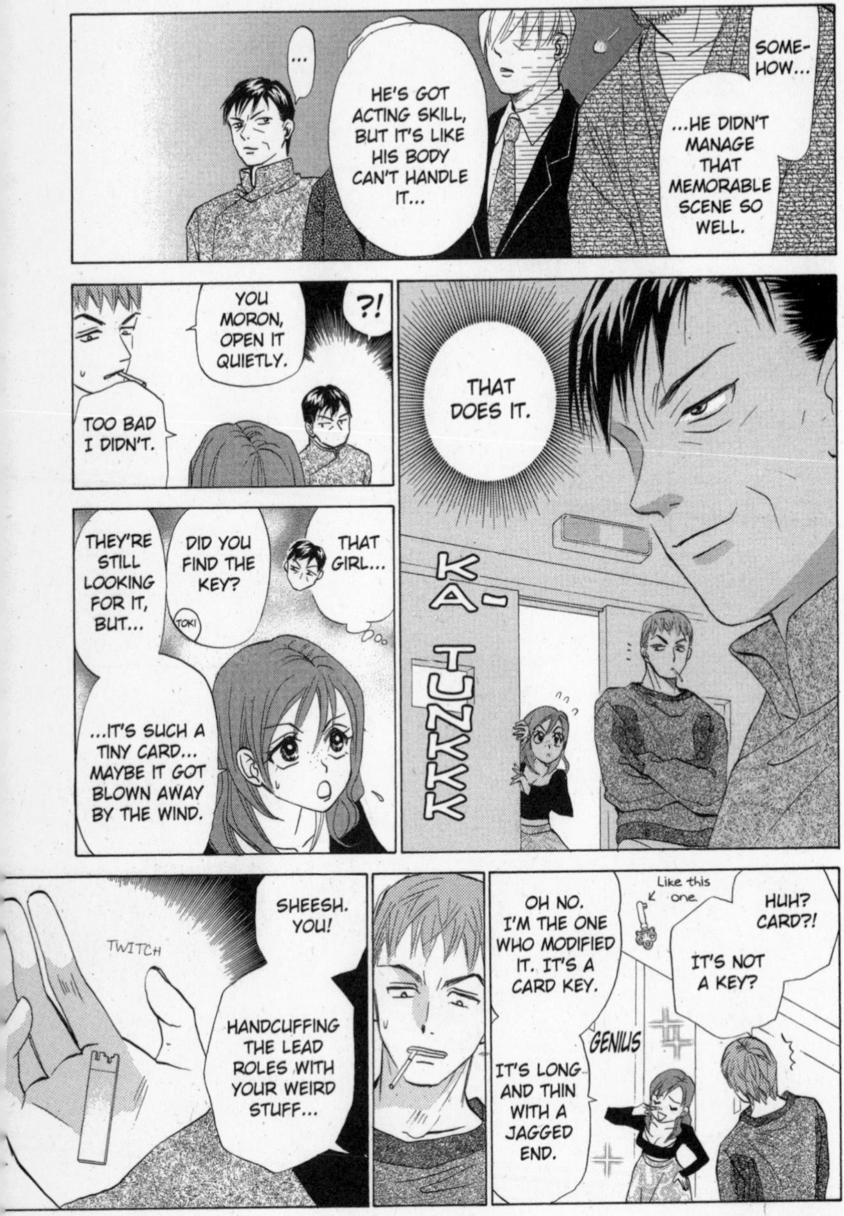
SOME-HOW...
...HE DIDN'T MANAGE THAT MEMORABLE SCENE SO WELL.
HE'S GOT ACTING SKILL, BUT IT'S LIKE HIS BODY CAN'T HANDLE IT...
...
THAT DOES IT.
KA-TUNKKK
?!
YOU MORON, OPEN IT QUIETLY.
TOO BAD I DIDN'T.
THAT GIRL...
DID YOU FIND THE KEY?
TOKI
THEY'RE STILL LOOKING FOR IT, BUT...
...IT'S SUCH A TINY CARD... MAYBE IT GOT BLOWN AWAY BY THE WIND.
HUH? CARD?!
IT'S NOT A KEY?
Like this one.
OH NO. I'M THE ONE WHO MODIFIED IT. IT'S A CARD KEY.
GENIUS
IT'S LONG AND THIN WITH A JAGGED END.
SHEESH. YOU!
HANDCUFFING THE LEAD ROLES WITH YOUR WEIRD STUFF...
TWITCH

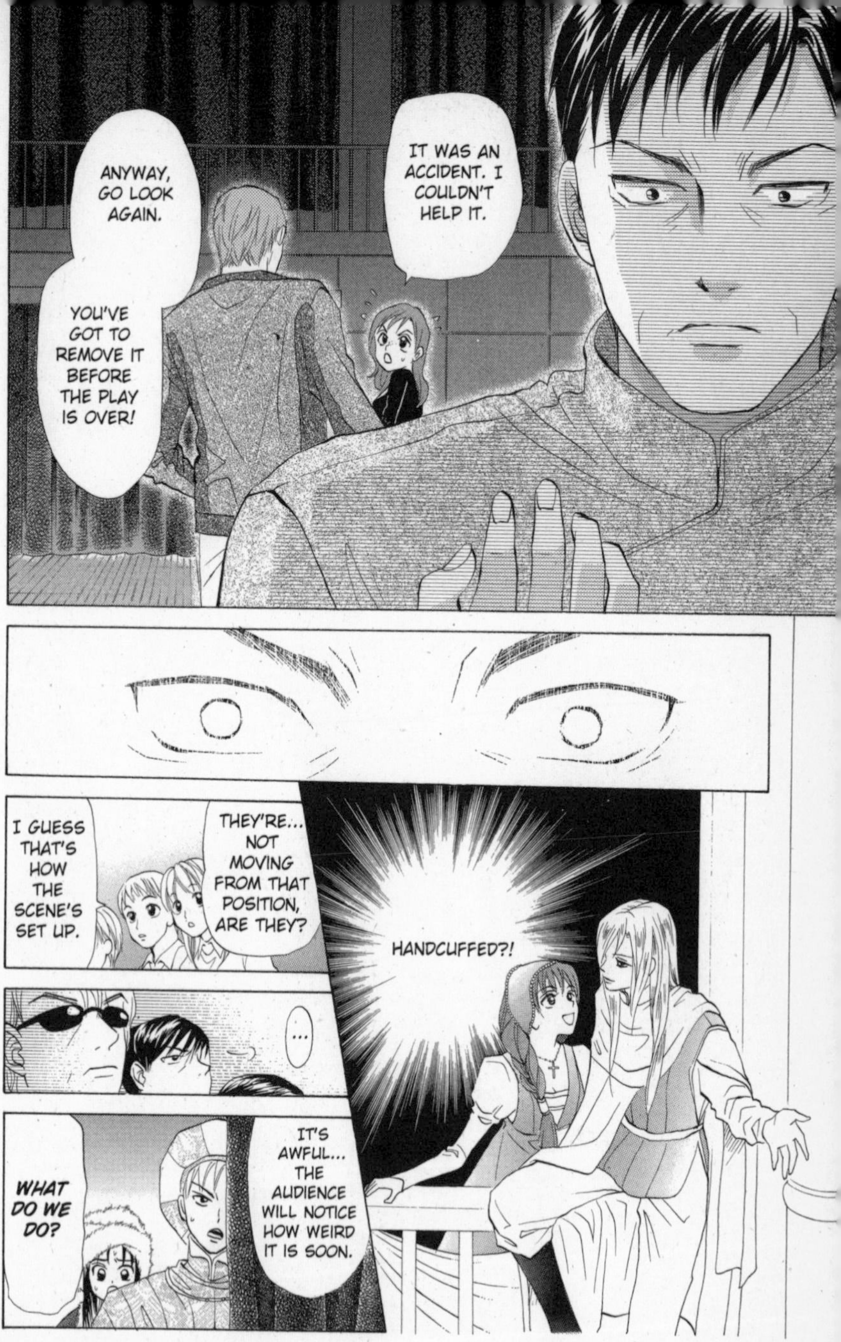
IT WAS AN ACCIDENT. I COULDN'T HELP IT.
ANYWAY, GO LOOK AGAIN.
YOU'VE GOT TO REMOVE IT BEFORE THE PLAY IS OVER!
HANDCUFFED?!
THEY'RE... NOT MOVING FROM THAT POSITION, ARE THEY?
I GUESS THAT'S HOW THE SCENE'S SET UP.
...
IT'S AWFUL... THE AUDIENCE WILL NOTICE HOW WEIRD IT IS SOON.
WHAT DO WE DO?

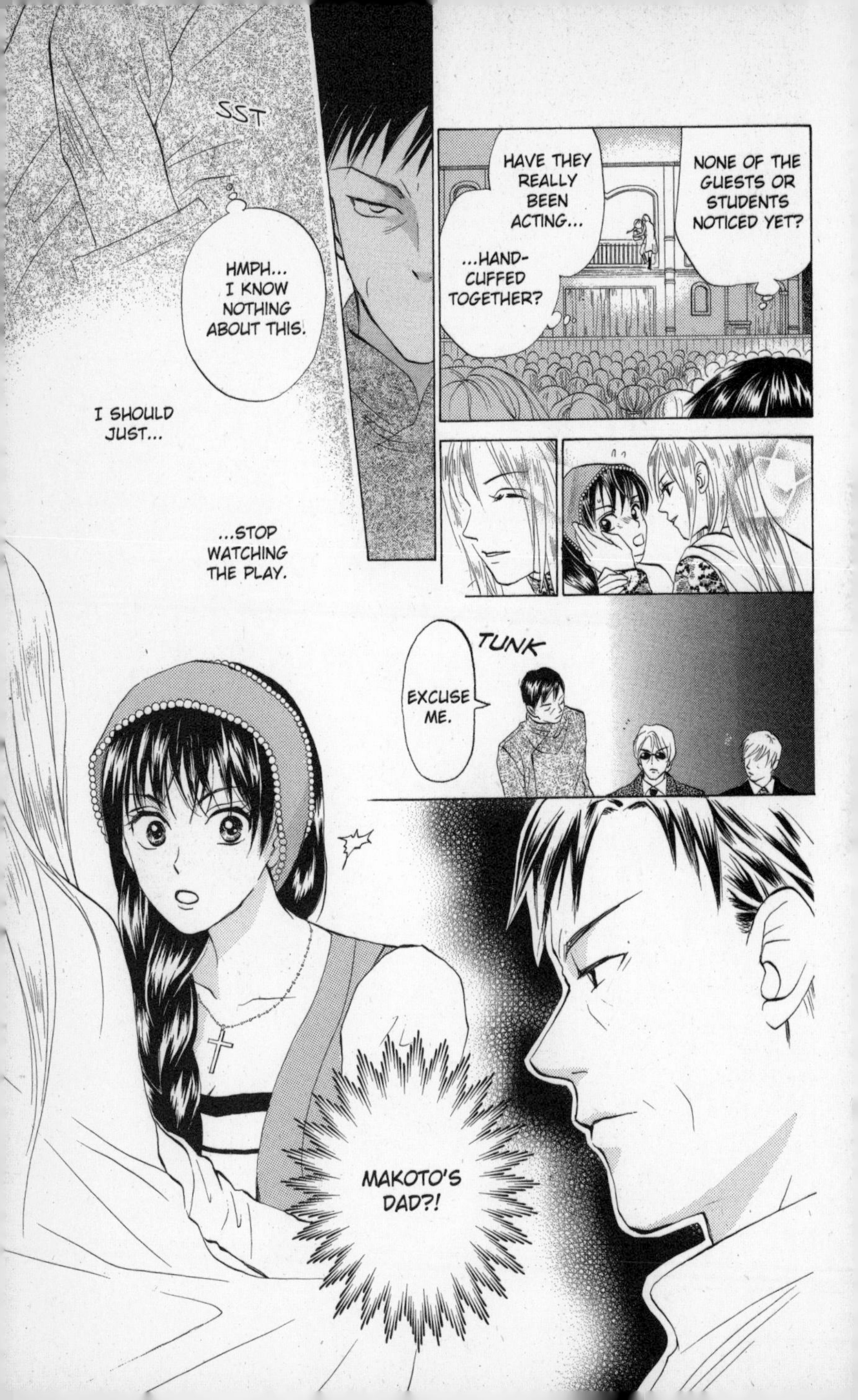
NONE OF THE GUESTS OR STUDENTS NOTICED YET?
HAVE THEY REALLY BEEN ACTING...
...HAND-CUFFED TOGETHER?
SST
HMPH... I KNOW NOTHING ABOUT THIS.
I SHOULD JUST...
...STOP WATCHING THE PLAY.
TUNK
EXCUSE ME.
MAKOTO'S DAD?!

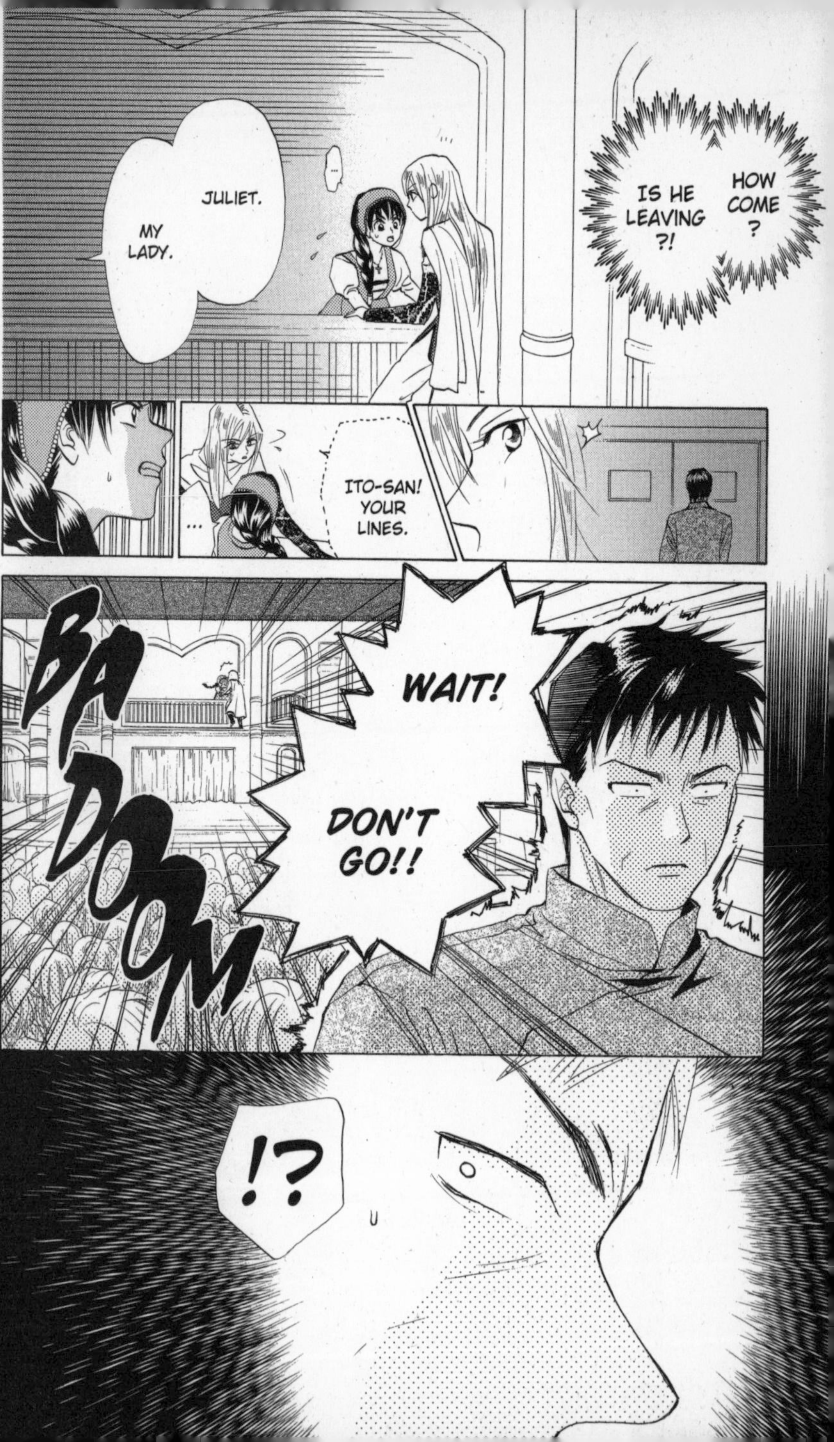

HOW COME?
IS HE LEAVING?!
...
JULIET.
MY LADY.
ITO-SAN! YOUR LINES.
...
WAIT!
DON'T GO!!
BA DOOM
!?

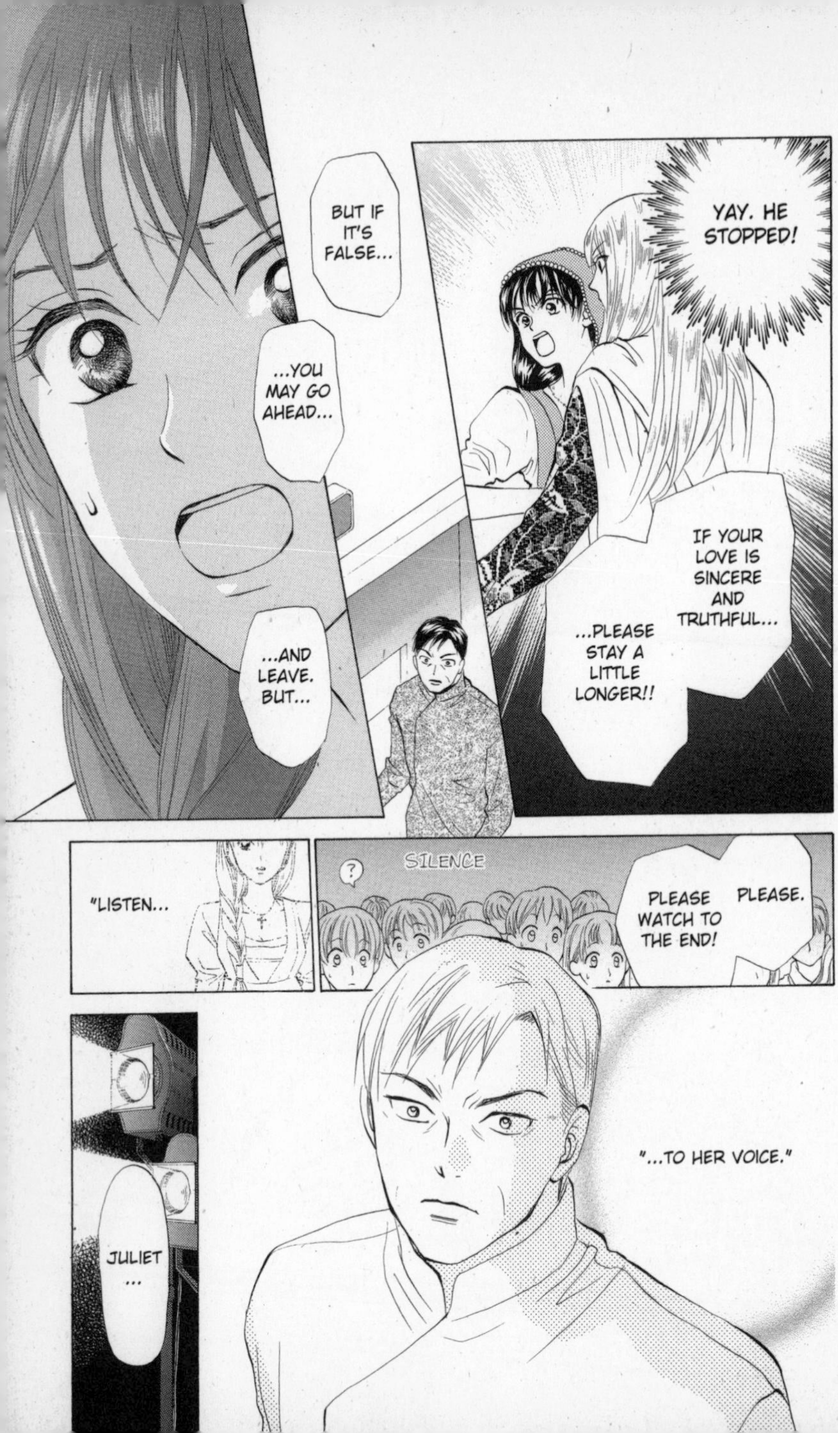
YAY. HE STOPPED!
IF YOUR LOVE IS SINCERE AND TRUTHFUL...
...PLEASE STAY A LITTLE LONGER!!
BUT IF IT'S FALSE...
...YOU MAY GO AHEAD...
...AND LEAVE. BUT...
PLEASE.
PLEASE WATCH TO THE END!
SILENCE
?
"LISTEN...
"...TO HER VOICE."
JULIET ...

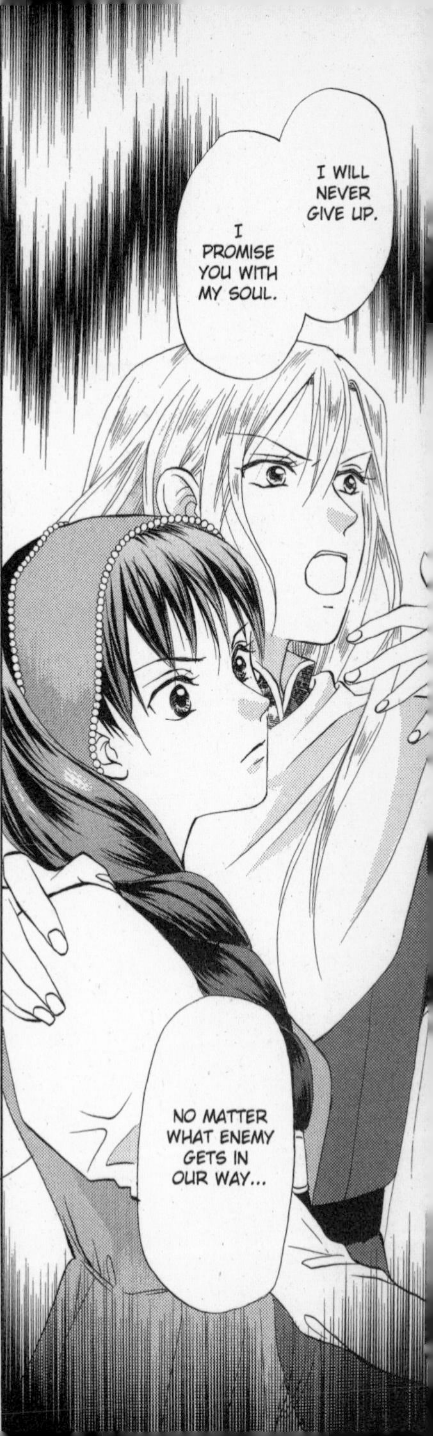
I WILL NEVER GIVE UP.
I PROMISE YOU WITH MY SOUL.
NO MATTER WHAT ENEMY GETS IN OUR WAY...

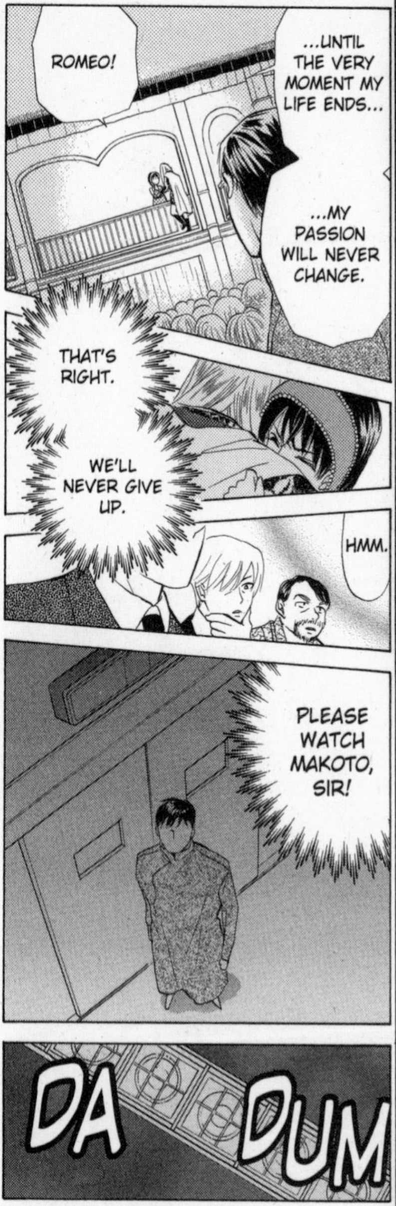
...UNTIL THE VERY MOMENT MY LIFE ENDS...
...MY PASSION WILL NEVER CHANGE.
ROMEO!
THAT'S RIGHT.
WE'LL NEVER GIVE UP.
HMM.
PLEASE WATCH MAKOTO, SIR!
DA
DUM

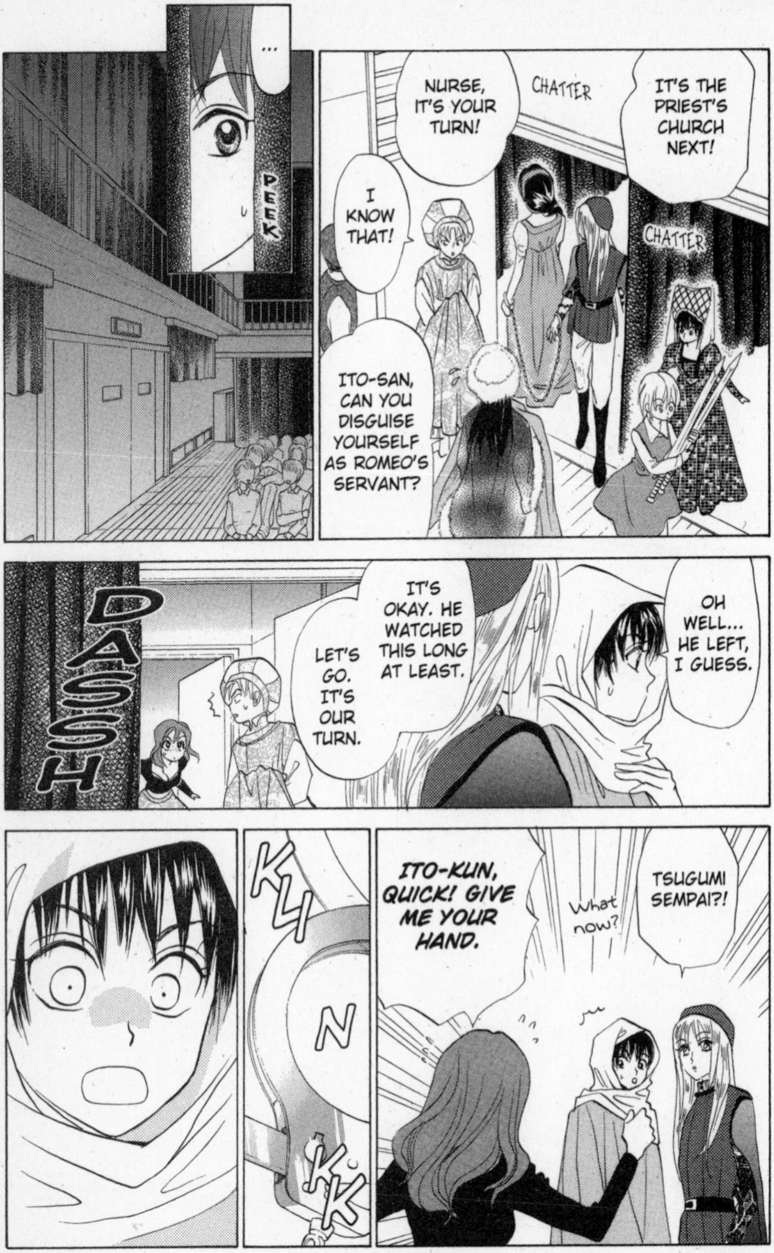
IT'S THE PRIEST'S CHURCH NEXT!
CHATTER
NURSE, IT'S YOUR TURN!
CHATTER
I KNOW THAT!
ITO-SAN, CAN YOU DISGUISE YOURSELF AS ROMEO'S SERVANT?
...
PEEK
OH WELL... HE LEFT, I GUESS.
IT'S OKAY. HE WATCHED THIS LONG AT LEAST.
LET'S GO. IT'S OUR TURN.
DASSH
TSUGUMI SEMPAI?!
What now?
ITO-KUN, QUICK! GIVE ME YOUR HAND.
KLI
N
KK

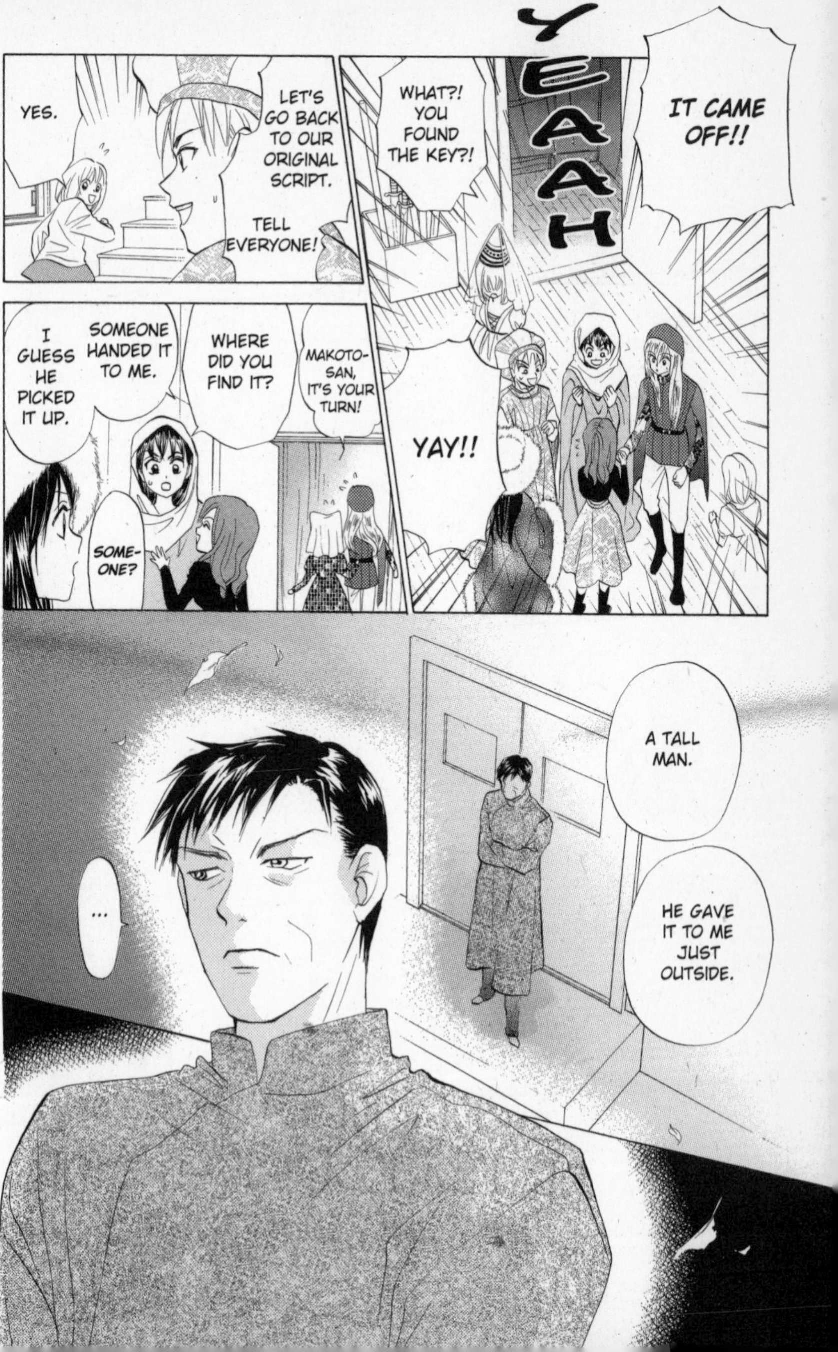
YEAH
IT CAME OFF!!
WHAT?! YOU FOUND THE KEY?!
YAY!!
LET'S GO BACK TO OUR ORIGINAL SCRIPT.
TELL EVERYONE!
YES.
MAKOTO-SAN, IT'S YOUR TURN!
WHERE DID YOU FIND IT?
SOMEONE HANDED IT TO ME.
I GUESS HE PICKED IT UP.
SOME-ONE?
A TALL MAN.
HE GAVE IT TO ME JUST OUTSIDE.
...

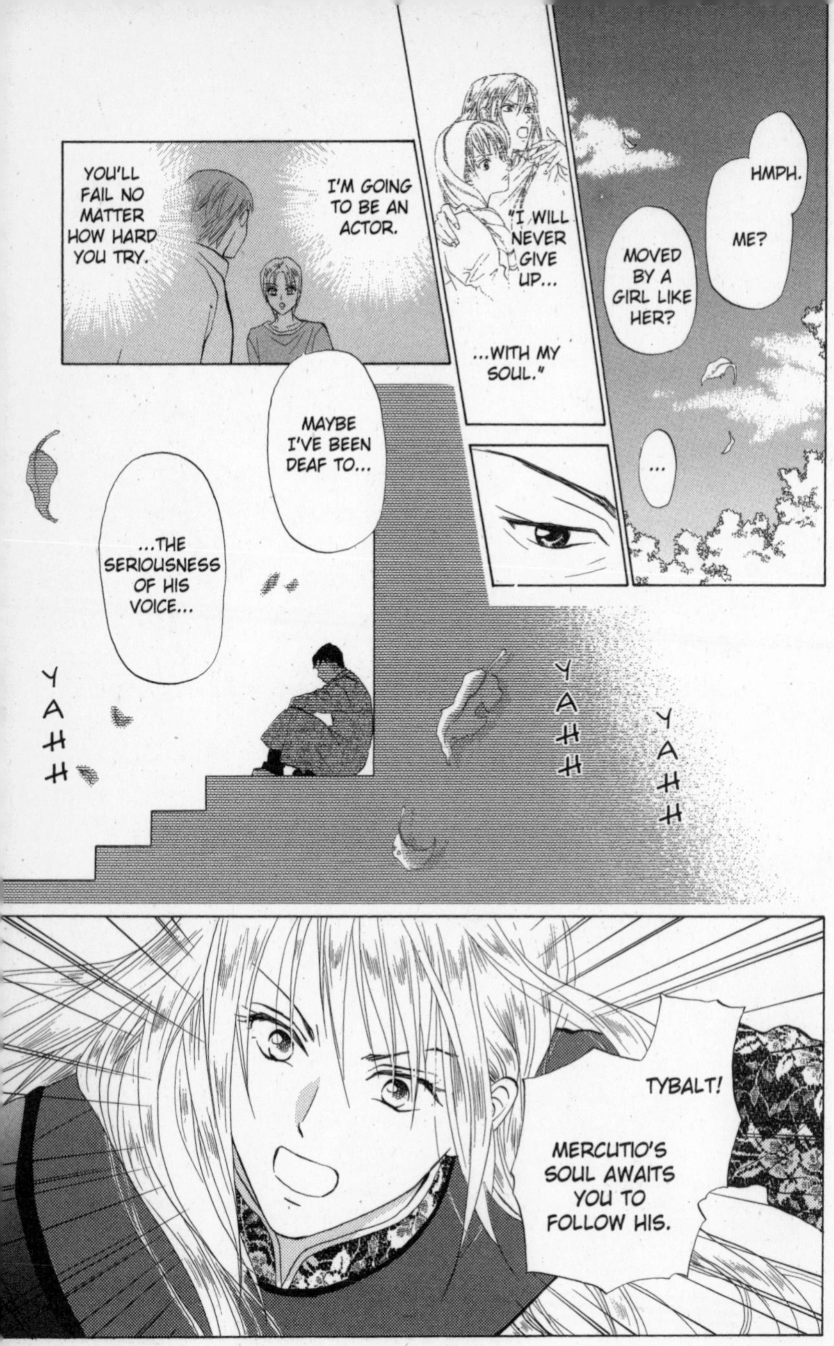
HMPH.
ME?
MOVED BY A GIRL LIKE HER?
"I WILL NEVER GIVE UP...
...WITH MY SOUL."
I'M GOING TO BE AN ACTOR.
YOU'LL FAIL NO MATTER HOW HARD YOU TRY.
...
MAYBE I'VE BEEN DEAF TO...
...THE SERIOUSNESS OF HIS VOICE...
YAHH
YAHH
YAHH
TYBALT!
MERCUTIO'S SOUL AWAITS YOU TO FOLLOW HIS.

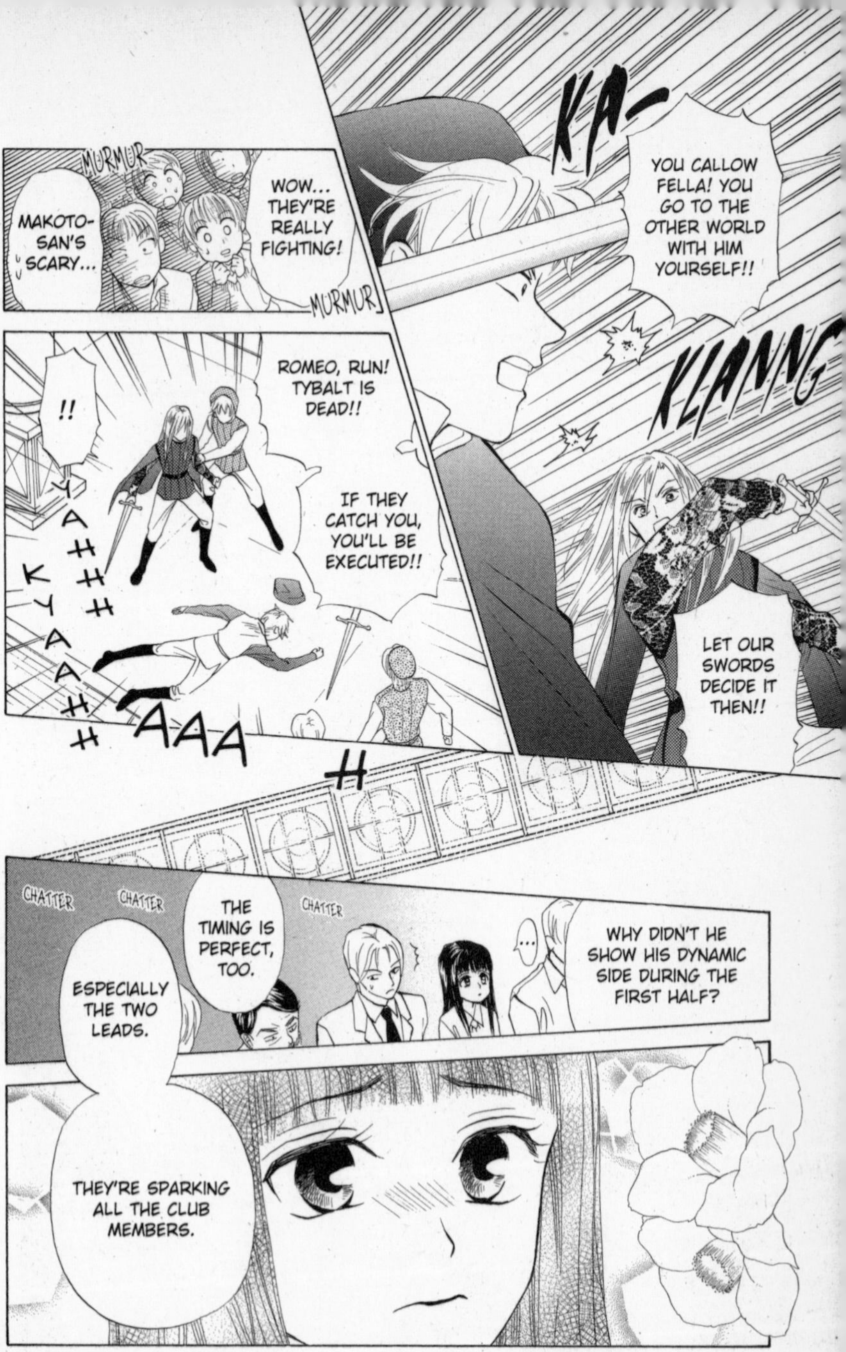
KA-
YOU CALLOW FELLA! YOU GO TO THE OTHER WORLD WITH HIM YOURSELF!!
KLANNG
LET OUR SWORDS DECIDE IT THEN!!
WOW... THEY'RE REALLY FIGHTING!
MURMUR
MAKOTO-SAN'S SCARY...
MURMUR
ROMEO, RUN! TYBALT IS DEAD!!
IF THEY CATCH YOU, YOU'LL BE EXECUTED!!
!!
YAHHHH
KYAAAHH
AAAH
WHY DIDN'T HE SHOW HIS DYNAMIC SIDE DURING THE FIRST HALF?
...
CHATTER
THE TIMING IS PERFECT, TOO.
CHATTER
ESPECIALLY THE TWO LEADS.
CHATTER
THEY'RE SPARKING ALL THE CLUB MEMBERS.

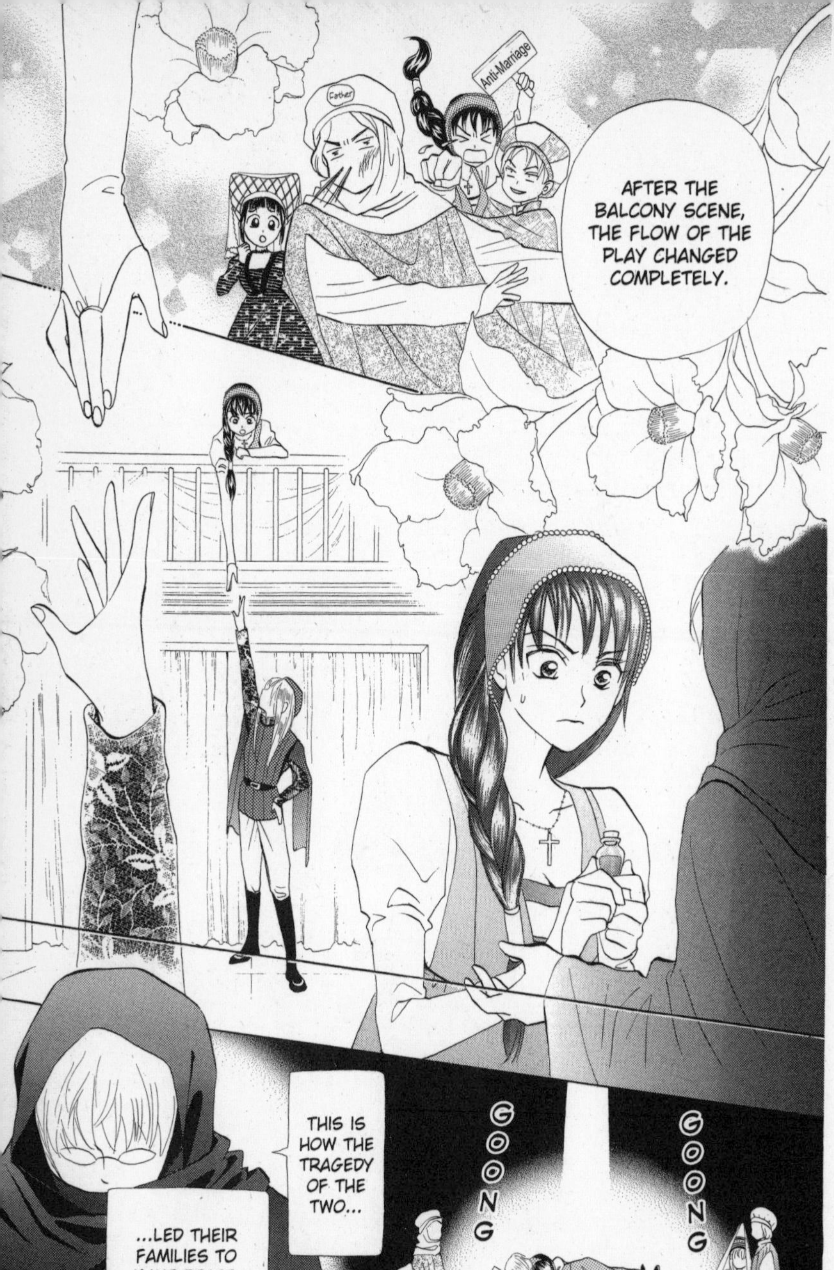
AFTER THE BALCONY SCENE, THE FLOW OF THE PLAY CHANGED COMPLETELY.
Father
Anti-Marriage
GOONG GOONG
THIS IS HOW THE TRAGEDY OF THE TWO...
...LED THEIR FAMILIES TO MAKE PEACE.

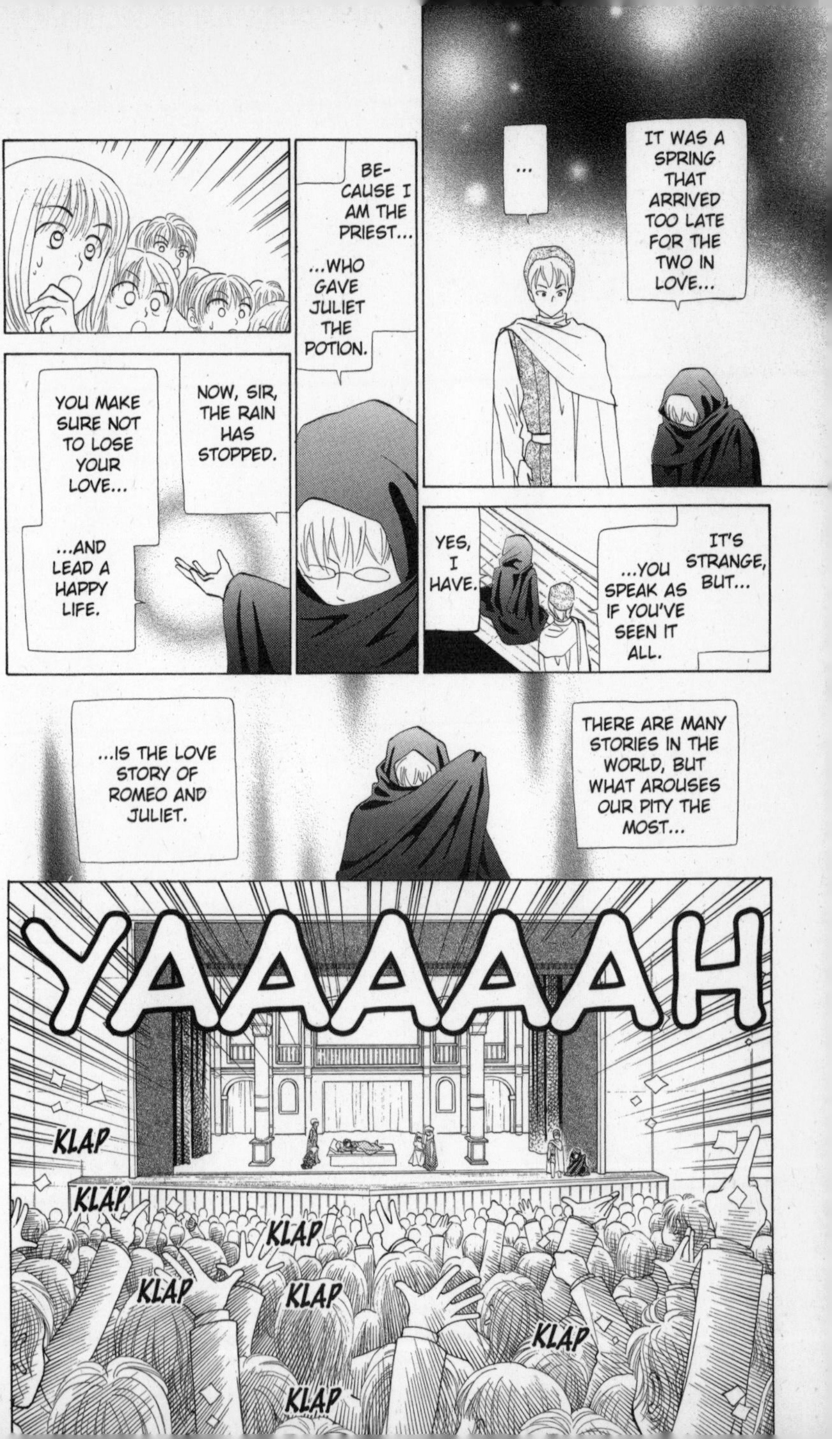
IT WAS A SPRING THAT ARRIVED TOO LATE FOR THE TWO IN LOVE...
...
IT'S STRANGE, BUT...
...YOU SPEAK AS IF YOU'VE SEEN IT ALL.
YES, I HAVE.
BE-CAUSE I AM THE PRIEST...
...WHO GAVE JULIET THE POTION.
NOW, SIR, THE RAIN HAS STOPPED.
YOU MAKE SURE NOT TO LOSE YOUR LOVE...
...AND LEAD A HAPPY LIFE.
THERE ARE MANY STORIES IN THE WORLD, BUT WHAT AROUSES OUR PITY THE MOST...
...IS THE LOVE STORY OF ROMEO AND JULIET.
YAAAAAH
KLAP
KLAP
KLAP
KLAP
KLAP
KLAP
KLAP

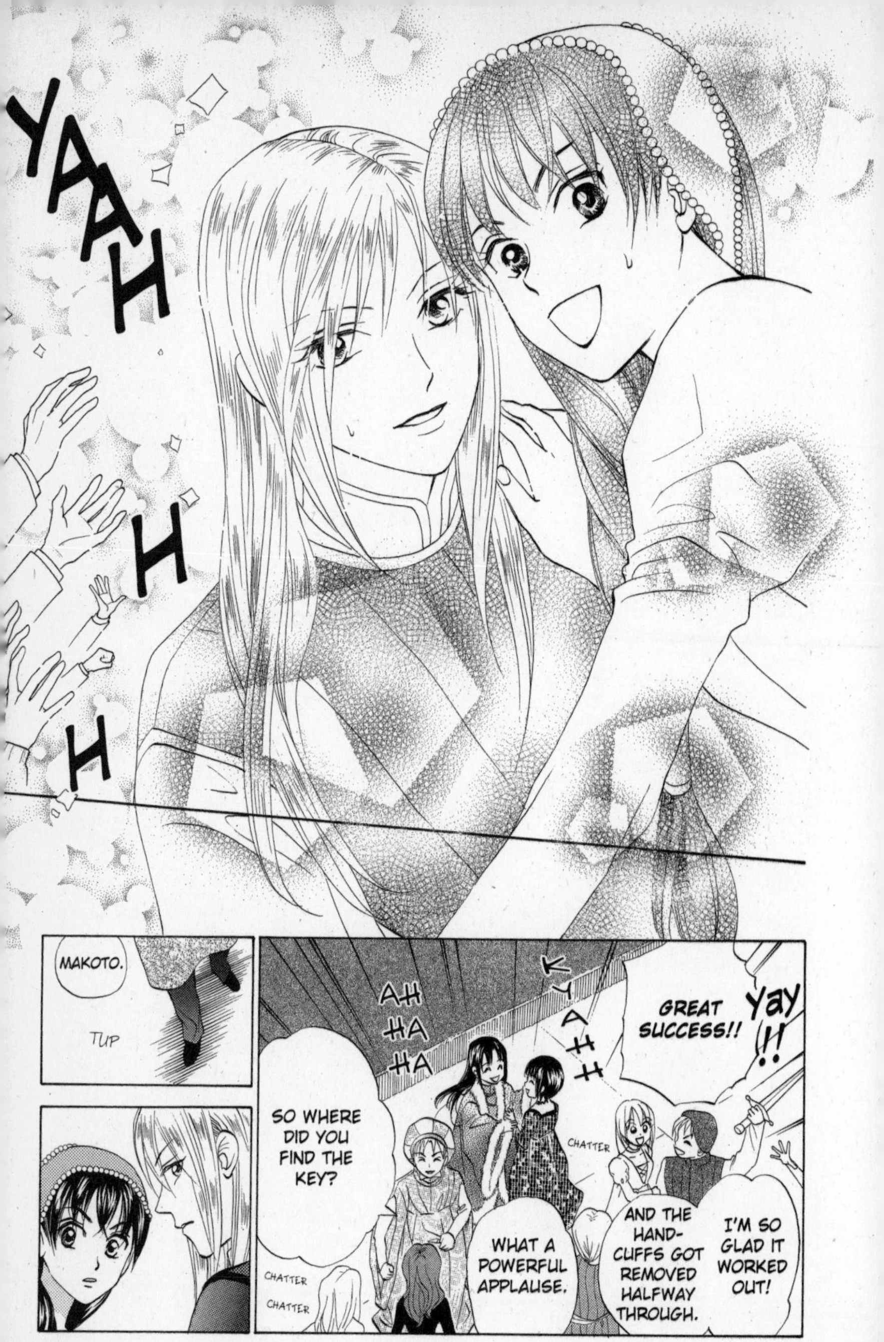
YAAAHH
H
H
Yay!!
GREAT SUCCESS!!
KYAHH
AH HA HA
SO WHERE DID YOU FIND THE KEY?
CHATTER
I'M SO GLAD IT WORKED OUT!
AND THE HAND-CUFFS GOT REMOVED HALFWAY THROUGH.
WHAT A POWERFUL APPLAUSE.
CHATTER
CHATTER
MAKOTO.
TUP

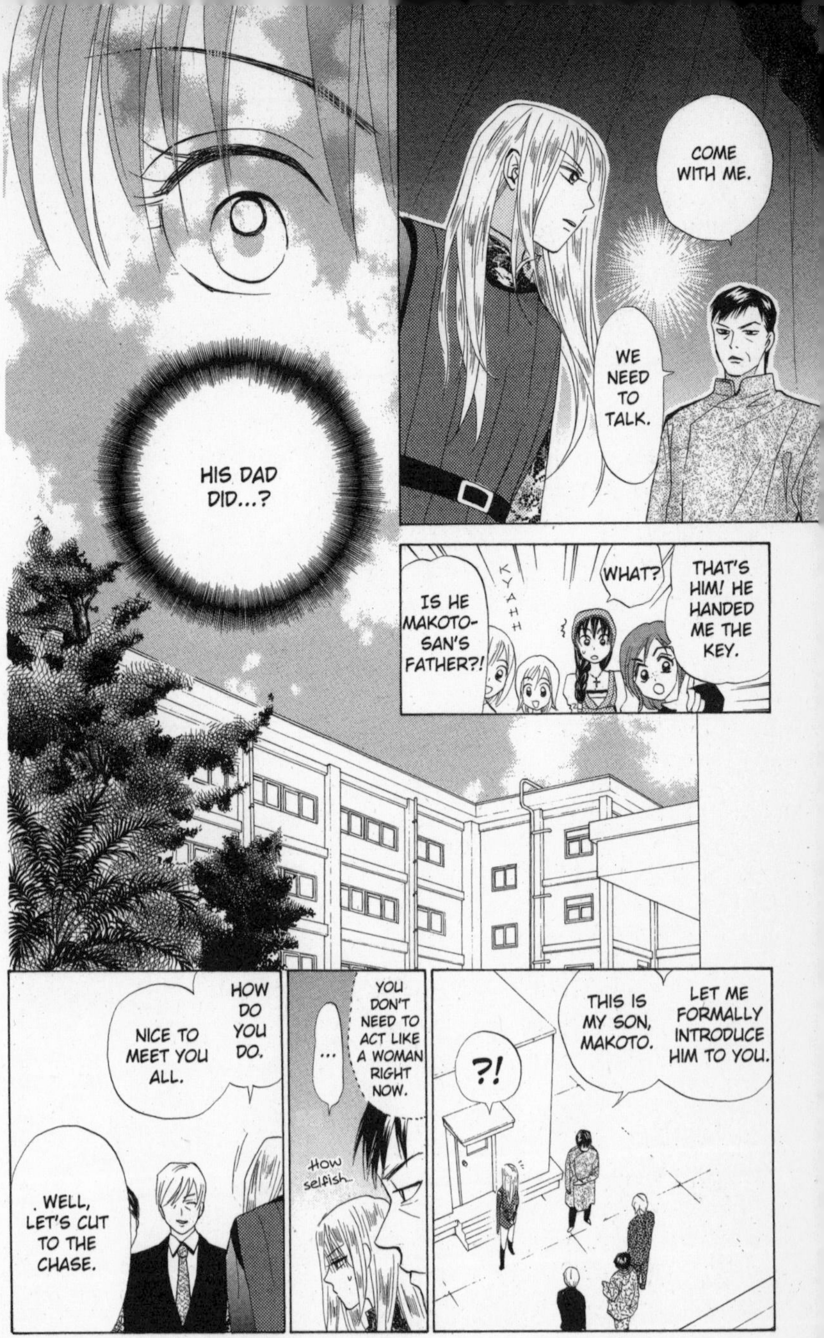
COME WITH ME.
WE NEED TO TALK.
THAT'S HIM! HE HANDED ME THE KEY.
WHAT?
KYAHH
IS HE MAKOTO-SAN'S FATHER?!
HIS DAD DID...?
LET ME FORMALLY INTRODUCE HIM TO YOU.
THIS IS MY SON, MAKOTO.
?!
YOU DON'T NEED TO ACT LIKE A WOMAN RIGHT NOW.
...
How selfish..
HOW DO YOU DO.
NICE TO MEET YOU ALL.
. WELL, LET'S CUT TO THE CHASE.

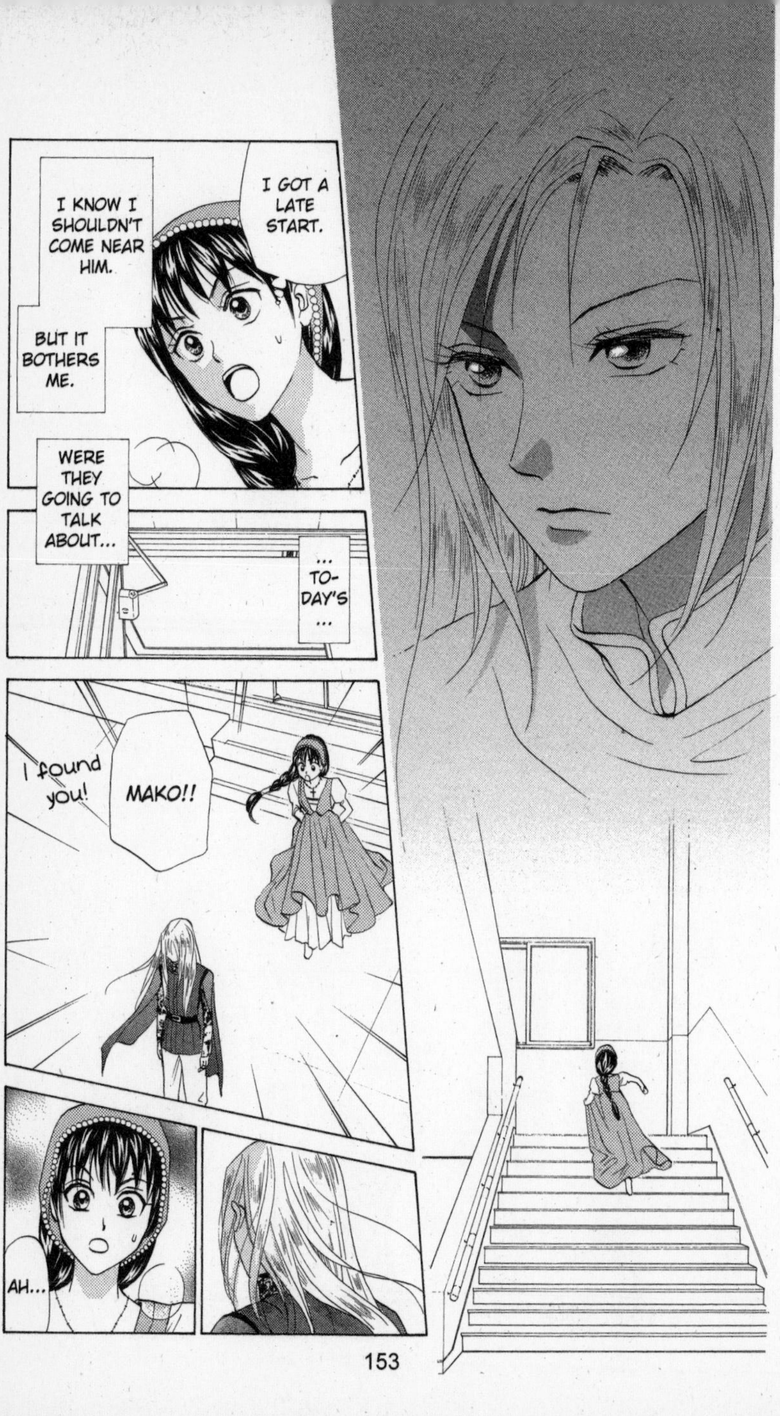
I GOT A LATE START.
I KNOW I SHOULDN'T COME NEAR HIM.
BUT IT BOTHERS ME.
WERE THEY GOING TO TALK ABOUT...
...TO-DAY'S...
MAKO!!
I found you!
AH...

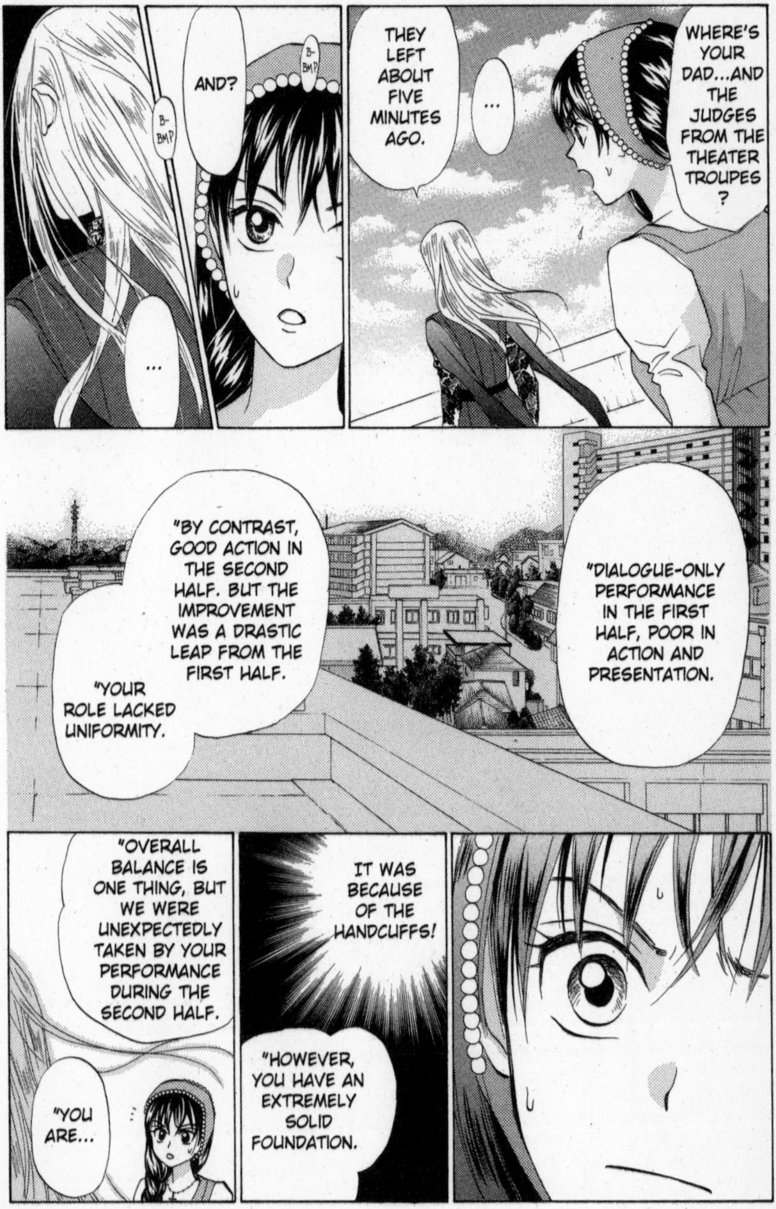
WHERE'S YOUR DAD...AND THE JUDGES FROM THE THEATER TROUPES?
...
THEY LEFT ABOUT FIVE MINUTES AGO.
B-BMP
AND?
B-BMP
...
"DIALOGUE-ONLY PERFORMANCE IN THE FIRST HALF, POOR IN ACTION AND PRESENTATION.
"BY CONTRAST, GOOD ACTION IN THE SECOND HALF. BUT THE IMPROVEMENT WAS A DRASTIC LEAP FROM THE FIRST HALF.
"YOUR ROLE LACKED UNIFORMITY.
IT WAS BECAUSE OF THE HANDCUFFS!
"HOWEVER, YOU HAVE AN EXTREMELY SOLID FOUNDATION.
"OVERALL BALANCE IS ONE THING, BUT WE WERE UNEXPECTEDLY TAKEN BY YOUR PERFORMANCE DURING THE SECOND HALF.
"YOU ARE...

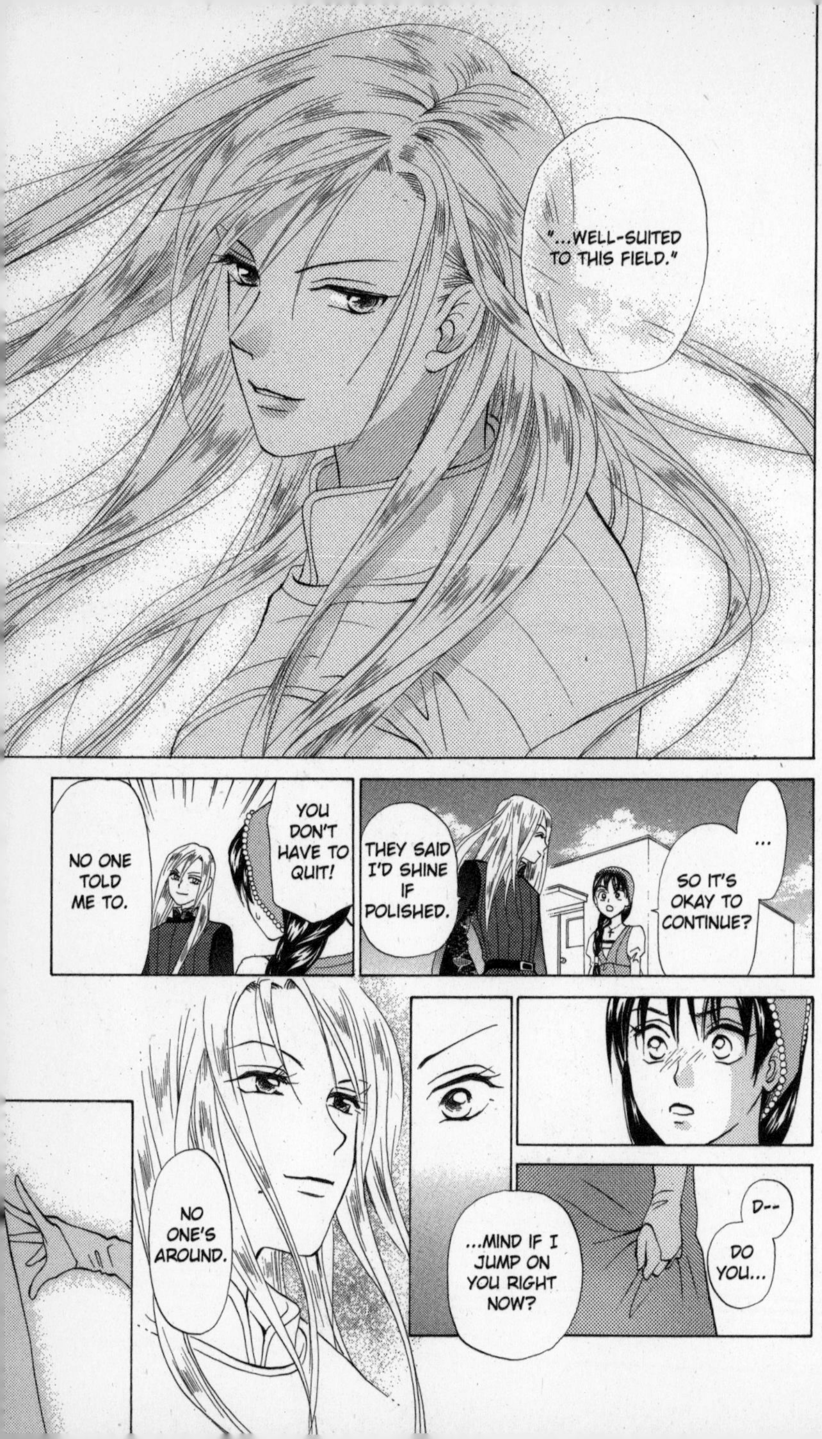

"...WELL-SUITED TO THIS FIELD."
...
SO IT'S OKAY TO CONTINUE?
THEY SAID I'D SHINE IF POLISHED.
YOU DON'T HAVE TO QUIT!
NO ONE TOLD ME TO.
D--
DO YOU...
...MIND IF I JUMP ON YOU RIGHT NOW?
NO ONE'S AROUND.

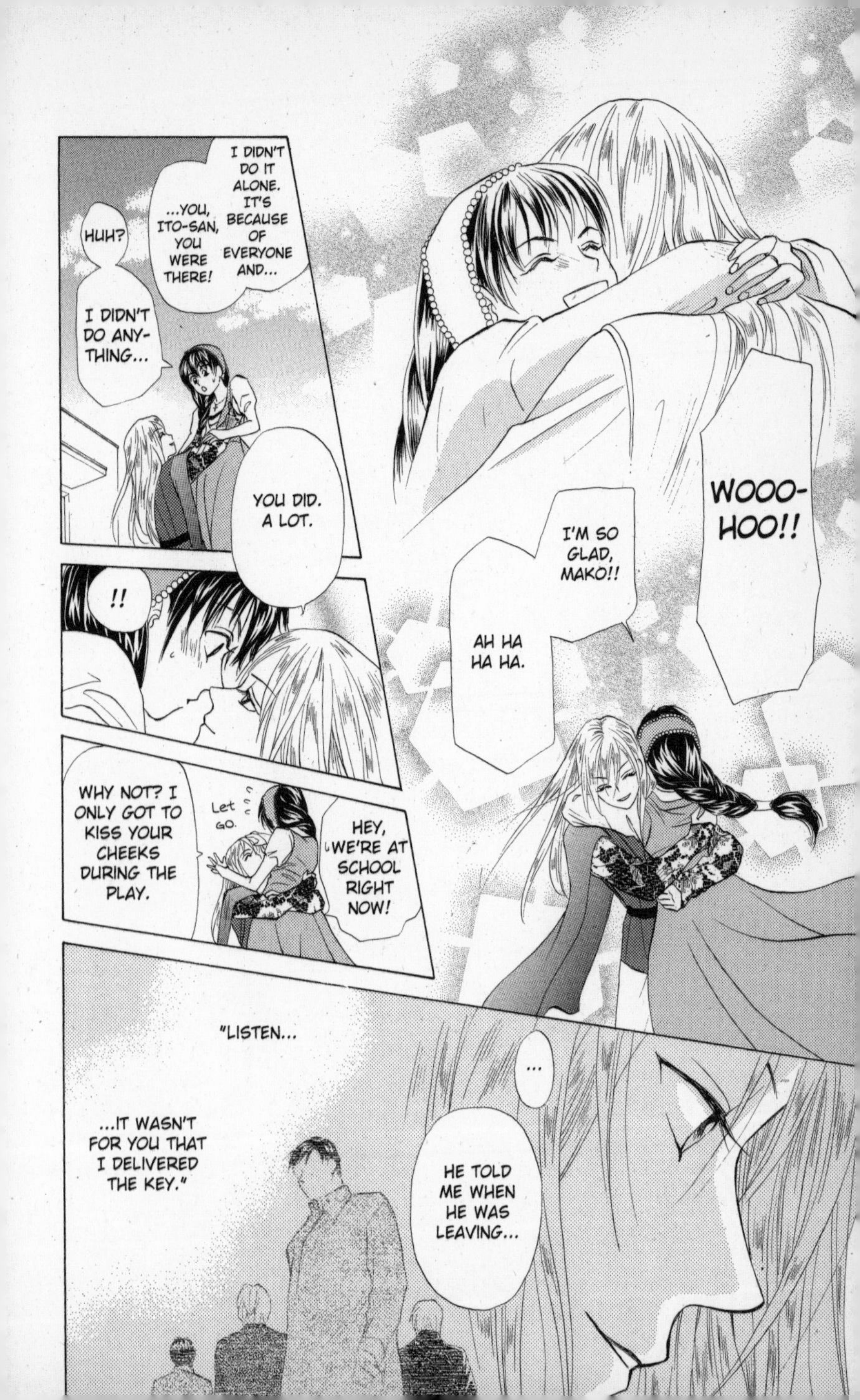
WOOO-HOO!!
I'M SO GLAD, MAKO!!
AH HA HA HA.
I DIDN'T DO IT ALONE. IT'S BECAUSE OF EVERYONE AND...
...YOU, ITO-SAN, YOU WERE THERE!
HUH?
I DIDN'T DO ANY-THING...
YOU DID. A LOT.
!!
HEY, WE'RE AT SCHOOL RIGHT NOW!
Let GO.
WHY NOT? I ONLY GOT TO KISS YOUR CHEEKS DURING THE PLAY.
...
HE TOLD ME WHEN HE WAS LEAVING...
"LISTEN...
...IT WASN'T FOR YOU THAT I DELIVERED THE KEY."

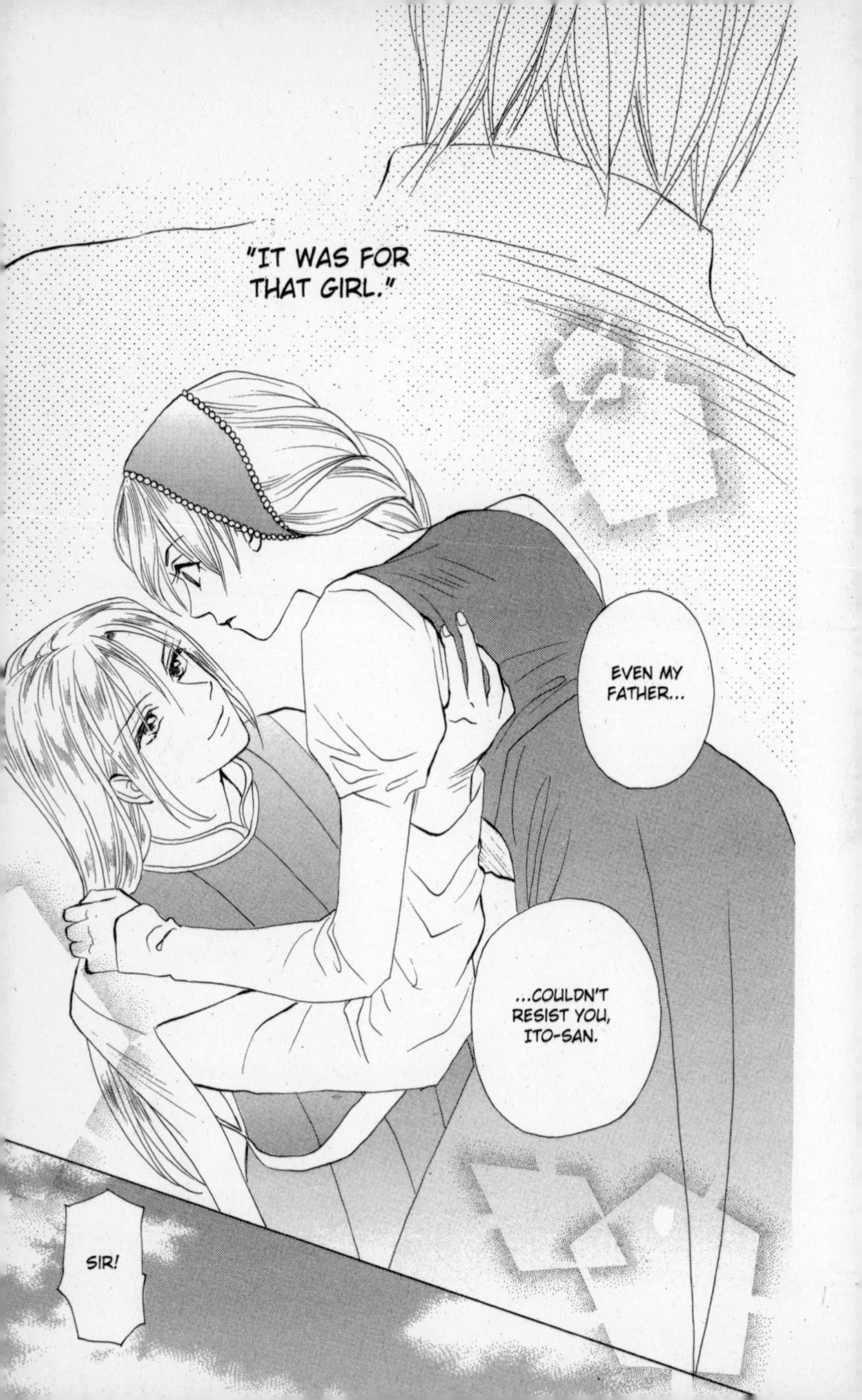
"IT WAS FOR THAT GIRL."
EVEN MY FATHER...
...COULDN'T RESIST YOU, ITO-SAN.
SIR!

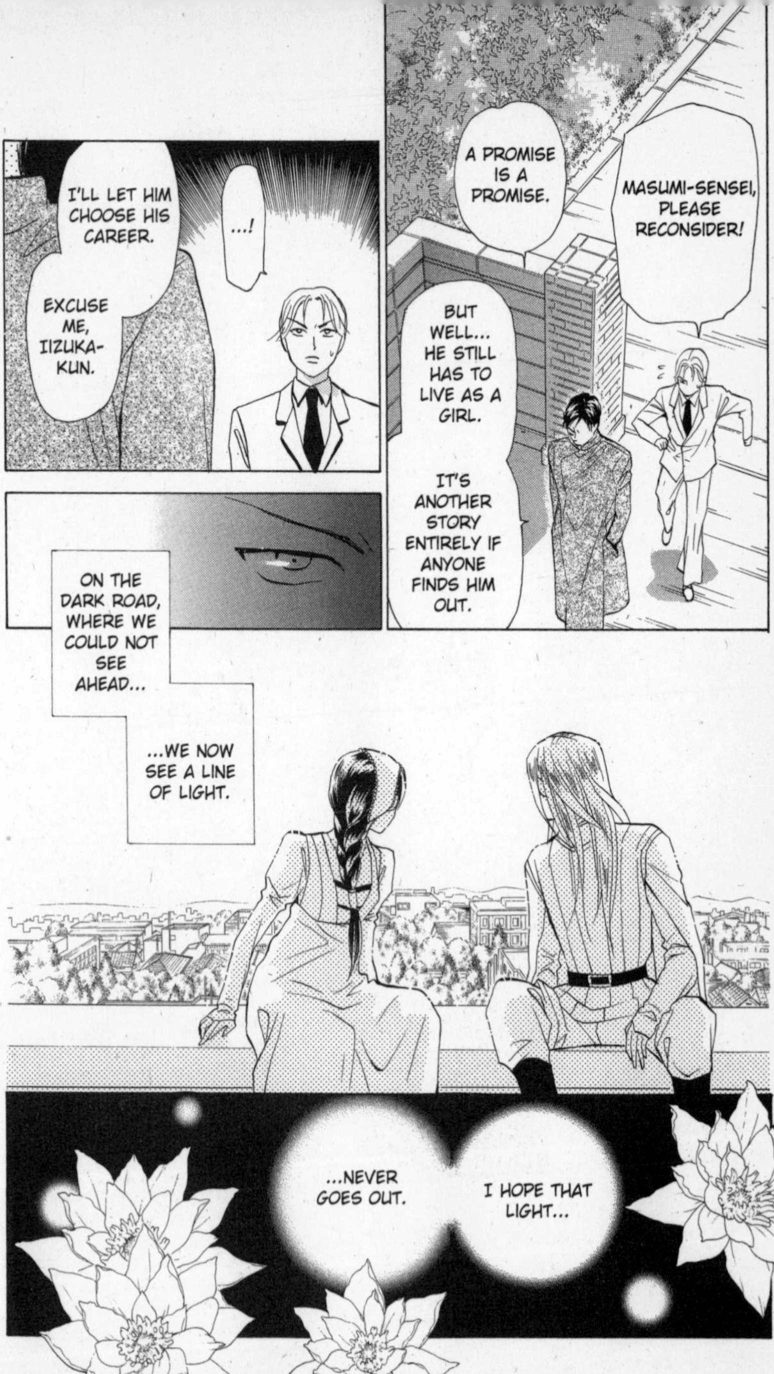
MASUMI-SENSEI, PLEASE RECONSIDER!
A PROMISE IS A PROMISE.
BUT WELL... HE STILL HAS TO LIVE AS A GIRL.
IT'S ANOTHER STORY ENTIRELY IF ANYONE FINDS HIM OUT.
I'LL LET HIM CHOOSE HIS CAREER.
...!
EXCUSE ME, IIZUKA-KUN.
ON THE DARK ROAD, WHERE WE COULD NOT SEE AHEAD...
...WE NOW SEE A LINE OF LIGHT.
I HOPE THAT LIGHT...
...NEVER GOES OUT.

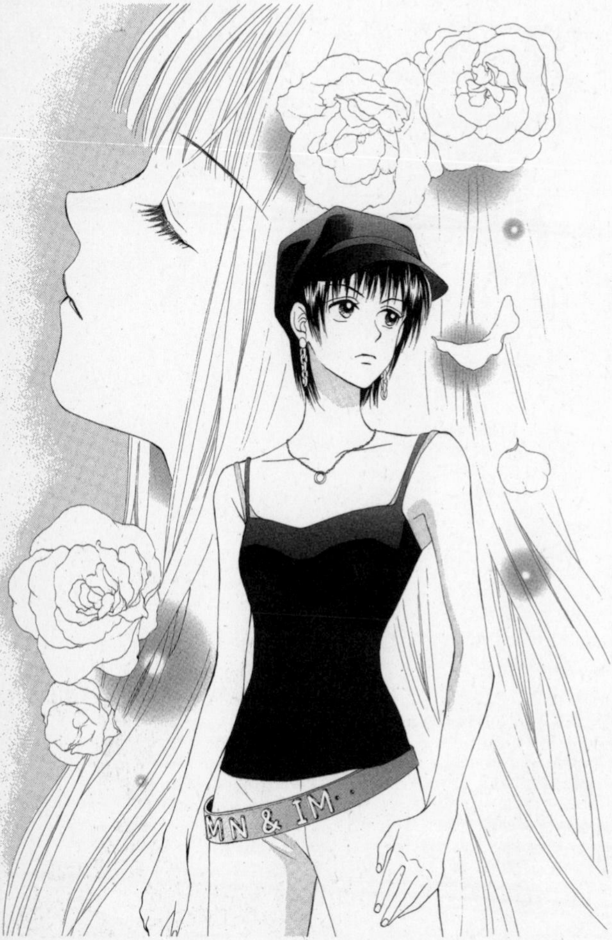
MN & IM

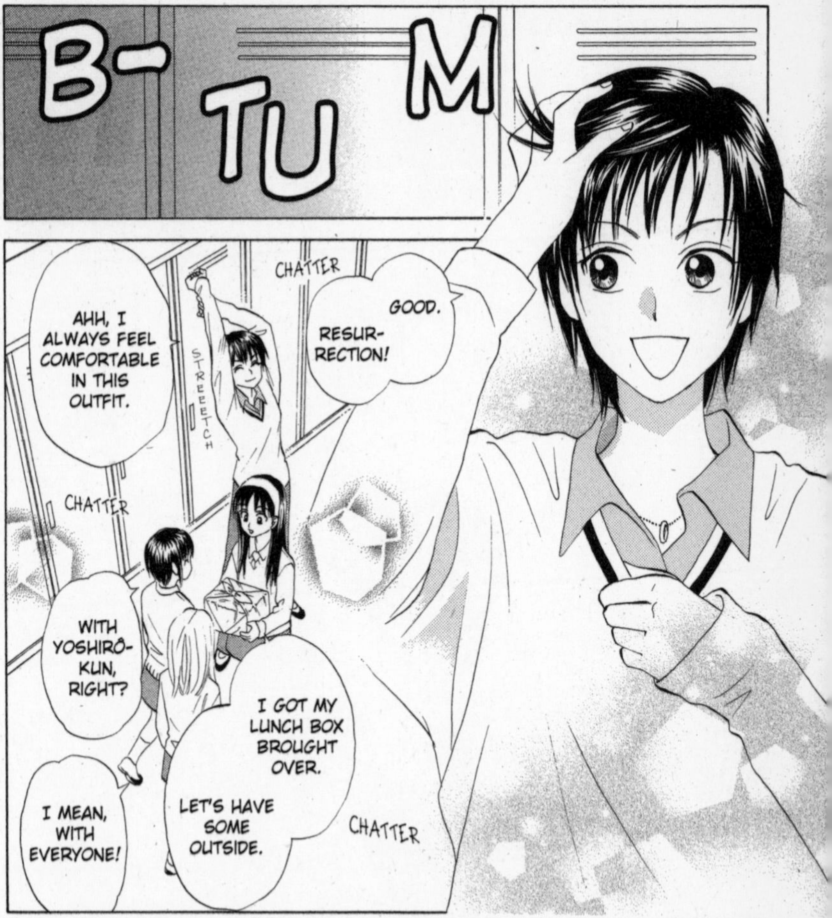
B-TU M
CHATTER
GOOD. RESURRECTION!
AHH, I ALWAYS FEEL COMFORTABLE IN THIS OUTFIT.
STREEETCH
CHATTER
I GOT MY LUNCH BOX BROUGHT OVER.
LET'S HAVE SOME OUTSIDE.
WITH YOSHIRŌ-KUN, RIGHT?
I MEAN, WITH EVERYONE!
CHATTER

—Behind the Scenes Story ⑥—

You know what? Takayo-chan's popularity shot up after this episode. Yes, big time! (Laugh) I love that slap on the face and the picnic scene with Ito myself. Especially the picnic scene--I was going to do that no matter what it took. Takayo-chan knew what was going to happen long ago, and maybe she needed something to help her move on. And, only those who read the magazine installment would understand, but the "lunch box"... That was just too much of a stretch, no matter how I cut it. (Laugh) That's why I revised the opening dialogue. Oh well, sorry about that.

There's no way she could've made a lunch box during that accident...

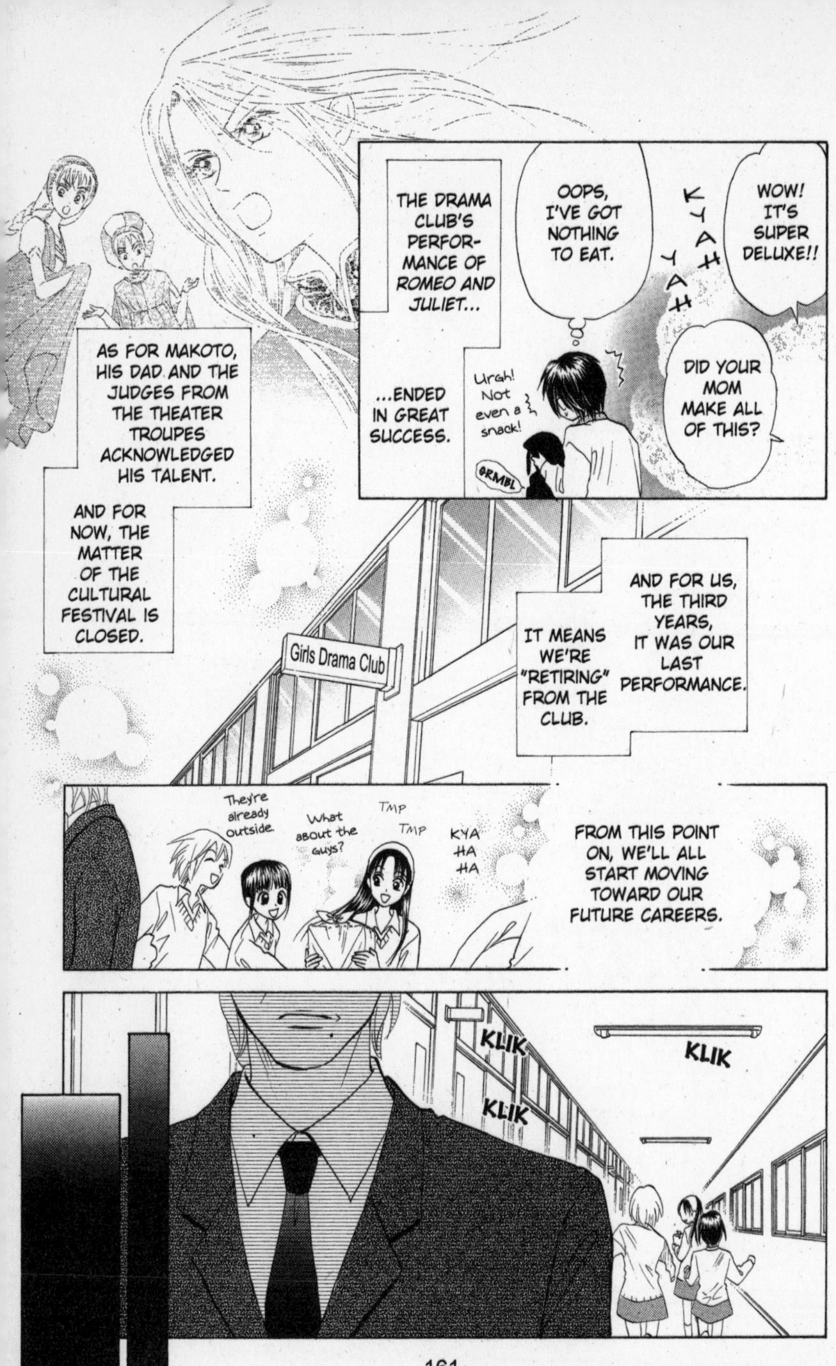
WOW! IT'S SUPER DELUXE!!
KYAH YAH
OOPS, I'VE GOT NOTHING TO EAT.
THE DRAMA CLUB'S PERFOR-MANCE OF ROMEO AND JULIET...
DID YOUR MOM MAKE ALL OF THIS?
Urgh! Not even a snack!
GRMBL
...ENDED IN GREAT SUCCESS.
AS FOR MAKOTO, HIS DAD AND THE JUDGES FROM THE THEATER TROUPES ACKNOWLEDGED HIS TALENT.
AND FOR NOW, THE MATTER OF THE CULTURAL FESTIVAL IS CLOSED.
AND FOR US, THE THIRD YEARS, IT WAS OUR LAST PERFORMANCE.
IT MEANS WE'RE "RETIRING" FROM THE CLUB.
Girls Drama Club
FROM THIS POINT ON, WE'LL ALL START MOVING TOWARD OUR FUTURE CAREERS.
KYA HA HA
TMP TMP
What about the guys?
They're already outside.
KLIK
KLIK
KLIK

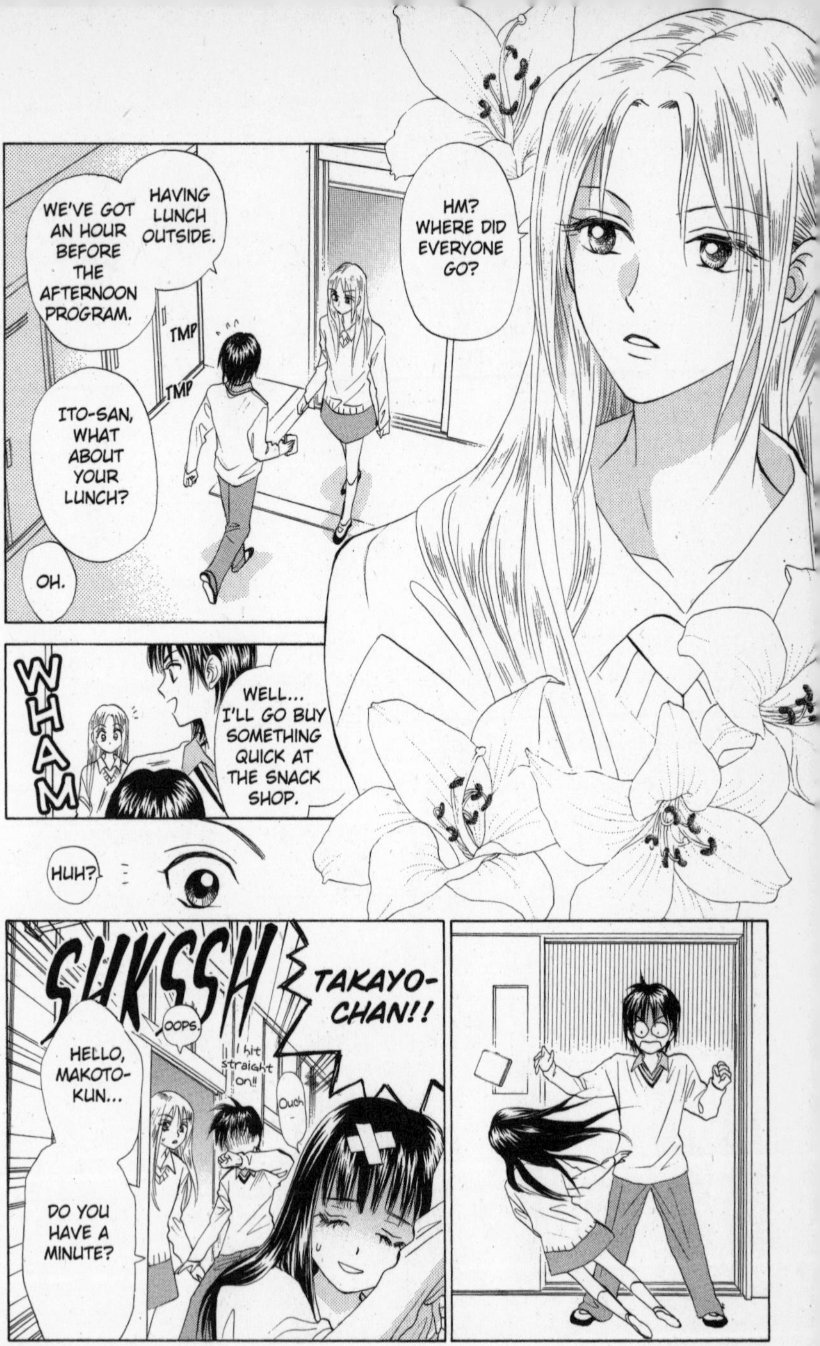
HM? WHERE DID EVERYONE GO?
HAVING LUNCH OUTSIDE.
WE'VE GOT AN HOUR BEFORE THE AFTERNOON PROGRAM.
TMP
TMP
ITO-SAN, WHAT ABOUT YOUR LUNCH?
OH.
WELL... I'LL GO BUY SOMETHING QUICK AT THE SNACK SHOP.
WHAM
HUH?
TAKAYO-CHAN!!
SUKSSH
OOPS.
I hit straight on!!
Ouch
HELLO, MAKOTO-KUN...
DO YOU HAVE A MINUTE?

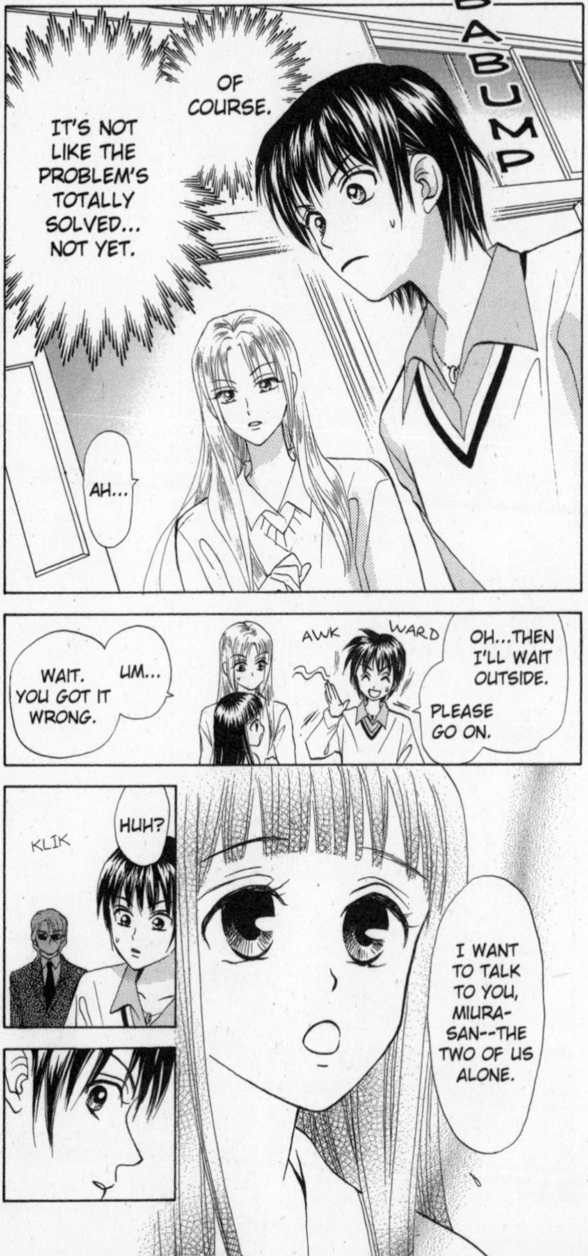
BABUMP
OF COURSE.
IT'S NOT LIKE THE PROBLEM'S TOTALLY SOLVED... NOT YET.
AH...
OH...THEN I'LL WAIT OUTSIDE.
PLEASE GO ON.
AWKWARD
UM...
WAIT. YOU GOT IT WRONG.
I WANT TO TALK TO YOU, MIURA-SAN--THE TWO OF US ALONE.
HUH?
KLIK

And the No. 3 is mine--but it's not as strong as my mom's or sis's.

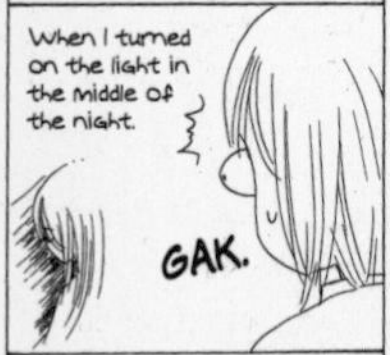
When I turned on the light in the middle of the night.
GAK.

I saw scales for a second. (It disappeared right away.)

And I bit someone else's finger when I felt paralyzed. That's just about it.

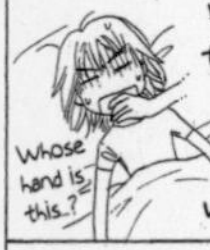
Whose hand is this..?

When I bit the finger, the paralyzing feeling went away.

The president of the publishing company gave me an amulet when I traveled to Taiwan, and once I started wearing it, I felt more settled. Apparently, it's been made with things like my birthday in mind, and according to my mom, it radiates an incredibly good aura.

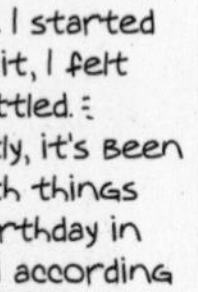

Maybe it drives away evil. I should've asked more about it.

Anyhow, see you again in volume 13. ♪

2002. 9. 17

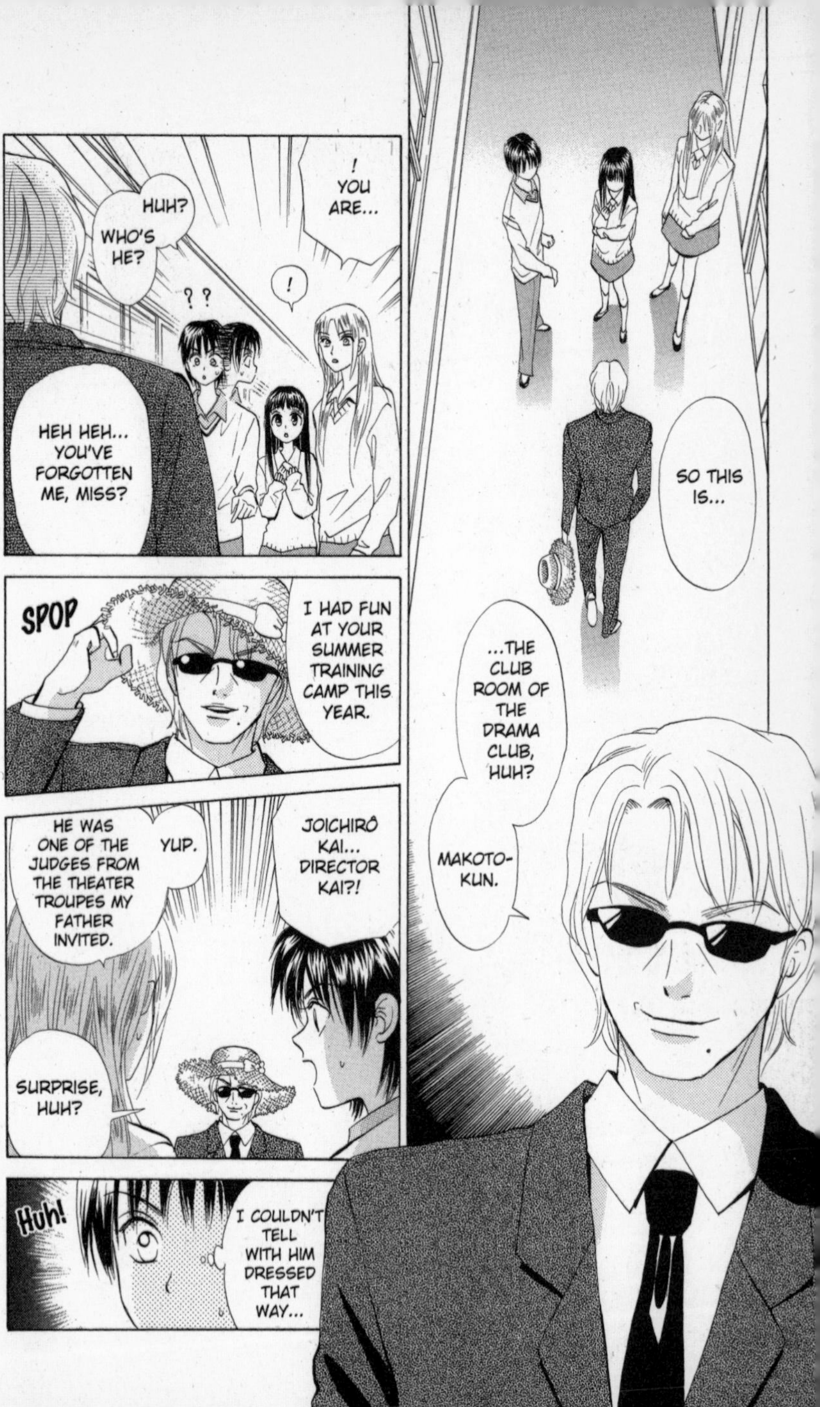
SO THIS IS...
...THE CLUB ROOM OF THE DRAMA CLUB, HUH?
MAKOTO-KUN.
! YOU ARE...
!
HUH? WHO'S HE?
? ?
HEH HEH... YOU'VE FORGOTTEN ME, MISS?
I HAD FUN AT YOUR SUMMER TRAINING CAMP THIS YEAR.
SPOP
JOICHIRÔ KAI... DIRECTOR KAI?!
YUP.
HE WAS ONE OF THE JUDGES FROM THE THEATER TROUPES MY FATHER INVITED.
SURPRISE, HUH?
I COULDN'T TELL WITH HIM DRESSED THAT WAY...
Huh!

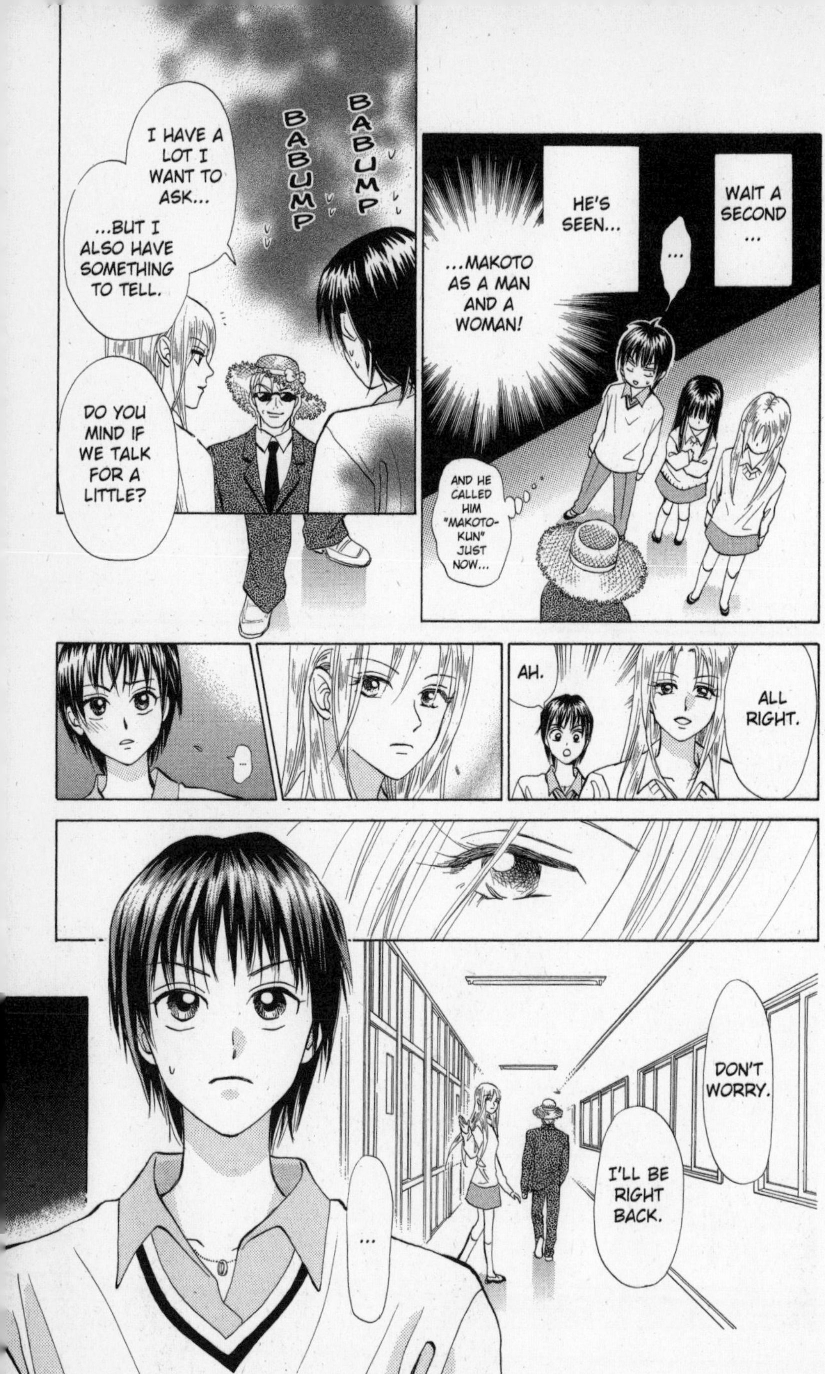
WAIT A SECOND ...
...
HE'S SEEN...
...MAKOTO AS A MAN AND A WOMAN!
AND HE CALLED HIM "MAKOTO-KUN" JUST NOW...
BABUMP
BABUMP
I HAVE A LOT I WANT TO ASK...
...BUT I ALSO HAVE SOMETHING TO TELL.
DO YOU MIND IF WE TALK FOR A LITTLE?
ALL RIGHT.
AH.
...
DON'T WORRY.
I'LL BE RIGHT BACK.
...

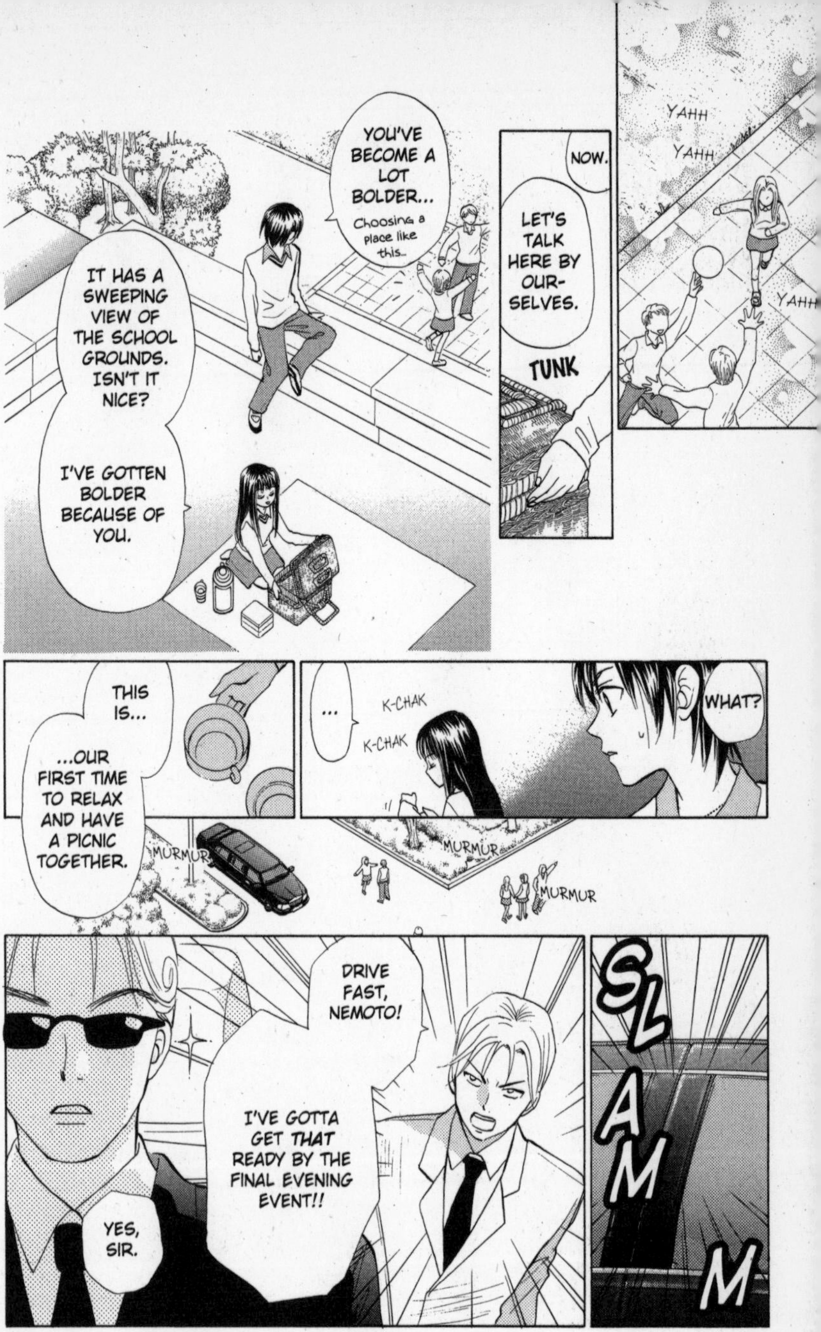
YAHH
YAHH
YAHH
NOW.
LET'S TALK HERE BY OUR-SELVES.
TUNK
YOU'VE BECOME A LOT BOLDER...
Choosing a place like this..
IT HAS A SWEEPING VIEW OF THE SCHOOL GROUNDS. ISN'T IT NICE?
I'VE GOTTEN BOLDER BECAUSE OF YOU.
WHAT?
...
K-CHAK
K-CHAK
THIS IS...
...OUR FIRST TIME TO RELAX AND HAVE A PICNIC TOGETHER.
MURMUR
MURMUR
MURMUR
SLAMM
DRIVE FAST, NEMOTO!
I'VE GOTTA GET THAT READY BY THE FINAL EVENING EVENT!!
YES, SIR.

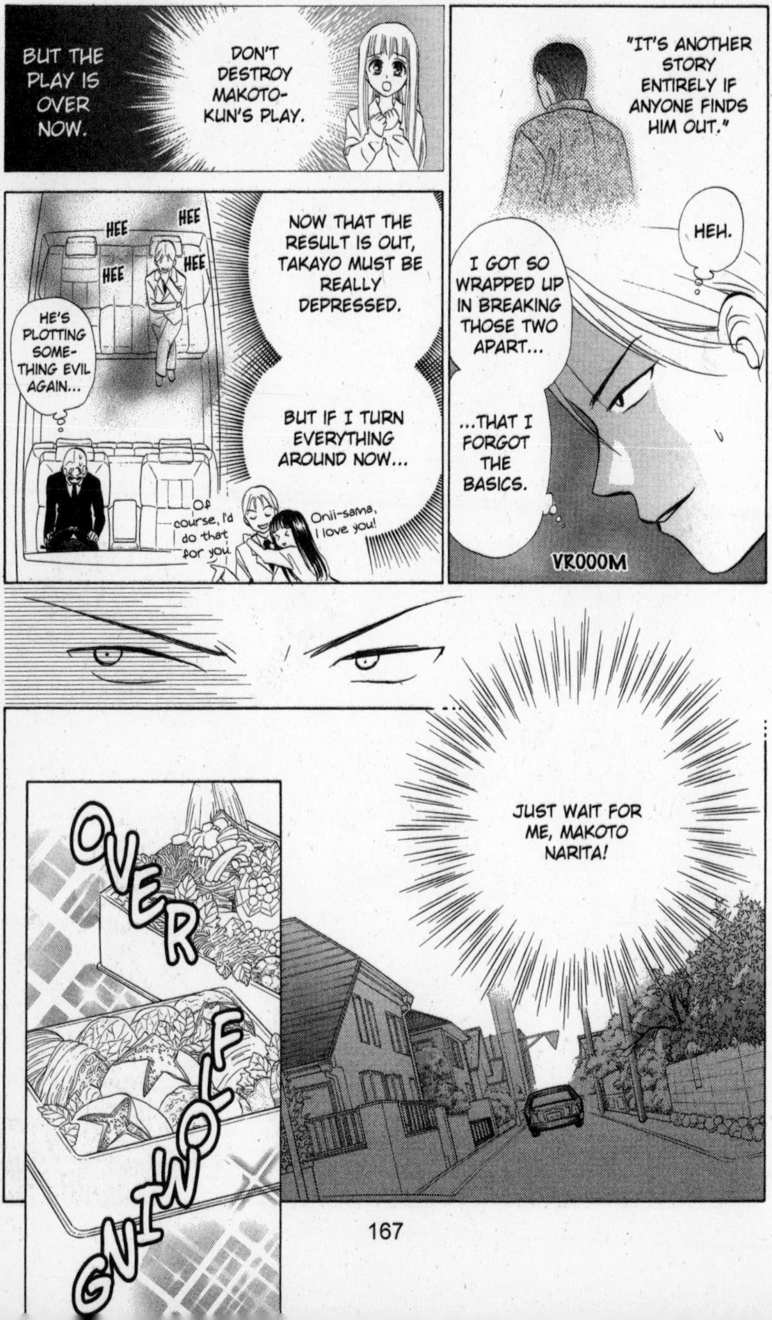
"IT'S ANOTHER STORY ENTIRELY IF ANYONE FINDS HIM OUT."
HEH.
I GOT SO WRAPPED UP IN BREAKING THOSE TWO APART...
...THAT I FORGOT THE BASICS.
VROOOM
DON'T DESTROY MAKOTO-KUN'S PLAY.
BUT THE PLAY IS OVER NOW.
NOW THAT THE RESULT IS OUT, TAKAYO MUST BE REALLY DEPRESSED.
HEE HEE HEE HEE
BUT IF I TURN EVERYTHING AROUND NOW...
Onii-sama, I love you!
Of course, I'd do that for you.
HE'S PLOTTING SOMETHING EVIL AGAIN...
...
JUST WAIT FOR ME, MAKOTO NARITA!
OVERFLOWING

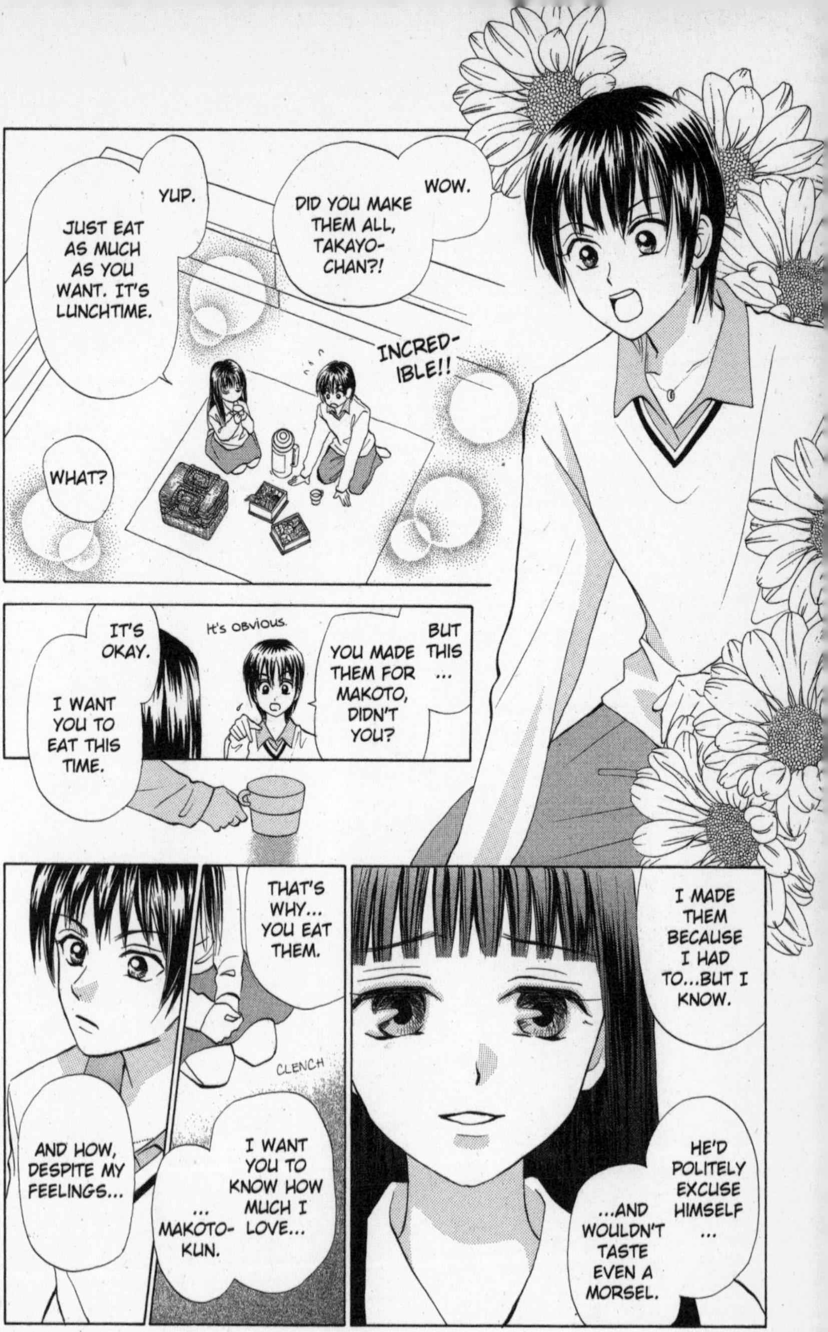

WOW.
DID YOU MAKE THEM ALL, TAKAYO-CHAN?!
YUP.
JUST EAT AS MUCH AS YOU WANT. IT'S LUNCHTIME.
INCRED-IBLE!!
WHAT?
BUT THIS ...
YOU MADE THEM FOR MAKOTO, DIDN'T YOU?
It's obvious.
IT'S OKAY.
I WANT YOU TO EAT THIS TIME.
I MADE THEM BECAUSE I HAD TO...BUT I KNOW.
HE'D POLITELY EXCUSE HIMSELF ...
...AND WOULDN'T TASTE EVEN A MORSEL.
THAT'S WHY... YOU EAT THEM.
CLENCH
I WANT YOU TO KNOW HOW MUCH I LOVE...
... MAKOTO-KUN.
AND HOW, DESPITE MY FEELINGS...

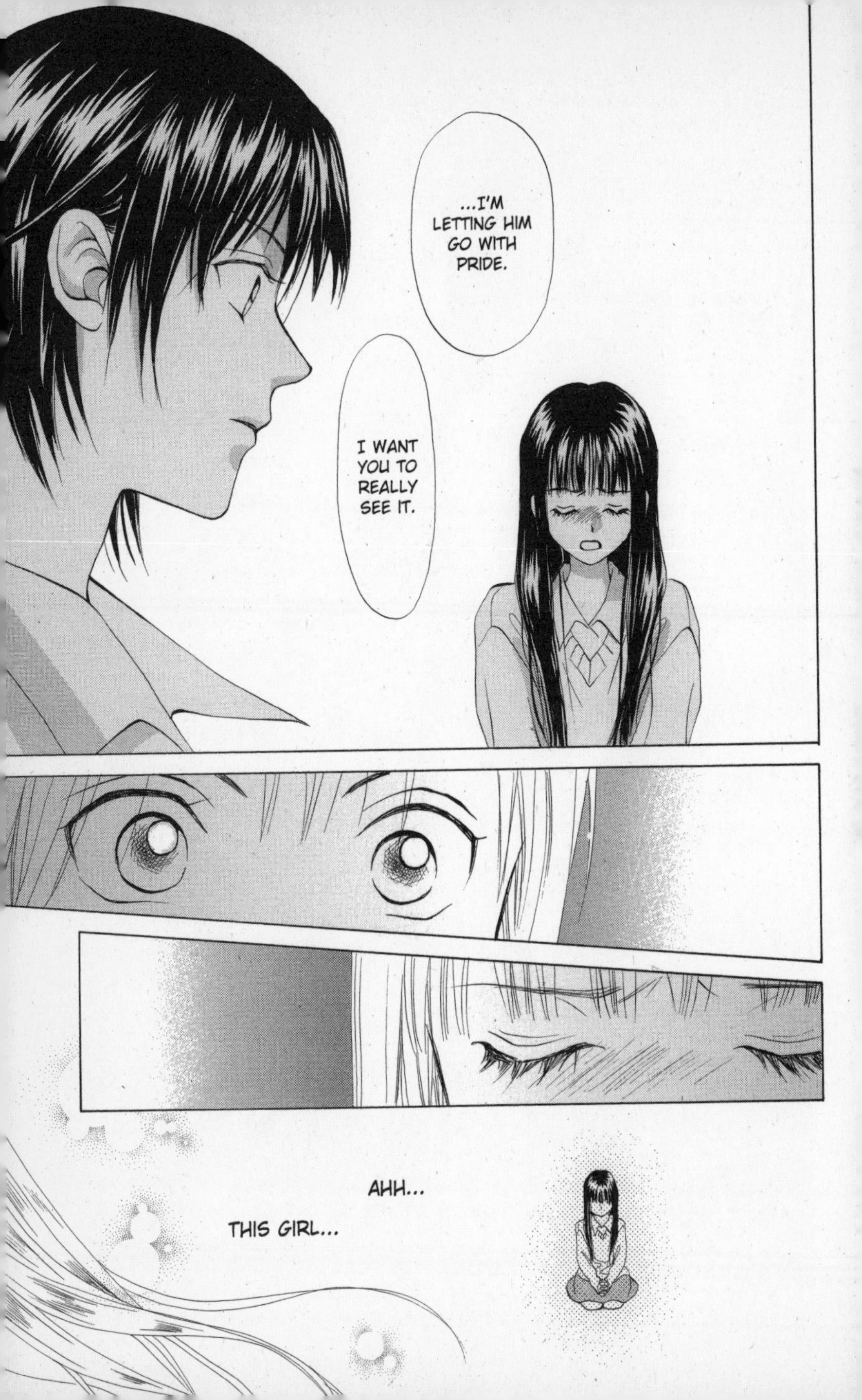
...I'M LETTING HIM GO WITH PRIDE.
I WANT YOU TO REALLY SEE IT.
AHH...
THIS GIRL...

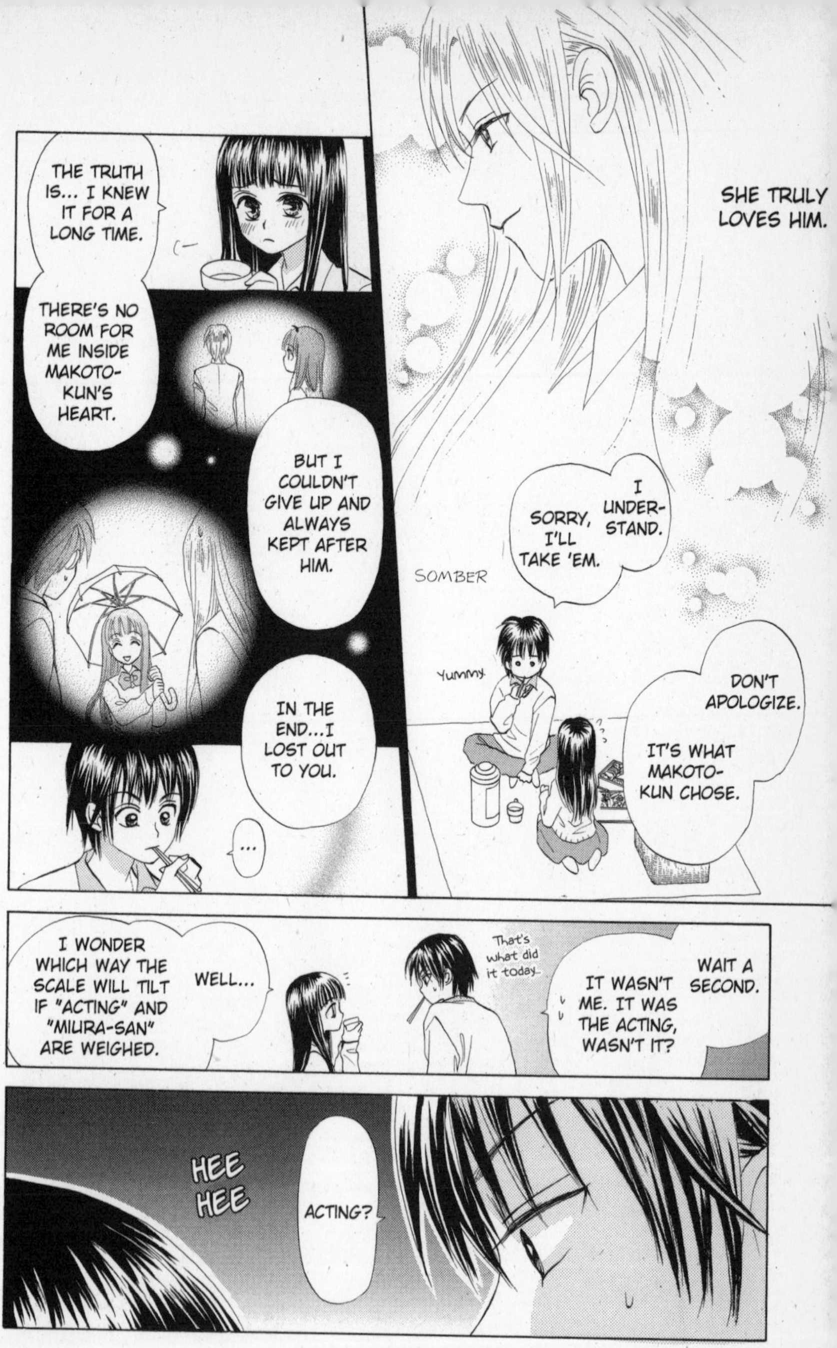

SHE TRULY LOVES HIM.
I UNDER-STAND.
SORRY, I'LL TAKE 'EM.
SOMBER
DON'T APOLOGIZE.
IT'S WHAT MAKOTO-KUN CHOSE.
Yummy.
THE TRUTH IS... I KNEW IT FOR A LONG TIME.
THERE'S NO ROOM FOR ME INSIDE MAKOTO-KUN'S HEART.
BUT I COULDN'T GIVE UP AND ALWAYS KEPT AFTER HIM.
IN THE END...I LOST OUT TO YOU.
...
WAIT A SECOND.
IT WASN'T ME. IT WAS THE ACTING, WASN'T IT?
That's what did it today.
WELL...
I WONDER WHICH WAY THE SCALE WILL TILT IF "ACTING" AND "MIURA-SAN" ARE WEIGHED.
ACTING?
HEE HEE

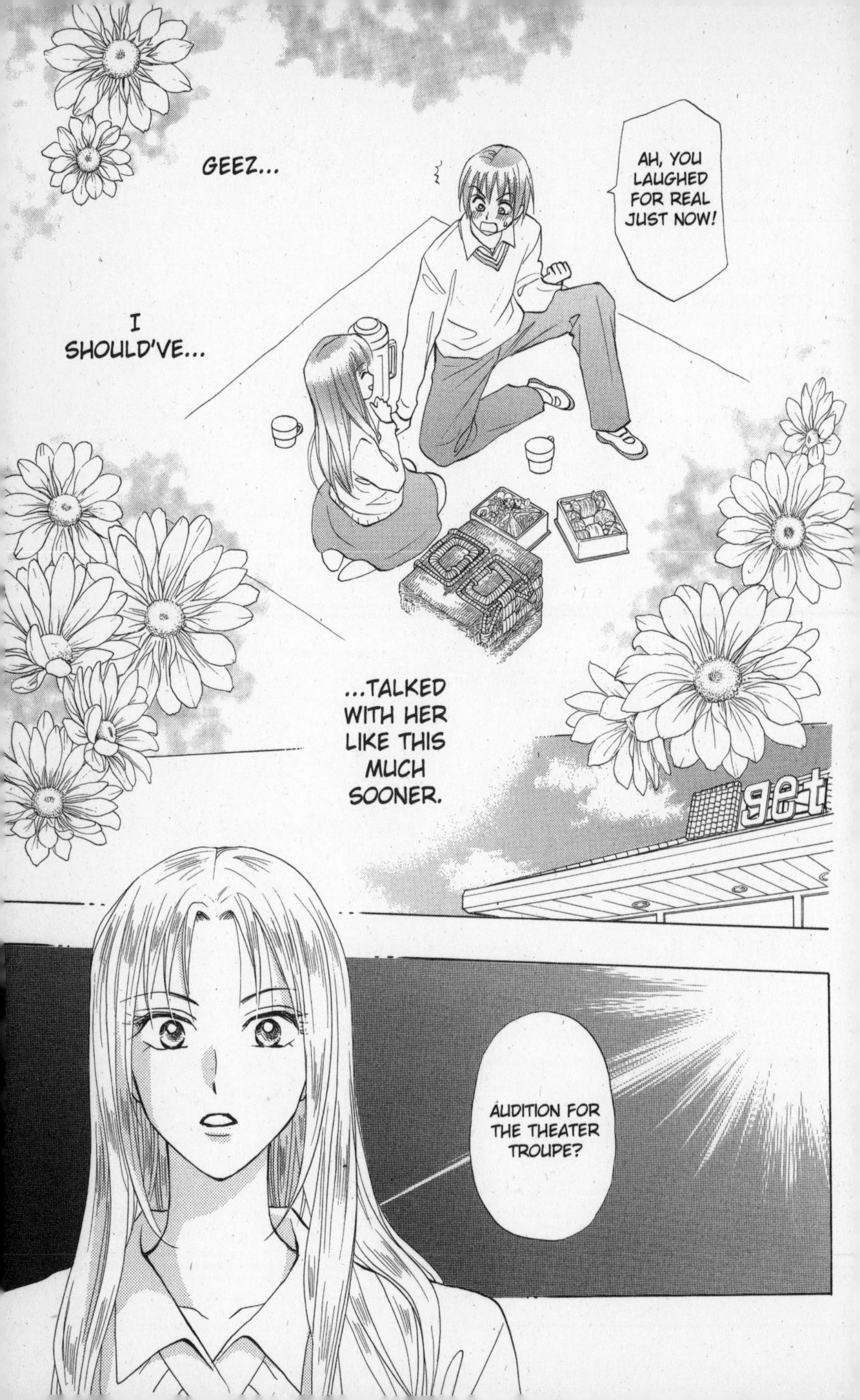
AH, YOU LAUGHED FOR REAL JUST NOW!
GEEZ...
I SHOULD'VE...
...TALKED WITH HER LIKE THIS MUCH SOONER.
AUDITION FOR THE THEATER TROUPE?

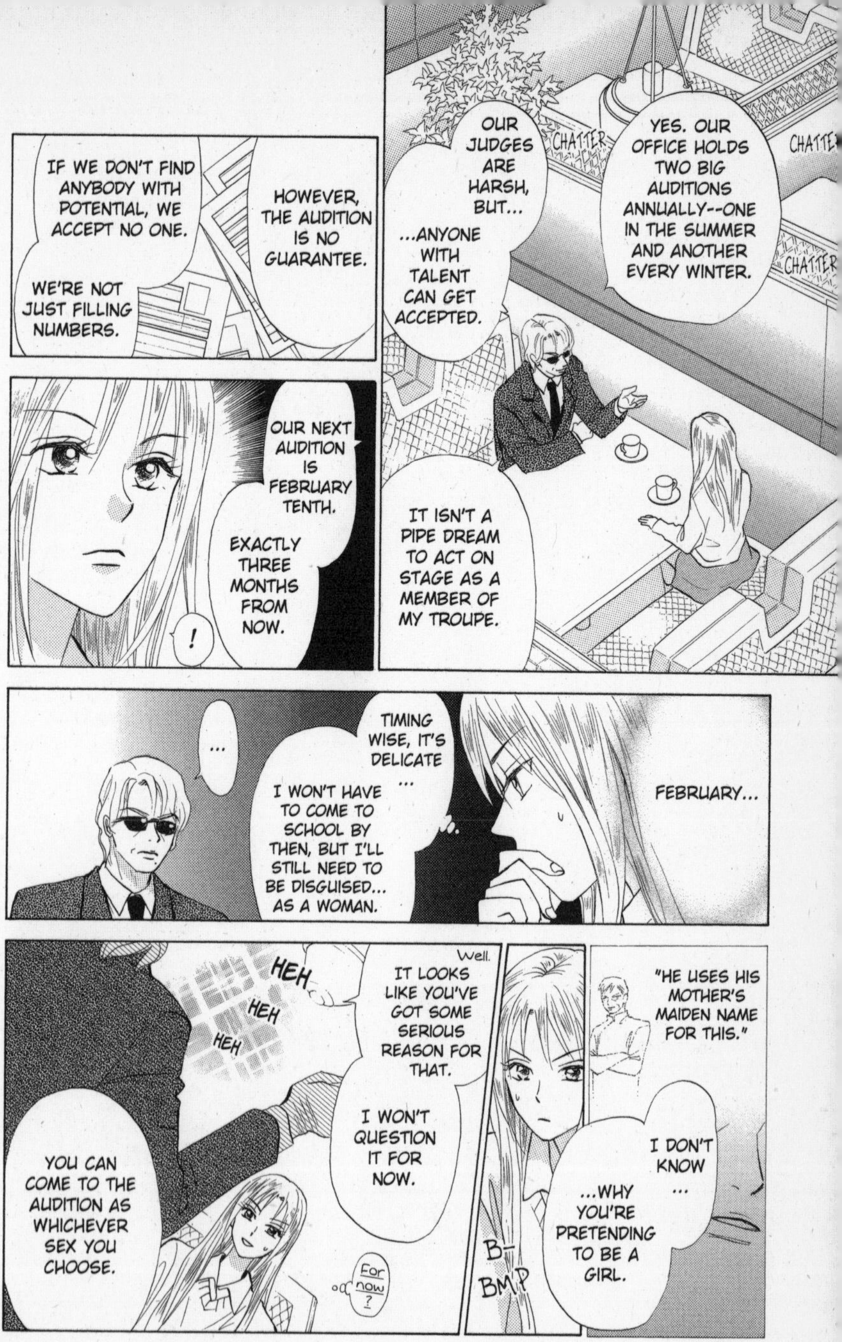
YES. OUR OFFICE HOLDS TWO BIG AUDITIONS ANNUALLY--ONE IN THE SUMMER AND ANOTHER EVERY WINTER.
CHATTER
CHATTER
CHATTER
OUR JUDGES ARE HARSH, BUT...
...ANYONE WITH TALENT CAN GET ACCEPTED.
IT ISN'T A PIPE DREAM TO ACT ON STAGE AS A MEMBER OF MY TROUPE.
HOWEVER, THE AUDITION IS NO GUARANTEE.
IF WE DON'T FIND ANYBODY WITH POTENTIAL, WE ACCEPT NO ONE.
WE'RE NOT JUST FILLING NUMBERS.
OUR NEXT AUDITION IS FEBRUARY TENTH.
EXACTLY THREE MONTHS FROM NOW.
!
FEBRUARY...
TIMING WISE, IT'S DELICATE ...
I WON'T HAVE TO COME TO SCHOOL BY THEN, BUT I'LL STILL NEED TO BE DISGUISED... AS A WOMAN.
...
"HE USES HIS MOTHER'S MAIDEN NAME FOR THIS."
I DON'T KNOW ...
...WHY YOU'RE PRETENDING TO BE A GIRL.
B-BMP
Well.
IT LOOKS LIKE YOU'VE GOT SOME SERIOUS REASON FOR THAT.
I WON'T QUESTION IT FOR NOW.
HEH
HEH
HEH
YOU CAN COME TO THE AUDITION AS WHICHEVER SEX YOU CHOOSE.
For now?

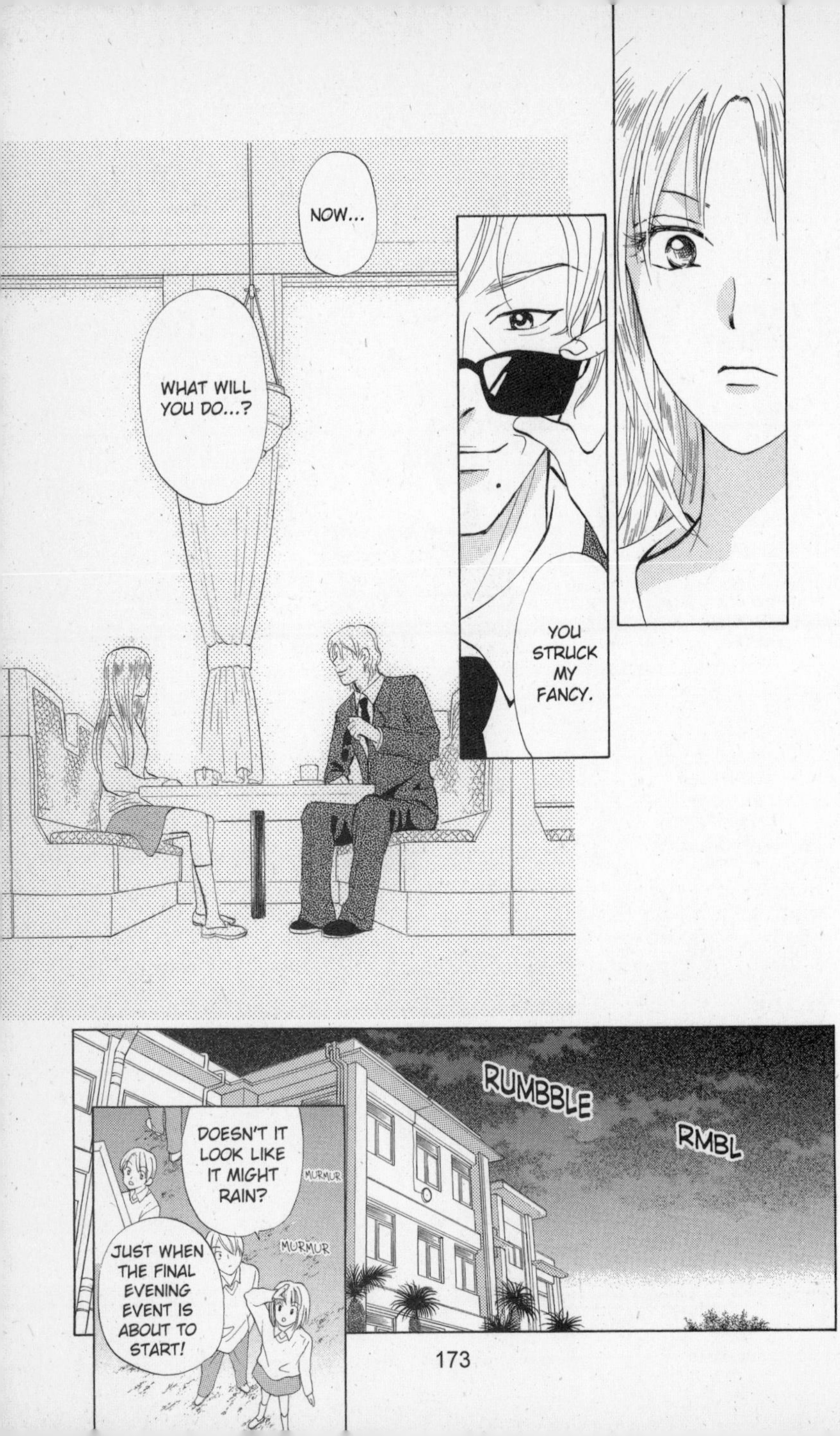
YOU STRUCK MY FANCY.
NOW...
WHAT WILL YOU DO...?
RUMBBLE
RMBL
DOESN'T IT LOOK LIKE IT MIGHT RAIN?
MURMUR
MURMUR
JUST WHEN THE FINAL EVENING EVENT IS ABOUT TO START!

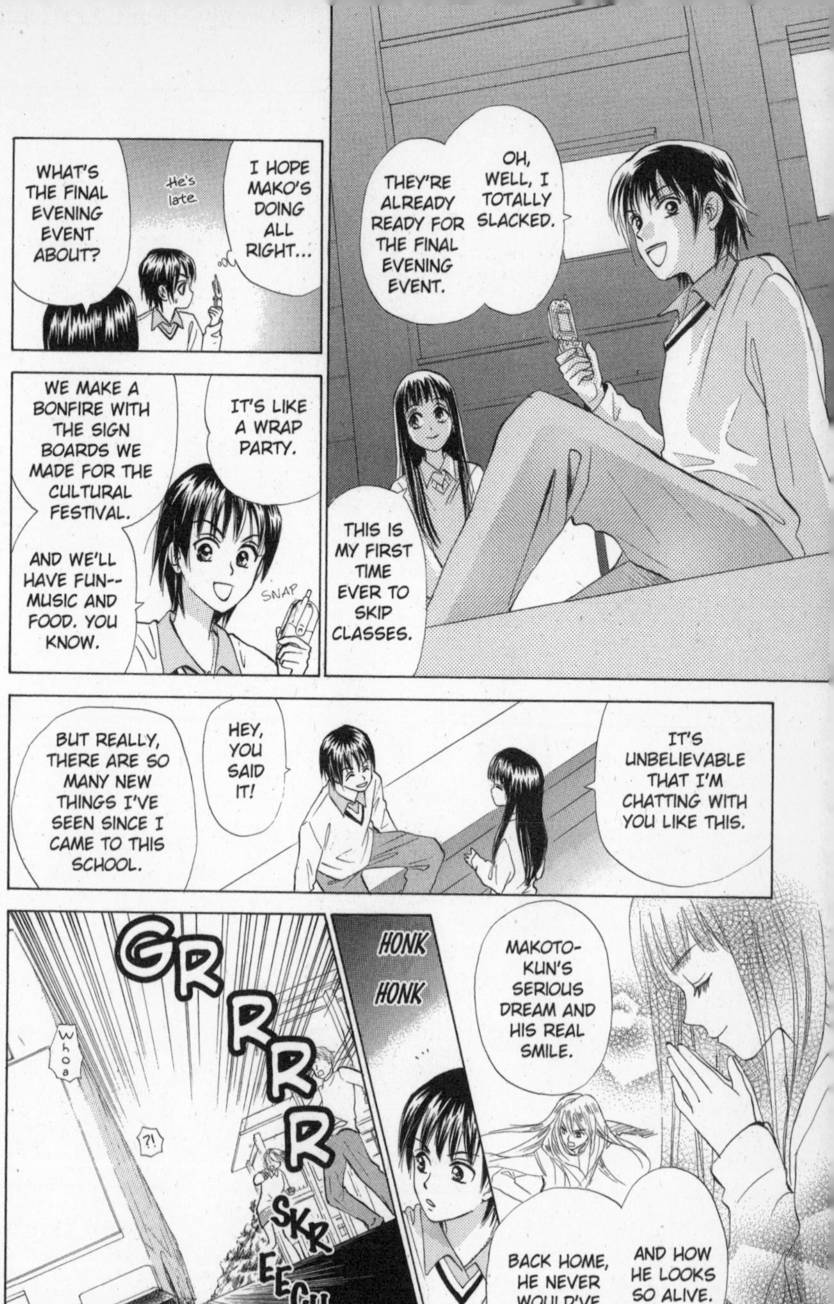
OH, WELL, I TOTALLY SLACKED.
THEY'RE ALREADY READY FOR THE FINAL EVENING EVENT.
THIS IS MY FIRST TIME EVER TO SKIP CLASSES.
I HOPE MAKO'S DOING ALL RIGHT...
He's late
WHAT'S THE FINAL EVENING EVENT ABOUT?
IT'S LIKE A WRAP PARTY.
WE MAKE A BONFIRE WITH THE SIGN BOARDS WE MADE FOR THE CULTURAL FESTIVAL.
AND WE'LL HAVE FUN-- MUSIC AND FOOD. YOU KNOW.
SNAP
IT'S UNBELIEVABLE THAT I'M CHATTING WITH YOU LIKE THIS.
HEY, YOU SAID IT!
BUT REALLY, THERE ARE SO MANY NEW THINGS I'VE SEEN SINCE I CAME TO THIS SCHOOL.
MAKOTO-KUN'S SERIOUS DREAM AND HIS REAL SMILE.
AND HOW HE LOOKS SO ALIVE.
BACK HOME, HE NEVER WOULD'VE SHOWN THAT.
...
HONK
HONK
GRRRRR
SKREEECH
Whoa
?!

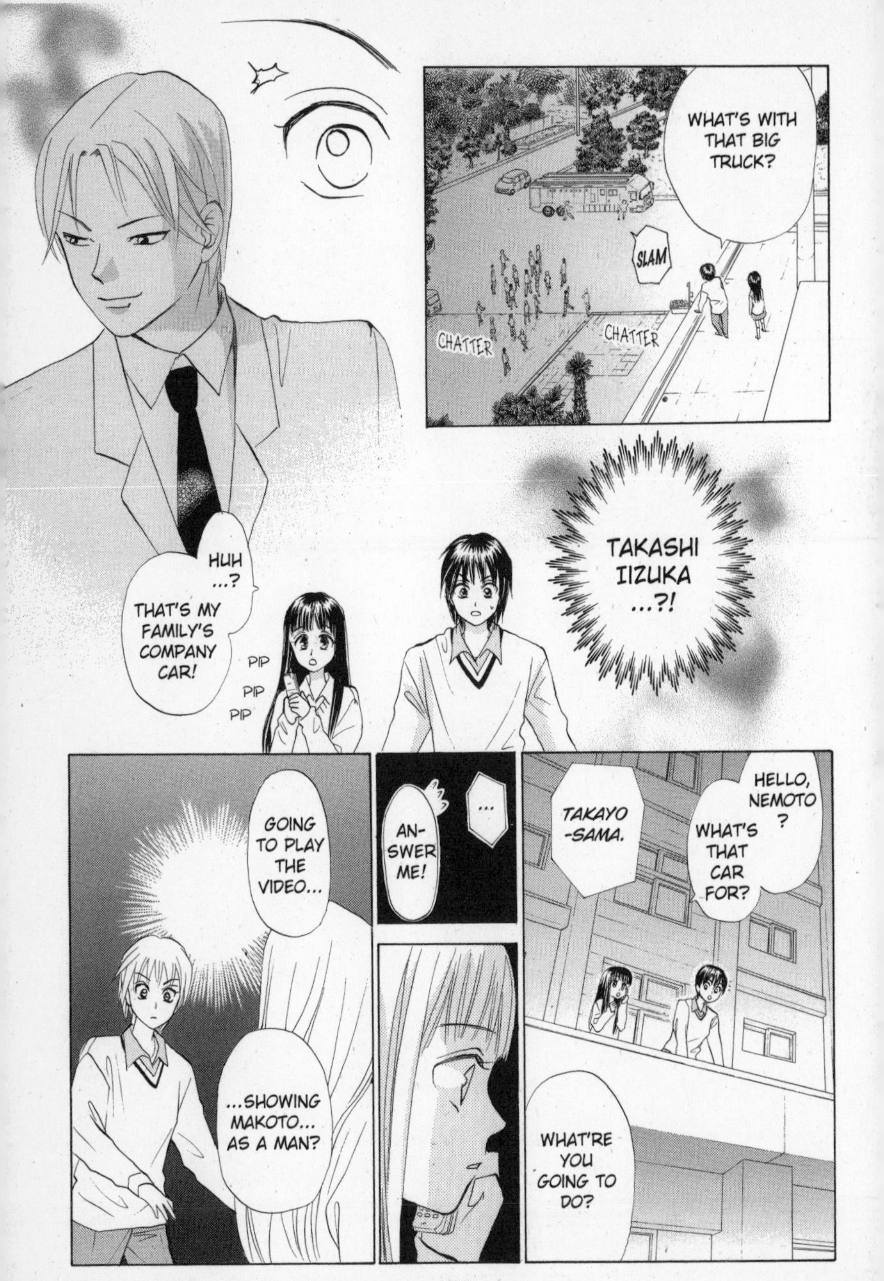
WHAT'S WITH THAT BIG TRUCK?
SLAM
CHATTER
CHATTER
TAKASHI IIZUKA ...?!
HUH ...?
THAT'S MY FAMILY'S COMPANY CAR!
PIP
PIP
PIP
HELLO, NEMOTO?
WHAT'S THAT CAR FOR?
TAKAYO-SAMA.
WHAT'RE YOU GOING TO DO?
...
AN-SWER ME!
GOING TO PLAY THE VIDEO...
...SHOWING MAKOTO... AS A MAN?

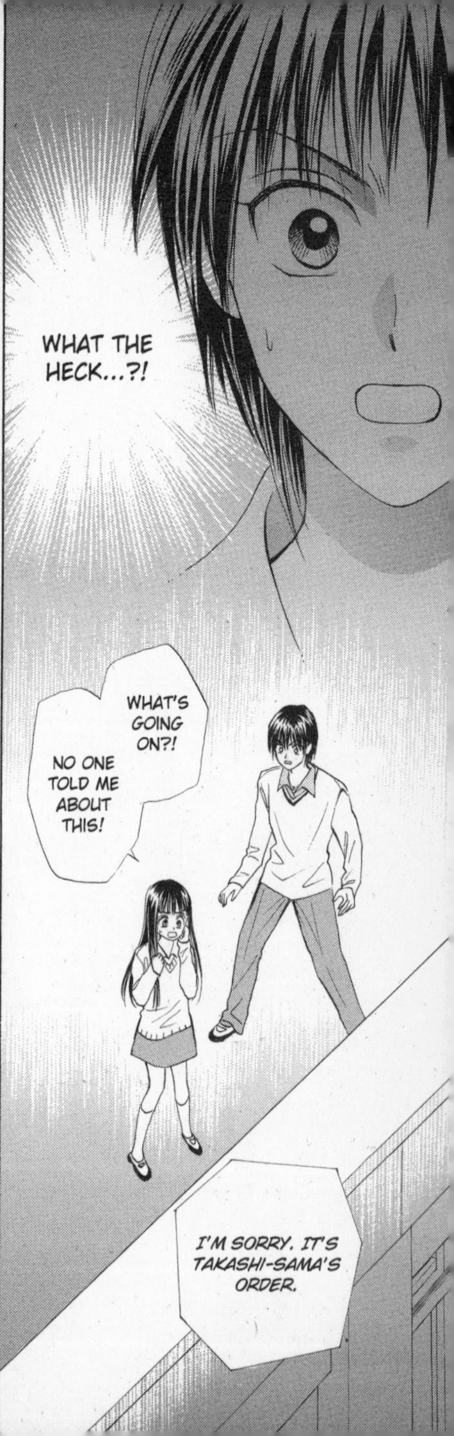
WHAT THE HECK...?!
WHAT'S GOING ON?!
NO ONE TOLD ME ABOUT THIS!
I'M SORRY. IT'S TAKASHI-SAMA'S ORDER.
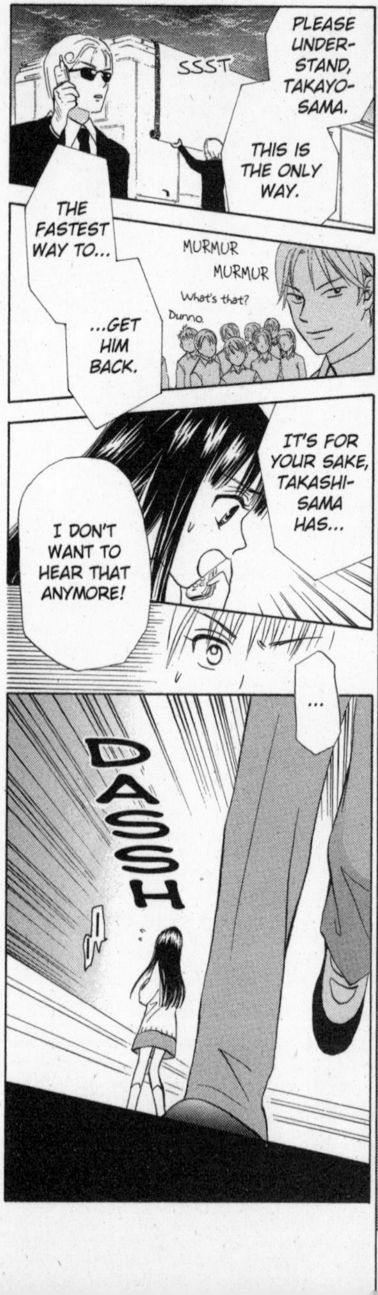
PLEASE UNDER-STAND, TAKAYO-SAMA.
SSST
THIS IS THE ONLY WAY.
THE FASTEST WAY TO...
MURMUR
MURMUR
What's that?
Dunno.
...GET HIM BACK.
IT'S FOR YOUR SAKE, TAKASHI-SAMA HAS...
I DON'T WANT TO HEAR THAT ANYMORE!
...
DASSH

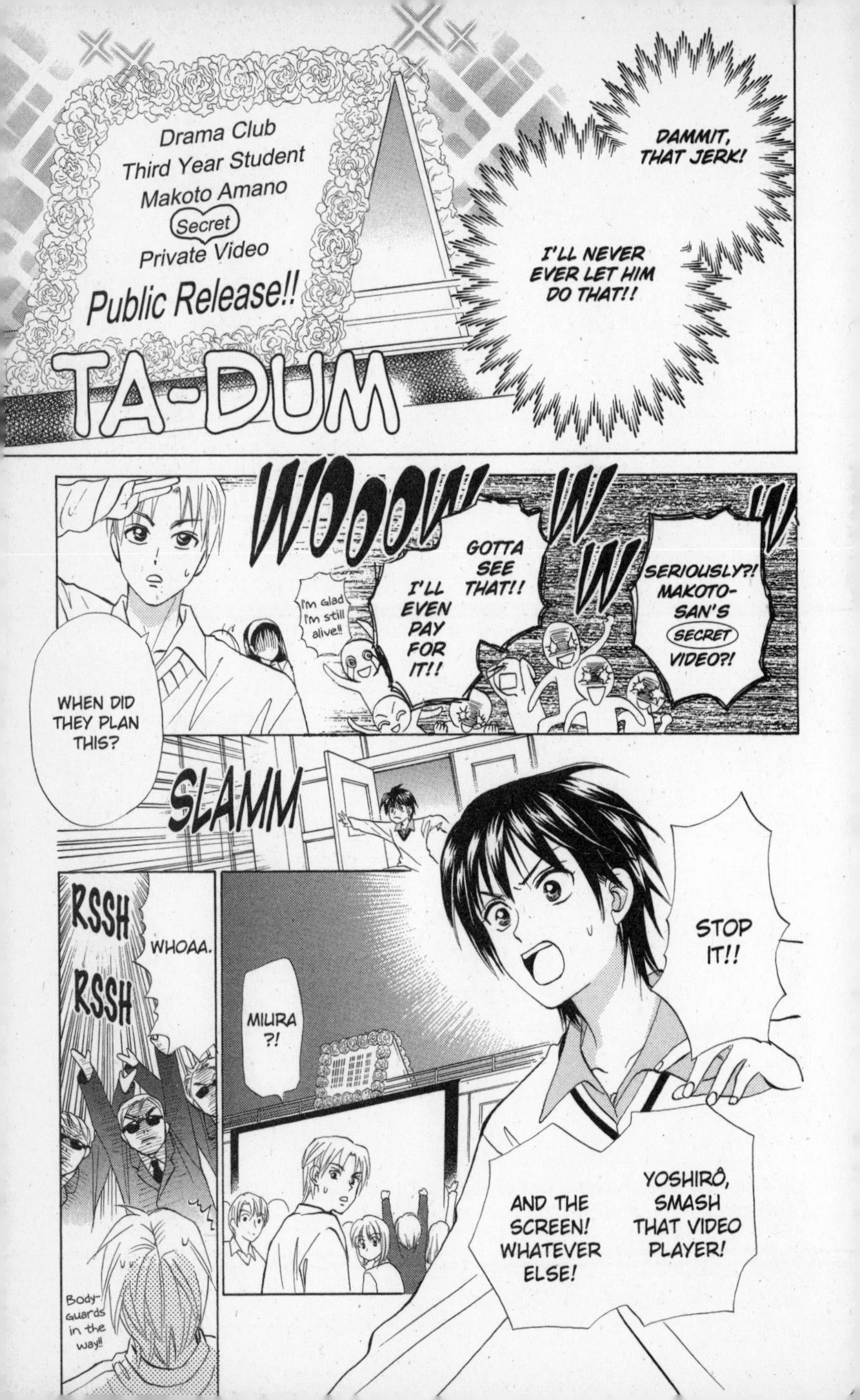
DAMMIT, THAT JERK!
I'LL NEVER EVER LET HIM DO THAT!!
Drama Club
Third Year Student
Makoto Amano
Secret
Private Video
Public Release!!
TA-DUM
WOOOW W W W
SERIOUSLY?! MAKOTO-SAN'S SECRET VIDEO?!
GOTTA SEE THAT!!
I'LL EVEN PAY FOR IT!!
I'm Glad I'm still alive!!
WHEN DID THEY PLAN THIS?
SLAMM
STOP IT!!
YOSHIRÔ, SMASH THAT VIDEO PLAYER!
AND THE SCREEN! WHATEVER ELSE!
MIURA ?!
RSSH
RSSH
WHOAA.
Body-Guards in the way!!

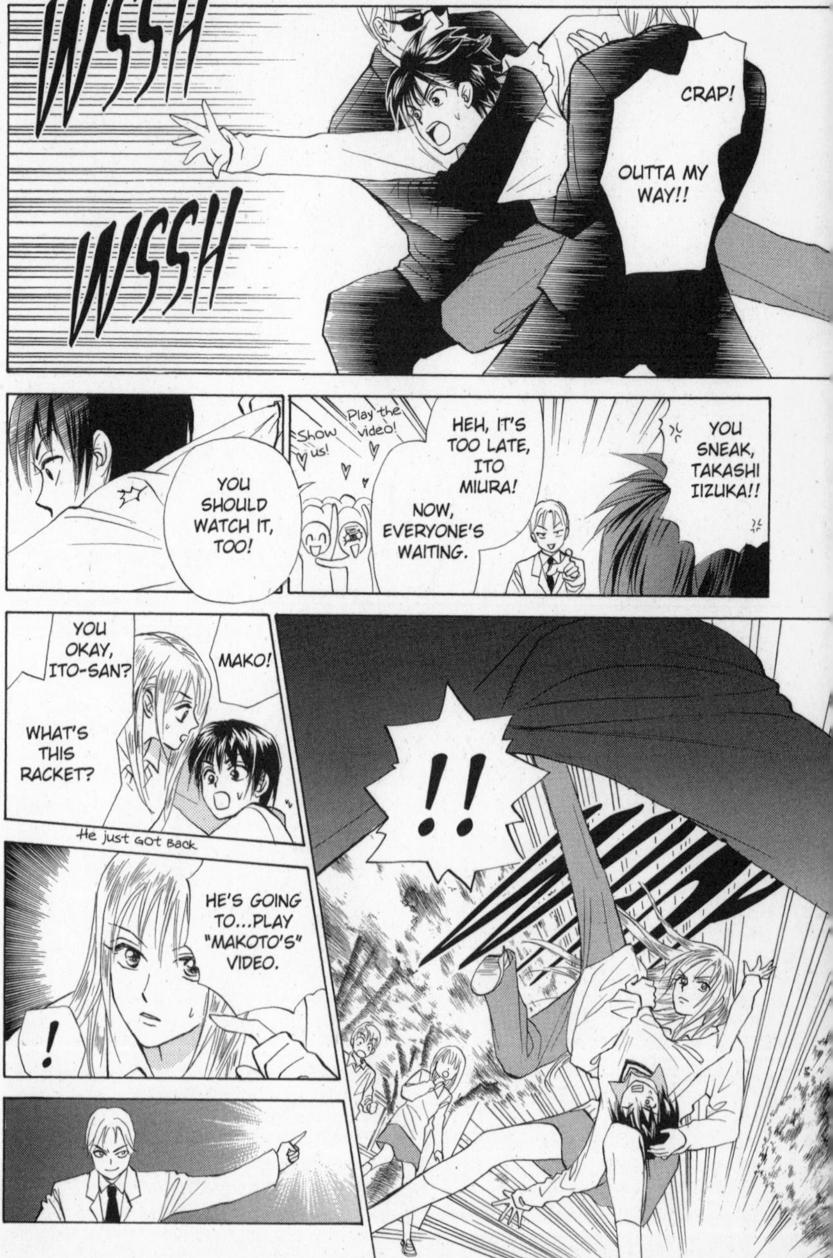
CRAP!
OUTTA MY WAY!!
WSSH
WSSH
YOU SNEAK, TAKASHI IIZUKA!!
HEH, IT'S TOO LATE, ITO MIURA!
NOW, EVERYONE'S WAITING.
Play the video!
Show us!
YOU SHOULD WATCH IT, TOO!
!!
MAKO!
YOU OKAY, ITO-SAN?
WHAT'S THIS RACKET?
He just GOT Back
HE'S GOING TO...PLAY "MAKOTO'S" VIDEO.
!

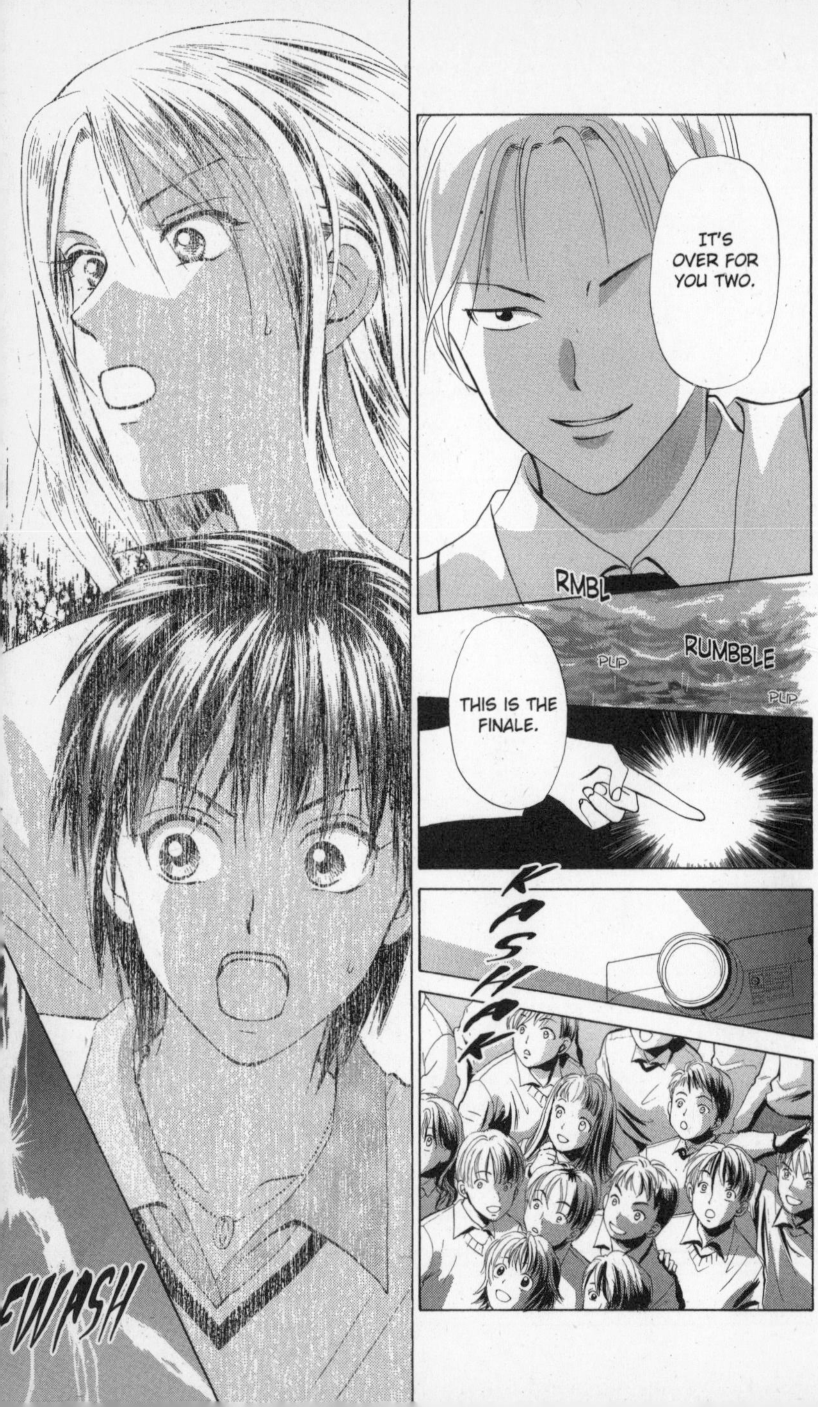
IT'S OVER FOR YOU TWO.
RMBL
RUMBBLE
PLIP
PLIP
THIS IS THE FINALE.
KASHAK
SWISH

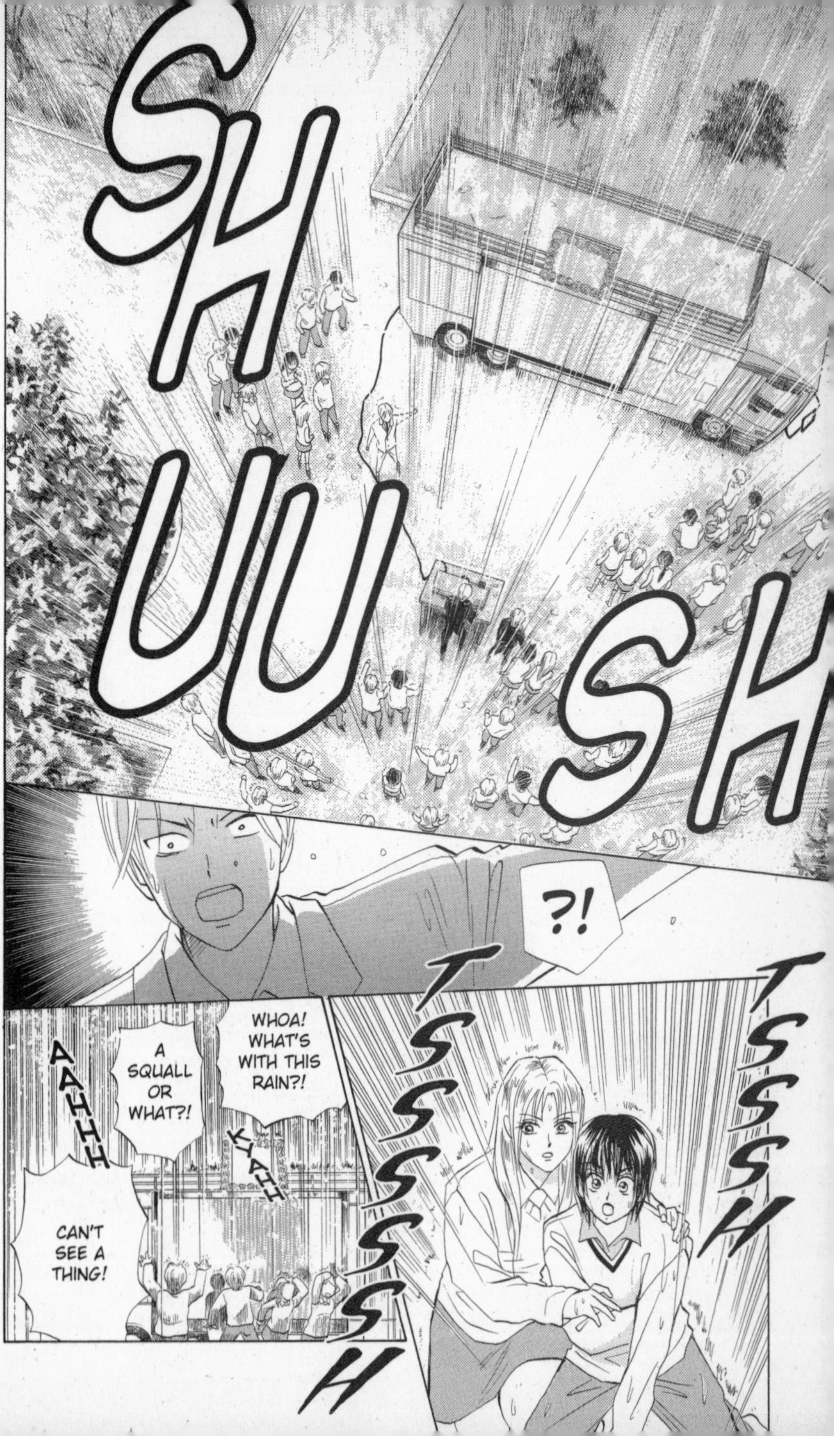
SHUUSH
?!
TSSSSH
TSSSSSSH
WHOA! WHAT'S WITH THIS RAIN?!
A SQUALL OR WHAT?!
KYAHH
AAHHH
CAN'T SEE A THING!

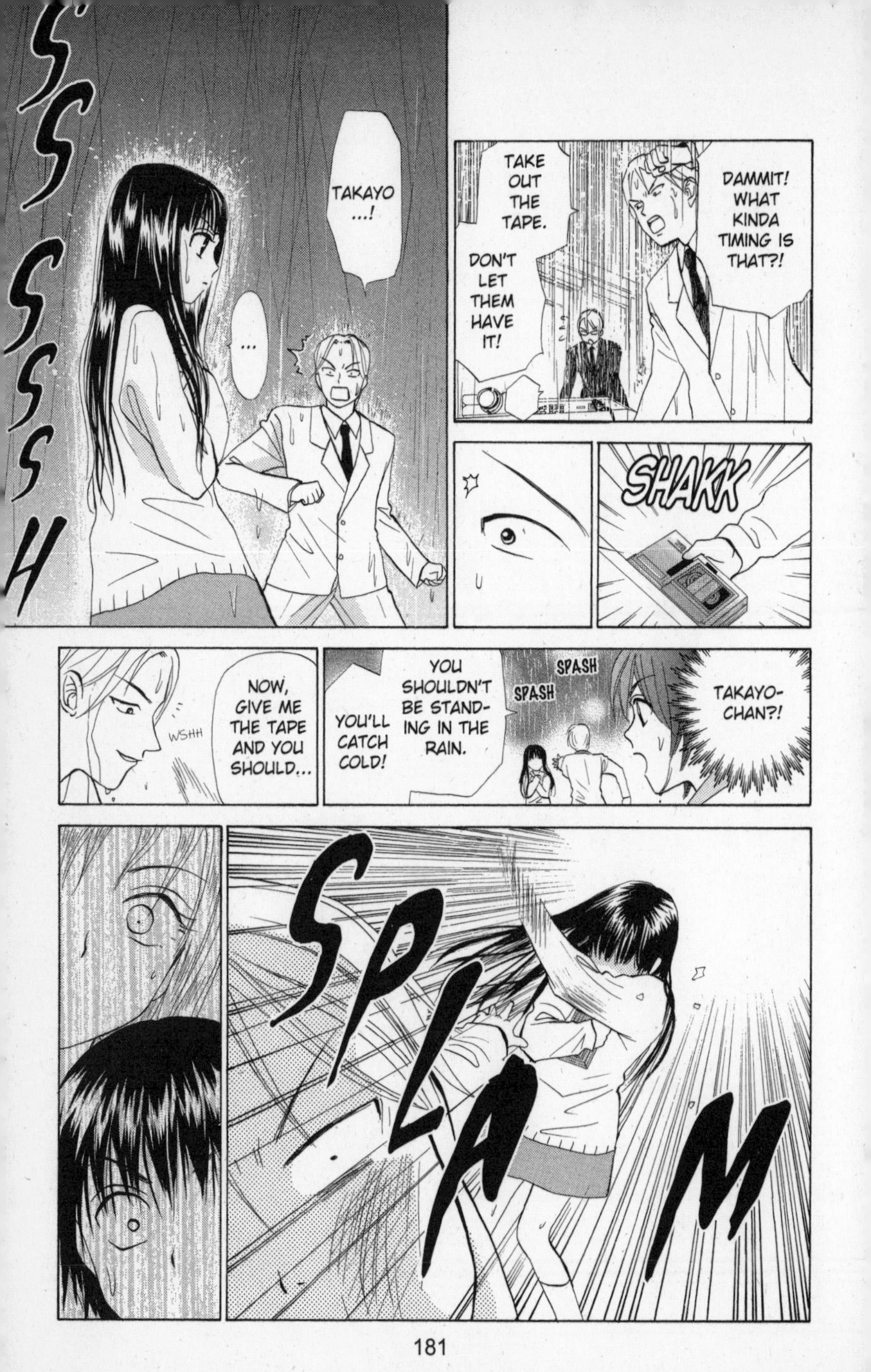
DAMMIT! WHAT KINDA TIMING IS THAT?!
TAKE OUT THE TAPE.
DON'T LET THEM HAVE IT!
SHAKK
TAKAYO ...!
...
SSSSSH
TAKAYO-CHAN?!
SPASH
SPASH
YOU SHOULDN'T BE STANDING IN THE RAIN.
YOU'LL CATCH COLD!
NOW, GIVE ME THE TAPE AND YOU SHOULD...
WSHH
SPLAM

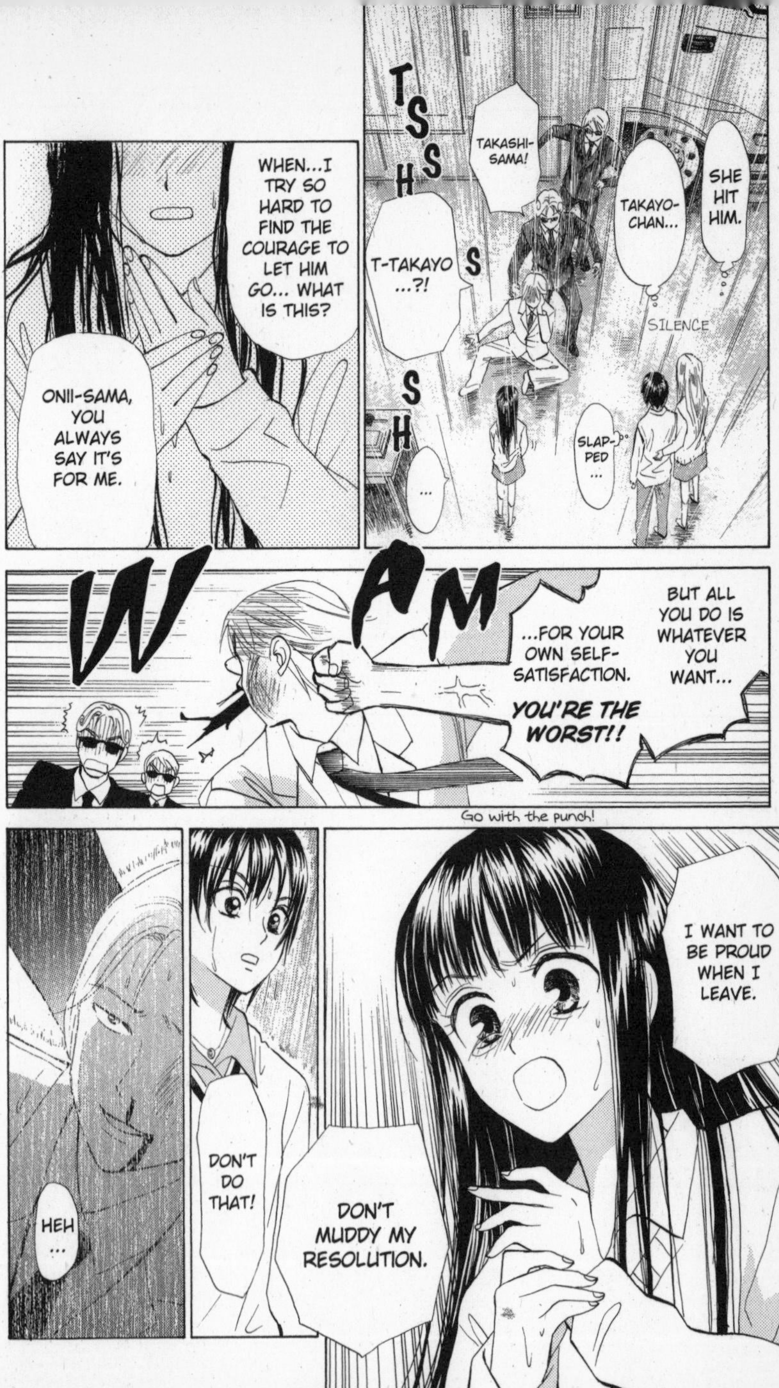
SHE HIT HIM.
TAKAYO-CHAN...
TAKASHI-SAMA!
T-TAKAYO...?!
TSSHSSH
SILENCE
SLAPPED...
...
WHEN...I TRY SO HARD TO FIND THE COURAGE TO LET HIM GO... WHAT IS THIS?
ONII-SAMA, YOU ALWAYS SAY IT'S FOR ME.
BUT ALL YOU DO IS WHATEVER YOU WANT...
...FOR YOUR OWN SELF-SATISFACTION.
YOU'RE THE WORST!!
WAM
Go with the punch!
I WANT TO BE PROUD WHEN I LEAVE.
DON'T MUDDY MY RESOLUTION.
DON'T DO THAT!
HEH...

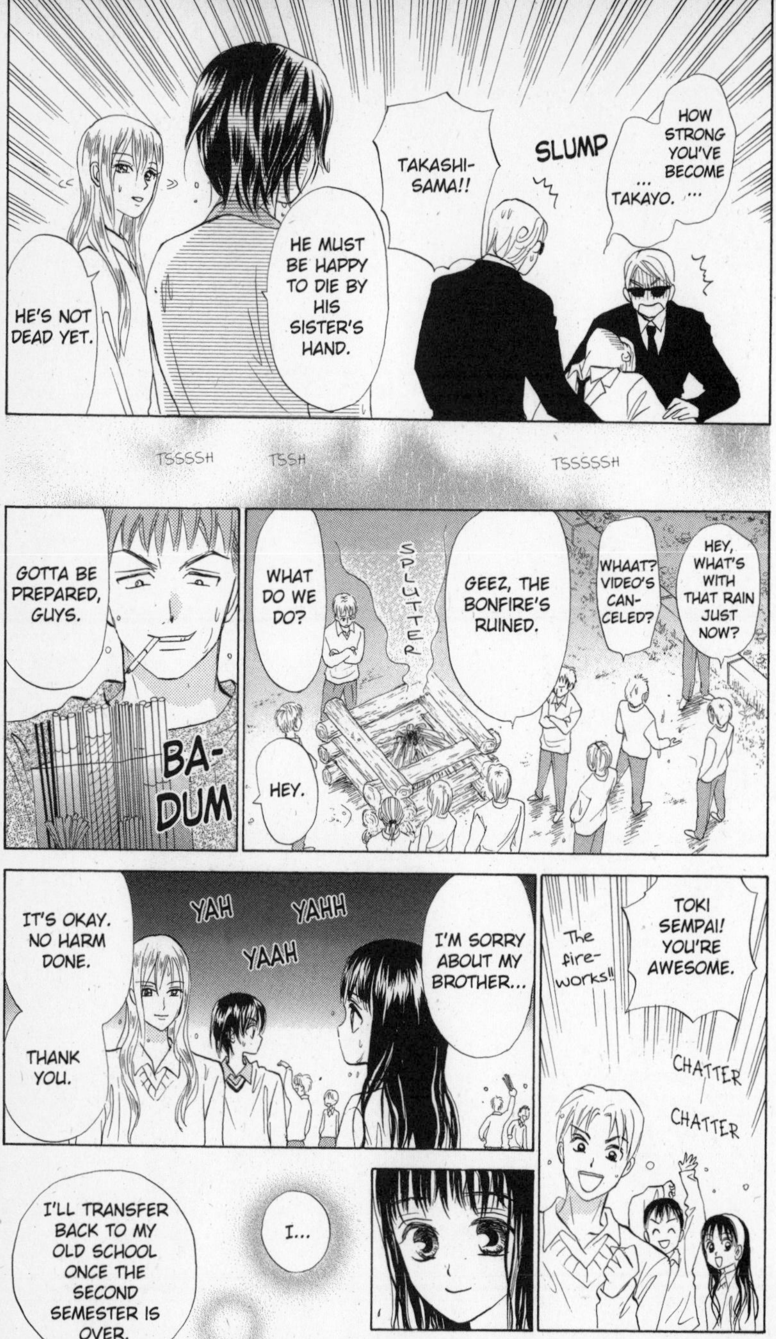
HOW STRONG YOU'VE BECOME ... TAKAYO. ...
SLUMP
TAKASHI-SAMA!!
HE MUST BE HAPPY TO DIE BY HIS SISTER'S HAND.
HE'S NOT DEAD YET.
TSSSSSH
TSSH
TSSSSH
HEY, WHAT'S WITH THAT RAIN JUST NOW?
WHAAT? VIDEO'S CAN-CELED?
GEEZ, THE BONFIRE'S RUINED.
SPLUTTER
WHAT DO WE DO?
HEY.
GOTTA BE PREPARED, GUYS.
BA-DUM
TOKI SEMPAI! YOU'RE AWESOME.
The fire-works!!
CHATTER
CHATTER
I'M SORRY ABOUT MY BROTHER...
YAHH
YAH
YAAH
IT'S OKAY. NO HARM DONE.
THANK YOU.
I...
I'LL TRANSFER BACK TO MY OLD SCHOOL ONCE THE SECOND SEMESTER IS OVER.

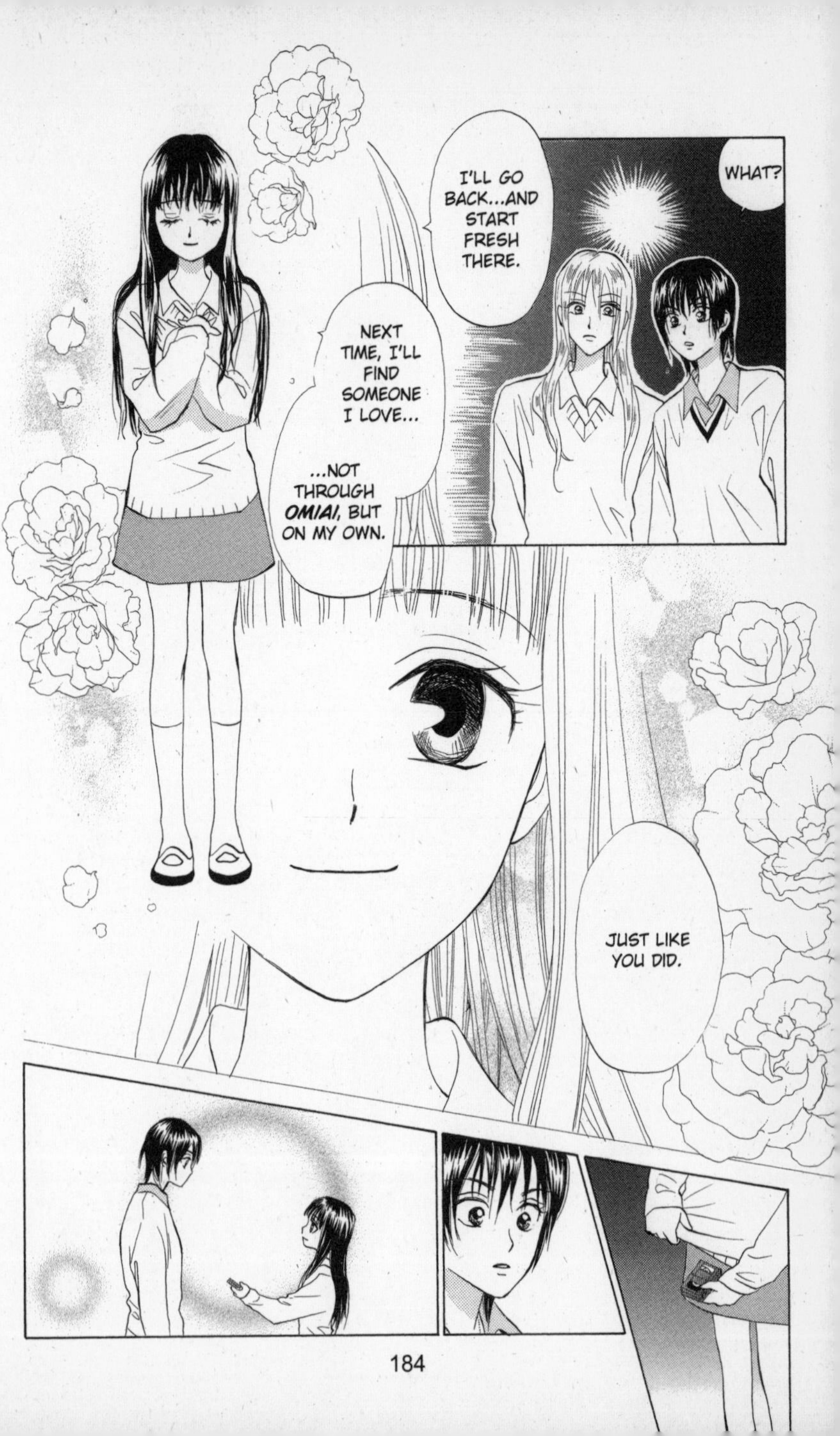
WHAT?
I'LL GO BACK...AND START FRESH THERE.
NEXT TIME, I'LL FIND SOMEONE I LOVE...
...NOT THROUGH OMIAI, BUT ON MY OWN.
JUST LIKE YOU DID.

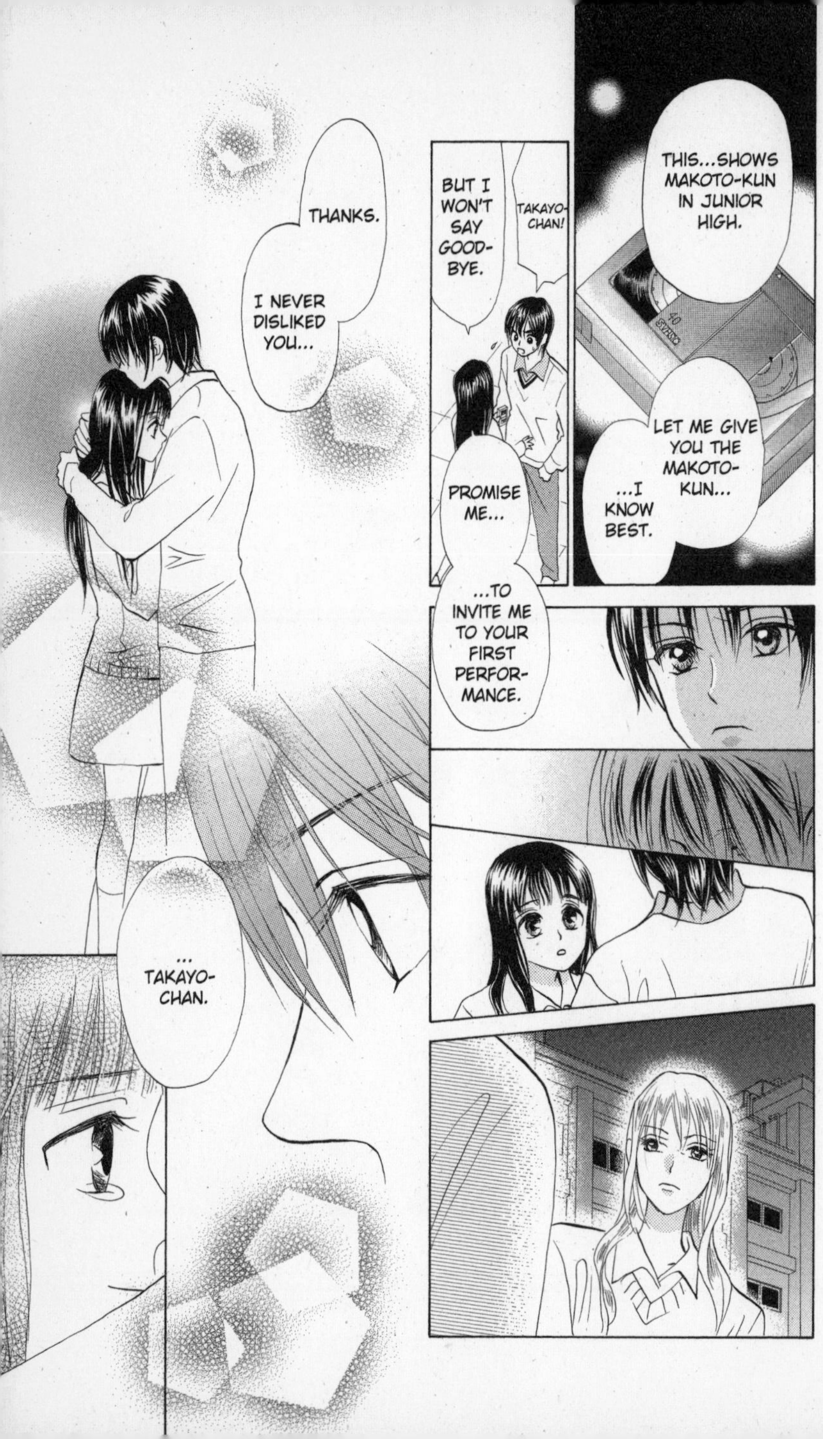
THIS...SHOWS MAKOTO-KUN IN JUNIOR HIGH.
LET ME GIVE YOU THE MAKOTO-KUN...
...I KNOW BEST.
TAKAYO-CHAN!
BUT I WON'T SAY GOOD-BYE.
PROMISE ME...
...TO INVITE ME TO YOUR FIRST PERFORMANCE.
THANKS.
I NEVER DISLIKED YOU...
...TAKAYO-CHAN.

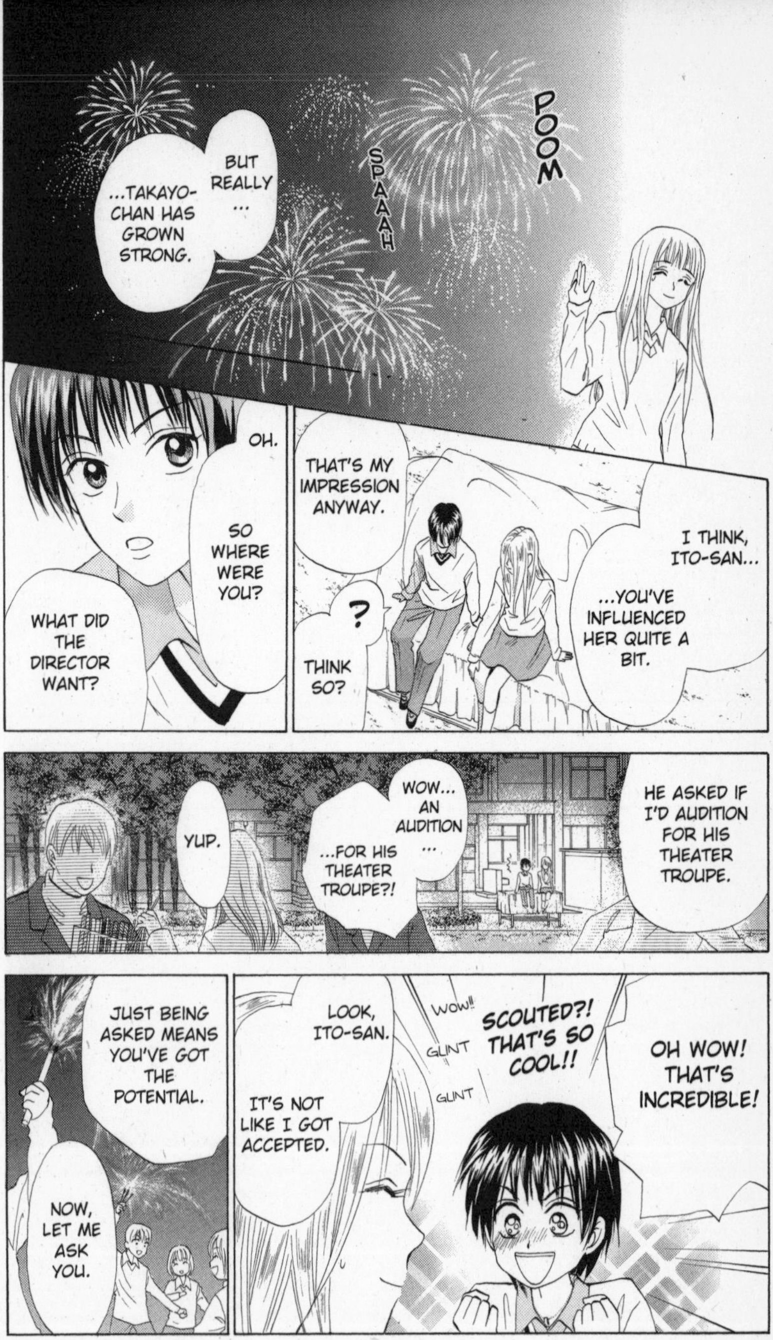

POOM
SPAAAH
BUT REALLY...
...TAKAYO-CHAN HAS GROWN STRONG.
I THINK, ITO-SAN...
...YOU'VE INFLUENCED HER QUITE A BIT.
THAT'S MY IMPRESSION ANYWAY.
?
THINK SO?
OH.
SO WHERE WERE YOU?
WHAT DID THE DIRECTOR WANT?
HE ASKED IF I'D AUDITION FOR HIS THEATER TROUPE.
WOW... AN AUDITION...
...FOR HIS THEATER TROUPE?!
YUP.
OH WOW! THAT'S INCREDIBLE!
SCOUTED?! THAT'S SO COOL!!
WOW!!
GLINT
GLINT
LOOK, ITO-SAN.
IT'S NOT LIKE I GOT ACCEPTED.
JUST BEING ASKED MEANS YOU'VE GOT THE POTENTIAL.
NOW, LET ME ASK YOU.

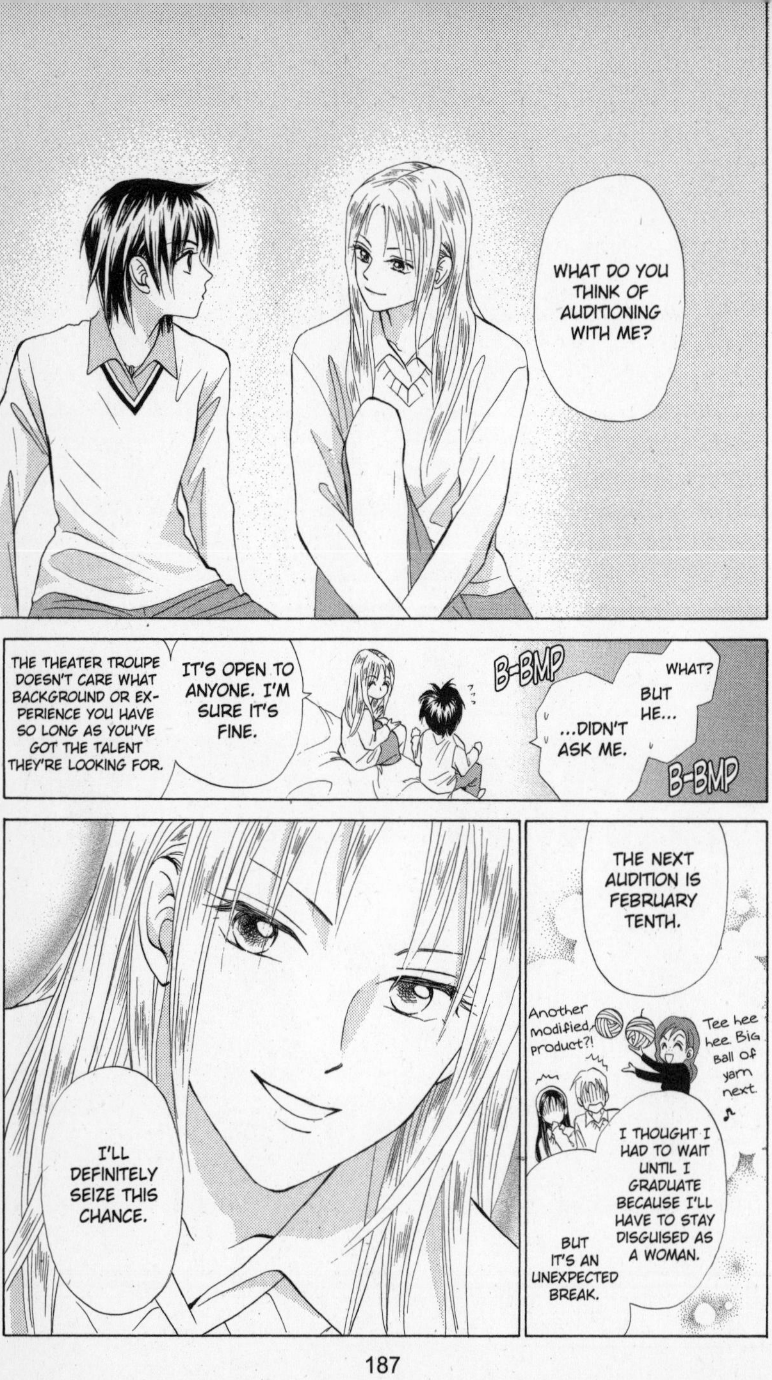
WHAT DO YOU THINK OF AUDITIONING WITH ME?
WHAT? BUT HE...
...DIDN'T ASK ME.
B-BMP
B-BMP
IT'S OPEN TO ANYONE. I'M SURE IT'S FINE.
THE THEATER TROUPE DOESN'T CARE WHAT BACKGROUND OR EX-PERIENCE YOU HAVE SO LONG AS YOU'VE GOT THE TALENT THEY'RE LOOKING FOR.
THE NEXT AUDITION IS FEBRUARY TENTH.
Tee hee hee. Big ball of yarn next.
Another modified product?!
I THOUGHT I HAD TO WAIT UNTIL I GRADUATE BECAUSE I'LL HAVE TO STAY DISGUISED AS A WOMAN.
BUT IT'S AN UNEXPECTED BREAK.
I'LL DEFINITELY SEIZE THIS CHANCE.

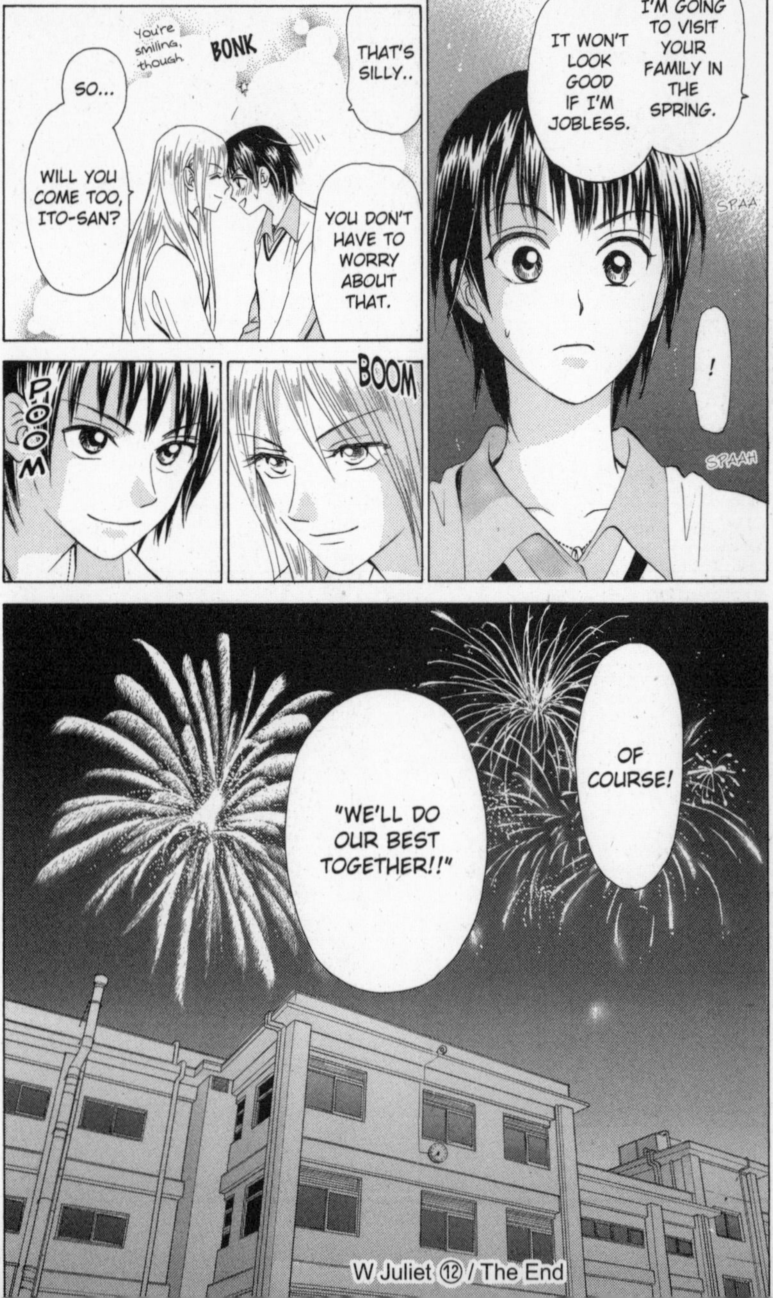
BESIDES, I'M GOING TO VISIT YOUR FAMILY IN THE SPRING.
IT WON'T LOOK GOOD IF I'M JOBLESS.
SPAA
!
SPAAH
THAT'S SILLY..
BONK
You're smiling, though.
YOU DON'T HAVE TO WORRY ABOUT THAT.
SO...
WILL YOU COME TOO, ITO-SAN?
BOOM
POOM
OF COURSE!
"WE'LL DO OUR BEST TOGETHER!!"
W Juliet ⑫ / The End

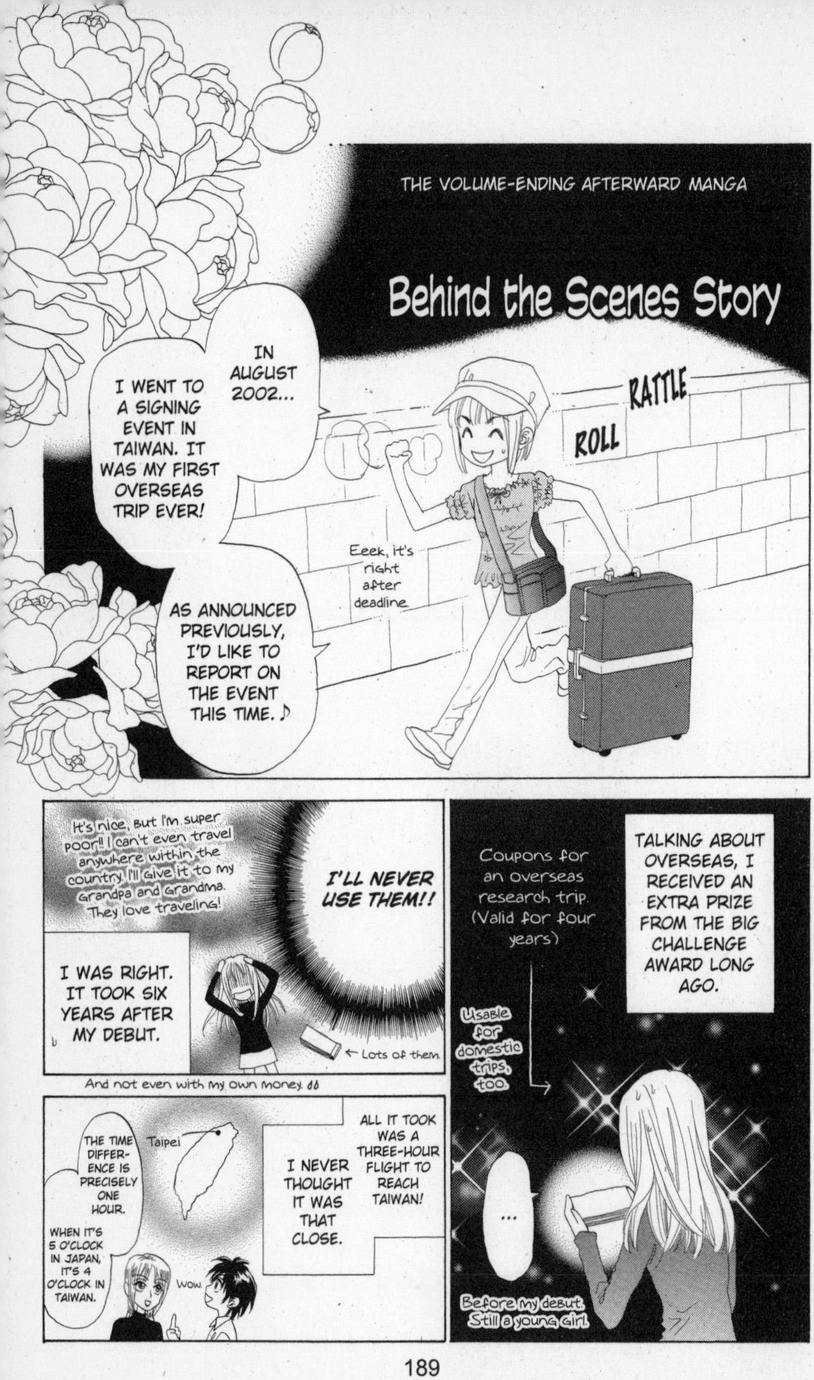
THE VOLUME-ENDING AFTERWARD MANGA
Behind the Scenes Story
RATTLE
ROLL
IN AUGUST 2002... I WENT TO A SIGNING EVENT IN TAIWAN. IT WAS MY FIRST OVERSEAS TRIP EVER!
Eeek, it's right after deadline.
AS ANNOUNCED PREVIOUSLY, I'D LIKE TO REPORT ON THE EVENT THIS TIME. ♪
TALKING ABOUT OVERSEAS, I RECEIVED AN EXTRA PRIZE FROM THE BIG CHALLENGE AWARD LONG AGO.
Coupons for an overseas research trip. (Valid for four years)
Usable for domestic trips, too.
...
Before my debut. Still a young girl.
I'LL NEVER USE THEM!!
It's nice, but I'm super poor!! I can't even travel anywhere within the country. I'll give it to my Grandpa and Grandma. They love traveling!
I WAS RIGHT. IT TOOK SIX YEARS AFTER MY DEBUT.
← Lots of them.
And not even with my own money.
ALL IT TOOK WAS A THREE-HOUR FLIGHT TO REACH TAIWAN!
I NEVER THOUGHT IT WAS THAT CLOSE.
Taipei
THE TIME DIFFERENCE IS PRECISELY ONE HOUR.
WHEN IT'S 5 O'CLOCK IN JAPAN, IT'S 4 O'CLOCK IN TAIWAN.
Wow.

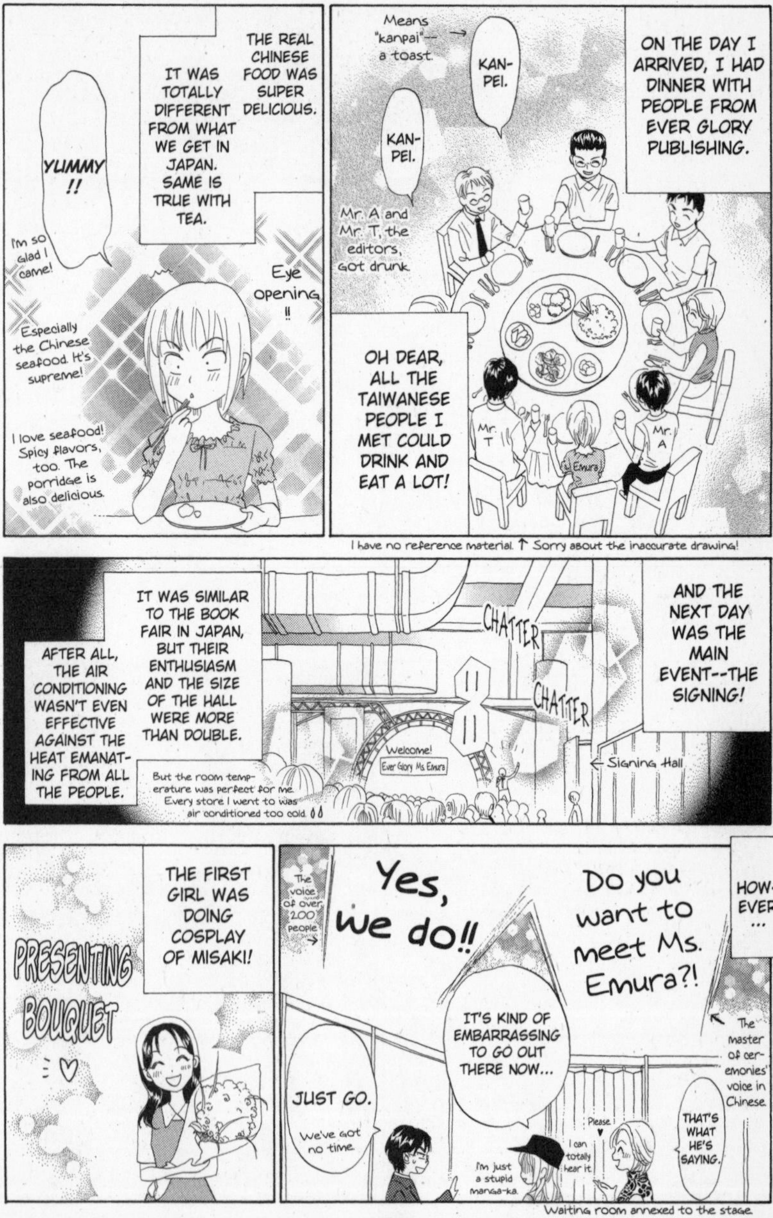
ON THE DAY I ARRIVED, I HAD DINNER WITH PEOPLE FROM EVER GLORY PUBLISHING.
KAN-PEI.
Means "kanpai"-- a toast.
KAN-PEI.
Mr. A and Mr. T, the editors, got drunk
OH DEAR, ALL THE TAIWANESE PEOPLE I MET COULD DRINK AND EAT A LOT!
Mr. T
Emura
Mr. A
I have no reference material. ↑ Sorry about the inaccurate drawing!
THE REAL CHINESE FOOD WAS SUPER DELICIOUS.
IT WAS TOTALLY DIFFERENT FROM WHAT WE GET IN JAPAN. SAME IS TRUE WITH TEA.
YUMMY!!
I'm so glad I came!
Eye opening!!
Especially the Chinese seafood. It's supreme!
I love seafood! Spicy flavors, too. The porridge is also delicious.
AND THE NEXT DAY WAS THE MAIN EVENT--THE SIGNING!
CHATTER
CHATTER
IT WAS SIMILAR TO THE BOOK FAIR IN JAPAN, BUT THEIR ENTHUSIASM AND THE SIZE OF THE HALL WERE MORE THAN DOUBLE.
AFTER ALL, THE AIR CONDITIONING WASN'T EVEN EFFECTIVE AGAINST THE HEAT EMANAT-ING FROM ALL THE PEOPLE.
← Signing Hall
Welcome!
Ever Glory Ms. Emura
But the room temp-erature was perfect for me. Every store I went to was air conditioned too cold.
HOW-EVER...
Do you want to meet Ms. Emura?!
The master of cer-emonies' voice in Chinese
Yes, we do!!
The voice of over 200 people →
IT'S KIND OF EMBARRASSING TO GO OUT THERE NOW...
THAT'S WHAT HE'S SAYING.
Please ♥
I can totally hear it
I'm just a stupid manga-ka.
JUST GO.
We've got no time
Waiting room annexed to the stage
THE FIRST GIRL WAS DOING COSPLAY OF MISAKI!
PRESENTING BOUQUET
♥

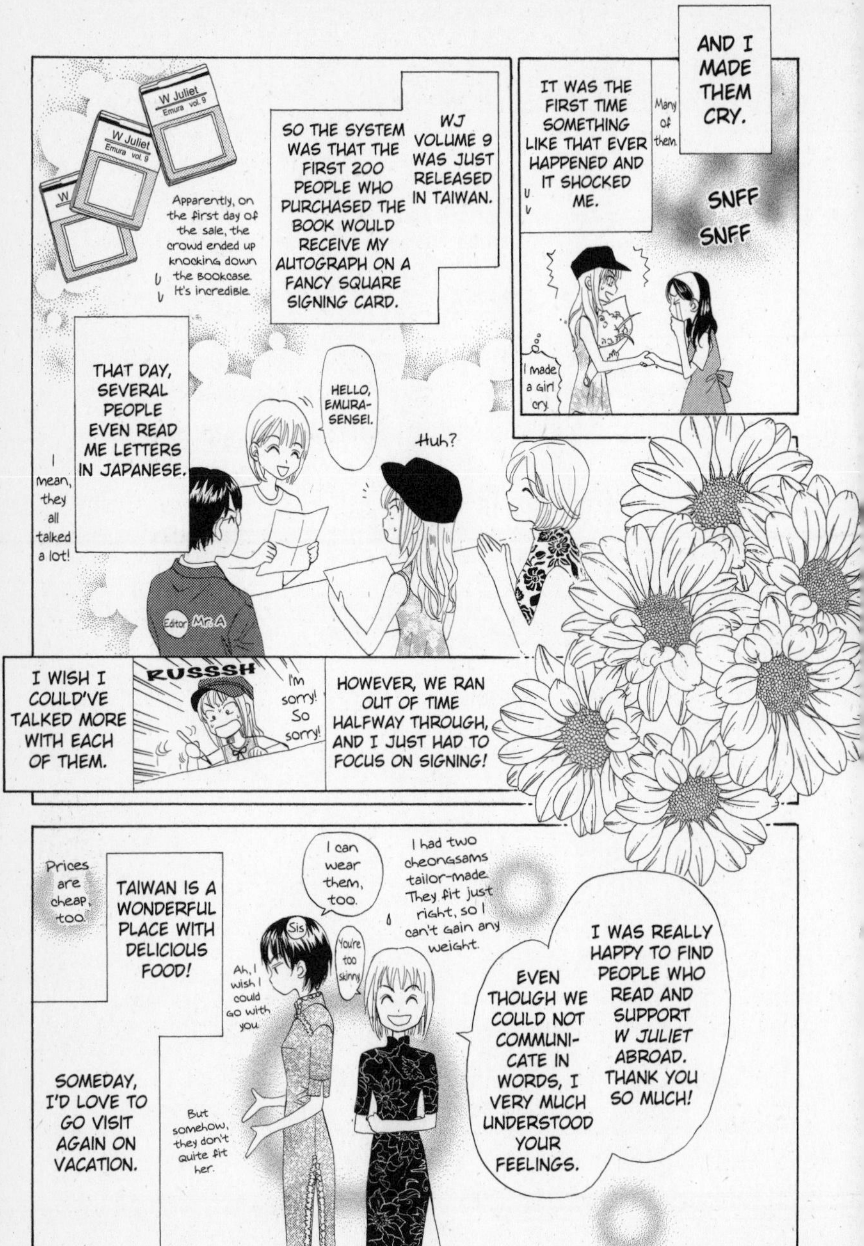
AND I MADE THEM CRY.
Many of them.
IT WAS THE FIRST TIME SOMETHING LIKE THAT EVER HAPPENED AND IT SHOCKED ME.
SNFF
SNFF
I made a girl cry.
WJ VOLUME 9 WAS JUST RELEASED IN TAIWAN.
SO THE SYSTEM WAS THAT THE FIRST 200 PEOPLE WHO PURCHASED THE BOOK WOULD RECEIVE MY AUTOGRAPH ON A FANCY SQUARE SIGNING CARD.
W Juliet Emura vol. 9
W Juliet Emura vol. 9
Apparently, on the first day of the sale, the crowd ended up knocking down the bookcase. It's incredible.
THAT DAY, SEVERAL PEOPLE EVEN READ ME LETTERS IN JAPANESE.
HELLO, EMURA-SENSEI.
Huh?
I mean, they all talked a lot!
Editor Mr. A
HOWEVER, WE RAN OUT OF TIME HALFWAY THROUGH, AND I JUST HAD TO FOCUS ON SIGNING!
I'm sorry! So sorry!
RUSSSH
I WISH I COULD'VE TALKED MORE WITH EACH OF THEM.
I WAS REALLY HAPPY TO FIND PEOPLE WHO READ AND SUPPORT W JULIET ABROAD. THANK YOU SO MUCH!
EVEN THOUGH WE COULD NOT COMMUNI-CATE IN WORDS, I VERY MUCH UNDERSTOOD YOUR FEELINGS.
I had two cheongsams tailor-made. They fit just right, so I can't gain any weight.
You're too skinny
I can wear them, too.
Sis
Ah, I wish I could go with you.
TAIWAN IS A WONDERFUL PLACE WITH DELICIOUS FOOD!
Prices are cheap, too.
But somehow, they don't quite fit her.
SOMEDAY, I'D LOVE TO GO VISIT AGAIN ON VACATION.

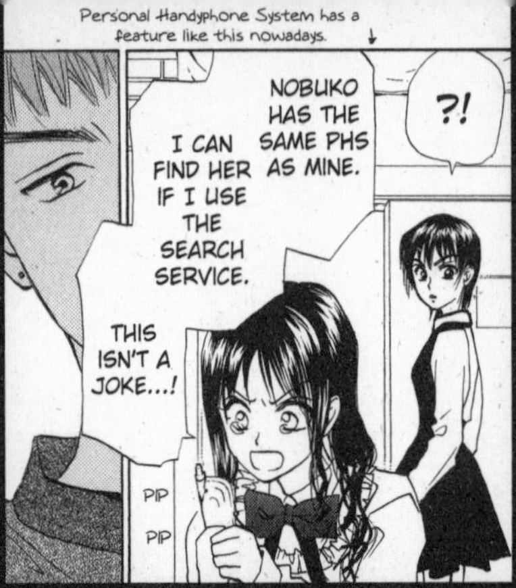
Personal Handyphone System has a feature like this nowadays.
?!
NOBUKO HAS THE SAME PHS AS MINE.
I CAN FIND HER IF I USE THE SEARCH SERVICE.
THIS ISN'T A JOKE...!
PIP
PIP

PHS

[reference page 33] PHS sta
"Personal Handyphone Syst
looks like a cell phone, but i
a digital cordless telephone
Functionally, PHS can opera
as a cordless telephone, but
outdoor public mobile comr
system or transceiver. Comp
cell phone system its transn
power is small, with limited

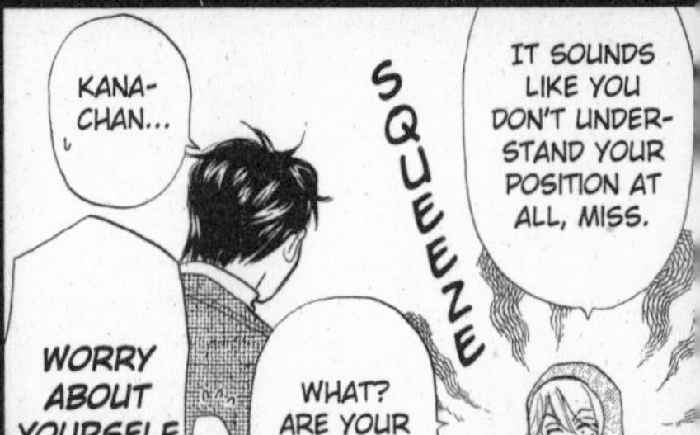
IT SOUNDS LIKE YOU DON'T UNDER-STAND YOUR POSITION AT ALL, MISS.
SQUEEZE
KANA-CHAN...
WHAT? ARE YOUR CHEEKS MADE OF OMANJU OR WHAT?
MPFF
WORRY ABOUT YOURSELF INSTEAD OF US!

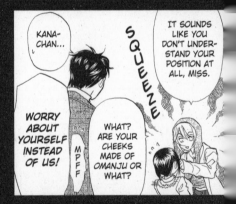

Omanju

[reference page 42] *Omanju*, or *manju*, is a traditional confection
Japan. There are many varieties, but most of them have an outsi
made of flour or rice dough and an inside filling of sweet bean p
This treat's texture is soft and flexible, so when Kanako pinches
Nobuko's cheeks, she means that they're pliant like dough—like
those of an innocent baby rather than those of a hardened adul

Osekihan

[reference page 108]

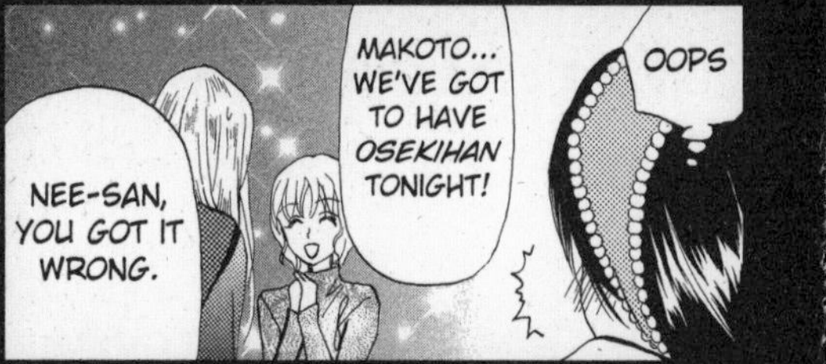
OOPS
MAKOTO... WE'VE GOT TO HAVE OSEKIHAN TONIGHT!
NEE-SAN, YOU GOT IT WRONG.

Osekihan (or *sekihan*) is a traditional Japanese dish of sticky rice steamed with azuki beans (small red beans) that is served on special occasions like birthdays, weddings and graduation days. Literally, *sekihan* translates to "red rice"; when steamed with azuki beans, the rice turns red. And, yes, red in Japan evokes images of auspicious or happy occasions, and that's precisely why *sekihan* is often prepared for celebration.

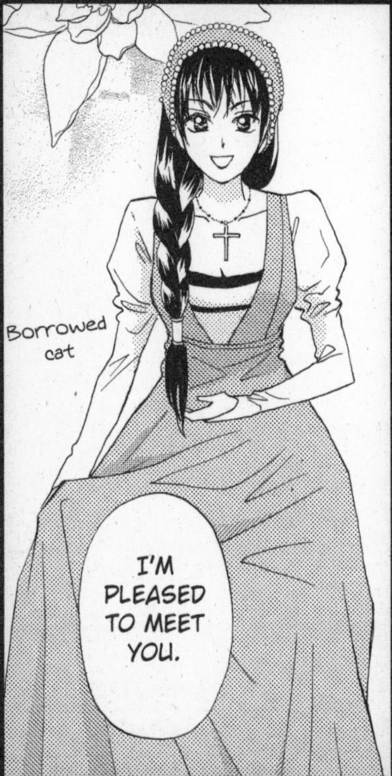
Borrowed cat
I'M PLEASED TO MEET YOU.

Borrowed cat

[reference page 114] "Borrowed cat" is a Japanese idiom that describes someone who is behaving in an uncharacteristically quiet or well-behaved manner as opposed to his true nature, just like a cat in unfamiliar territory.

What happens when the hottest guy in school is a girl?!?

Find out in the popular manga series!

With original artwork by series creator Hisaya Nakajo, your favorite characters come to life in this art book!

Hana-Kimi

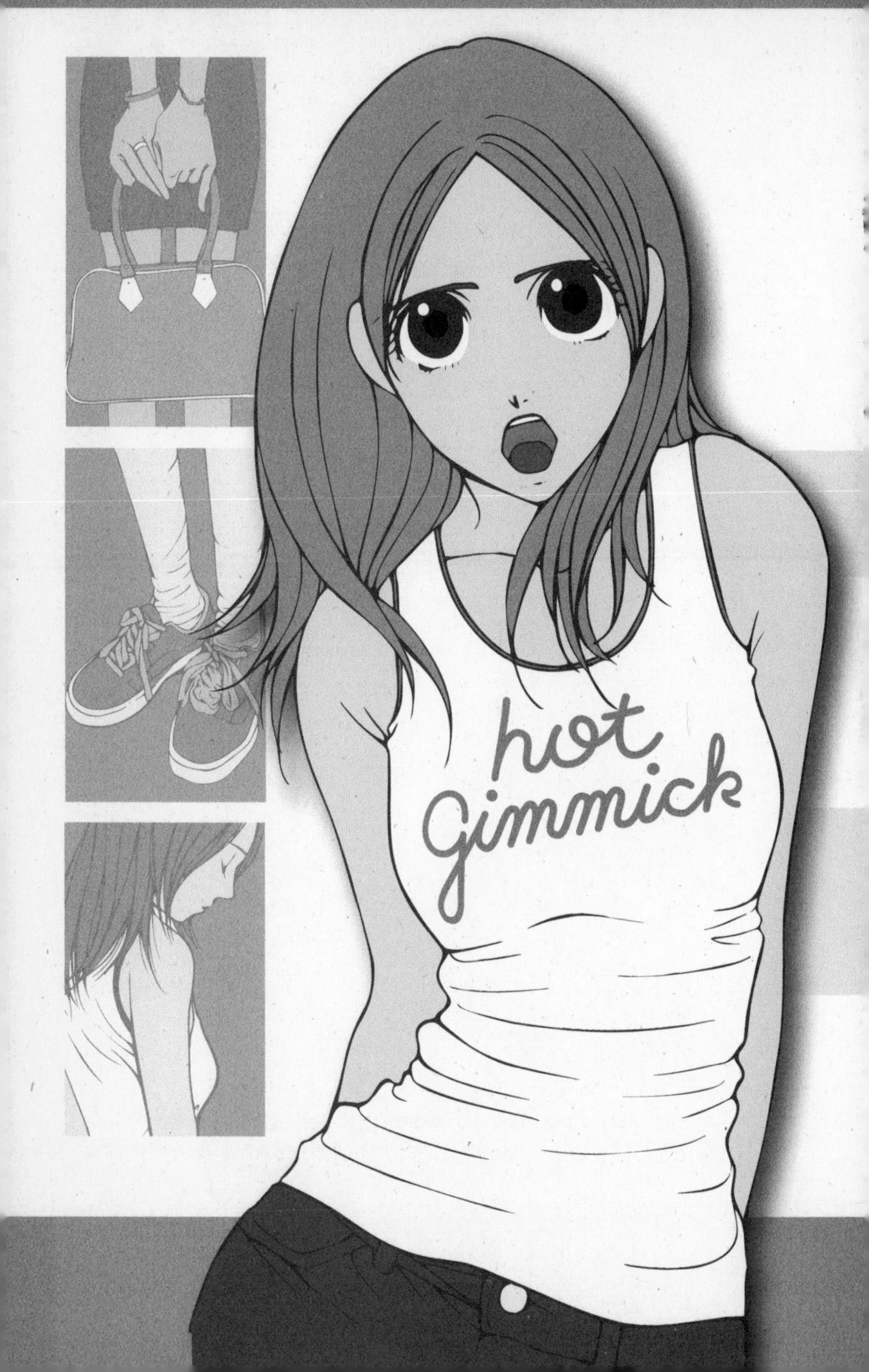
hot
Gimmick

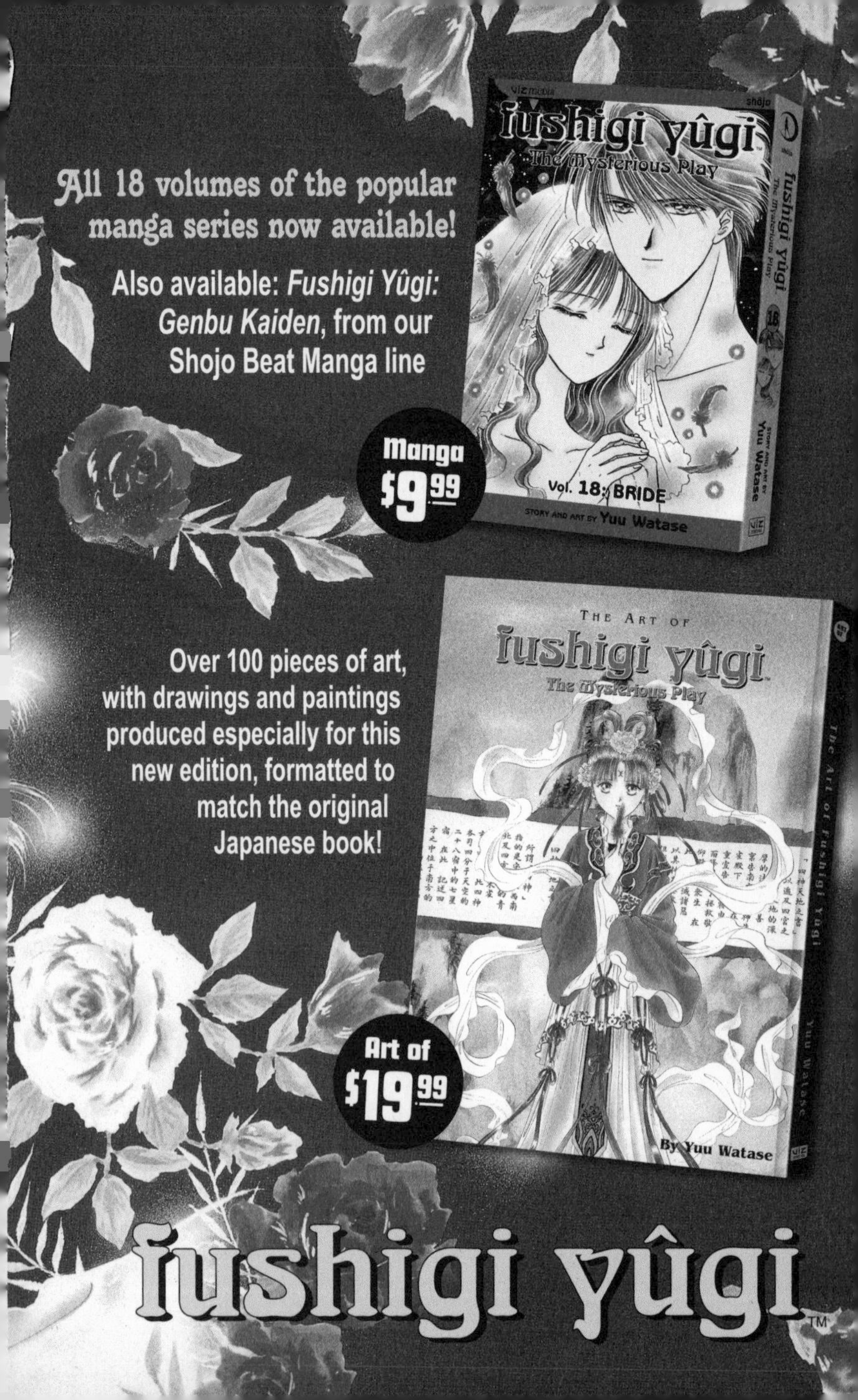
All 18 volumes of the popular manga series now available!
Also available: *Fushigi Yûgi: Genbu Kaiden*, from our Shojo Beat Manga line
fushigi yûgi
The Mysterious Play
Vol. 18: BRIDE
STORY AND ART BY Yuu Watase
Manga $9.99
Over 100 pieces of art, with drawings and paintings produced especially for this new edition, formatted to match the original Japanese book!
THE ART OF
fushigi yûgi
The Mysterious Play
By Yuu Watase
Art of $19.99
fushigi yûgi™

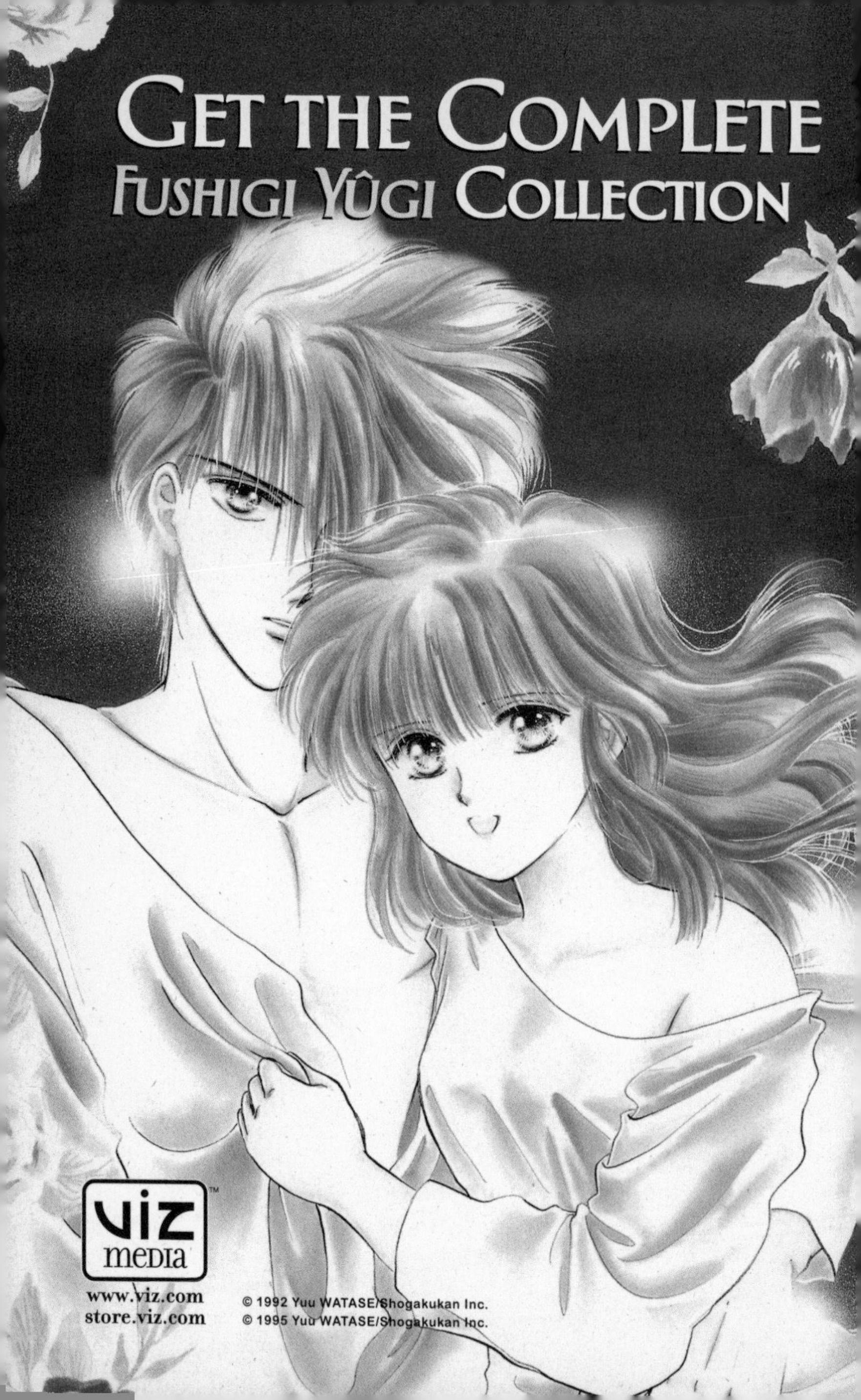
GET THE COMPLETE
FUSHIGI YÛGI COLLECTION
viz media
www.viz.com
store.viz.com
© 1992 Yuu WATASE/Shogakukan Inc.
© 1995 Yuu WATASE/Shogakukan Inc.

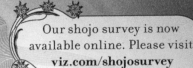

Love Shojo Manga?
Let us know what you think!

Our shojo survey is now available online. Please visit **viz.com/shojosurvey**

Help us make the manga you love better!